Film
Review
2003-2004

Includes video releases and websites

Film Review

2003-2004

ADAM KEEN

Executive editor: James Cameron-Wilson

Reynolds & Hearn Ltd
London

To Adeline... quo vadis

Acknowledgements

The editor would like to thank Mr Tan, the owner of the dodgy Kuala Lumpur video store who let a spotty 12-year-old watch just about anything he could pull off the shelves; my parents, for crediting me with the sense to tell fact from fiction, and right from wrong; James Cameron-Wilson, for ambushing me with an ambition I never knew I had; and F Maurice Speed, for starting the whole *Film Review* institution.

This book would also not exist without David Miller, Mansel Stimpson and Scot Woodward Myers and their generous support of the annual and its long traditions. Thanks also to The Joel Finler Collection and The Tony Hillman Collection for additional picture research.

Not least, I would like to thank Marcus Hearn and Richard Reynolds, for taking a chance on a long shot.

First published in 2003 by
Reynolds & Hearn Ltd
61a Priory Road
Kew Gardens
Richmond
Surrey TW9 3DH

A CIP catalogue record for this book is available from the British Library.

ISBN 1 903111 68 4

Designed by James King and Paul Chamberlain
Cover designed by Paul Chamberlain

Printed and bound in Great Britain by
Biddles Ltd, Guildford, Surrey.

Contents

Right: Johnny Depp steers his ship through tumultuous waters in the surprise hit, *Pirates of the Caribbean: The Curse of the Black Pearl* (from Buena Vista International)

Introduction

In my last introduction, I grumbled about the number of sequels in the marketplace. Silly me. This year saw a record number of the things, confirming Hollywood's lazy reliance on a sure bet. Silly them. With global marketing budgets soaring to an average $75 million per title (ouch), films like *Charlie's Angels: Full Throttle, Lara Croft Tomb Raider: The Cradle of Life* and *Dumb and Dumberer: When Harry Met Lloyd* lost a good deal of cash at the box-office. Even the much-hyped *The Matrix Reloaded*, which accrued a respectable $280m in the US, failed to live up to expectations.

For once, audiences seemed bored of recycled ideas and were impatient to embrace something new. The biggest movie of the summer, *Finding Nemo*, turned out to be a total original. The story of a harassed clown fish and a blue tang with short-term memory loss, *Nemo* was actually inspired by a 1992 visit to Marine World by its director and co-writer (Andrew Stanton). Never underestimate an outing with the kids.

The year's second surprise – *Pirates of the Caribbean: The Curse of the Black Pearl* – was also from Disney. And what a surprise it was. In recent times, pirate films have notoriously sunk at the box-office (cf *CutThroat Island, The Pirate Movie* and *Pirates*); Johnny Depp is an established non-starter (even his commercial ventures have been flops); and the film was based on nothing so inspiring as Disney's own theme park of the same name. Now a sequel is already in the works (will Hollywood *ever* learn?), and no doubt other pirate scripts are being dusted off and given a fresh lick of paint.

If the last 12 months revealed anything, it was that women have a higher stake in the commercial marketplace, making their presence felt in every genre going. The chick flick excelled (cf *Freaky Friday, Legally Blonde 2, Bend it Like Beckham*), the Oscar voters were spoilt for choice and even actioners were strictly equal opportunity (think *Charlie's Angels, Lara Croft*, Halle Berry, Famke Janssen, Rebecca Romijn-Stamos, Anna Paquin and Kelly Hu in *X-Men 2*, not to mention Kristanna Loken trouncing Arnie in *Terminator 3: Rise of the Machines*). Everywhere you looked, the fairer sex was muscling in on the action.

This trend was reflected in the pay packet of the Hollywood actress, with the likes of Cameron Diaz, Reese Witherspoon and Renée Zellweger demanding – and getting – massive sums, while the female-driven *Chicago* resurrected the musical virtually single-handedly; *Phantom of the Opera, Urinetown* and *Sweeney Todd* are all in pre-production.

In the spirit of brushing away the cobwebs, a new editor has come on board with this edition. First published in 1945 by MacDonald & Co and edited by F Maurice Speed, this annual has undergone many changes. As Maurice noted in his very first foreword, 'what the ordinary moviegoer lacks is a more or less complete annual record, in picture and story, of his year's filmgoing. Ironically enough, it wasn't until the war came along, and I had been discharged from the Army, that I decided, as nobody else seemed so inclined, I might as well attempt to fill the void myself.' Since then countless film annuals have come and gone, but *Film Review* remains, being a testament to Maurice's vision.

It's extraordinary that, in its 59 incarnations, it has only had three editors. I personally became involved in 1978 when Maurice asked me to contribute a feature on the *Carry On* phenomenon. Two years later I established the regular feature 'Faces of the Year' (initially called 'The Young Ones') and showcased such newcomers as Bo Derek, Bette Midler, Sigourney Weaver and Robin Williams (and, on a whim, the character actor Paul Dooley!). From then on my editorial duties gradually increased, until it was unclear who was actually in charge of *F Maurice Speed's Film Review*.

Today, Maurice (who died in 1998) would not approve of many of the films out there (I'd hate to think what he would say about *Irréversible*, or even *American Wedding*). So it seems apt that a young journalist with his finger on the pulse should take over from myself. While I might not concur with every opinion that Adam Keen has to offer, he is certainly more in tune with today's audience than I am. And to steer a ship through such tumultuous waters, you need to know your ocean. So I doff my captain's hat to the new admiral and hope that he derives as much pleasure from his duties as I did. It's a lousy job, but somebody's got to do it.

James Cameron-Wilson
September 2003

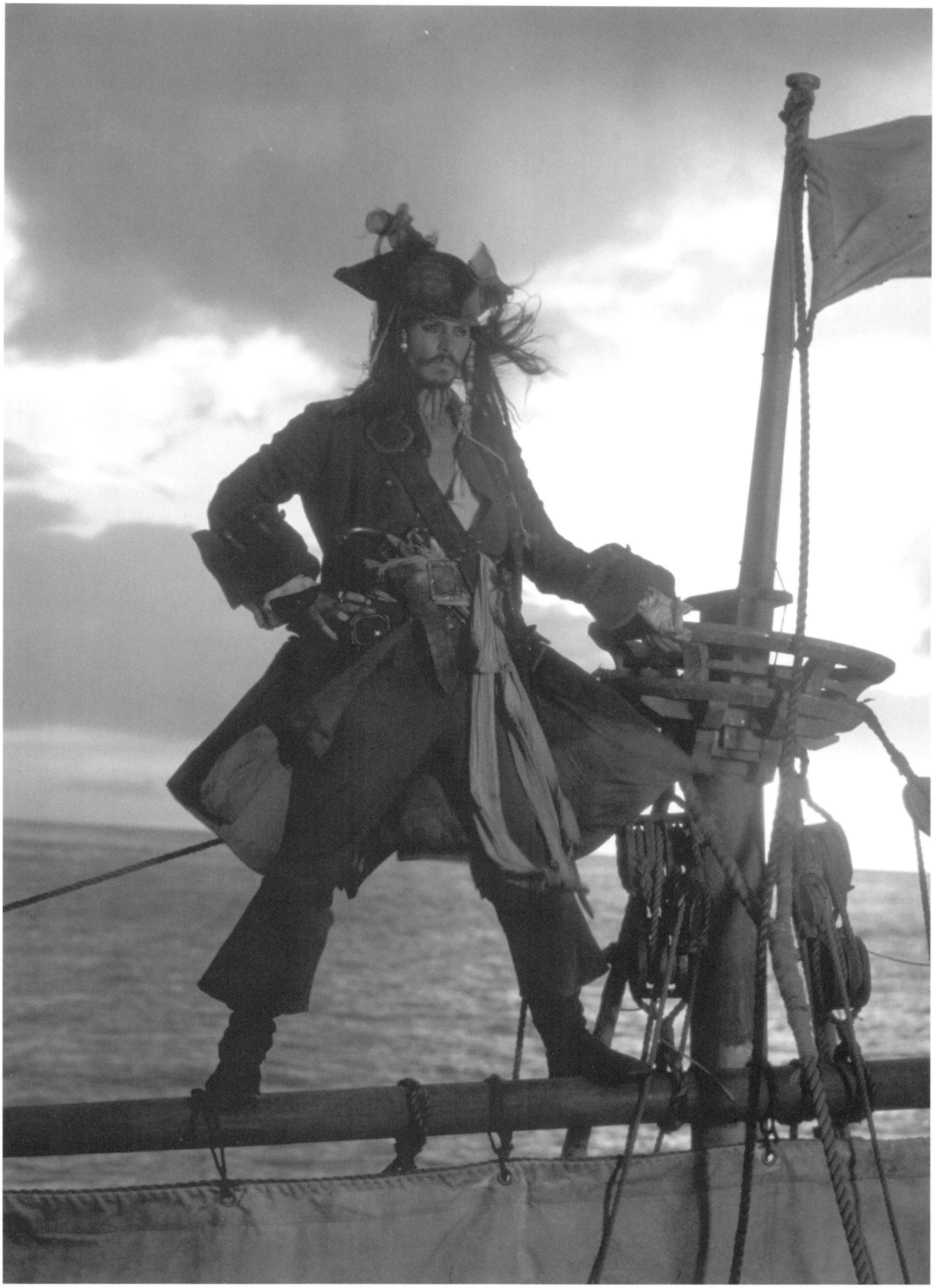

Top 20 UK Box-Office Hits
July 2002 – June 2003

1. The Lord of the Rings: The Two Towers
2. Harry Potter and the Chamber of Secrets
3. Die Another Day
4. The Matrix Reloaded
5. Spider-Man
6. Austin Powers in Goldmember
7. X-Men 2
8. Men in Black II
9. Scooby-Doo
10. Johnny English
11. Minority Report
12. Chicago
13. Signs
14. Catch Me if You Can
15. Bruce Almighty
16. My Big Fat Greek Wedding
17. Two Weeks Notice
18. Lilo & Stitch
19. 8 Mile
20. xXx

Top 10 Box-Office Stars

Star of the Year: Leonardo DiCaprio

At a time when computer-generated monstrosities and rabid machines ruled the box-office, it was hard for a mere thespian to make an impression. Indeed, only one actor cropped up in two concurrent box-office hits – *Catch Me if You Can* and *Gangs of New York* – which makes Leonardo DiCaprio front-runner for star of the year, repeating his win of 1998.

In second place, Mike Myers proved his enduring appeal as the gormless Austin Powers, the megalomaniac Dr Evil, the unintelligible Goldmember and the grotesque Fat Bastard – all in the same comedy, *Austin Powers in Goldmember*. Following his vocal work as the irascible Scottish ogre in *Shrek*, Myers seems almost boundless in his comic invention; indeed, he was the funniest thing in the disappointing *View from the Top*, in which he plays a boss-eyed flight instructor with an inferiority complex.

In *Die Another Day*, Pierce Brosnan's 007 demonstrated that he could compete with Sean Connery, while Halle Berry, his leading lady, seemed to be everywhere. So successful was her portrayal of Jinx, the plucky undercover agent in *Die Another Day*, that she's been lined up for a spin-off series.

However, in spite of the critical reception afford *The Hours* and other films, women did not fare well at the box-office. Only Renée Zellweger seemed to flourish, following the triumph of *Bridget Jones's Diary* with the amazing success of *Chicago*. For the record, runners-up this year include Jim Carrey, Hugh Grant, Sandra Bullock, Eminem, Anthony Hopkins and Tom Hanks.
JC-W

2. Mike Myers
3. Pierce Brosnan
4. Will Smith
5. Keanu Reeves
6. Mel Gibson
7. Rowan Atkinson
8. Tom Cruise
9. Halle Berry
10. Tommy Lee Jones

Releases of the Year

This section contains details of all the films released in Great Britain from 1 July 2002 to the end of June 2003 – the period covered by all the reference features in this book.

Leading actors are normally credited with the roles they played, followed by a summary of supporting players. Where an actor further down a cast list is of special interest then his/her role is generally credited as well.

For technical credits the normal abbreviations operate, and are as follows: Dir – for Director; Pro – for Producer; Ex Pro – for Executive Producer; Co Pro – for Co-Producer; Ass Pro – for Associate Producer; Line Pro – for Line Producer; Scr – for Screenwriter; Ph – for Cinematographer; Ed – for Editor; Pro Des – for Production Designer; and M – for composer.

Abbreviations for the names of film companies are also obvious when used, such as Fox for Twentieth Century Fox, and UIP for Universal International Pictures. The production company (or companies) is given first, the distribution company last.

Information at the foot of each entry is presented in the following order: running time/country of origin/year of copyright/ date of British release/British certification.

Reviewers: Adam Keen and Mansel Stimpson, with additional contributions from Charles Bacon, James Cameron-Wilson, Danny Graydon, Marcus Hearn, David Miller, Jonathan Rigby and Scot Woodward Myers.

Star ratings

★★★★★ Wonderful
★★★★ Very good
★★★ Good
★★ Mediocre
★ Insulting

Abouna

See *Our Father*

About Schmidt ★★★★

Warren Schmidt's orderly existence drifts into late-life limbo when his stalwart wife suddenly dies. Feeling profoundly confused – and mad after discovering an ancient incidence of his late wife's infidelity – he embarks on an eventful cross-country tour in a luxury Winnebago, perhaps to save his estranged daughter from a marriage to a nice-but-dim 'loser'. Like David Lynch's *The Straight Story*, the art to Alexander Payne's apparently mundane tale lies in its gentle subtleties and restrained appetite for irony. His masterstroke was to cast Jack Nicholson utterly against type as the helpless and confused Schmidt (referencing his role in *Easy Rider* by playing George Hanson's time-warped twin), a role he takes to with uncanny sensitivity and humour. And Nicholson is backed up by solid work from a wonderful supporting cast. AK

• *Warren Schmidt* Jack Nicholson *Roberta Hertzel* Kathy Bates *Jeannie* Hope Davis *Randall Hertzel* Dermot Mulroney *Larry* Howard Hesseman *Ray* Len Cariou *Helen Schmidt* June Squibb
• *Dir* Alexander Payne *Scr* Payne and Jim Taylor, based on the novel by Louis Begley *Ph* James Glennon *Ed* Kevin Tent *M* Rolfe Kent *Pro Des* Jane Ann Stewart *Pro* Harry Gittes, Michael Besman

Avery Pix / New Line Cinema / Entertainment Film 125 mins. US 2002. Rel: 25 January 2003. Cert 15.

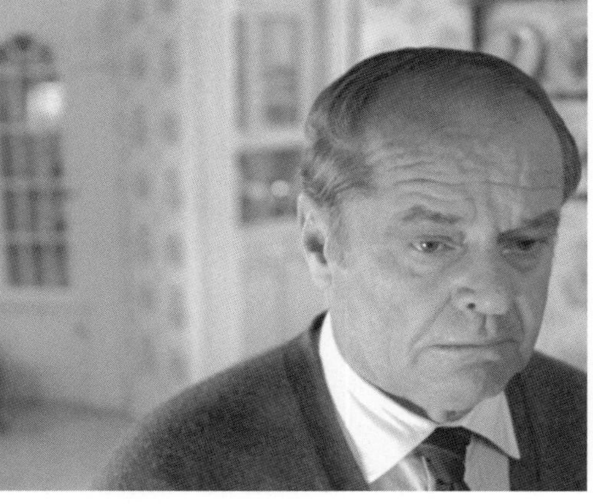

Left: The brilliant Jack Nicholson, cast against type in *About Schmidt* (from Entertainment)

The Actors ★★½

Further proof that a film can't get by with a bad script, this Dublin-based comedy features actors planning a robbery involving disguises. It blends elements of *The Lavender Hill Mob* and *The Producers*, although here it's the actors who are supposed to be bad, not the play. To work it needs to treat the plot logically instead of adopting the notion that anything, however exaggerated, will get a laugh. As the inept star actor and chief plotter, Sir Michael Caine attempts a real characterisation. So do Sir Michael Gambon as a minor criminal and child actress Abigail Iversen, who advises with suitable gravitas. Film newcomer Dylan Moran is very assured too. But, as writer and director, Conor McPherson throws credibility to the winds and it all becomes desperately silly. His cast tries hard and valiantly, but it just doesn't play. MS

Right: Michael Caine gets Dylan Moran into another fine mess in the middling farce *The Actors* (from Momentum)

• *O'Malley* Michael Caine *Tom* Dylan Moran *Barreller* Michael Gambon *Magnani* Miranda Richardson *Dolores* Lena Headey
• *Dir* Conor McPherson *Scr* Neil Jordan, McPherson *Ass Pro* John Erraught *Ex Pro* Paul Webster, Hanno Huth *Pro* Jordan, Redmond Morris, Stephen Woolley *Ph* Seamus McGarvey *Ed* Declan McGrath

Bórd Scannán na hÉireann / Close Call Films / Company of Wolves / DreamWorks / FilmFour / Four Provinces Films / Scala Productions / Senator Film Produktion / Momentum
91 mins. UK/Germany/Ireland 2003. Rel: 16 May 2003. Cert 15.

Adam Sandler's Eight Crazy Nights

See *Eight Crazy Nights*

Right: Nicolas Cage and Meryl Streep don't quite meet in Spike Jonze's stunningly original *Adaptation* (from Columbia Tristar)

Adaptation ★★★

Intent on following up *Being John Malkovich* with a film no less singular, director Spike Jonze and writer Charlie Kaufman achieve their aim for much of the time. Inventing a fictional version of Charlie Kaufman and giving him a twin brother (both played by Nicolas Cage on top form), this film shows them caught up in a problematic adaptation of a book by one Susan Orlean. The authoress exists in real life but is fictionalised to become Charlie's unresponsive object of desire, the role being played by Meryl Streep. As a comedy about scripting films, this zany and original piece is easily as entertaining as Robert Guédiguian's *À l'attaque.* Brian Cox's cameo performance as the writing expert Robert McKee is a highlight, but *Adaptation* is so ambitious that it is, in parts, uneven. MS

• *Charlie Kaufman/Donald Kaufman* Nicolas Cage *Susan Orlean* Meryl Streep *John Laroche* Chris Cooper *Valerie* Tilda Swinton *Amelia* Cara Seymour *Robert McKee* Brian Cox *Alice the waitress* Judy Greer *Caroline* Maggie Gyllenhaal *Marty* Ron Livingston *Matthew Osceola* Jay Tavare
• *Dir* Spike Jonze *Scr* Charlie Kaufman, Donald Kaufman, based on the book *The Orchid Thief* by Susan Orlean *Ph* Lance Acord *Ed* Eric Zumbrunnen *M* Carter Burwell *Pro Des* K K Barrett *Pro* Edward Saxon, Vincent Landay, Jonathan Demme

Beverly Detroit / Clinica Estetico Ltd / Good Machine / Intermedia / Magnet Productions / Propaganda Films / Columbia Tristar
114 mins. US 2002. Rel: 28 February 2003. Cert 15.

The Adventures of Pluto Nash ★½

2087, The Moon. Suave and successful club owner and legendary ex-smuggler Pluto Nash falls into the laser-sights of a mysterious mobster when he refuses to sell his club. With only a sexy aspiring lounge singer, a clunky robot bodyguard, and his blackalicious Mom to help him, he outsmarts the gangsters and makes a shocking discovery – that all this time he has been fighting himself! A dismal script and rickety effects sink even the best attempts by an experienced crew to stir a laugh. The movie crashed and burned on release, blowing right past 'so bad it's good' to just 'so bad'. AK

• *Pluto Nash* Eddie Murphy *Bruno* Randy Quaid *Dina Lake* Rosario Dawson *Mogan* Joe Pantoliano *Tony Francis* Jay Mohr *Felix Laranga* Luis Guzmán *Belcher* James Rebhorn *Rowland* Peter Boyle *Gino* Burt Young *Miguel* Miguel A Nuñez Jr *Flura Nash* Pam Grier *Dr Mona Zimmer* Illeana Douglas *James* John Cleese
• *Dir* Ron Underwood *Scr* Neil Cuthbert *Ph* Oliver Wood *Ed* Paul Hirsch and Alan Heim *M* John Powell *Pro Des* Bill Brzeski *Pro* Martin Bregman, Michael Bregman and Louis A Stroller

Castle Rock Entertainment / NPV Entertainment / Village Roadshow Productions / Warner Bros
94 mins. USA 2002. Rel 30 August 2002. Cert PG.

AKA ★★★

Duncan Roy's first feature, set in 1979, echoes Mike Figgis' *Time Code* in telling its story through three images seen side by side. It's an ambitious notion, but it's easier to admire the cheek than the quality since the script, purportedly based on a true story, is much less sophisticated than the visuals. Matthew Leitch is an Essex youth, son of a waitress, who climbs onward and upward, taking advantage of gay men who are attracted to him and copying Patricia Highsmith's Tom Ripley by passing himself off as a member of high society. The rich characters frequently emerge as stereotypes, and details that would make events more credible are often lacking. For all the genuine enterprise involved, the piece plays like no more than a gay novelette, but you have to admire its chutzpah. MS

• *Dean Page* Matthew Leitch *Lady Tryffoyn* Diana Quick *David* George Asprey *Georgie* Lindsey Coulson *Alexander Griffoyn* Blake Ritson *Benjamin* Peter Youngblood Hills *Brian Page* Geoff Bell *Hannah Yelland* Camille Sturton *Jamie Page* Daniel Lee *Uncle Louis Gryffoyn* Bill Nighy *Lee Page* David Kendall *Sarah* Fenella Woolgar *Tim Lyttleton* Sean Gilder *Neil Frost* Robin Soans *Dermot* Stephen Boxer *Marcus* Neil Maskell *Jeremy* Reginald S Bundy
• *Dir / Scr* Duncan Roy *Pro* Richard West *Ass Pro* Julian Alexander *Ex Pro* Julian Hayward, Roy *M* Matt Rowe *Ph* Ingrid Domeij, Steve Smith, Scott Taylor, Claire Vinson *Ed* Lawrence Catford, John Cross, Jackie Ophir *Pro Des* Philip Robinson, Dean Clegg *Sets* Gemma Ryan (uncredited)

Third Rock Ltd / Julian Hayward / Bard Entertainments / Film Council / City Screen
123 mins. UK 2002. Rel: 14 October 2002. Cert 18.

À la folie pas du tout

See *He Loves Me, He Loves Me Not*

All or Nothing ★★★½

Mike Leigh returns to his spiritual home in this unwashed soap opera set in the grimy council estates

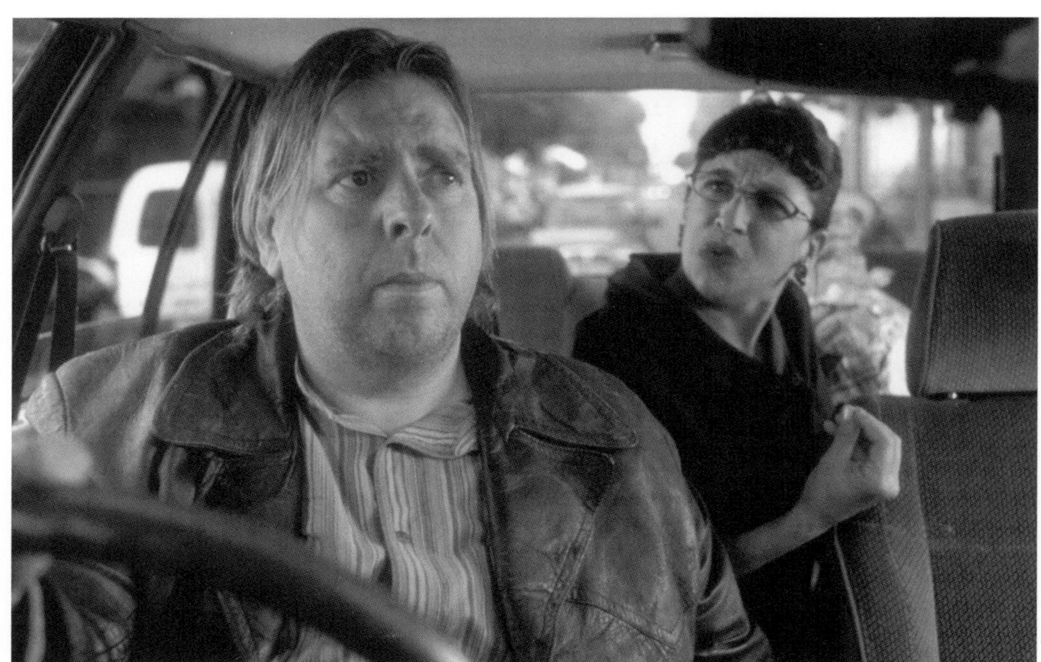

Left: Timothy Spall and Kathryn Hunter in Mike Leigh's drama *All Or Nothing* (from UGC)

of South East London. With a circus of archetypes ranging from Timothy Spall's existentially traumatised cabbie to Ruth Sheen's long-suffering pragmatic, and from their emotionally stunted children to their angrily desperate friends and neighbours, Leigh's art is to set his characters loose in one other's company in order to extract some facet of truth about their circumstances. In one sense there is nothing very surprising about Leigh's latest outing (unlike his previous film, the highly uncharacteristic *Topsy Turvy*), but the lack of thematic novelty fades away when one considers the poverty of good films made on Leigh's turf. AK

• *Phil* Timothy Spall *Penny* Lesley Manville *Rachel* Alison Garland *Rory* James Corden *Maureen* Ruth Sheen *Carol* Marion Bailey *Ron* Paul Jesson *Sid* Sam Kelly *Donna* Helen Coker *Samantha* Sally Hawkins *Cecile* Kathryn Hunter
• *Dir / Scr* Mike Leigh *Ph* Dick Pope *Ed* Lesley Walker *M* Andrew Dickson *Pro Des* Eve Stewart *Pro* Alain Sarde, Simon Channing Williams

Cloud Nine Films Ltd / Les Films Alain Sarde / Studio Canal / Thin Man Films / UGC Films UK
128 mins. UK/France 2002. Rel: 18 October 2002. Cert 18.

Amen ★★★

The best films of Costa-Gavras, including the famous *Z*, have been political dramas drawing on real-life events. In line with that, this adaptation of a play by Rolf Hochhuth tackles the issue of the failure of the Catholic Church at the time of the Holocaust to speak out against the Nazis. It's a subject well worth addressing, and the film does it by telling the story of an SS officer, Kurt Gerstein. Both his Christian beliefs and his knowledge of the use to which poison gas is being put result in his making an alliance with a Jesuit, Riccardo, to alert the Pope to the need to take a stand. Ulrich Tukur and Mathieu Kassovitz do well in these roles, but the film fails to deliver, being seriously compromised by the fact that, while Gerstein really existed, Riccardo is a fictional character used to milk the emotions of the audience. MS

• *Kurt Gerstein* Ulrich Tukur *Ricardo Fontana* Mathieu Kassovitz *the doctor* Ulrich Mühe *the Cardinal* Michel Duchaussoy *the Pope* Marcel Iures *Count Fontana* Ion Caramitru *Grawitz* Hanns Zischler
• *Dir* Costa-Gavras *Pro* Claude Berri *Ex Pro* Michèle Ray *Scr* Costa-Gavras and Jean-Claude Grumberg *Ph* Patrick Blossier *Pro Des* Ari Hantke and Maria Miu *Ed* Yannick Kergoat *M* Armand Amar *Costumes* Édith Vespérini

Katharina / Renn Prods / TF1 Films / Canal Plus-Pathé
130 mins. France 2002. Rel: 12 July 2002. Cert. 15.

Analyze That ★½

Sequels don't come much cheaper than this. Billy Crystal and Robert De Niro follow up their enormously successful farce *Analyze This* with a limp extension of a fine scenario, ie, a mobster's relationship with his shrink. Plot: Paul Vitti suddenly becomes the target of prison assassination attempts and plays crazy so that Dr Ben Sobel is hoodwinked into taking custody of his old patient. The original film allowed Cystal to indulge his neurotic mannerisms to the max while De Niro relished the opportunity to send up the New York gangster-roles that launched his career. The encore, however, is a toothless mutt lost in a fog of uninspired jokes and lazy acting. AK

• *Paul Vitti* Robert De Niro *Ben Sobel* Billy Crystal *Laura Sobel* Lisa Kudrow *Jelly* Joe Viterelli *Patti Lo Presti* Cathy Moriarty-Gentile *Anthony Bella* Anthony LaPaglia
• *Dir* Harold Ramis *Scr* Peter Steinfeld, Ramis and Peter Tolan *Ph* Ellen Kuras *Ed* Andrew Mondshein *M* David Holmes *Pro Des* Wynn Thomas *Pro* Paula Weinstein and Jane Rosenthal

Baltimore Spring Creek Productions / Face Productions / NPV Entertainment / Tribeca Productions / Village Roadshow Productions / Warner Bros
95 mins. US 2003. Rel: 28 February 2003. Cert 15.

Anger Management ★★★½

Dave Buznik has a dead-end career path and a lovely girlfriend he can barely kiss in public. A shocking episode on a plane puts him in the dock for assault and he is committed to the care of renowned anger therapist Buddy Rydell. Years of repressed emotion have apparently had a deeper effect on David than he knows, because another fight leads to Buddy moving in with him to administer a 24/7 intensive therapy program… Adam Sandler and Jack Nicholson are perfectly matched in this deliciously satisfying take on the classic 'odd couple' comedy. Nicholson turns on his devilish charm to full effect as he makes life for Sandler a living hell. On the side, a chorus of wacky angry-types hit the cheap laughs with unerring accuracy. A New York comedy that floweth over with star power, *Anger Management* successfully plays dumb like a standard Sandler-franchise taste vacation, while also being unusually clever. Until, that is, the syrupy ending spoils it all. AK

• *Dave Buznik* Adam Sandler *Buddy Rydell* Jack Nicholson *Linda* Marisa Tomei *Chuck* John Turturro *Frank* Kurt Fuller *Lou* Luis Guzmán *Andrew* Allen Covert *Judge Daniels* Lynne Thigpen *Galaxia/security guard* Woody Harrelson *Kendra* Heather Graham *himself* Robert Merrill
• *Dir* Peter Segal *Scr* David Dorfman

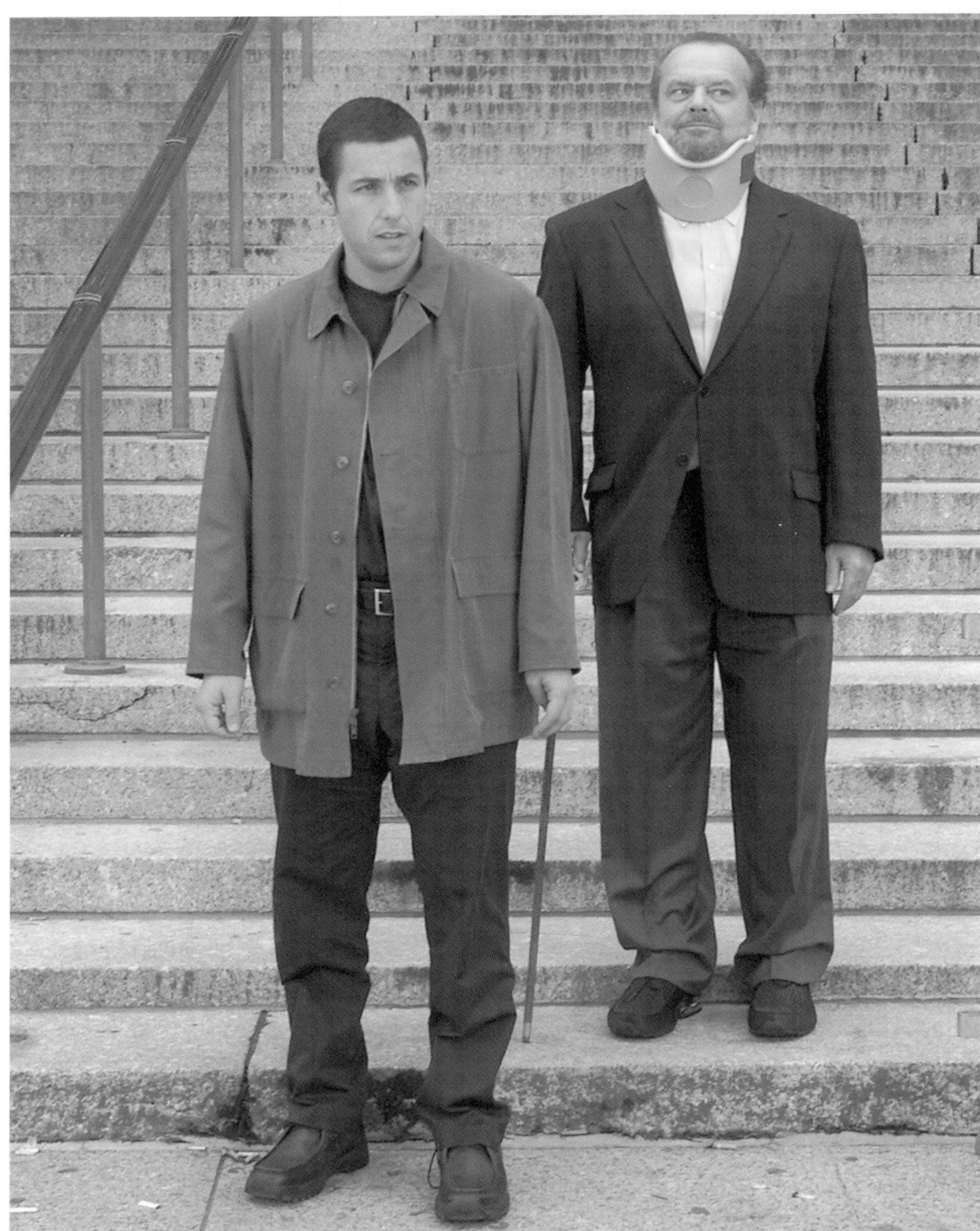

Left: Adam Sandler and Jack Nicholson in the harebrained but effective *Anger Management* (from Columbia Tristar)

Ph Donald M McAlpine *E* Jeff Gourson *M* Teddy Castellucci *Pro Des* Alan Au *Pro* Jack Giarraputo, Barry Bernardi

Happy Madison / Jack Giarraputo Productions / Revolution Studios / Columbia Tristar 106 mins. US 2003. Rel: 6 June 2003. Cert 15.

Animal Factory ★★★½

A rare and uncomfortable pleasure, *Animal Factory* lifts the lid on prison life looking through the eyes of Ron Decker, a youthful small-time dealer crucified by the system and sentenced to hard time. Ron's long lashes and wiry charm catch the eye of Earl Copen, a veteran jailbird who runs the prison yard via his connections with the guards. Unlike the heated, amped-up dramas that usually trademark the genre, *Animal Factory* is an insidious and actorly drama, focused almost entirely on the motives and machinations of its characters. Violent altercations, the inevitable rape scene, and the bid for escape almost appear incidental to the developments each character goes through. Willem Defoe confirms once again his status as perhaps the most underrated actor in Hollywood, while the rest of the cast deliver some stunningly original performances. AK

Above: Chandeep Uppal and Anita Brewster test the bonds of friendship in *Anita & Me* (from Icon)

• *Earl Copen* Willem Dafoe *Ron Decker* Edward Furlong *Jan the actress* Mickey Rourke *Buck Rowan* Tom Arnold *A R Hosspack* Steve Buscemi *James Decker* John Heard *Buzzard* Edward Bunker • *Dir* Steve Buscemi *Scr* Edward Bunker and John Steppling, based on Bunker's novel *Ph* Phil Parmet *Ed* Kate Williams *M* John Lurie *Pro Des* Steven Rosenzweig *Pro* Julie Yorn, Elie Samaha, Andrew Stevens and Buscemi

Animal Productions / Arts Production Corporation Franchise Pictures / Industry Entertainment / Phoenician Entertainment / Optimum Releasing 95 mins. US 2000. Rel: 4 July 2003. Cert 15.

Anita & Me ★★½

West Midlands, 1972. A Hindu family move into a nice-but-sheltered working class village. Their daughter, Meena, is a hopeful writer who, desperate to shed the stigma of her Asian-ness, throws herself into a one-sided friendship with the Nordically proportioned and prophetically surnamed Anita Rutter. But boys, puberty, family crises and the greater pressures of social change encroach on their private world, and their friendship is further tested by the prejudices of the day… While occasionally delightful, *Anita & Me* nevertheless fails to stick to a recognisable tune. Farce crashes into breezy wit, then jostles with social realism and teenage angst. Not really bittersweet, it throws up all the usual notes about racism and the summer of love in a coming of age setting that does not quite gel. The best moments are comic vignettes that play on nostalgia, filial rivalry, cultural misunderstanding, and a grinning, machete-wielding grandmother from India. AK

• *Meena* Chandeep Uppal *Anita Rutter* Anna Brewster *Hairy Neddy* Max Beesley *Papa* Sanjeev Bhaskar *Mama* Ayesha Dharkar *Deidre Rutter* Kathy Burke *Uncle Amman* Omid Djalili *Sam Lowbridge* Alex Freehorn *Mrs Ormerod* Lynn Redgrave *Auntie Sheila* Meera Syal *Zohra Segal* Nanima *Vicar* Mark Williams *Yeti* Kabir Bedi • *Dir* Metin Huseyin *Pro* Paul Raphael *Ex Pro* Paul Tribjis, David M Thompson, Peter Carlton, Bill Allan, Tristan Whalley *Scr* and *Co Pro* Meera Syal *Ph* Cinders Forshaw *Pro Des* Caroline Hanania *Ed* Annie Kocur *M* Nitin Sawhney

Take 3.1, 3.2, 3.3, 3.4 Partnerships / Portman Film / The Film Council / BBC Films / Icon Film Distribution 92 mins. UK 2002. Rel: 22 November 2002. Cert 12A.

Antwone Fisher ★★★½

(US title: *The Antwone Fisher Story*)
Newcomer Derek Luke, reminiscent of the young Sidney Poitier, impresses in the title role of Denzel Washington's promising debut as director. As actor, Washington offers unselfish support playing the Navy psychiatrist who helped when Fisher was sent to him after striking a non-commissioned officer in response to what he had interpreted as a racial slur. Flashbacks reveal Antwone growing up without parents and becoming the victim of a sexual abuser and a cruel foster-mother, experiences which have

Above: Gérard Depardieu and Christian Claver mug shamelessly in *Asterix & Obelix: Mission Cleopatra* (from Pathé)

left our hero with an anger problem. He needs to re-channel the energy to better himself and to come to terms with his past. Well-meaning and sympathetic but way too long, the film's increasing sentimentality disappoints. Based on a true story (the screenplay was written by Fisher himself), it incorporates fictional elements and would have worked better as a TV series. MS

• *Antwone Fisher* Derek Luke *Cheryl* Joy Bryant *Jerome Davenport* Denzel Washington *Berta* Salli Richardson *James* Earl Billings *Slim* Kevin Connolly *Nadine* Yolanda Ross *Mrs Tate* Novella Nelson
• *Dir* Denzel Washington *Scr* Antwone Fisher *Ph* Philippe Rousselot *Ed* Conrad Buff *M* Mychael Danna *Pro Des* Nelson Coates *Pro* Todd Black, Randa Haines, Washington

Antwone Fisher Productions / Hofflund/Polone / MDP Worldwide / Mundy Lane Entertainment / 20th Century Fox 119 mins. US 2003. Rel: 16 May 2003. Cert 15.

Ararat ★★★★

The Canadian-based Atom Egoyan is of Armenian descent, and this latest work is probably his most personal. It seeks to bring to wider notice the genocide of the Armenians in 1915, an event denied even now by the Turkish authorities. Instead of creating an historical epic, Egoyan has devised a film about film-making in which Charles Aznavour plays a director making a movie on this subject. This enables Egoyan to bring in many elements: reflections on Armenian culture, generational clashes and the role that tradition usefully fills in helping individuals to find themselves. Arguably, it's a bit over-loaded and calculated, but it's always interesting and magnificently photographed by Paul Sarossy. There's also a splendid score from composer Mychael Danna reflecting the general emphasis on things Armenian. A film from the heart. MS

• *Edward* Charles Aznavour *Rouben* Eric Bogosian *Philip* Brent Carver *Celia* Marie-Josée Croze *Martin/Clarence Ussher* Bruce Greenwood *Ani* Arsinée Khanjian *Ali/Jedvet Bey* Elias Koteas *Ashile Gorky* Simon Abkarian *David* Christopher Plummer *Raffi* David Alpay *Shusan Gorky* Lousnak
• *Dir / Scr* Atom Egoyan *Ph* Paul Sarossy *Ed* Susan Shipton *Pro Des* Phillip Barker *Pro* Robert Lantos, Egoyan

ARP Sélection / Alliance Atlantis Communications / Astral Films / Ego Film Arts / Serendipity Point Films / Super Écran / The Harold Greenberg Fund / The Movie Network / Téléfilm Canada / Momentum115 mins. Canada/France 2002. Rel: 18 April 2003. Cert 15.

Asterix & Obelix: Mission Cleopatra ★★★½

(*Astérix et Obélix: Mission Cléopâtre*)
A superior transposition of the much-loved comic set during the time of Caesar and featuring a village of

indomitable Gauls fortified by the magic potions of their druid Getafix, this is the second time Asterix & Obelix have been put on the big screen in live-action form. This time, the movie does a much better job of incorporating the comic's essential elements of farce, juvenile wordplay and historical revisionism. Monica Bellucci is in high camp heaven as the lovely Cleopatra, who instructs a hapless architect (Edifis) to build a palace in 30 days in order to impress upon Rome the greatness of Egypt, or else be served up to the sacred crocodiles. An impossible task, thinks Edifis, unless he turns his workers into supermen with the potions of his old friends, Asterix and Obelix. The prospect of an Egyptian holiday seems harmless enough, except for the backstabbing treachery that awaits them in Cleopatra's court. Wonderfully entertaining, provided you enjoy the special flavour of its comic-book origins. AK

• *Obélix* Gérard Depardieu *Astérix* Christian Clavier *Numérobis* Jamel Debbouze *Cléopâtre* Monica Bellucci *Jules César* Alain Chabat *Panoramix (Miraculix)* Claude Rich *Amonbofis (Pyradonis)* Gérard Darmon *Otis* Edouard Baer *Caius Céplus* Dieudonné *Baba, la vigie des pirates* Mouss Diouf *Sucettalanis* Marina Foïs *Barbe-Rouge le pirate* Bernard Farcy *Malococsis* Jean Benguigui *Triple Patte* Michel Crémadès *Caius Antivirus* Jean-Paul Rouve

• *Dir / Co Pro / Scr* Alain Chabat, based on the comic books by René Goscinny and Albert Uderzo *Pro* Claude Berri *Ex Pro* Pierre Grunstein *Ass Pro* Thomas Langmann, Dieter Meyer, Roland Pellegrino *M* Philippe Chany, Snoop Dogg *Ph* Laurent Dailland *Ed* Stéphane Pereira *Pro Des* Hoang Thanh At

CP Medien AG / Centre National de la Cinématographie / Chez Wam / KC Medien / Katharina / La Petite Reine / Le Studio Canal+ / Pathé Entertainment / Renn Productions / TF1 Films Productions / Pathé
108 mins. France/Germany 2002. Rel: 18 October 2002. Cert PG.

L'auberge Espagnole
See *Pot Luck*

Austin Powers in Goldmember
★★★½

Once again the world is at the mercy of a ruthless criminal mastermind. This time the villain is a certain Goldmember, a Dutch disco dictator with an impenetrable accent, elastic legs and, yes, a gold love muscle. And only the shagadelic Austin Powers can stop him... There are a lot of laughs in this third instalment of the Swinging Sixties spoof, but just as many misfires. In an unbridled attempt to make

Below: Mike Myers shows off his alter-ego's improved dental work in *Austin Powers in Goldmember* (from New Line)

every moment count, writer-producer-star Mike Myers (who was paid $25 million, plus 21 per cent of the gross) hurls everything he can into his high-octane stew. So, from the hilarious prologue on, Myers juggles sight gags, verbal wit, parody and toilet humour with wild abandon, spoofing *Singin' in the Rain* one minute and labouring the scatological references the next. Still, for every groan there is a genuine guffaw, which is more than can be said for most Hollywood comedies this summer. To quote Dr Evil, 'I haven't laughed that hard since I was a little girl.' JC-W

• *Austin Powers/ Dr Evil/ Goldmember/ Fat Bastard* Mike Myers *Foxxy Cleopatra* Beyoncé Knowles *Nigel Powers* Michael Caine *Scott Evil* Seth Green *Basil Exposition* Michael York *Number Two* Robert Wagner *Frau Farbissina* Mindy Sterling *Mini Me* Verne Troyer *Number Three* Fred Savage *Fook Mi* Diane Mizota *Fook Yu* Carrie Ann Inaba *Queen Elizabeth II* Jeannette Charles *with* Nobuyuki 'Nobu' Matsuhisa, Neil Mullarkey, Tommy 'Tiny' Lister, Clint Howard, Michael McDonald and (uncredited) Tom Cruise, *Dixie Normous* Gwyneth Paltrow, Kevin Spacey, Danny DeVito, John Travolta, Steven Spielberg, Britney Spears, Quincy Jones, Burt Bacharach, Nathan Lane, Rob Lowe, Ozzy Osbourne
• *Dir* Jay Roach *Pro* Suzanne Todd, Jennifer Todd, Demi Moore, Eric McLeod, John Lyons and Myers *Ex Pro* Toby Emmerich and Richard Brener *Co Pro* Gregg Taylor *Scr* Myers and Michael McCullers *Ph* Peter Deming *Pro Des* Rusty Smith *Ed* Jon Poll and Greg Hayden *M* George S Clinton; songs performed by George S Clinton, Britney Spears, Mike Myers, The Rolling Stones, Smash Mouth, Earth Wind & Fire, Beyoncé Knowles, Devin Vasquez and Solange, ELO, Freddy Flesh and Fatboy Slim, Bobby Darin, Burt Bacharach, Susanna Hoffs, etc *Costumes* Deena Appel *Visual effects* David D Johnson *Choreography* Marguerite Derricks

New Line Cinema / Gratitude International / Team Todd / Moving Pictures Entertainment
94 mins. USA 2002. Rel: 26 July 2002. Cert 12.

Auto Focus ★★★

From Paul Schrader (director but not writer on this occasion) we expect something better than a film which just gets by. Those familiar with the TV sitcom *Hogan's Heroes* and its lead actor Bob Crane, played here by Greg Kinnear, may be more readily drawn in by this tale. It's the story of a man whose sexual obsessions, encouraged by his companion John Carpenter (Willem Dafoe), led to the break-up of his marriage, the collapse of his career and, ultimately, his own murder. Although the film posits Carpenter as the killer, it seems that the evidence is in reality inconclusive. Gay connotations are not investigated, leaving this as no more than a well-acted but thoroughly seedy narrative told without insight or perspective. 'Guys gotta have fun' may be the ironic 'moral', but the film itself seems as indulgent as Crane. MS

• *Bob Crane* Greg Kinnear *John Carpenter* Willem Dafoe *Anne Crane* Rita Wilson *Patricia Crane* Maria Bello *Lenny* Ron Leibman *Feldman* Bruce Solomon *Richard Dawson* Michael Rodgers *Werner Klemperer* Kurt Fuller *Robert Clary* Christopher Neiman *John Banner* Lyle Kanouse
• *Dir* Paul Schrader *Scr* Michael Gerbosi, based on the book by Robert Graysmith *Ph* Fred Murphy *Ed* Kristina Boden *M* Angelo Badalamenti *Pro Des* James Chinlund *Pro* Scott Alexander, Larry Karaszewski, Todd Rosken, Pat Dollard, Alicia Allain

Focus Puller Inc / Good Machine / Propaganda Films / Columbia TriStar
105 mins. US 2002. Rel: 7 March 2003. Cert 18.

Avalon ★★★★

Sadly undervalued by British critics, this visionary futuristic tale may disappoint those who are looking for high-powered action, but it's a genuinely original work of art and a unique blend of east and west. It's the first live-action feature by Japan's Mamoru Oshii but, filmed in Poland with a European cast, it takes on a Kafkaesque atmosphere while also recalling the Russian filmmaker Tarkovsky. The excellently cast Matgorzata Foremniak is the heroine whose devotion to illegal virtual reality war games enables her as a competitor to break through into other worlds that are either beyond or still part of the game. As an allegory about human existence being subject to God or only to the illusion of an outside power, this is ultimately more obscure than one would wish but never less than fascinating. The music is great. MS

• *Ash* Malgorzata Foremniak *Game Master* Wladyslaw Kowalski *Murphy* Jerzy Gudejko *Bishop* Dariusz Biskupski *Stunner* Bartek Swiderski *receptionist* Katarzyna Bargielowska *Gill* Alicja Sapryk *Murphy of Nine Sisters* Michal Breitenwald *Ghost* Zuzanna Kasz *Player A* Adam Szyszkowski *Player B* Krzysztof Szczerbinski *Player C* Marek Stawinski *Cooper (voice)* Jaroslaw Budnik *Cusinart (voice)* Andrzej Debski
• *Dir* Mamoru Oshii *Scr* Kazunori Itô *Ex Pro* Tetsu Kayama, Naoyuki Sakagami, Toru Shiobara, Shigeru Watanabe *Pro* Atsushi Kubo *M* Kenji Kawai *Ph* Grzegorz Kedzierski *Pro Des* Barbara Nowak *Digital art director* Hiroyuki Hayashi *Visual effects supervisor* Nobuaki Koga

A-Film Distribution / Central Partnership / Cinévia Films / Herald Film Company / Kinowelt Home Entertainment / Miramax Films / Blue Dolphin
106 mins. Japan 2002. Rel: 8 November 2002. Cert 12A.

Bad Company ★½

Separated at birth from his twin, small-time hustler Kevin Pope is stunned to discover (a) that his brother was the CIA's top agent, and (b) that he was killed in action. Because Kevin is the only one capable of taking over where his identical twin left off, the CIA strong-arms him into a crash course in high-level espionage... A cheesy waltz through Ian Fleming-land, *Bad Company* is oddly conflicted. For Chris Rock, it is a step up for his acting to hold his own against the likes of Anthony Hopkins (if constant scattershot wisecracking counts as 'acting'). As for Hopkins, he embarrasses himself badly, looking decrepit and stale in a nuance-free performance. What real fun there is in this limp comic thriller owes a debt to *Trading Places*, while the stunts are high-impact and low-logic fare, fading from memory almost instantly. AK

• *Oakes* Anthony Hopkins *Jake Hayes / Kevin Pope* Chris Rock *Dragan Adjanic* Matthew Marsh *Seale* Gabriel Macht *Adrik Vas* Peter Stormare *Officer Swanson* Brooke Smith *Julie* Kerry Washington
• *Dir* Joel Schumacher *Scr* Jason Richman and Michael Browning, based on a story by Gary Goodman and David Himmelstein *Ph* Dariusz A Wolski *Ed* Mark Goldblatt *M* Trevor Rabin *Pro Des* Jan Roelfs *Pro* Jerry Bruckheimer and Mike Stenson

Touchstone Pictures / Buena Vista
116 mins. US 2002. Rel: 12 July 2002. Cert 12A.

Balzac and the Little Chinese Seamstress ★★★

Dai Sijie's film version of his novel is set in a remote Chinese location in 1971, a time when Chairman Mao ensured that members of reactionary families were sent away for re-education. It's a well-publicised fact that the 19-year-old central character, Ma (Liu Ye), represents Dai Sijie himself and the book *Wild Swans* has illustrated how a true story of survival can be popular without sacrificing quality. Here, however, with Ma and a close friend both attracted to the same girl and music by Mozart ruthlessly adapted to provide a recurring theme tune, authenticity loses out to fictional clichés and sentimentality. A more individual theme, albeit inadequately handled, is the power of literature, and here familiarity with Balzac's *Ursule Mirouët* is an advantage. MS

• *little Chinese seamstress* Xun Zhou *Luo* Kun Chen *Ma* Ye Liu *village head* Shuangbao Wang *old tailor* Zhijun Cong *Four Eyes* Hong Wei Wang
• *Dir* Dai Sijie *Scr* Dai Sijie, Nadine Perront *Pro* Lise Fayolle *Ex Pro* Bernard Lorain, Pujian Wang *M* Pujian Wang *Ph* Jean-Marie Dreujou *Ed* Luc Barnier, Julia Gregory *Pro Des* Juiping Cao

Les Films de la Suane / TF1 Films Productions / Soda Pictures
110 mins. France/China 2002.
Rel: 9 May 2003. Cert 12A.

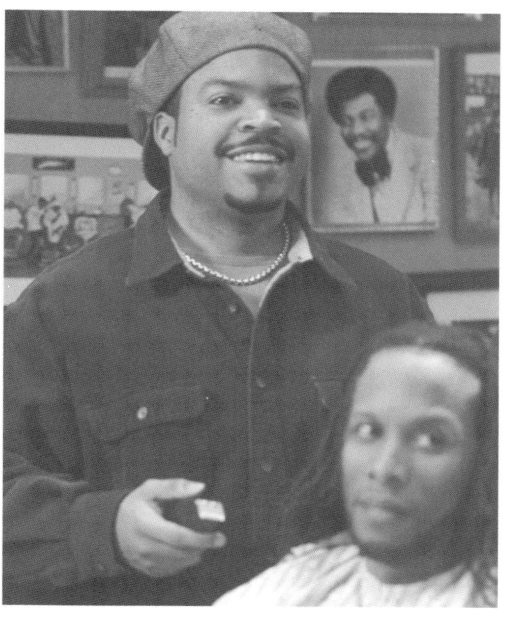

Right: Ice Cube cuts a fine figure in *Barbershop* (from Fox)

Barbershop ★★★

24 hours in a Chicago neighbourhood barbershop prove more exciting than you'd imagine. In this chat-heavy comic drama, Ice Cube slopes through his starring role as Calvin Palmer, the third generation proprietor of a family barbershop. Thankfully, the supporting ensemble livens up this portrait of a black community with spirited performances. Anthony Anderson is predictably excellent in his trademark funny-man role, while hip-hop star Eve is surprisingly watchable as the 'sistah' with the no-good boyfriend. The film is most rewarding the further it strays from the central plot strand, a tired refrain about whether Calvin will rescue the family store from the vicious loan shark Eddie. AK

• *Calvin Palmer* Ice Cube *JD* Anthony Anderson *Jimmy James* Sean Patrick Thomas *Terri Jones* Eve *Isaace Rosebberg* Troy Garity *Ricky Nash* Michael Ealy *Dinka* Leonard Earl Howze *Lester* Keith David *Billy* Lahmard Tate *Eddie* Cedric the Entertainer *Jennifer Palmer* Jazsmin Lewis
• *Dir* Tim Story *Scr* Mark Brown, Don D Scott, Marshall Todd *Pro* Robert Teitel, George Tillman Jr, Brown *Ph* Tom Priestley *Ed* John Carter *M* Terence Blanchard *Pro Des* Roger Fortune

Cube Vision / MGM / State Street Pictures / Twentieth Century Fox
102 mins. US 2002. Rel: 14 March 2003. Cert 12A.

Basic ½

Panama, the present. A training exercise goes horribly wrong, leaving a team of US Rangers missing in action with only two survivors (both with conflicting memories) to help unravel the truth. When the Navy's own interrogator, Julia Osborne, fails to crack the witness, the Colonel calls in DEA Agent and ex-Ranger Tom Hardy to 'unofficially' assist in the investigation... John McTiernan fails again to re-establish his psycho-suspense thriller credentials in this messy mongrel mixture of *Rashomon* and *A Few Good Men*. The film's migraine-inducing fascination with weather effects mates badly with an incomprehensible Gordian Knot of a plot that is eventually sliced apart by a ludicrous resolution. This competes strongly as the biggest waste of acting talent I've seen all year. AK

• *Tom Hardy* John Travolta *Julia Orborne* Connie Nielsen *Nathan West* Samuel L Jackson *Levi Kendall* Giovanni Ribisi *Raymond Dunbar* Brian Van Holt *Pike* Taye Diggs *Castro* Cristián de la Fuente *Mueller* Dash Mihok *Bill Styles* Tim Daly *Nunez* Roselyn Sanchez *Pete Vilmer* Harry Connick Jr
• *Dir* John McTiernan *Scr* James Vanderbilt *Ph* Steve Mason *Ed* George Folsey Jr *M* Klaus Badelt *Pro Des* Dennis Bradford *Pro* Mike Medavoy, Arnie Messer, Vanderbilt, Michael Tadross

InterMedia Film Equities Ltd / Orbit Entertainment Group / Phoenix Pictures / Icon
98 mins. US 2003. Rel: 20 June 2003. Cert 15.

Biker Boyz ★★

Purporting to be a mainstream exposé on superbiking weekend warriors, *Biker Boyz* is essentially an old-school Western on two wheels. 'Kid' Jalil has the talent for speed but it takes the death of his father to put his ambitions into gear. He starts his own club, the Biker Boyz, and immediately challenges Smoke, the veteran 'King of Cali' and leader of the Black Knights crew. But things take a hard corner when Kid's mother reveals that Smoke is his (sigh) father. As biker movies go, this one rides like a turbocharged neon Vespa. The comic asides that pass for 'cool' – like wheel-spinning bike tricks and military-style grand processions – extinguish any hope of our empathising with these reckless racers. Neither does the movie really build on the thrilling opening race scene. The final challenge, held on a dirt track surrounded by cows, is anticlimactic flimflam so sentimental that what trace of edgy attitude the film had skids away into the dust. AK

• *Smoke* Laurence Fishburne *Kid Jalil* Derek Luke *Soul Train* Orlando Jones *Motherland* Djimon Hounsou *Queenie* Lisa Bonet *Stuntman* Brendan Fehr *Wood* Larenz Tate *Dogg* Kid Rock *Slick Will* Eriq La Salle *Anita* Vanessa Bell Calloway *Tina* Meagan Good *Donny* Tyson Beckford
• *Dir* Reggie Rock Bythewood *Scr* Craig Fernandez and Bythewood, based on a *New Times* article by Michael Gougis *Ph* Gregory Gardiner *Ed* Terilyn A Shropshire and Caroline Ross *M* Camara Kambon *Pro Des* Cecilia Montiel *Pro* Stephanie Allain, Gina Prince- Bythewood, Erwin Stoff

3 Art Entertainment / DreamWorks SKG / UIP
111 mins. US 2003. Rel: 27 June 2003. Cert 12A.

Black Knight ★

It's nice that Martin Lawrence's new film starts with a taste warning: if you can stand to watch him brush, floss, pluck and primp himself during the opening credits, you will probably survive the film. Lawrence plays Jamal 'Sky' Walker, a self-centred

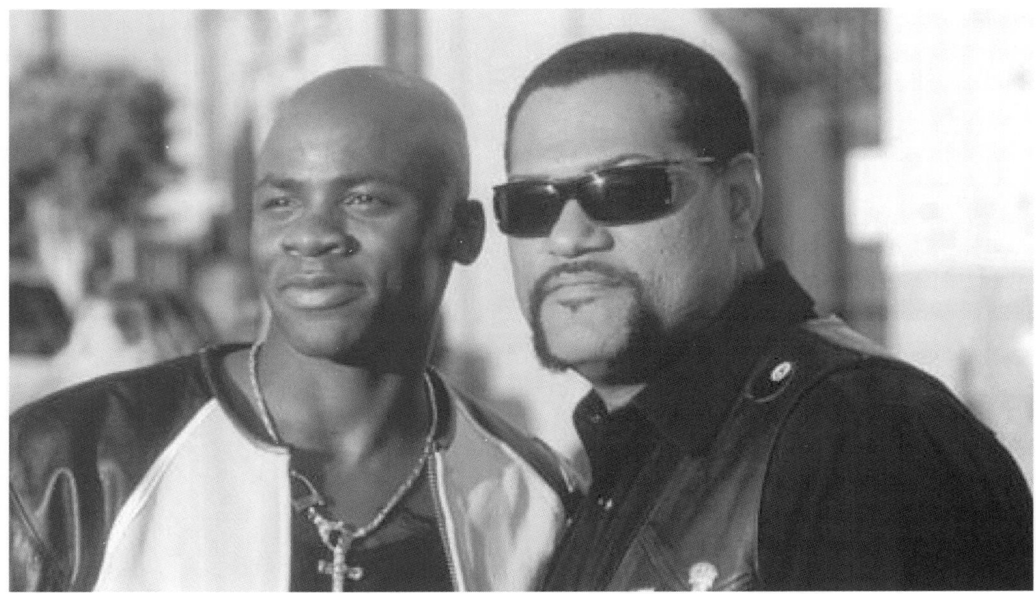

Left: Newcomer Derek Luke with Laurence Fishburne in the slick urban drama *Biker Boyz*. (from UIP)

brother from modern LA who is transported to 14th century England, setting up a 'Nubians in Camelot' *Carry On* farce. Cue anachronistic gags and screeds of dialogue beginning with 'Behold!', all in the dodgiest taste possible. Blatantly a Lawrence vehicle, only the sheer energy of his manic clowning keeps the film from drowning. Scripted by the team that brought us the abysmal *Say It Isn't So*, the dialogue is, unsurprisingly, witless stuff. "'Tis roadkill, man!" and "Brother lost in the woods? Not good!" says Lawrence. He has a point. AK

• *Jamal Walker* Martin Lawrence *Victoria* Marsha Thomason *Knolte* Tom Wilkinson *Percival* Vincent Regan *Steve* Daryl Mitchell *King Leo* Kevin Conway
• *Dir* Gil Junger *Scr* Darryl J Quarles, Peter Gaulke and Gerry Swallow *Ph* Ueli Steiger *Ed* Michael R Miller *M* Randy Edelman *Pro Des* Leslie Dilley *Pro* Arnon Milchan, Quarles, Michael Green and Paul Schiff

Twentieth Century Fox / New Regency Pictures / Regency Enterprises / Runteldat Entertainment / The Firm / Twentieth Century Fox
97 mins. US 2002. Rel: 23 August 2002. Cert PG.

Blood Work ★★

Clint Eastwood is on familiar ground here as FBI 'profiler' Terry McCaleb, towering over his co-stars like a granite institution, squinting disapprovingly at the wisecracks of his one-dimensional colleagues. There's a serial killer on the loose and, like so many screen psychos before him, this one is playing mind games with his hunter. At the scene of one particularly nasty murder, McCaleb spots the killer in the crowd and chases him down the alleyways of Los Angeles. It's kind of ridiculous to see the 72-year-old Eastwood speeding after a man several decades his junior, but there's a twist: McCaleb suffers a heart attack. Two years later, the fed is retired and recovering from a heart transplant. He then discovers that the donor of his new ticker is the female victim of a homicide and, piqued by an entreaty from the donor's sister, he starts to investigate her murder. Eastwood is always good value, both as director and icon, and can even make a formulaic thriller like this seem interesting – up to a point. However, some awkward dialogue and poorly executed action scenes reduce this to very routine fare. JC-W

• *Terry McCaleb* Clint Eastwood *Buddy Noone* Jeff Daniels *Graciella Rivers* Wanda De Jesùs *Det Ronaldo Arrango* Paul Rodriguez *Dr Bonnie Fox* Anjelica Huston *Jaye Winston* Tina Lifford *Det John Waller* Dylan Walsh *Raymond* Mason Lucero *with* Gerry Becker, Rick Hoffman, Alix Koromzay, Igor Jijikine, Dina Eastwood, Glenn Morshower
• *Dir* and *Pro* Clint Eastwood *Ex Pro* Robert Lorenz *Co Pro* Judie G Hoyt *Scr* Brian Helgeland, based on the novel by Michael Connelly *Ph* Tom Stern *Pro Des* Henry Bumstead *Ed* Joel Cox *M* Lennie Niehaus *Costumes* Deborah Hopper

Warner/Malpaso-Warner.
108 mins. US 2002. Rel: 27 December 2002. Cert 15.

Blue Crush ★★½

Lithe, blonde and talented, Anne Marie is a hotel maid by day and a dedicated surfer every other waking minute. An opportunity to hit the big time comes along with a wildcard to compete in the legendary Pipe Masters Competition. But memories of a nearly fatal accident and a budding romance with a hunky football player distract her from fulfilling her dreams... *Blue Crush* is perhaps the first decent surfing film that doesn't reduce the women in the sport to jiggling, bikinied wipeout fodder. Based on a magazine article about the real 'Surf Girls of Maui', it melds authentic elements of the insular surfing mafia on the Hawaiin islands with a story that is pure Hollywood. The action sequences take full advantage of digital hi-tech, delivering gut-juddering effects powerful enough to justify its 'extreme sports' marketing façade. AK

• *Anne Marie* Kate Bosworth *Eden* Michelle Rodriguez *Matt* Matthew Davis *Lena* Sanoe Lake *Penny* Mika Boorem *Leslie* Faizon Love
• *Dir* John Stockwell *Scr* Lizzy Weiss and Stockwell, based on the magazine article 'Surf Girls of Maui' by Susan Orlean *Ph* David Hennings *Ed* Emma E Hickox *M* Paul Haslinger *Pro Des* Tom Meyer *Pro* Brian Grazer and Karen Kehela

Imagine Entertainment / Shutt/Jones Productions / Universal Pictures / UIP
109 mins. US 2002. Rel: 4 April 2003. Cert 12A.

Boat Trip ★★½

Where do you go after you've vomited on your fiancé while trying to propose? Answer: a singles cruise with your raunchy best friend. Jerry and Nick take to the high seas in an attempt to find new romance. The problem is, it's an all-gay cruise. But even after they finally figure this out, one look at sexy Vivica A Fox and the Swedish Bikini Team has the two men deciding to stay on board and play along... Cuba Gooding Jr is as good as the material allows and it's great to see Horatio Sanz on the big screen. Roger Moore steals the show as a camp septuagenarian and a cameo by Richard Roundtree as Vivica's dad is a hoot. Credibility is strained but the story is affable enough, with a few genuine laughs peppered among the groans. SWM

• *Jerry* Cuba Gooding Jr *Nick* Horatio Sanz *Gabriella* Roselyn Sanchez *Felicia* Vivica A Fox *Hector* Maurice

Godin *Lloyd* Roger Moore *Sonya* Lin Shaye *Inga* Victoria Silvsted
• *Dir* Mort Nathan *Pro* Brad Krevoy, Gerhard Schmidt, Frank Hubner, Andrew Sugerman *Ex Pro* Sabine Müller *Scr* Nathan and William Bigelow *Ph* Shawn Maurer *Ed* John Axness *M* Robert Folk *Pro Des* Charles Breen

ApolloMedia / Boat Trip LLC / Erste Productions KG / Gemini Filmproduktions GmbH / International West Pictures / Motion Picture Corporation of America / Entertainment
93 mins. US/Germany 2002. Rel: 4 October 2002. Cert 15.

El Bola ★★★★

(aka *Pellet*)
Reaching us belatedly – Achero Mañas made this Spanish award-winner in 2000 – this grim slice of life proves reminiscent of Mike Leigh's *All or Nothing.* Set in Madrid, it starts with schoolboys dicing with death on a railway track and then concentrates on two families. In each case there's a young son – 12-year-old Pablo, known as Pellet (Juan José Ballesta), and his friend Alfredo (Pablo Galán) – who plays a key role. In the second half of the film comes the revelation that Pellet, too frightened to speak out, is being regularly disciplined and beaten up by his brutal father. Able filming, distinguished acting (both child actors are first class) and strong emotional involvement are let down, if only slightly, by a couple of unconvincing moments and by swearing so excessive as to seem unjustified. MS

• *Pablo* aka '*El Bola'* Juan José Ballesta *Alfredo* Pablo Galan *José* Alberto Gimenez *Mariano* Mañuel Maron *Laura* Ana Wagener *Marisa* Nieve de Medina *Aurora* Gloria Munoz
• *Dir / Scr* Achero Manas *Ex Pro* José Antonio Felez *Ph* Juan Carlos Gomez *Art Dir* Satur Idarreta *Ed* Nacho Ruiz Capillas *M* Eduardo Arbide

Tesela / TVE / Via Digital-Axiom Films
88 mins. Spain 2000. Rel: 4 April 2003. Cert 15.

Bollywood/Hollywood ★★★

Handsome dotcom millionaire Rahul is tired of his mother and grandmother's exaggerated interest in his love life. They're even prepared to cancel his sister's wedding, so keen are they for him to settle down. As a result, he decides to acquire a bogus fiancée in the shape of escort Sunita Singh… Deepa Metha's placing of Bollywood conventions in a Canadian setting might not have the splash of its Bombay-based counterparts, but it still manages to be a lively and frequently funny culture-clash comedy. Rahul Khanna and Lisa Ray make an appealing lead couple as Rahul and Sue, but the film really belongs to the veterans: Grandma Dina Pathak (in her final performance), the versatile comedienne Moushumi Chatterjee and Kulbhushan Kharbanda, who plays Sue's drunken father. It's a thoroughly predictable tale featuring all manner of clichés, but it's dominated by a sure sense of fun along with some effervescent song-and-dance sequences, ensuring that it's never less than an enjoyable watch. DG

• *Rahul Seth* Rahul Khanna *Sue Singh* Lisa Ray *Twinky Seth* Rishma Malick *Bobby* Jazz Mann *Mrs Seth* (mother) Moushumi Chatterjee *Mrs Seth* (grandmother) Dina Pathak *Mr Singh* Kulbhushan Kharbanda *Rocky* Ranjit Chowdry *Lucy* Leesa Gaspari *Go* Arjun Lombardi-Singh
• *Dir / Scr* Deepa Metha *Pro* David Hamilton *Ex Pro* Camelia Frehberg, Ajay Virmani *Co Pro* Robert Wertheimer *Ph* Douglas Koch *Ed* Barry Farrell *M* Sandeepo Chowta *Pro Des* Tamara Deverell *Art Dir* Jason Graham *Costume* Anne Dixon, Ritu Kumar

Magnolia Pictures / Mongrel Media / Different Tree Same Wood / iDream Productions / Momentum
105 mins. US 2002. Rel: 14 February 2003 Cert 12A.

Below: Matt Damon is on a steep learning curve for his first action hero role in *The Bourne Identity* (from UIP)

The Bourne Identity ★★★★

Rescued from drowning by Marseilles fishermen, the only clue to his identity a numbered deposit box in Switzerland, Jason Bourne falls into a rabbit hole of assassins and sleeper agents when he tries to discover who – and what – he is… Robert Ludlum's amnesiac spy story gets a very hip update at the hands of Doug Liman, whose masterstroke was to cast Matt Damon as Bourne. Damon brings intellectual integrity to what might otherwise have been just another adrenaline-chasing spook hunt. The highly focused reserve he gives to the role is the epitome of cool, matching the blue-grey cast of the film's continental winter setting. Like the stunningly effective fighting style Bourne uses, the film works on a fluid economy of expression that is profoundly refreshing in a genre dedicated to just blowing up the next biggest thing. With Franka Potente as the bystander swept up by the storm, the film achieves a substantial emotional centre to anchor the hurricane of stylish action. AK

• *Jason Bourne* Matt Damon *Marie Kreutz* Franka Potente *Ted Conklin* Chris Cooper *the Professor* Clive Owen *Ward Abbott* Brian Cox *Nykwana Wombosi* Adewale Akinnuoye-Agbaje
• *Dir* Doug Liman *Scr* Tony Gilroy and William Blake Herron, based on the novel by Robert Ludlum *Ph* Oliver Wood *Ed* Saar Klein *M* John Powell *Pro Des* Dan Weil *Pro* Liman, Patrick Crowley, Richard N Gladstein

Hypnotic / Kalima Productions / The Kennedy/Marshall Company / UIP
118 mins. US 2002. Rel: 6 September 2002. Cert 12A.

Bowling for Columbine ★★★★

Michael Moore, America's most prominent liberal critic, trudges across a warped landscape of 'normal' Americans who treasure their right to gun ownership the way other people treasure drinking water. The question he disingenuously poses is, "Why, when Americans kill over 11,000 fellow Americans each year, is the private ownership of firearms not more strictly controlled?" From the opening scene where Moore is offered a free rifle for opening a bank account ("Don't you think it's a little dangerous handing out guns in a bank?") to his encounters with characters like 'Oklahoma Bomber' Tim McVeigh's brother, Charlton Heston (spokesperson for the National Rifle Association) and the kids from Columbine High School, Moore chips away at the credibility of the pro-gun faction in a hilariously one-sided polemic. AK

• *with* Michael Moore, Dick Clark, Charlton Heston, James Nichols, Marilyn Manson, John Nichols and Matt Stone
• *Dir / Scr* Michael Moore *Ph* Brian Danitz and Michael McDonough *Ed* Kurt Engfehr *M* Jeff Gibbs *Pro* Charles Bishop, Michael Donovan, Kathleen Glynn, Jim Czarnecki, Moore

Alliance Atlantis Communications / Dog Eat Dog Films / Salter Street Films International / United Broadcasting Inc / VIF Babelsberger Filmproduktion GmbH & Co Zweite KG (VIF 2) / Momentum
120 mins. US / Canada / Germany 2002. Rel: 15 November 2002. Cert 15.

Bringing Down the House ★★½

In recent years Steve Martin has been building on his reputation as a dramatic actor, novelist and playwright. Now 57, his forays into screen comedy have become scarcer and scarcer, so it's almost nostalgic to see him goofing off in this out-and-out farce. *Bringing Down the House* features Martin as the sort of character he has been playing on-and-off for the last 12 years or so: an anal, suburban professional with a huge reservoir of wild and crazy energy under the surface. Here, he's Peter Sanderson, a sly, divorced lawyer who's never really stopped

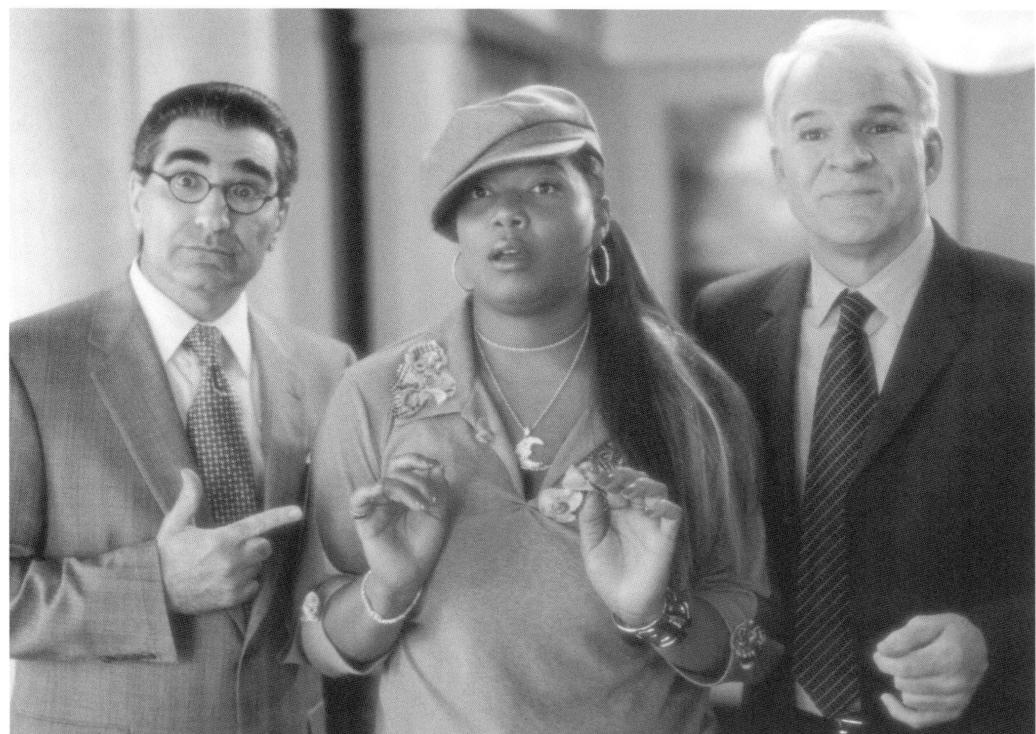

Right: Eugene Levy, Queen Latifah and Steve Martin in *Bringing Down the House* (from Buena Vista)

carrying a torch for his ex-wife but who's too busy to spend quality time with his kids. What spare time he has, he devotes to an anonymous pen friend he's found in an Internet chat room. When the latter – who's been posing as a blonde, beautiful barrister – turns out to be a loud-mouthed sister from the 'hood, she refuses to leave his house. Thanks to the comic chemistry brewed up by Martin and Queen Latifah, what follows is some fun, even though a number of asinine set pieces outstay their welcome. Previously known as *In the Houze.* JC-W

• *Peter Sanderson* Steve Martin *Charlene Morton* Queen Latifah *Howie Rottman* Eugene Levy *Kate* Jean Smart *Mrs Arness* Joan Plowright *Sarah Sanderson* Kimberly J Brown *Georgey Sanderson* Angus T Jones *Ashley* Missi Pyle *Todd Gendler* Michael Rosenbaum *Mrs Kline* Betty White *Widow* Steve Harris *Ed Tobias* Jim Haynie *with* Aengus James, Michael Ensign, John Prosky, Deezer D, Kelly Price
• *Dir* Adam Shankman *Pro* David Hoberman, Ashok Amritraj *Ex Pro* Jane Bartelme, Queen Latifah *Co Pro* Todd Lieberman *Scr* Jason Filardi *Ph* Julio Macat *Pro Des* Linda DeScenna *Ed* Jerry Greenberg *M* Lalo Schifrin; songs performed by Foxy Brown, The Time, Robert Palmer, Bishop, Jonny Was, Calvin Richardson, Kelly Price, Barry White, Jamie Dunlap, Just Shawn, Iceberg, Floetry, Redman, The Unit, Lil' Wayne, Eve, N.E.R.D., Mr Cheeks, Queen Latifah *Costumes* Pam Withers-Chilton

Touchstone Pictures / Hyde Park Entertainment / Buena Vista
105 mins. USA 2003. Rel: 30 May 2003. Cert 12A.

Broken Wings ★★★

(*Knafayim Shvurot*)
This Jewish drama about the stresses of family life is reminiscent of Mike Leigh's *All or Nothing.* But since it shows a family struggling to come to terms after being traumatised and rendered dysfunctional by a sudden death, it is even closer to *The Son's Room.* Initially, and with the aid of a good cast, it seems possible that this award winner will be of comparable quality to those earlier films. But where *The Son's Room* had the wisdom to recognise that there are no easy adjustments to life after bereavement, this film opts for increasingly unlikely developments and contrived, neat resolutions. In short, Nir Bergman's film ultimately reveals itself as a soap opera, with real life left behind. On that level it could be worse, but it promised so much more. MS

• *Dafna Ulman* Orly Silbersatz Banai *Maya Ulman* Maya Maron *Yair Ulman* Nitai Gaviratz *Dr Valentin Goldman* Vladimir Friedman *Iris* Dana Ivgi *Yoram* Danny Niv (as Danny 'mooki' Niv) *Ido Ulman* Daniel Magon *Bahr Ulman* Eliana Magon
• *Dir / Scr* Nir Bergman *Pro* Assaf Amir *Ex Pro* Yoav Roeh *M* Avi Belleli *Ph* Valentin Belonogov *Ed* Einat Glaser-Zarhin

Israeli Film Fund / Norma Productions Ltd / Yes-DBD Satellite Services / Optimum Releasing
83 mins. Israel 2002. Rel: 6 June 2003. Cert 15.

Brown Sugar ★★½

Sidney and Dre grew up with hip-hop and continue to live for the music, she as the new editor of *XXL* magazine and he as a record producer. Their easy friendship is jolted when Dre announces his marriage to the ultra-buppie Reese (trans 'black yuppie')... A standard romcom given a neo-cultural spin by presenting a history of hip-hop in parallel to the generic boy-girl-career tennis game. The metaphors and analogies applied to the music – which end up representing love, life, and the meaning of the universe (almost) – ultimately stretch what credibility there could have been, leaving the sense that the film is merely cashing in on the spirit of the movement in exactly the way it criticises others for doing. AK

Right Jim Carrey draws down the moon for an astonished Jennifer Aniston in the divine comedy *Bruce Almighty* (from Buena Vista)

Below: Nicole Ari Parker is delighted with her zippy new wardrobe in *Brown Sugar* (from Fox)

• *Dre* Taye Diggs *Sidney* Sanaa Lathan *Chris* Mos Def *Reese* Nicole Ari Parker *Kelby* Boris Kodjoe *Francine* Queen Latifah.
• *Dir* Rick Famuyiwa *Scr* Michael Elliot and Famuyiwa *Ph* Enrique Chediak *Ed* Dirk Westervelt *M* Robert Hurst *Pro Des* Kalina Ivanov *Pro* Peter Heller

Evergreen Productions / Heller Highwater Productions / Magic Johnson Entertainment / 20th Century Fox
109 mins. US 2003. Rel: 18 July 2003. Cert 12A.

Bruce Almighty ★★★½

Pigeonholed as the 'joke news guy', frustrated TV reporter Bruce Nolan self-destructs on live TV when he loses an anchor position to a rival. He is fired, and then beaten up for helping a bum. That is just the start of the worst day of Bruce's life. At the end of it, Bruce angrily challenges the heavens, claiming that if *he* were God, he'd have the world fixed in a week. Lo and behold, God takes Bruce up on the offer, granting him all his heavenly powers, which Bruce usefully expends by looking up ladies' skirts and magically parting red soup... Jim Carrey's lightweight romcom knocked *The Matrix Reloaded* off the US No 1 spot and concedes that his best talents lie in rubber-faced comedy, not the serious drama of last year's floppy *The Majestic.* Morgan Freeman – a spookily convincing Almighty – silkily foils Carrey's mounting outrageousness, which is on a masterly level unseen since *The Mask.* Surrealistic pratfalls mix with a philosophical (though ultimately melodramatic) line about love and happiness, and Carrey makes the devilishly tricky task of making an audience laugh seem almost as simple as proclaiming "Let There Be Light Comedy!" AK

• *Bruce Nolan* Jim Carrey *God* Morgan Freeman *Grace Connelly* Jennifer Aniston *Jack Keller* Philip Baker Hall *Sisan Ortega* Catherine Bell *Debbie* Lisa Ann Walter
• *Dir* Tom Shadyac *Scr* Steve Koren, Mark O'Keefe, Steve Oedekerk *Ph* Dean Semler *Ed* Scott Hill *M* John Debney *Pro Des* Linda Descenna *Pro* Shadyac, Carrey, James D Brubaker, Michael Bostick, Koren, O'Keefe

Universal Pictures / Shady Acres Entertainment / The Pitbull Co / Beverly Detroit / Interscope Communications / Partizan / Pit Bull Productions / Spyglass Entertainment / Buena Vista
101 mins. US 2003. Rel: 27 June 2003. Cert 12A.

Bulletproof Monk ★★½

A nameless Tibetan monk on the run from a psychotic old Nazi (aren't they all?) meets Kar, the unlikely protector of a sacred scroll of power… In a comic-book adaptation of such startling derivativeness (featuring a 'chosen one' who can dodge bullets, defy gravity and deliver 'enlightenment' chased by gunmen in black suits and rimless shades; yes, it's *The Matrix Reheated*!), not even Chow Yun Fat's legendary Cheshire Cat grin and charming cotton-mouthed delivery can compensate for a plot riddled with leaps of logic only the wisdom of Buddha could comprehend. How did Kar know where to find his lady-love, Jade? And are we seriously expected to believe that a diet of Hong Kong martial arts movies trained him to such competent martial artistry? However, the kung-fu is good (it really is), and there is a small kick to be got from the script's fortune-cookie philosophising, unconcerned though it is with either relevance or wit. AK

• *Monk With No Name* Chow Yun-Fat *Kar* Seann William Scott *Jade / Bad Girl* Jaime King *Struker* Karel Roden *Nina* Victoria Smurfit *Mr Funktastic* Marcus Jean Pirae *Master Monk* Roger Yuan
• *Dir* Paul Hunter *Scr* Ethan Reiff and Cyrus Voris, based on the Flypaper Press comic book *Ph* Stefan Czapsky *Ed* Robert K Lambert *M* Eric Serra *Pro Des* Deborah Evans *Pro* Charles Roven, Douglas Segal, Terence Chang, John Woo

Cub Five Productions / Flypaper Press / Lakeshore Entertainment / Lion Rock / Mosaic Media Group / Signpost Films / Pathé
103 mins. US 2003. Rel: 18 April 2003. Cert 12A.

Bundy ★★★½

This film tells of 1970s serial killer Ted Bundy and uses his eventual execution as an opportunity to mount an attack on capital punishment in the manner of *Monster's Ball.* But such righteous indignation hardly fits with what has until then been a Corman-style semi-exploitation piece featuring women in jeopardy. However, on its own terms Matthew Bright's film is well made, and it does seek to examine Bundy's past history (he was an illegitimate child who discovered that his real mother was the person he knew as his sister) to suggest reasons why as an adult he became a psychopath. Furthermore, the women are not reduced to being victims and nothing more: Zarah Little wins our admiration for an abductee who escapes and Boti Ann Bliss as Bundy's unsuspecting girlfriend also impresses. MS

• *Ted Bundy* Michael Reilly Burke *Lee* Boti Ann Bliss *Professor* Julianna McCarthy *Julie* Steffani Brass *Vincennes* Tricia Dickson *Welch* Meadow Sisto
• *Dir* Matthew Bright *Scr* Stephen Johnston, Bright *Ph* Sonja Rom *Ed* Paul Heiman *M* Kennard Ramsey *Pro Des* Chris Anthony Miller *Pro* Hamish McAlpine, Michael Muscal

First Look Media / Incessant Barking Productions / Tartan Films / Metro Tartan

Right Blind terror in the dying days of the Second World War for the cast of *The Bunker* (from Salvation)

99 mins. US/ UK. 2002. Rel: 22 November 2002. Cert 18.

The Bunker ★★½

The Black Forest, 1944: A platoon of bedraggled German soldiers hide from advancing Allied forces in an abandoned concrete bunker. Their refuge soon becomes a prison, and claustrophobia amplifies their insecurity and paranoia. As their ammunition runs low they come to the grim realisation that their only means of escape is via a labyrinth of dank tunnels. But the bunker was built on the site of unspeakable horrors, and the tunnels seem to harbour a terrifying, murderous presence... Rob Green's earthy debut feature is clearly influenced by the classic Val Lewton/Jacques Tourneur thrillers, but the novel backdrop and convincing performances from Jason Flemyng and John Carlisle help compensate for the familiarity of the routine. Green struggles to maintain the pace and coherence of the narrative, however, and the absence of any female cast members similarly dents the commercial potential of this otherwise unsettling film. MH

• *Corporal Baumann* Jason Flemyng *Lance Corporal Ebert* Jack Davenport *Sergeant Heydrich* Christopher Fairbank *Private Mirus* John Carlisle *Private Neumann* Andrew Lee Potts
• *Dir* Rob Green *Scr* Clive Dawson *Ph* John Pardue *Ed* Richard Milward *M* Russell Currie *Pro Des* Richard Campling *Pro* Daniel Figuero, David Reid

Millennium Pictures / Salvation Films
92 mins. UK 2001. Rel: 27 September 2002. Cert 15.

Butterfly Man ★★½

The directorial debut of the British-born Kaprice Lea, ***Butterfly Man*** is seldom less than ravishing to look at but reveals the inexperience of its maker in matters of dialogue and character development. Covering ground previously explored with considerable accomplishment by Danny Boyle in ***The Beach*** (callow Western backpacker seduced by the exotica of Thailand), Lea's film is best at exploring the minutiae of Thai life, complete with its mysticism and exploitation. Where it comes unstuck is in its interaction between stock characters, particularly with an unconvincing element of criminal activity. Still, the young Thai actress Napakpapha M Nakprasitte is a revelation as a local masseuse, her broken English and complete beauty a tonic to the soul. Less successful is Stuart Laing as the story's English protagonist, who, having just broken up with his girlfriend, flits from woman to woman like a 'butterfly man'. To be fair, though, Laing is provided with some pretty indigestible dialogue ("I thought I knew what life was in England"). JC-W

• *Adam* Stuart Laing *Em* Napakpapha 'Mamee' Nakprasitte *Joey* Francis Magee *Bill Kincaid* Gavan O'Herlihy *No Name* Abigail Good *Kate* Kirsty Mitchell *Noi* Vasa Vatcharayon
• *Dir / Scr* Kaprice Lea *Pro* Tom Waller *Ass Pro* Pairoj Roljertanya *Ph* Mark Duffield *Pro Des* Fay Garrett *Ed* Atisthan Sangawut and William Watts *M* Steve Bentley-Klein *Costumes* Juliana Ross *Sound* Peter Michael Sullivan

De Warrenne Pictures-De Warrenne Pictures
95 mins. UK 2002. Rel: 6 December 2002. Cert 15.

Catch Me If You Can ★★★½

Frank Abagnale Jr, just 16 years old, flees the bleak realities of a broken home to become the greatest fraudster in American history (politicians aside). Using an uncommon wit, he transforms himself into an airline pilot, a paediatrician, and then a lawyer, all within the space of three years. But Frank's happiness depends on staying one step ahead of the law, particularly the dogged FBI agent Carl Hanratty… Based on Frank's fantastic memoirs, Spielberg assembles a peerless cast to bring his story to life. Fastidiously styled and warmly presented, the movie runs a little slowly in the middle act, when we are told more than we need to know about Frank's escapades. Spielberg also shies away from portraying any moral ambiguity, plumping instead for the line that Frank was merely a misunderstood kid struggling to get along in a cruel world, when the reality was perhaps a little less romantic. Given a tighter budget, and a less family-friendly brief, *Catch Me If You Can* could have been a true modern classic instead of merely another polished notch on Spielberg's belt. AK

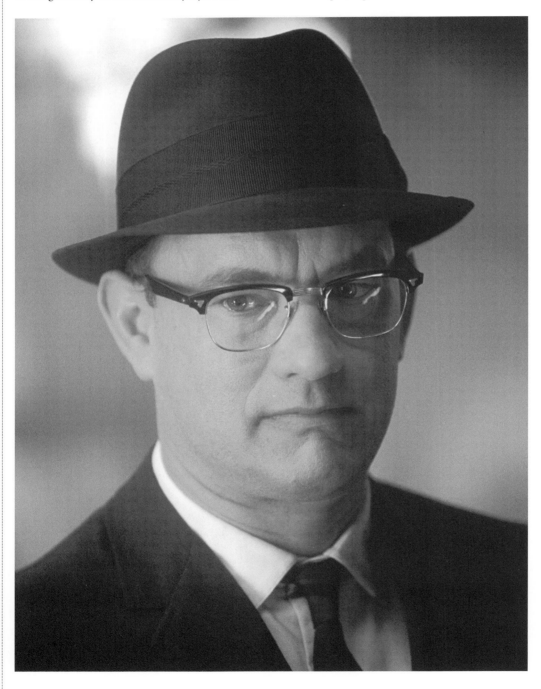

Left: Tom Hanks in Spielberg's slick dramatisation of a young con artist's adventures, *Catch Me If You Can* (from UIP)

• *Frank Abagnale Jr* Leonardo DiCaprio *Carl Hanratty* Tom Hanks *Frank Abagnale Sr* Christopher Walken *Roger Strong* Martin Sheen *Paula Abagnale* Nathalie Baye *Brenda Strong* Amy Adams *Jack Barnes* James Brolin
• *Dir* Steven Spielberg *Scr* Jeff Nathanson, based on the book by Frank W Abagnale Jr and Stan Redding *Ph* Janusz Kaminski *Ed* Michael Kahn *M* John Williams *Pro Des* Jeannine Oppewall *Pro* Spielberg, Walter F Parkes

Amblin Entertainment / Bungalow 78 Productions / DreamWorks SKG / Kemp Company / Magellan Filmed Entertainment / Parkes/MacDonald / Splendid Pictures Inc. / UIP
141 mins. US 2002. Rel: 31 January 2003. Cert 12A.

Changing Lanes ★★★

The paths of recovering alcoholic Doyle Gipson and hotshot attorney Gavin Baneck collide on a New York freeway, prompting a bout of bad Samaritanism that results in Doyle losing custody of his children for being late to court and Gavin being embarrassed by the lack of a key piece of evidence that Doyle now possesses. In a moralistic tale about small choices with big consequences, Gavin and Doyle proceed to make each other's lives hell in an increasingly mean-spirited game of one-upmanship, coming full circle when Doyle forces Gavin into another freeway collision. The edgy look of the film (which somewhat predictably constrasts the dirty concrete of inner-city New York with the lofty glamour of Manhattan) and the insistently jagged soundtrack don't quite gel with the soft-centred script, which eventually jumps through some barely credible hoops in order to make things come out right in the end. AK

• *Gavin Banek* Ben Affleck *Doyle Gipson* Samuel L Jackson *Valerie Gipson* Kim Staunton *Michelle* Toni Collette *Andrew Delano* Sydney Pollack *Mrs Delano* Tina Sloan *Cynthia Banek* Amanda Peet *Walter Arnell* Richard Jenkins *Sponsor* William Hurt
• *Dir* Roger Michell *Scr* Chap Taylor and Michael Tolkin *Ph* Salvatore Totino *Ed* Christopher Tellefsen *M* David Arnold *Pro Des* Kristi Zea *Pro* Scott Rudin

Scott Rudin Productions / Paramount / UIP
99 mins. US 2002. Rel: 1 November 2002. Cert 15.

Charlie's Angels: Full Throttle ★★★★

When two coded titanium bands containing the secret identities of everyone placed in the FBI's Witness Protection Program go missing, it's up to the gals of the Charles Townsend Detective Agency to save the day… This second outing for Charlie's Angels truly deserves the *Full Throttle* sobriquet. It's all-out action balanced with just the right blend of humour and drama. Never taking itself too seriously, it's unashamedly over-the-top in characterisation, plot, action and special effects. Gratuitously borrowing themes from a host of films (from *Cape Fear* to *Spider-Man*), *CA:FT* is nothing short of dazzling. At the same time, it's a genuine homage to the show that inspired it (note the Jaclyn Smith cameo). It's obvious that Drew Barrymore, Cameron Diaz and Lucy Liu had a blast making this sequel and the addition of Bernie Mac as Bosley rounds out the team perfectly. SWM

• *Natalie Cook* Cameron Diaz *Dylan Sanders* Drew Barrymore *Alex Munday* Lucy Liu *Jimmy Bosley* Bernie Mac *The Thin Man* Crispin Glover *Seamus O'Grady* Justin Theroux *Ray Carter* Robert Patrick *Madison Lee* Demi Moore *Randy Emmers* Rodrigo Santoro *Pete* Luke Wilson *Max* Shia LaBeouf *Jason* Matt LeBlanc *Mother Superior* Carrie Fisher *Mr Munday* John Cleese *[voice of] Charlie* John Forsythe *Future Angels* Ashley Olsen and Mary-Kate Olsen [uncredited] *Mexican Bar Angel* Jaclyn Smith [uncredited] *William Rose Bailey* Bruce Willis [uncredited]
• *Dir* McG *Scr* John August, Cormac Wibberley, Marianne Wibberley *Ph* Russell Carpenter *Ed* Wayne Wahrman *M* Edward Shearmur *Pro Des* J Michael Riva *Pro* Leonard Goldberg, Drew Barrymore, Nancy Juvonen

Columbia Pictures Corporation / Flower Films (Barrymore/Juvonen) / Tall Trees Productions / Wonderland Sound and Vision / Columbia Tristar
106 mins. US 2003. Rel: 1 July 2003. Cert 12A.

Chicago ★★★★

Rob Marshall's Oscar-winning musical illustrates how to make a semi-silk purse out of a semi-sow's ear. The score by John Kander with librettist Fred Ebb is simply not in the same league as their *Cabaret*, but that just provides the opportunity to create a work of cinematic energy based on fast editing and the personal enthusiasm of all five leading players. The twenties plot, filmed in 1942 as *Roxie Hart*, features cynical comedy in a tale of two female killers (Zellweger and Zeta-Jones) and the lawyer (Gere) who takes on their cases. He treats legal 'justice' as a form of showbusiness in which, after 15 minutes of fame, every murderer becomes old hat. This is quite good fun, but the point of the piece is the treatment of the music. Baz Luhrmann's *Moulin Rouge!* insulted great songs by cutting them up, but Marshall and his editor Martin Walsh are far neater and – the prime point here – are dealing with a score that benefits from everything they do with it. MS

• *Roxie Hart* Renée Zellweger *Velma Kelly* Catherine Zeta-Jones *Billy Flynn* Richard Gere *Matron Mam Morton* Queen Latifah *Amos Hart* John C Reilly *Kitty Baxter* Lucy Liu *bandleader* Taye Diggs

Left: Renée Zellweger and Richard Gere in the razzle-dazzling *Chicago* (from Buena Vista)

Harrison Colm Feore *Mary Sunshine* Christine Baranski *Fred Casely* Dominic West *Nickie* Chita Rivera
• *Dir / Choreography* Rob Marshall *Scr* Bill Condon, based on the musical by Bob Fosse and Fred Ebb and the play by Maurine Dallas Watkins *Ch* Dion Beebe *Ed* Martin Walsh *M* John Kander, Fred Ebb, Danny Elfman *Pro Des* John Myhre *Pro* Martin Richards *Costumes* Colleen Atwood

Loop Films / Miramax Films / The Producers Circle Co. / Buena Vista
107 mins. US 2002. Rel: 27 December 2002. Cert 15.

Chiwaseon

See *Drunk on Women and Poetry*

Chop Suey ★★★★½

Bruce Weber's pot-pourri of a movie ought not to work, but it undoubtedly does. Despite a few longueurs, it's a fascinating mix in which the unexpected frequently occurs (Robert Mitchum singing with Dr John; glimpses of performers ranging from Sophie Tucker to Miss Peggy Lee). Three elements are crucial: a kind of autobiography (mainly career-centred), a fond portrait of the lesbian jazz singer Frances Faye and a survey of the changing photographic scene over recent decades, including fashionable magazines adjusting to homoerotic imagery. The latter, whether or not centred on Weber's model Peter Johnson, is a potent element in his pictures, and this film achieves unity through its romantic celebration of life and of the human body. The screen images are stunning, but it's also well edited and fed by the use of unusually varied background music. Terrific. MS

• *with* Peter Johnson, Frances Faye (archive footage), Herbie Fletcher, Dibi Fletcher, Christian Fletcher, Nathan Fletcher, Rickson Gracie, Robert Mitchum (archive footage), Sir Wilfred Thesiger (archive footage), Jan-Michael Vincent, Diana Vreeland (archive footage), Teri Shepherd, Teddy Antolini, Jason Maves, Ryan Mickelson
• *Dir* Bruce Weber *Ex Pro* Nan Bush *Scr* Weber, Maribeth Edwards *Ph* Lance Accord, Douglas Cooper, Jim Fealy *Ed* Angelo Corrao *M* John Leftwich *Pro Des* Dimitri Levas

Just Blue Films Inc / BFI
98 mins. US 2000. Rel: 5 July 2002. Cert 15.

Christie Malry's Own Double-Entry ★½

An ambitious black comedy that doubletracks the invention of the double-entry book-keeping system in 15th century Italy with the deeply psychotic quest of repressed accountant Christie Malry to pay back every injustice visited upon him with bloody, violent interest. The ambition is to be admired, but the wildly veering tone of the various narrative lines breaks down what, presumably, was intended as the cohesive theme of justice and balance. The mounting violence also breaks down into hysteria whatever satirical value the film might have had. Nick Moran performs well, and the director makes good use of his naturally sneering expressions, but even as a cult film this doesn't quite add up. AK

• *Christie Malry* Nick Moran *Headlam* Neil Stuke *Carol* Kate Ashfield *Leonardo* Mattia Sbragia *Pacioli* Marcello Mazzarella *Giacomo* Salvatore Lazzaro *Duke Ludovice* Sergio Albelli *Salai* Francesco Giuffrida *Mary* Shirley Anne Field *Wagner* Peter Sullivan
• *Dir* Paul Tickell *Scr* Simon Bent, based on the novel by B S Johnson *Pro* Kees Kasander *M* Luke Haines *Ph* Reinier van Brummelen *Ed* Chris Wyatt *Pro Des* Wilbert Can Dorp, Tom Pye *Costumes* Heleen Heintjes

Delux Productions / Movie Masters / The Kasander Film Company / Woodline Films / Ratpack
94 mins. UK/Netherlands/Luxembourg 2000. Rel: 16 August 2002. Cert 18.

Chuen jik sat sau

See *Fulltime Killer*

Cidade de Deus

See *City of God*

City by the Sea ★★★

The city of the title is Long Beach, where a police investigation follows after a drug dealer meets a violent end. But the film is only partly a thriller because the axis of the tale resides in the fact that the cop in charge (Robert De Niro) discovers that the chief suspect is his own estranged son (James Franco), a drug taker. The tale (freely adapted from real-life events) is centred on the way the divorced cop, who feels that he has been a bad father, uses these desperate circumstances to bring about a reconciliation with his son. However, this is a concept which in its sentimentality is more likely to appeal to American than to British audiences. A good cast (Patti LuPone scores as the cop's wife but Frances McDormand is wasted as his girlfriend) is unable to rise above sometimes banal dialogue. Passable, but not more. MS

• *Vincent LaMarca* Robert De Niro *Michelle* Frances McDormand *Joey* James Franco *Gina* Eliza Dushku *Spyder* William Forsythe *Dave Simon* Anson Mount *Maggie* Patti LuPone
• *Dir* Michael Caton-Jones *Scr* Ken Hixon, based on a 1997 *Esquire* magazine article, 'Mark of a Murderer', by Michael McAlary *Ph* Karl Walter Lindenlaub *Ed* Jim Clark *M* John Murphy *Pro Des* Jane Musky *Pro* Brad Grey, Elie Samaha, Caton-Jones and Matthew Baer

Brad Grey Pictures / Franchise Pictures / Sea Breeze Productions Inc / Warner Bros
108 mins. US 2002. Rel: 9 January 2003.

City of God ★★★½

(*Cidade de Deus*)

The first two thirds of this highly acclaimed Brazilian film by Fernando Meirelles suggests that lightning has struck twice. This portrayal of life in the toughest and poorest quarter of Rio de Janeiro, covering three decades from the sixties onwards, has the energy and directorial panache that made *Amores Perros* one of the best films of 2001. But with the emphasis on rival gangs involved with drugs, the film ultimately becomes a wearying catalogue of killings, with the large cast of characters coming and going without ever achieving the individuality which might cause us to be moved. A comparison with Ken Loach's films immediately reveals that Meirelles is more concerned with the pyrotechnics of the violent action movie than with expressing a deep sense of social outrage over the fate of the underprivileged. The view that this is what cinema was created for is disheartening in the extreme. MS

• *Knockout Ned* Seu Jorge *Rocket* Alexandre Rodrigues *Li'l Zé* Leandro Firmino da Hora *Benny* Phellipe Haagensen *Li'l Dice* Douglas Silva *Steak & Fries* Darlan Cunha
• *Dir* Fernando Meirelles *Scr* Braulio Mantovani, based on the novel by Paulo Lins *Ph* Cesar Charlone *Ed* Daniel Rezende *M* Antônio Pinto, Ed Côrtes *Pro Des* Tulé Peake *Pro* Andrea Barata Ribeiro, Maurício Andrade Ramos

Globo Filmes / Lumiere Productions / O2 Filmes / Studio Canal / VideoFilmes / Wild Bunch / Buena Vista 130 mins. Brazil 2002. Rel: 3 January 2003. Cert 18.

Clockstoppers ★½

Jesse Bradford takes a dive from *Swimf@n.* Where the latter's bid at doing *Fatal Attraction* in Speedos at least took itself seriously, *Clockstoppers* suffers a complete lack of self-respect. The film opens with a dizzying flood of clichéd images, through which we meet Zak Gibbs, the rebel child of a brilliant physics professor who is drawn into a secret project to develop a time-freezing device. However, for something that relies heavily on high (albeit silly) science, the movie's tone is remarkably lowbrow. The presence of Identikit teen-movie components (the black best friend, the gob-smackingly beautiful foreign student, freestyle stunts on bicycles) emphasises the creative black hole at the centre of the movie. There remains only the charm offensive of the young cast and the clever special effects. Being dazzled by bright teeth, clear complexions and freaky photography is fun.. for about eight minutes. Unfortunately, *Clockstoppers* goes on way longer than that. AK

• *Zak Gibbs* Jesse Bradford *Earl Dopler* French Stewart *Francesca* Paula Garcés *Henry Gates* Michael Biehn *Dr Gibbs* Robin Thomas *Meeker* Garikayi Mutambirwa *Jenny Gibbs* Julia Sweeney *Kelly Gibbs* Lindze Letherman *Richard* Jason Winston George *Jay* Linda Kim *Agent Moore* Ken Jenkins
• *Dir* Jonathan Frakes *Pro* Gale Anne Hurd,

Above: Douglas Silva as the juvenile gangster Li'l Dice in the gritty Brazilian import *City of God* (from Buena Vista)

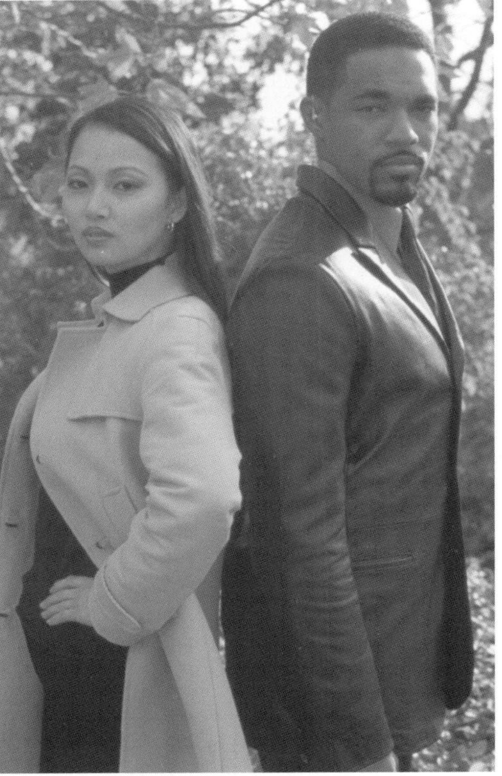

Left: Paula Garcés and Jason Winston George in the disappointing *Clockstoppers* (from UIP)

Julia Pistor *Ex Pro* Albie Hecht *Scr* Rob Hedden, J David Stem & David N Weiss, story by Rob Hedden & Andy Hedden and J David Stem & David N Weiss *Ph* Tim Suhrstedt *Ed* Peter E Berger *Costumes* Deborah Everton *M* Jamshied Sharifi *Pro Des* Marek Dobrowolski

Nickelodeon Movies / Pacific Western / Valhalla Motion Pictures / UIP
94 mins. US 2002. Rel: 11 October 2002. Cert PG.

Club le Monde ★★★★

Not yet as famous as Nottingham's Shane Meadows, Simon Rumley is one of the few British filmmakers to have found a cinematic style of his own aligned with his ability to write dialogue that seems wholly authentic. Following *Strong Language* and *The Truth Game*, this completes a London trilogy centred on young people. Affectionate yet critical too, *Club le Monde* casts a comic but perceptive eye on the club scene which flourished on the periphery of the West End around 1993. Rumley touches in the lives of 32 characters with masterful clarity, but the material is likely to appeal most to those who were part of this scene. Nevertheless, expert casting and Rumley's refusal to mock his characters make this a real achievement. The interesting question now is: where does Rumley go from here? MS

• *Mr Sunglasses* Danny Nussbaum *Yas* Emma Pike *Kelly* Tania Emery *Chas* Lee Oakes *Ra* Emma Handy *Anthony* Tom Connolly *Patrick* Tom Halstead *Steve* Daniel Ainsleigh *Tanita* Mr Darcy *Karina* Tom Fisher *Mosh* Tony Maudsley *Terry* Bruce Byron *Ali* Allison McKenzie *Jaqui* Dawn Steele *Mike* Brad Gorton
• *Dir / Scr* Simon Rumley *Ex Pro* Douglas Abbott, John Jaquiss *Pro* Rumley, Piers Jackson *M* Edmund Butt *Ph* Simon Starling *Ed* Eddie Hamilton *Pro Des* Mark Larkin

2M Films / Screen Production Associates
79 mins. UK 2002. Rel: 11 October 2002. Cert 18.

Confessions of a Dangerous Mind ★½

Chuck Barris, formerly a game-show celebrity on American television, wrote an autobiography asserting that he was at the same time a paid assassin working for the CIA. Many suspect this claim to be bogus but, in adapting the book for the screen, Charlie Kaufman (of *Being John Malkovich* and *Adaptation*) presents the supposed facts deadpan, without offering any opinion. However, as told, the tale lacks any sense of credibility, so there's neither tension nor suspense and precious little humour to relish (the only real exception, oddly enough, being the last sentences in the movie, which are brilliant). As Barris, Sam Rockwell is totally lacking in charisma and Julia Roberts is wasted in a secondary

Right: Sam Rockwell shakes it up as the TV producer cum government assassin Chuck Barris in *Confessions of a Dangerous Mind* (from Buena Vista)

female role. Drew Barrymore at least has presence and George Clooney directs as well as appearing. The photography is outstanding, but the material is so ill-judged, so boring, that this becomes the kind of film that gives sophisticated cinema a bad name. MS

• *Penny* Drew Barrymore *Jim Byrd* George Clooney *Patricia* Julia Roberts *Chuck Barris* Sam Rockwell *Keeler* Rutger Hauer
• *Dir* George Clooney *Scr* Charlie Kaufman, based on the book by Chuck Barris *Ph* Newton Thomas Sigel *Ed* Stephen Mirrione *M* Alex Wurman *Pro Des* James D Bissell *Pro* Andrew Lazar

Allied Filmmakers / Kushner-Locke Company / Mad Chance / Miramax Films / NPV Entertainment / Section Eight Ltd / Village Roadshow Productions / Buena Vista
113 mins. US 2002. Rel: 14 March 2003. Cert 15.

The Core ★★★

After a series of especially harrowing natural disasters occurs around the world, scientists discover that the Earth's molten core is about to stop spinning, promising still more global havoc. Unless geophysicist Dr Joshua Keyes and his team of crack

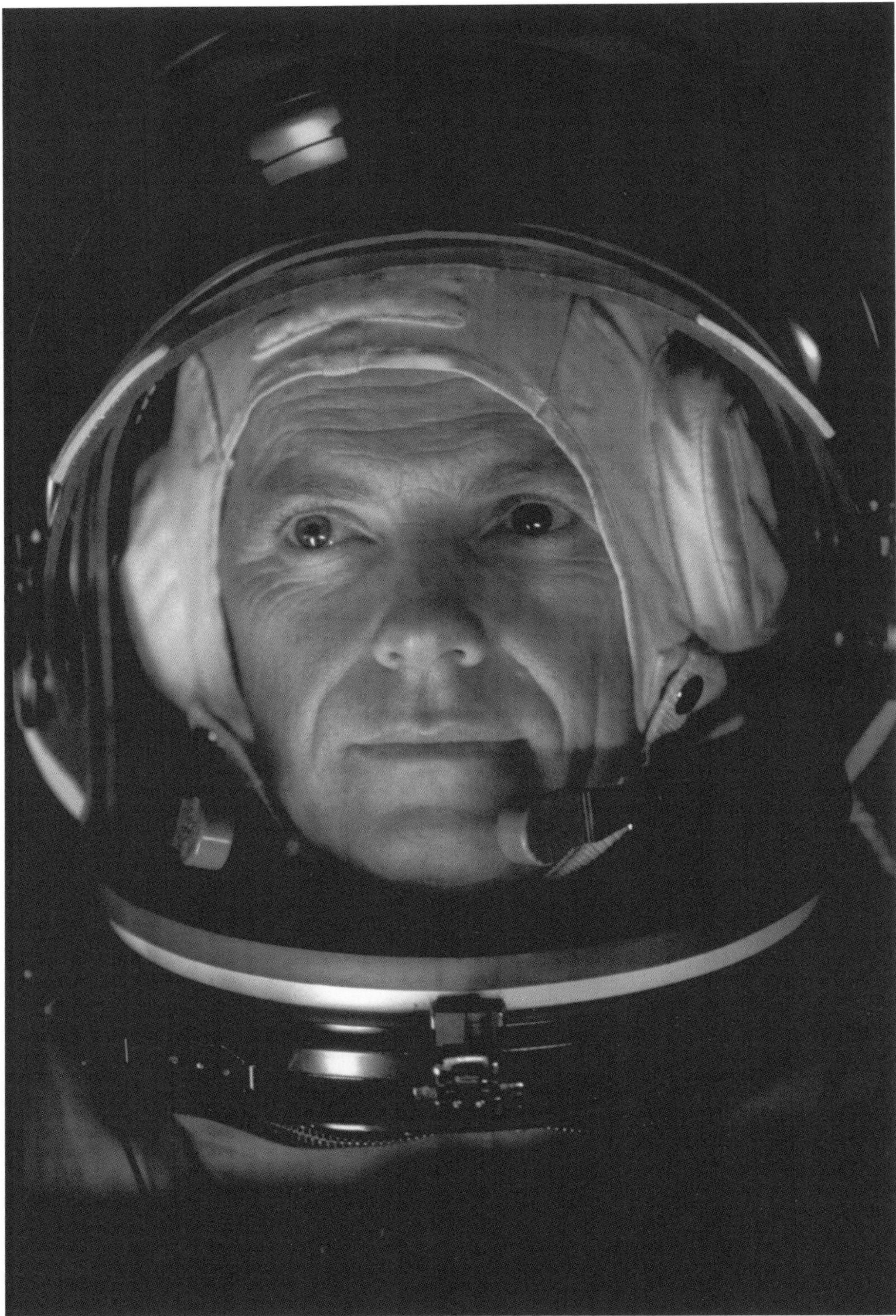

Left: Bruce Greenwood as Commander Richard Iverson in the disaster fantasy *The Core* (from UIP)

'Terranauts' can journey to the Earth's core and detonate a nuclear device to restart the core's normal rotation, life as we know it will end... Despite its predictability, *The Core* invokes many of the disaster/sci-fi flicks of the 1950s to positive effect.

Director Jon Amiel has come a long way from 1993's *Somersby*. Sadly, he treads all too familiar ground while giving physicists front-row seats as action heroes. It's small wonder that writer John Rogers earned a degree in Physics before penning this paean to the oft-overlooked geologist. Still, great Saturday afternoon fare and Aaron Eckhart and Hilary Swank are always delicious. SWM

• *Dr Josh Keyes* Aaron Eckhart *Maj Rebecca Childs* Hilary Swank *Dr Ed Brazzleton* Delroy Lindo *Dr Conrad Zimsky* Stanley Tucci *Rat* D J Qualls *Gen Thomas Purcell* Richard Jenkins *Dr Sergei Leveque* Tcheky Karyo *Col Robert Iverson* Bruce Greenwood *'Stick'* Alfre Woodard
• *Dir* Jon Amiel *Pro* David Foster, Cooper Layne, Sean Bailey *Scr* Cooper Lane, John Rogers *Ph* John Lindley *Ed* Terry Rawlings *Costumes* Dan Lester *M* Christopher Young *Pro Des* Philip Harrison, Sandra Tanaka

Core Prods Inc / Horsepower Films / UIP
135 mins. US/UK 2003. Rel: 28 March 2003. Cert 12A.

Cradle 2 the Grave ★½

A flamboyant, hare-brained jewel heist opens the movie, trading screen time with shots of a cool, sun-shaded Jet Li showing off his kung-fu in a spectacular cat-burgling stunt. Sadly, the opening sequence is all that's worth watching in this chopped-up, flashy hip-hop wet dream that takes the worst aspects of *Romeo Must Die* (idiotic plot) and *Exit Wounds* (idiotic performances) to produce an extended music video. Complete with a trite urban 'gangstuh' setting (focusing on a professional thief who engages in ever more ridiculous heists to save his kidnapped daughter), it is an insult to action fans who revere Jet Li as the one true successor to Bruce Lee. Potentially elegant fight sequences, the real stars of films like these, are mutilated into a deeply unsatisfying 'highlights' reel. Even the final all-important showdown between Li and star martialist Mark Dacascos is a flaming let-down which no amount of knowing post-credits irony can excuse. AK

• *Su* Jet Li *Tony Fait* DMX *Ling* Mark Dacascos *Tommy* Anthony Anderson *Sona* Kelly Hu *Archie* Tom Arnold *Daria* Gabrielle Union *Odion Drag-On* Michael Jace *Hurd* Miles Paige *Chamber* Vanessa Chi McBride
• *Dir* Andrzej Bartkowiak *Scr* John O'Brien, Channing Gibson *Ch* Corey Yuen *Ph* Daryn Okada *Pro* Joel Silver *M* Tina Davis, Damon Blackman *Co Pro* Melina Kevorkian, Susan Levin *Ed* Derek Brechin *Ex Pro* Herbert W Gains, Ray Copeland *Pro Des* David F Klassen

Silver Pictures / Warner Bros
101 mins. US 2003. Rel: 28 March 2003. Cert 15.

The Crime of Father Amaro ★★½

(*El crimen del padre Amaro*)
Not altogether wisely, this ably directed film from Mexico's Carlos Carrera takes a novel of 1875 and reworks it in a contemporary setting. It's the story of how a young priest, Father Amaro, discovers the extent of corruption in the Catholic Church, and our expectation is that he will grow up to become the hero who challenges the behaviour he uncovers. Instead, one early generous gesture apart, he turns out to be a total shit. This means that his story is unappealing and that, as with Stephen Frears' *Liam*, the film's anti-religious slant appears simplistic and extremist. Consequently the talented Gael García Bernel (*Amores Perros, And Your Mother Too*) can make nothing interesting out of Amaro, but those who get a kick out of anti-Catholic ranting will love it. *The Magdalene Sisters*, a genuinely angry yet deeply considered exposé, is everything that this film isn't. MS

• *Amaro* Gael Garcia Bernal *Padre* Benito Sancho Gracia *Amelia* Ana Claudia Talancón *Sanjuanera* Angélica Aragón *Dionisia* Luisa Huertasa *Padre Natalio* Damián Alcázar *municipal president* Pedro Armendáriz
• *Dir* Carlos Carrera *Pro* Alfredo Ripstein and Daniel Birman Ripstein *Co Pro* José María Morales *Scr* Vicente Leñero, from the novel by José María Eça de Queiroz *Ph* Guillermo Granillo *Ed* Oscar Figueroa *M* Rosino Serrano

Alameda Films / Blu Films / Artcam-Columbia TriStar
118 mins. Mexico/France/Argentina/Spain 2002.
Rel: 20 June 2003. Cert 15.

Crocodile Hunter: The Collision Course ★★★½

Welcome to a wildlife documentary disguised as a movie about CIA agents sent 'Down Under' to recover a satellite swallowed by an ornery croc. But the G-men haven't a hope of overcoming the mighty forces of Steve and Terri Irwin, perhaps the planet's most famous conservationist warriors, who want to relocate the croc to safety. The fearless, flamboyant and intensely ebullient style of Steve 'The Crocodile Hunter' Irwin has propelled him to international stardom with an audience of over 200 million for his TV shows. To protect the Irwins' magic, filmmaker John Stainton kept the script from them until the last minute, ensuring their natural charm remained unspoilt amid some fairly ridiculous movie-style nonsense. Bear in mind that 'natural' for the Irwins includes kissing deadly snakes, manhandling evil reptiles and caressing some of the planet's most dangerous creatures. It sometimes feels like watching an instructional-safety film about swallowing razor blades. AK

• *himself* Steve Irwin *herself* Terri Irwin *Brozzie Drewitt* Magda Szubanksi *Sam Flynn* David Wenham *Agent Bob Wheeler* Lachy Hulme *Agent*

Vaughan Archer Kenneth Ransom *Kate Beahan* Jo Buckley • *Dir* John Stainton *Scr* Holly Goldberg Sloan *Ph* David Burr, Gary Phillips *Ed* Suresh Ayyar, Bob Blasadall *Pro Des* Jon Dowding *Pro* Bruce Willis, Arnold Rifkin, Judi Bailey, Stainton

Animal Planet / Best Picture Show Company / Cheyenne Enterprises / Discovery Channel Pictures / J&M Entertainment / Metro-Goldwyn-Mayer / Winchester Films / 20th Century Fox
89 mins. Australia/US 2002. Rel: 26 July 2002. Cert PG.

The Curse of the Jade Scorpion

★★★½

Woody Allen's nostalgic evocation of the popular movies of the forties is set in that era and features Woody himself as an insurance claims investigator. This light-hearted tale, minor Allen, involves a master criminal, robberies and hypnosis. Unfortunately the plot is over-stretched at full feature length, but there are plenty of good one-liners and Helen Hunt playing an efficiency expert enters into the mood of it splendidly. Those critics who damned Allen for getting the girl fail to appreciate the extent to which he sends himself up in this respect. Forgettable but fun. MS

• *C W Briggs* Woody Allen *Chris Magruder* Dan Aykroyd *Jill* Elizabeth Berkley *Betty Ann Fitzgerald* Helen Hunt *George Bond* Wallace Shawn *Voltan* David Ogden Stiers *Laura Kensington* Charlize Theron *Al* Brian Markinson *with* John Schuck, Peter Gerety, Dick Hyman, Howard Erskine, Ira Wheeler • *Dir / Scr* Woody Allen *Pro* Letty Aronson *Ex Pro* Stephen Tenenbaum *Co Pro* Helen Robin *Co-Ex Pro* Datty Ruth, Jack Rollins and Charles H Joffe *Ph* Zhao Fei *Pro Des* Santo Loquasto *Ed* Alisa Lepselter *M* various; numbers performed by Duke Ellington, Earl 'Fatha' Hines, Dick Hyman, Wilbur de Paris, Harry James, and Glenn Miller *Costumes* Suzanne McCabe

DreamWorks / VCL / Gravier-UIP
104 mins. USA 2001. Rel: 6 December 2002. Cert 12A.

Above: Elizabeth Berkley falls for Woody Allen's irresistible charms in his noir pastiche *Curse of the Jade Scorpion* (from UIP)

D

The Dancer Upstairs ★★★½

Set in a generically corrupt South American dictatorship, *The Dancer Upstairs* is a concentrated actor's piece with the wonderful Javier Bardem as an undercover police captain ordered to track down the terrorist leader Ezequiel. As he pursues his mission, it becomes apparent that he might be on the wrong side of this particular war. His work puts stress on his marriage and pushes him to find solace in the arms of his daughter's dance instructor, Yolanda. John Malkovich's directorial debut begins with pungent images of suicidal terrorism and symbolic cruelty. But his deftly executed romantic thriller, based loosely on the 'Shining Path' terrorists of Peru and the hunt for their leaders, is no cheap shocker but a deliciously ambiguous essay on the slim difference between terrorists and revolutionaries. But one wonders about the decision to shoot the film in such heavily accented English. Are subtitles really so difficult to digest? AK

• *Augustin Rejas* Javier Bardem *Yolanda* Laura Morante *Sucre* Juan Diego Botto *Llosa* Elvira Minguez *Sylvina* Alexandra Lencastre *General Merino* Oliver Cotton *Calderon* Luis Miguel Cintra *Clorindo* Javier Manrique *Ezequiel/Duran* Abel Folk *Laura* Marie-Anne Berganza

• *Dir* John Malkovich *Pro* Andres Vicente Gomez, Malkovich *Ex Pro* Lianne Halfon, Russel Smith *Scr* Nicholas Shakespeare, based on his novel *Ph* Jose Luis Alcaine *Ed* Mario Battistel *Pro Des* Pierre-Françoise Limbosch *Costumes* Bina Daigeler *M* Alberto Iglesias

Lolafilms SA /Adres Vicente Gomez / Mr Mudd / Antena 3 Television / Via Digital / Fox
133 mins. Spain/US 2002. Rel: 6 December 2002. Cert 15.

Daredevil ★★

Blinded as a child by strange chemicals in an accident, Matt Murdock's other senses became superheroically sensitive. He grows up to become the Daredevil, a costumed vigilante in Hell's Kitchen. A struggling lawyer by day, he shelves his dysfunctional identity at night and dons his red leathers to deal in rough justice with preternatural acrobatics and the deadliest blind man's cane ever invented... Yet another glossy film adaptation from the Marvel Comics Universe, it is frustrating to see one of the most substantial and morally ambiguous characters since Batman in such a jejune and commercial treatment. Forget sexy and dark, director Mark Steven Johnson emasculates Daredevil in

Below: Blind lawyer by day, vigilant crime fighter by night, Ben Affleck is the *Daredevil* (from Fox)

perhaps the hottest story in the character's history (his tragic love affair with the assassin Elektra and his duel with the supervillain Bullseye), delivering instead a Saturday matinée flick that might as well have remained in two dimensions. AK

• *Matt Murdock / Daredevil* Ben Affleck *Elektra* Jennifer Garner *Bullseye* Colin Farrell *Kingpin / Wilson Fisk* Michael Clarke Duncan *Franklin Nelson* Jon Favreau *young Matt Murdock* Scott Terra *Karen Page* Ellen Pompeo *Jack Murdock* David Keith *Father Everett* Derrick O'Connor *Urich* Joe Pantoliano *Bully* Robert Iler *man with pen in head* Frank Miller *forensic assistant* Kevin Smith
• *Dir / Scr* Mark Steven Johnson, based on the Marvel Comics character created by Stan Lee and Bill Everett *Ph* Ericson Core *Ed* Dennis Virkler, Armen Minasian *M* Graeme Revell *Pro Des* Barry Chusid *Pro* Arnon Milchan, Gary Foster, Avi Arad *Costumes* James Acheson *Stunt Coordinator* Jeff Imada *Action Dir* Cheung-Yan Yuen *Fight Coordinator* Daxing Zhang

20th Century Fox / Horseshoe Bay Productions / Marvel Entertainment / New Regency Pictures / Regency Enterprises / Fox
103 mins. US 2003. Rel: 14 February 2003. Cert 15.

Dark Water ★★★★

(*Honogurai Mizu No Soko Kara*)
Itsumi, a young mother caught in the toils of an ugly divorce settlement, moves with her six-year-old daughter into a supremely baleful apartment block. There she becomes plagued by watery manifestations guaranteed to play directly into the hands of her vengeful husband, whose lawyers will naturally consider her insane... Here is a small supernatural gem from the director (Hideo Nakata) and writer (Koji Suzuki) of the much-acclaimed *Ring*, trading in much the same imagery with no diminution in effect. Nakata isn't too proud to recycle effects from other people's movies (*The Innocents, Don't Look Now* and *The Shining*, in this case), but the miasmic unpleasantness of *Dark Water* is all his own. And miasmic is exactly the word: the film's original title translates literally as 'Out of the Murky Depths', and if you see it you'll know why. In addition to his trademark glimpses of the half-seen, Nakata adds a real emotional force to the climactic scene of self-sacrifice while making the ghost girl, though thoroughly malign, a deeply tragic figure. And a haunting 15-minute coda, dismissed by some critics as an irrelevance, may well cause the viewer to reach for his hanky as well as a tranquiliser. JR

• *Itsumi Matsubara* Hitomi Kuroki *Ikuko, age six* Rio Kanno *Mitsuko Kawai* Mirei Oguchi *Ikuko, age 16* Asami Mizukawa
• *Dir* Hideo Nakata *Scr* Ken-ichi Suzuki, Yoshihiro Nakamura *Ed* Nobuyuki Takahashi *M* Kenji Kawai *Pro* Taka Ichise *Pro Des* Katsumi Nakazawa *Ph* Junichiro Hayashi

Simpatico / Metro Tartan
101 mins. Japan 2002. Rel: 6 June 2003. Cert 15.

Above: Emma Caulfield, Lee Cornie and Chaney Kley in *Darkness Falls* (from Columbia Tristar)

Darkness Falls ★★★

A curse lies on the New England-ish town of Darkness Falls. The ghost of Matilda Dixon, unjustly burned at the stake a century ago, has become the vicious 'Tooth Fairy', who preys on children who have (quite silly this) lost their last milk teeth. But one kid, Michael Greene, sees her coming and refuses to sleep. His sister Cat looks for help from the only person she knows who has survived the 'Tooth Fairy', childhood sweetheart Kyle Walsh. Once he's in the picture, it's a duel, with flashlights till dawn... Jonathan Liebesman might have had the notion that subverting a popular myth via *Pitch Black* and *A Nightmare on Elm Street* might just be silly enough to work, but that it works at all is thanks largely to master foley artist Gary Hecker, whose intensely chilling sonics (an essential component of any good horror flick) breathe into undead life an atmosphere thick enough to choke on. The kills are sharp and bloody, and the shocks escalate to formula. However, in the finale the movie stumbles badly with the stock elements it otherwise ran so well with. AK

• *Kyle Wals* Chaney Kley *Cat Greene* Emma Caulfield *Michael Greene* Lee Cornie *Matt Henry* Sullivan Stapleton *Larry Fleishman* Grant Piro *Officer Matt Henry* Sullivan Stapleton *Tooth Fairy vocal effects* Gary A Hecker
• *Dir* Jonathan Liebesman *Pro* John Hegeman, John Fasano, William Sherak, Jason Shuman *Ex Pro* Derek Dauchy, Lou Arkoff *Scr* Fasano, James Vanderbilt, Joe Harris *Ph* Dan Lausten *Ed* Steve Mirkovich, Tim Alverson *M* Brian Tyler *Creature design* Stan Winston Studio *Costumes* Anna Borghesi *Pro Des* George Liddle, Tom Nursey

Blue Star Productions / Distant Corners Entertainment Group Inc / Revolution Studios / Village Roadshow Productions / Columbia Tristar
85 mins. US/Australia. 2002. Rel: 9 May 2003. Cert 15.

Deathwatch ★½

1917, the Western Front. A company of stranded soldiers capture a German trench and, along with it, a prisoner terrified of a deadly evil therein... Another example of the British resurgence in the horror genre, *Deathwatch* at least adopts a Gothic feel which goes well with trench warfare setting. However, in light of the kind of bloody realism audiences have come to expect from their war movies, the oblique (and clearly budget-constrained) representations of the carnage of war in the opening sequence are theatrical rather than visceral. This contributes to the sense of caricature that plagues the film in spite of fine attempts by the actors to give the movie some heart. This is not a good thing when the genre depends on audience identification to help us care about the poor bastards getting killed off one by one. Unfortunately, feeling sorry for the actors suffering through what looks like a truly uncomfortable shoot is no substitute. AK

• *Charlie Shakespeare* Jamie Bell *Pvt Chevasse* Rúaidhrí Conroy *Captain Jennings* Laurence Fox *Pvt McNess* Dean Lennox Kelly *Friedrich* Torben Liebrecht *Pvt Starinski* Kris Marshall *Pvt Hawkstone* Hans Matheson *McNess* James McAvoy *Bradford* Hugh O'Conor *'Doc' Fairweather* Matthew Rhys *Pvt Quinn* Andy Serkis *Sergeant Tate* Hugo Speer
• *Dir / Scr* Michael J Bassett *Pro* Mike Downey, Frank Hübner *Ass Pro* Michael Bischoff , Ralph Kamp *Ex Pro* Caroline Hewitt, Sam Lavender, Dan Maag, Sam Taylor *M* Curt Cress, Robert Lane, Chris Weller *Ph* Hubert Taczanowski *Ed* Anne Sopel *Pro Des* Aleksandar Denic

ApolloMedia / ApolloProMedia / Bavaria Film / Canal+ / CiBy 2000 / F.A.M.E. Film and Music Entertainment Ltd. / Medusa Produzione / Odyssey Entertainment / Portobello Pictures / Q&Q Medien GmbH / Pathé
94 mins. UK/France/Germany/Italy. 2002.
Rel: 6 December 2002. Cert 15.

Deep Breath ★★★½

(*Le Souffle*)

This French film offers yet another study of adolescence, but an individual one since writer/director Damien Odoul has his own style. There is an unorthodox emphasis on close-ups and he opts tellingly for black-and-white photography. Odoul also obtains a remarkable performance from Pierre-Louis Bonnetblanc, non-professional like the rest of the cast. He plays the 15-year-old youth whose growing problems, leading to disaster, are central to this rural tale. It's a gritty work reminiscent of Ken Loach's *Sweet Sixteen* but, short as it is (77 minutes), it drifts in its final stages. This tells against a frequently impressive work, albeit one that, with characters more real than appealing, doesn't eclipse memories of other treatments of similar themes that made us care more. MS

• *David* Pierre-Louis Bonnetblanc *Jacques* Dominique Chevallier *Paul* Maxime Dalbrut *John* Jean-Claude Lecante *Mr Milford* Jean Milford *Stef* Stéphane Terpereau
• *Dir / Scr* Damien Odoul *Ph* Pascale Granel *Ed* Gwénola Heaulme *Pro Des* Hélène Melani *Pro* Gérard Lacroix

Centre National de la Cinématographie / Morgane Productions / Région Limousin / Metro Tartan
77 mins. France 2001. Rel: 11 April 2003. Cert 15.

Die Another Day ★★★★

Forty years on and, suddenly, James Bond has grown up. In North Korea on business, 007 finds himself involved in a spectacular hovercraft chase through a minefield, after which he is captured by the enemy. He is then summarily tortured – over the stylish opening credits – and later flits from Hong Kong to Cuba to London to Iceland in his pursuit of justice... Of course, the amazing gadgets, outrageous stunts, exotic locations, cosmetically perfect babes and feeble one-liners are all present and accounted for. However, this Bond packs a far greater wallop than previous entries. Indeed, *Die Another Day* exhibits a fresh cinematic flourish, paying a stylistic debt to the oeuvre of David Fincher and the Wachowski brothers. In the hands of New Zealand director Lee Tamahori, the yarn moves at a cracking pace and repeatedly manages to surprise. For starters, Bond's double-O status is revoked and he's forced to find his own way in an impudent plot involving, um, world domination, DNA gene therapy and even strong echoes of Ronald Reagan's 'Star Wars' programme. In addition, there is a splendidly plucky heroine in Halle Berry, an impressive car chase through a melting palace of ice, and even the time-honoured English villain devised with a cocktail dash of Richard Branson and Kim Il-Sung. JC-W

• *James Bond* Pierce Brosnan *Jinx Jordan* Halle Berry *Gustav Graves* Toby Stephens *Miranda Frost* Rosamund Pike *Zao* Rick Yune *Q* John Cleese *M* Judi Dench *Damian Falco* Michael Madsen *Colonel Moon* Will Yun Lee *Charles Robinson* Colin Salmon *Ms Moneypenny* Samantha Bond *with* Kenneth Tsang, Emilio Echevarrí, Michael Gorevoy, Rachel Grant, Ian Pirie, Deborah Moore [daughter of Roger], Michael G Wilson, Paul Darrow and (uncredited) *Verity* Madonna.
• *Dir* Lee Tamahori *Pro* Michael G Wilson and Barbara Broccoli *Ex Pro* Anthony Waye *Co Pro*

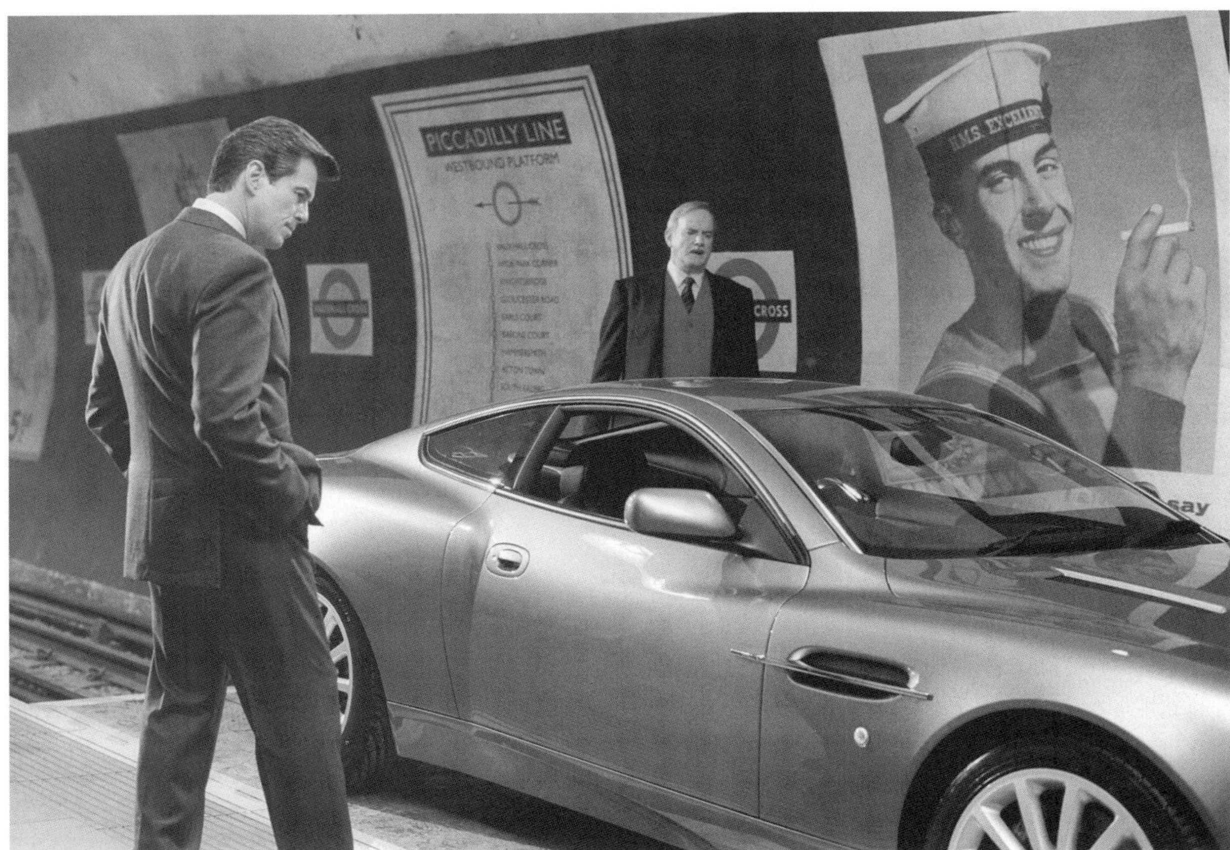

Above: Pierce Brosnan and John Cleese contemplate the life expectancy of James Bond's latest supercar in *Die Another Day* (from Fox)

Callum McDougall *Scr* Neal Purvis and Robert Wade *Ph* David Tattersall *Pro Des* Peter Lamont *Ed* Christian Wagner *M* David Arnold *title song* performed by Madonna *Costumes* Lindy Hemming *Second unit dir* Vic Armstrong

MGM / Eon Productions / Fox
135 mins. USA/UK 2002. Rel: 22 November 2002. Cert 12A.

Dirty Deeds ★★★

It is 1969, and the flood of American GIs holidaying in Sydney, Australia from the Vietnam war has given small-time gangster Barry the keys to his own fruit machine empire. But two rival Mafiosi arrive from the US to muscle in on Barry's territory, starting a bloodbath that is, apparently, supposed to be quite a laugh. Starting well with a fizzing visual style, you would need a Tarantino-esque predilection for blood and gore to catch the unapologetically violent joke that director David Caesar is making. Packed with enjoyable turns – Sam Neill and John Goodman in particular – and accompanied by an appropriately cheesy soundtrack, this is exactly what a *Lock, Stock and Two Barrels of Fosters* would look like. AK

• *Barry Ryan* Bryan Brown *Sharon* Toni Collette *Tony* John Goodman *Ray* Sam Neill *Darcy* Sam Worthington *Margaret* Kestie Morassi *Hollywood* William McInnes *Norm* Andrew S Gilbert *Freddie* Garry Waddell *Sal* Felix Williamson • *Dir / Scr* David Caesar *Pro* Deborah Balderstone, Bryan Brown *Exec Pro* Jennie Hughes, Xavier Marchand, Hugh Marks, Kris Noble *Line Pro* Helen Watts *M* Paul Healy, Tim Rogers *Ph* Geoffrey Hall *Ed* Mark Perry *Pro Des* Chris Kennedy

Alliance Atlantis Communications / Australian Film Finance Corporation / Haystack Productions Ltd / Macquarie Film Corporation / New South Wales Film & Television Office / New Town Films Pty Ltd / Nine Film & Television Pty Ltd / Momentum
97 mins. Australia 2002. Rel: 6 June 2003. Cert 18.

Dirty Pretty Things ★★★

Stephen Frears' film opened the 2002 London Film Festival and is a brave attempt at unveiling the underclass of urban British society. Chiwetel Ejiofor is magnificent as Okwe, a Nigerian illegal immigrant hustling a London living as a taxi driver by day and a hotel porter by night. Through his relationship with the nervous Senay, a Turkish refugee, he is drawn into a grim, merciless underworld that feeds on the desperation of the city's illegals. The acting is riveting, and the script laces its dark medicine with just enough humour (notably from Okwe's buddy,

Above: Audrey Tautou struggles to survive in London's seedy underworld in Stephen Frears' *Dirty Pretty Things* (from Buena Vista)

played by Benedict Wong) to remain palatable. A shame that it loses sense of its centre during a careless drive for an 'up' Hollywood-style ending that, after the preceding panorama of earnest urban drama, feels like a badly fitting shoe. AK

• *Okwe* Chiwetel Ejiofor *Senay* Audrey Tautou *Sneaky (Juan)* Sergi López *Juliette* Sophie Okonedo *Guo Yi* Benedict Wong *Ivan* Zlatko Buric
• *Dir* Stephen Frears *Scr* Steve Knight *Pro* Robert Jones, Tracey Seaward *Ex Pro* Julie Goldstein, Teresa Moneo, Allon Reich, Tracey Scoffield, Paul Smith, David M Thompson *M* Christian Henson, Nathan Larson *Ph* Chris Menges *Ed* Mick Audsley *Pro Des* Hugo Luczyc-Wyhowski

BBC / Celador Productions / Buena Vista
107 mins. UK 2002. Rel: 13 December 2002. Cert 15.

Divine Intervention ★★½

(*Yadon Ilaheyya*)

As original as it is unsatisfactory, Elia Suleiman's bizarre movie uses humour to comment on tensions in the Middle East. Initially there are some neat Tati-esque jokes, but, because they don't build, the first half-hour seems essentially plotless. Thereafter the film concentrates on a loving couple, both Palestinians. However, the man lives in Jerusalem and the woman in Ramallah and they are kept apart by the Israeli army checkpoint she is not allowed to cross. Such a situation could have yielded pointed comments blending pathos with those absurdities of life that have a comic as well as a tragic side. But Suleiman does nothing to make us care for his central characters, who remain cyphers, while the humour is extended inconsistently into surrealism and fantasy scenes involving Ninja fighting. It is well photographed and may please admirers of the equally off-beat Otar Iosseliani, but it's surely an acquired taste. MS

• *ES* Elia Suleiman *the woman* Manal Khader *the father* Nayef Fahoum Daher
• *Scr / Dir* Elia Suleiman *Ph* Marc-André Batigne *Ed* Véronique Langue *Pro Des* Miguel Markin, Denis Renault *Pro* Humbert Balsan

Sarjeromsirlot Productions Inc / Artificial Eye
93 mins. France/Morocco/Palestine 2000.
Rel: 17 January 2003. Cert 15.

Dog Days ★★★★

(*Hundstage*)

Six sets of Viennese suburbanites have their lives exposed to our intrusive gaze one sweltering weekend in the 'dog days' of July and August.

An arthouse project that took three and a half years to complete, Ulrich Seidl choreographs a cast of 'found' actors, some completely inexperienced, in a grotesque ballet of damaged people, including a sex-addicted teacher, a pair of warring ex-spouses, a mentally unstable hitchhiker, and a torpid old man and his coldly accommodating housekeeper. There is no story as such, but the dispassionate camera hypnotises us with the promise that, somewhere amid the emotional wreckage and soul-wearying behaviour, profound points may be gleaned about the ethical shape of the community under examination. Powerful and disturbing, the film damns by its grim poetry the society that bred these social victims. AK

• *Anna, the hitchhiker* Maria Hofstatter *Hruby, the alarm salesman* Alfred Mrva *Walter, the old man* Erich Finsches *Walter's housekeeper* Gerti Lehner *Klaudia, the young girl* Franziska Wel_ *Mario, Klaudia's boyfriend* Rene Wanko *the ex-wife* Claudia Martini *the ex-husband* Victor Rathbone *the masseur* Christian Bakonyi *the teacher* Christine Jirku *Wickerl, the teacher's lover* Victor Henneman *Lucky, Wickerl's friend* Georg Friedrich
• *Dir* Ulrich Seidl *Scr* Ulrich Seidl, Veronika Franz *Pro* Helmut Grasser, Phillippe Bober *Ph* Wolfgang Thaler *Ed* Andrea Wagner, Christof Schertenleib *M* Nicole Hencsei, Werner Geyer, Fritz Ostermayer

Allegro Film Production / The Coproduction Office / Metro Tartan
127 mins. Austria / Germany 2001. Rel: 8 September 2002. Cert 18.

Dogtown and Z-Boys ★★★½

The history of modern skateboarding, as told by the people who made it in the 1970s. The current boom in skateboard culture, that has even the geekiest pre-teen dreaming about 'flipping Ollies' and 'catching frontside', started out in the surfing ghettoes of 1970s Dogtown. A group of disaffected Californian youngsters transferred their love of surfing onto the asphalt and concrete wonderland, and transformed the sport into the gravity-defying spectacle it is today. Beautifully illustrated with Craig Stecyk's vintage photographs and grainy 8mm footage, the documentary successfully sells the energy of the bleached-out California setting that led to the all-conquering rise of the MTV generation's sport of choice. However, except for a thesis that trades on the pureness of heart of its pioneers, there isn't much in the way of emotional involvement to entice the viewer amid all the schoolyard bragging and chummy backslaps. Factoid: Stecyk and Peralta made this documentary specifically to beat *The Lords of Dogtown*, an 'unauthorised' version by David Fincher backed by Sony, to the punch. AK

• *narrator* Sean Penn *interviewees* Jay Adams (interviewed from prison), Tony Alva, Bob Biniak, Paul Constantineau, Shogo Kubo, Jim Muir, Peggy Oki, Stacy Peralta, Nathan Pratt, Wentzle Ruml, Allen Sarlo
• *Dir* Stacy Peralta *Scr* Peralta and Craig Stecyk *Ph* Peter Pilafian *Ed* Paul Crowder *M* Terry Wilson and Crowder *Pro Des* Stecyk *Pro* Agi Orsi

Agi Orsi Productions / Vans Off the Wall / Columbia Tristar
90 mins. US 2001. Rel: 5 July 2002. Cert 15.

Dolls ★★★½

For Western audiences, *Dolls* will come as something of a culture shock. For a start, its themes are inspired by the stories explored in the traditional form of 'Bunraku' (ie, Japanese puppet theatre). To stress the point, the film opens with a Bunraku performance filmed at Tokyo's National Theatre in front of a live audience. The production is Chikamatsu's classic tale of doomed love, *Meido No Nikaku* (aka *The Courier for Hell*). After the opening credits, the story is given a contemporary setting, one of three fables that are intertwined in a poignant contemplation of undying love. Deliberately paced and ravishingly photographed, *Dolls* exudes a poetry that creeps up on the viewer with an almost insidious power. While most cinemagoers are likely to find the film slow and irrelevant, those interested in eastern culture should discover much to admire. Indeed, there are some wonderful things here, from the haunting performance of Miho Kanno (as a young woman driven insane by unrequited love) to the spectacular landscapes of Japan revealed in all four seasons. If you let it, *Dolls* will haunt you. JC-W

• *Sawako* Miho Kanno *Matsumoto* Hidetoshi Nishijima *Hiro, the 'boss'* Tatsuya Mihashi *woman in the park* Chieko Matsubara *Haruna, the pop star* Kyoko Fukada Nukui *the fan* Tsutomu Takeshige.
• *Dir / Scr / Ed* Takeshi Kitano *Pro* Masayuki Mori, Takio Yoshida *Ph* Katsumi Yanagijima *Pro Des* Norihiro Isoda *M* Joe Hisaishi *Costumes* Yohji Yamamoto *Sound* Senji Horiuchi

Bandai Visual / TV Tokyo / Office Kitano / Artificial Eye
113 mins. Japan 2002. Rel: 30 May 2003. Cert 12A.

Donnie Darko ★★★★

Donnie Darko is a troubled suburban teen in therapy who is about to experience the strangest week of his life. Set in the moral surreality of 1980s America under Reagan, this creepy debut by writer/director Richard Kelly is intelligent, unsettling, evocative and utterly original. It straddles horror, sci-fi and straight drama like a petulant prodigy, refusing to accept genre boundaries. Perhaps for this reason it failed to dent the US box-office when it was first released; however, it immediately gained cult status upon secondary release on DVD. Jake Gyllenhaal delivers a star-making performance as Donnie Darko, and the supporting cast are on excellent form. The film's rarest attraction lies in qualities unheard-of for what is ostensibly a teen movie: too many smart ideas, intricately crafted and poetically arrayed. The soundtrack, too, is outstanding. AK

• *Donnie Darko* Jake Gyllenhaal *Gretchen Ross* Jena Malone *Karen Pomeroy* Drew Barrymore *Rose Darko* Mary McDonnell *Eddie Darko* Holmes Osborne *Dr Lillian Thurman* Katharine Ross *Jim Cunningham* Patrick Swayze *Dr Monnitoff* Noah Wyle *Elizabeth Darko* Maggie Gyllenhaal *Frank* James Duval *Kittie Farmer* Beth Grant
• *Dir / Scr* Richard Kelly *Ph* Steven Poster *Ed* Eric Strand, Sam Bauer *M* Michael Andrews *Pro Des* Alexander Hammond *Pro* Sean McKittrick, Nancy Juvonen

Adam Fields Productions / Flower Films (Barrymore/Juvonen) / Gaylord Films / Pandora Cinema / Metrodome
113 mins. US 2002. Rel: 25 October 2002. Cert 15.

Dreamcatcher ★★

Stephen King has contributed to the narrative of 76 films and TV productions, either directly as scenarist or indirectly as the writer of the original novel or short story. It's a wonder he has any ideas left. What is extraordinary about *Dreamcatcher*, Kasdan's adaptation of King's 2001 bestseller, is that it suffers from a *surfeit* of ideas. While it crosses territory already explored in King's own *Stand by Me*, *The Tommyknockers* and *The Stand* – not to mention touching on a variety of other sources – it does offer an original angle on the alien invasion theme. Having saved an otherworldly handicapped boy from bullies, four childhood friends find themselves gifted with the power of telepathy. Twenty years later they have turned into foul-mouthed men who join up for a weekend hunting trip in the woods. And, boy, do they need their telepathy now... Superbly crafted and intriguingly set up, *Dreamcatcher* starts off as the best King adaptation since, well, *The Shawshank Redemption*. It then overloads on special effects, story strands and some surprisingly inedible dialogue, culminating in a ludicrous – albeit entertaining – mess. JC-W

• *Colonel Abraham Curtis* Morgan Freeman *Dr Henry Devlin* Thomas Jane *Joe 'Beaver' Clarendon* Jason Lee *Professor Gary 'Jonesy' Jones* Damian Lewis *Pete Moore* Timothy Olyphant *Captain Owen Underhill* Tom Sizemore *Douglas 'Duddits' Cavell* Donnie Wahlberg *with* Michael O'Neill, Rosemary Dunsmore, Darrin Klimek, Campbell Lane, Eric Keenleyside, Ty Olsson, Jonathan Kasdan and (*uncredited*) Grant Heslov
• *Dir* Lawrence Kasdan *Pro* Kasdan and Charles Okun *Ex Pro* Bruce Berman *Scr* Kasdan and William Goldman *Ph* John Seale *Pro Des* Jon Hutman *Ed* Carol Littleton and Raul Davalos *M* James Newton Howard *Costumes* Molly Maginnis *Visual effects* Stefen Fangmeier *Creature Design* Crash McCreery *Sound* Yann Delpuech

Castle Rock Entertainment / Village Roadshow Pictures / NPV Entertainment / Kasdan Pictures-Warner
133 mins. USA 2003. Rel: 25 April 2003. Cert 15.

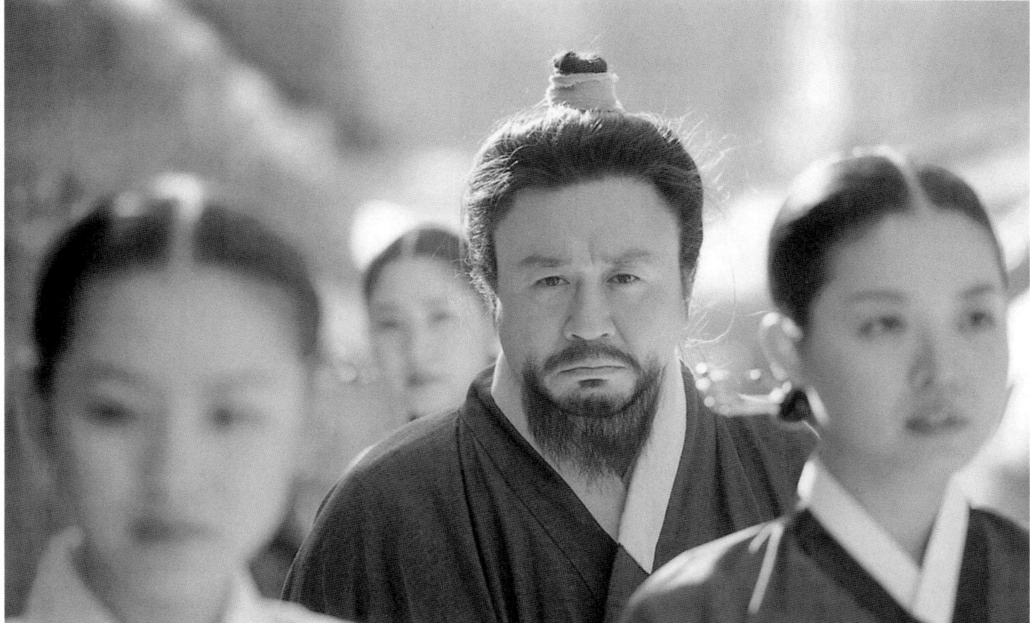

Right: Choi Min-Shik as the painter Jang Seung-Up in the striking *Drunk On Women and Poetry* (from Pathé)

Drunk on Women and Poetry ★★★★

(*Chiwaseon*)

Visually striking and classical in its approach, this film from the veteran Korean director Im Kuon Tack is a study of a real-life painter, Jang Seung-Up, and thus a comment on the position of the artist in society. It covers four decades in the life of this 19th century figure, about whom relatively little is known. Perhaps for this reason, depth and detail are missing and the film is more like a sketch than a fully realised drawing. But even if one is not fully engaged emotionally the film is mesmerisingly beautiful and also well cast: a feast for the eyes. The stress on women and drinking may sometimes suggest a stereotypical portrait of an artist but its view of the pressures both personal and social on such a man has universal resonance. AK

• *Jang Seung-Up* Choi Min-Shik *Kim Byung-Moon* Ahn Sung-Ki *Mae-Hyang* You Ho-Jeong *Jin-Hong* Kim Yeo-Jin *So-Woon* Son Ye-Jin *Lee Eung-Heon* Han Myung-Goo *teenage Jang Seung-Up* Jung Tae-Woo
• *Dir* Im Kwon-Taek *Scr* Kim Yong-Oak and Im *Ph* Jung Il-Sung *Ed* Park Soon-Duk *Pro Des* Ju Byoung-Do *Pro* Lee Tae-Won

Taehung Pictures / Pathé
116 mins. South Korea 2002. Rel: 6 June 2003. Cert 12A.

Dumb and Dumberer: When Harry Met Lloyd ★

Providence, Rhode Island, sometime in the 1980s: we are treated to the awesome spectacle of first contact between two of cinema's stupidest characters. The prequel to the Farrelly Brothers' classic 'gross-out' comedy *Dumb & Dumber* sports two young actors bearing an uncanny resemblance to Jim Carrey and Jeff Daniels as they appeared in the first film. Plot is almost redundant in a movie that is really about how imaginative the creatives could get with the most vulgar bodily functions available. There are also gay jokes and other mindless hi-jinks to pad out the moments that don't involve faecal humour. The trouble is that the young Harry and Lloyd aren't anywhere near charming enough to justify this film's existence. AK

• *Lloyd Christmas* Eric Christian Olsen *Harry Dunne* Derek Richardson *Jessica* Rachel Nichols *Ms Heller* Cheri Oteri *Clarence* Luis Guzman *Turk* Elden Henson *Carl* William Lee Scott *Mrs Dunne* Mimi Rogers *Principal Collins* Eugene Levy *Margie* Lin Shayne
• *Dir* Troy Miller *Scr* Robert Brenner, Brian Hartt, Miller *Ph* Anthony Richmond *Ex Pro* Toby Emmerich, Cale Boyter, Richard Brener, Bennett Yellin *M* Eban Schletter *Co Pro* Carl Mazzocone *Ed* Lawrence Jordan *Pro* Oren Koules, Charles B Wessler, Brad Krevoy, Steven Stabler, Miller *Pro Des* Paul Huggins

Avery Pix / Burg-Koules Productions / Dakota Pictures / New Line Cinema / Entertainment
85 mins. US 2003. Rel: 13 June 2003. Cert 12A.

Below: Eric Christian Olsen and Derek Richardson flunk out in the irredeemably daft *Dumb and Dumberer: When Harry Met Lloyd* (from Entertainment)

Eight Crazy Nights ★

A musical Jewish remix of *It's a Wonderful Life*, this is a mystifying waste of everybody's time. It's a miserable parody of the Christmas family film, and because it ultimately wants to sell a happy ending the scatological humour that forms the bulk of the script seems completely out of place. But the litany of offensive jokes, cringe-worthy musical numbers and tasteless *Jackass*-inspired images that rains down on the viewer from start to finish makes for a film only a delinquent could love. BBFC certification aside, it is as much of an animated 'family film' as *Fritz the Cat*. AK

• voices: *Davey, Whitey, Eleanore and Deer* Adam Sandler, *Jennifer* Jackie Titone *Benjamin* Austin Stout *Mayor* Kevin Nealon *Chinese waiter and narrator* Rob Schneider *Judge* Norm Crosby *Tom Baltezor* Jon Lovitz • *Dir* Seth Kearsley *Scr* Brooks Arthur, Allen Covert, Brad Isaacs and Adam Sandler *Ed* Amy Budden *M* Ray Ellis, Marc Ellis, Teddy Castellucci *Pro Des* Perry Andelin Blake *Pro* Sandler, Jack Giarraputo, Covert

Happy Madison / Meatball Animation / Columbia TriStar
76 mins. US 2002. Rel: 6 December 2002. Cert 12A.

Right: Rap star Eminem surprises the world with his acting debut in the highly charged *8 Mile* (from UIP)

8 Mile ★★★★★

Topical in casting but universal in theme, this film finds Eminem taking to acting. He appears as a Detroit youth with ambitions to escape from his impoverished environment, his plan being to take on black rappers and build a career as a performer. Thanks to Curtis Hanson's direction, Scott Silver's screenplay and some expert editing, this movie represents the best of Hollywood mainstream cinema. Any young person can identify with the hero's hopes and, since the climactic contest plays as dramatically as a boxing match, you don't even have to be a rap fan to appreciate this film. As cast here, Eminem looks like a screen natural, while Kim Basinger (mother) and Brittany Murphy (girlfriend) give strong support. It's welcome too that in passing the film also celebrates male camaraderie across racial divides. On its own terms, a total success. MS
• *Jimmy Smith Jr* Eminem *Stephanie* Kim Basinger *Alex* Brittany Murphy *Future* Mekhi Phifer, Omar Benson Miller *Cheddar Bob* Evan Jones *Wink* Eugene Byrd *DJ Iz* De'Angelo Wilson *Janeane* Taryn Manning *with* Anthony Mackie, Michael Shannon, Paul Bates • *Dir* Curtis Hanson *Pro* Hanson, Brian Grazer and Jimmy Iovine *Ex Pro* Carol Fenelon, James Whitaker, Gregory Goodman and Paul Rosenberg *Scr* Scott Silver *Ph* Rodrigo Prieto *Pro Des* Philip Messina *Ed* Jay Rabinowitz and Craig Kitson *M* Eminem *Costumes* Mark Bridges

Universal/Imagine Entertainment-UIP
110 mins. USA 2002. Rel: 17 January 2003. Cert 15.

Eight Legged Freaks ★★★

Prosperity, Arizona, the present. In the time-honoured tradition of 50s B-movie monster flicks, the toxins spilled by a truck into a small town's river happen to be the kind that grow things to enormous size, in this case, spiders. From tarantulas the size of watermelons to those the size of a small terrace, the monsters proceed to kill off the wilfully dumb inhabitants of Prosperity with sadistic glee. So why is it so disappointing? Somehow, the film manages to emasculate the terrific scare value of giant spiders after a fantastic first act job that has the entire audience holding its breath. After about the 20th victim is devoured in a jokey set-up, and the running gag about the family pets, the incessant genre-spoofing drums what suspense there is out of existence. Without that, you only have self-consciously stale dialogue and cheap laughs. AK

• *Chris McCormack* David Arquette *Sheriff Sam Parker* Kari Wuhrer *Mike Parker* Scott Terra *Ashley Parker* Scarlett Johansson *Harlan* Doug E Doug *Deputy Pete* Rick Overton *Wade* Leon Rippy *Bret* Matt Czuchry *Leon* Jay Arlen Jones *Gladys* Eileen Ryan *Randy* Riley Smith *Larry* Matt Holwick *Emma* Jane Edith Wilson
• *Dir* Ellory Elkayem *Scr* Jesse Alexande, Ellory Elkayem, based on a story by Elkayem and Randy Kornfield *Ch* John Bartley *Ed* David J Siegel *M* John Ottman *Pro Des* Charles Breen *Pro* Dean Devlin, Bruce Berman

Centropolis Entertainment / Electric Entertainment / NPV Entertainment / Village Roadshow Productions / Warner Bros
99 mins. US 2002. Rel: 9 August 2002. Cert 12A.

8 Women ★★

(*Huit femmes*)

Somewhere in the French countryside, a wealthy man is shot in his own maison by one of the eight women in his life. Amid a parade of kitsch song-and-dance routines, a detective mystery of sorts is played out as the film uncovers the secret tortures the women inflicted on him, and their individual

Left: Virginie Ledoyen, Danielle Darrieux, Fanny Ardant, Catherine Deneuve, Isabelle Huppert, Emanuelle Beart and Ludovine Sagnier in *8 Women* (from UGC)

motives for murder. François Ozon explains, somewhat bemusingly, that his estrogenic project demonstrates how redundant men have become in the new millennium, being a film where the sole male is only glimpsed. It also appears to show how redundant a thread of narrative sense can be when you persuade a near-definitive pantheon of the greatest French actresses alive to frolic in vividly photographed numbers, singing songs so arrogantly ironic and self-consciously uncool that it rapidly becomes really, *really* irritating. AK

• *Gaby* Catherine Deneuve *Augustine* Isabelle Huppert *Louise* Emmanuelle Béart *Pierrette* Fanny Ardant *Suzon* Virginie Ledoyen *Mamy* Danielle Darrieux *Catherine* Ludivine Sagnier *Madame Chanel* Firmine Richard
• *Dir* François Ozon *Scr* Ozon, Marina De Van, based on the play by Robert Thomas *Ph* Jeanne Lapoirie *Ed* Laurence Bawedin *M* Krishna Lévy *Ch* Sébastien Charles *Pro* Olivier Delbosc, Marc Missonnier

BIM / Centre National de la Cinématographie / Fidélité Productions / France 2 Cinéma / Gimages 5 / Le Studio Canal+ / Mars Films / UGC Films UK
110 mins. France / Italy 2002. Rel: 29 November 2002. Cert 15.

11' 09" 01 – September 11 ★★★

Eleven international directors were given carte blanche to comment on the tragic events of 11 September 2001, the only proviso being that each segment should last for eleven minutes, nine seconds and one frame. Ken Loach and Mira Nair rise to the occasion magnificently with cogent pieces that make their points quickly and Shohei Imamura broadens out the theme with a characteristically bizarre final episode that questions all wars. Danis Tanović and Samira Makhmalbaf also make worthwhile contributions, but the other directors (see credits below) disappoint, being confused, lightweight, pretentious (Iñárritu) or so sentimental as to be banal (Lelouch and Penn). A very mixed bag, then, but splendid at its best, with Loach looking at past history to attack the notion that America has the moral high ground and Nair raising the disturbing issue of how Muslims are seen now. MS

• *Pro* Alain Brigand
• *Dir* and *Scr* Samira Makhmalbaf, *with* Maryam Karimi
• *Dir* Claude Lelouch, *Scr* Lelouch and Pierre Uytterhoeven, *with* Emmanuelle Laborit and Jerome Horry
• *Dir / Scr* Youssef Chahine, *with* Nour el-Cherif
• *Dir / Scr* Danis Tanović, *with* Dzana Pinjo, Aleksandar Seksan and Tatjana Sojic
• *Dir / Scr* Idrissa Ouedraogo, *with* Lionel Zizreel Guire, Rene Aime Bassingra and Lionel Gael Folikoue
• *Dir* Ken Loach *Scr* Paul Laverty, *with* Vladimir Vega
• *Dir / Scr* Alejandro González Iñárritu
• *Dir* Amos Gitai *Scr* Gitai and Marie-Jose Sanselme, *with* Keren Mor, Liron Levo and Tomer Russo
• *Dir* Mira Nair *Scr* Sabrina Dhawan, *with* Tanvi Azmi, Kapil Bawa and Taleb Adlah
• *Dir / Scr* Sean Penn, *with* Ernest Borgnine
• *Dir* Shohei Imamura *Scr* Daisuke Tengan, *with* Tomorowo Taguchi, Kumiko Aso, Akira Emoto, Mitsuko Baisho and Tetsuro Tanba

BIM / Galatee Films / Canal Plus
135 mins. France 2002. Rel: 27 December 2002. Cert 12A.

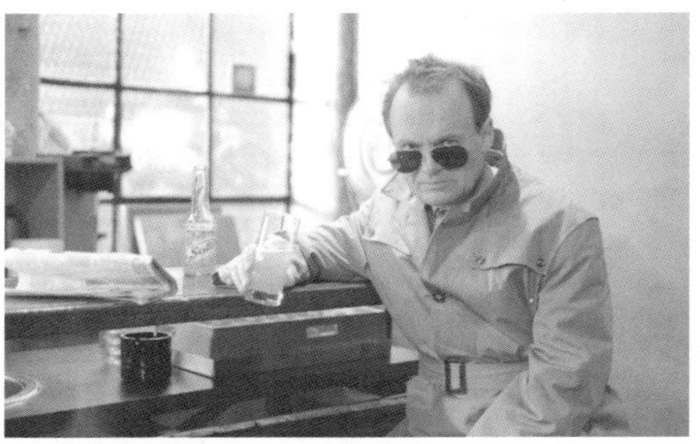

Left: Per Christian Ellefsen as the tortured poet in *Elling* (from UIP)

Elling ★★½

The non-sexual male bonding of two misfits is central to this Norwegian feature. Both men, Elling (Per Christian Ellefsen) and Kjell Bjarne (Sven Nordin), are adjusting to life after a period in an institution. Treated as a comedy complete with self-conscious gag lines, this emerges as a would-be feel-good movie about unbalanced people. The actors are fine, but for me (and this may well be a minority view) the piece never rings true. It is, of course, very difficult to blend the comic and the touching when dealing with the mentally dysfunctional, but last year's *Pauline and Paulette* did it perfectly, thereby showing just how phoney *Elling* is. Given the underlying seriousness of the characters' plight, it's just not good enough for such material to play like a variation on *The Odd Couple*. The direction by debutant Petter Næss is unexciting. MS

• *Elling* Per Christian Ellefsen *Kjell Bjarne* Sven Nordin *Alfons Jorgensen* Per Christensen *Frank Asli* Jorgen Langhelle *Reidun Nordsletten* Marit Pia Jacobsen

• *Dir* Petter Næss *Scr* Axel Hellstenius, based on the book *Brodre i Blodet* by Ingvar Ambjornsen *Ph* Svein Krovel *Ed* Inge-Lise Langfeldt *M* Lars Lillo Stenberg *Pro Des* Harald Egede-Nissen *Pro* Dag Alveberg

Arsenal / First Look Pictures Releasing / Golem Distribución SL / Italian International Film / Pretty Pictures / United International Pictures / Arts Alliance
88 mins. Norway / Sweden 2001. Rel: 14 March 2003. Cert 15.

Elsker dig for evigt

See *Open Hearts*

Embrassez qui vous voudrez

See *Summer Things*

Enough ★

Beautiful Billy Campbell plays against type as Mitch Hiller, the abusive, sociopathic husband who amazingly manages to hide all of his crueller habits from naïve wife Jennifer Lopez until she's truly trapped in his web. After a few scenes to establish Mitch as a sadist and the Lopez character, Slim Hiller, as gullible and downtrodden, she finally takes off with daughter Gracie. Crazy Mitch obsessively pursues her and endangers everyone she turns to for help. Finally, Slim has had enough and knows what she has to do. You've seen it all before, except better. As written, it could have been an acting tour de force for more talented actors, but the cast simply isn't up to the task. SWM

• *Slim Hiller* Jennifer Lopez *Mitch Hiller* Billy Campbell *Gracie Hiller* Tessa Allen *Ginny* Juliette Lewis *Joe* Dan Futterman *Robbie* Noah Wyle
• *Dir* Michael Apted *Pro* Irwin Winkler, Rob Cowan *Ex Pro* E Bennett Walsh *Scr* Nicholas Kazan *Ph* Rogier Stoffers *Ed* Rick Shaine *Costumes* Shay Cunliffe *M* David Arnold *Pro Des* Doug Kraner, Andrew Menzies

Columbia Pictures Corporation / Winkler Films / Columbia Tristar
115 mins. US 2002. Rel: 29 November 2002. Cert 15.

Equilibrium ★★½

Kurt Wimmer's debut as writer/director posits a future world controlled by one man, Father, who has made war a thing of the past. He has done this by requiring all individuals to be kept in a state of emotionless equilibrium through drugs. Christian Bale is the individual who rebels, but sadly Wimmer's concept is only a faint echo of existing works from *Metropolis* to *1984*. As though belatedly aware of this, the filmmaker changes gear halfway to introduce the kind of kung-fu fighting that might appeal to admirers of *The Matrix*. But the result is to turn what has been just about passable into outright absurdity. Pity Emily Watson for getting involved, but at least her role is brief. MS

Below: Christian Bale and Taye Diggs take a wrong turn on the way to Utopia in the frantic sci-fi thriller *Equilibrium* (from Momentum)

• *John Preston* Christian Bale *Mary O'Brien* Emily Watson *Brandt* Taye Diggs *Dupont* Angus MacFadyen *Partridge* Sean Bean *Robbie Preston* Matthew Harbour *Jurgen* William Fichtner *Father* Sean Pertwee
• *Dir / Scr* Kurt Wimmer *Ph* Dion Beebe *Ed* Tom Rolf, William Yeh *M* Klaus Badelt *Pro Des* Wolf Kroeger *Pro* Jan De Bont, Lucas Foster

Blue Tulip / Dimension Films / Momentum
107 mins. US 2002. Rel: 14 March 2003. Cert 12A.

Être et avoir ★★★★

(*To Be and To Have*)
This award-winning documentary is a simple, unhurried portrait of a dedicated teacher, Georges Lopes. For 20 years he has taught those children aged between four and ten living in the region of Saint-Etienne sur Usson. Both as a study of a man in a job that he loves, and as a record of young people guaranteed to bring back childhood memories to most audiences, this is a deeply sympathetic venture. It's also a memorial to those single classroom schools in rural areas where one teacher handles not only the initial nursery phase but also the later stages of primary education. Nicholas Philibert's film refuses to ingratiate itself with the audience and leaves you to come to it. Some may reject it for telling us nothing we didn't know already, but far more will love it for the privilege of observing George Lopes and his pupils. MS

• *Dir / Ed* Nicolas Philibert *Ph* Katell Djian, Laurent Didier, Hugues Gémignani *M* Philippe Hersant *Pro* Gilles Sandoz

Canal+ / Centre National de Documentation Pédagogique / Centre National de la Cinématographie (CNC) / Gimages 4 / Le Studio Canal+ / Les Films d'Ici / Maïa Films / arte France Cinéma / Metro Tartan
104 mins. France 2002. Rel: 20 June 2003. Cert U.

Evelyn ★★½

1950s Dublin, Ireland. Desmond Doyle has lost his wife and his job. He hits bottom when his three children are wrested away by the state, which then refuses to return them. When he asks why, they tell him the Family Act of 1941 denies single fathers the right to care for their children. "You'll never get them back," they say. "You just watch me," he replies… Based on Evelyn Doyle's memoirs, this family courtroom drama obeys all the laws of good storytelling thanks to Bruce Beresford being at the helm. But it lays it on a little thick. Touching moments throughout are nearly ruined by the permanent soft-focus setting, robbing the film of the emotional power it might otherwise have mustered. AK

• *Desmond Doyle* Pierce Brosnan *Nick Barron* Aidan Quinn *Bernadette Beattie* Julianna Margulies *Michael Beattie* Stephen Rea *Evelyn Doyle* Sophie Vavasseur

Left: Pierce Brosnan twinkles his Irish eyes at Julianna Margulies in the court drama *Evelyn* (from Pathé)

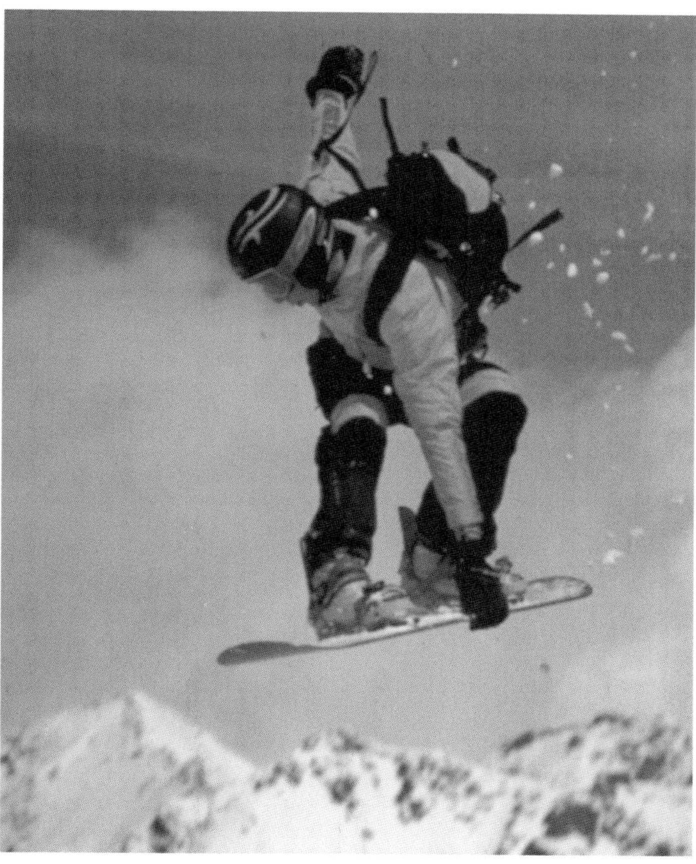

Above: High jinks in the overlong *Extreme Ops* (from UIP)

Dermot Doyle Niall Beagan *Maurice Doyle* Hugh MacDonagh *Tom Connolly* Alan Bates • *Dir* Bruce Beresford *Scr* Paul Pender *Ph* André Fleuren *Ed* Humphrey Dixon *M* Stephen Endelman *Pro* Pierce Brosnan, Beau St Clair, Michael Ohoveni

Irish Dreamtime / United Artists / Pathé
94 mins. UK/US/Ireland 2002. Rel: 21 March 2003. Cert PG.

Extreme Ops ★

Cocky advertising executive Ian Fintach wants to make the best commercial that money can buy. Unfortunately, he's already used up most of his budget, so he persuades gold medal skier Chloe Weston to flee an avalanche without the use of CGI effects. He also persuades a couple of adrenaline-junkies to join her for the ride, setting up a scenario of competitive jealousy, reckless risk-taking and soul-searching. As if this doesn't provide enough tension for one location shoot, the unit ends up sharing their Alpine digs with a gang of trigger-happy Serbian war criminals... A film about the making of a TV ad, *Extreme Ops* lacks the slick expertise of a real commercial and at 93 minutes feels about 90 minutes too long. Everybody is jolly good-looking (except for the war criminals) and the Alpine scenery is a bonus, but the characterisations are thin and the stunts are poorly filmed. JC-W

• *Will Flaky* Devon Sawa *Chloe Weston* Bridgette Wilson-Sampras *Jeffrey* Rupert Graves *Ian Fintach* Rufus Sewell *Mark* Heino Ferch *Silo* Joe Absolom *Kittie* Jana Pallaske *Yana* Liliana Komorowska *Slobovan Pavle* Klaus Lowitsch
• *Dir* Christian Duguay *Pro* Moshe Diamant and Jan Fantl *Ex Pro* Romain Schroeder, Rudy Cohen, Mark Damon and David Sanders *Scr* Michael Zaidan, from a story by Timothy Scott Bogart and Mark Mullan *Ph* Hannes Hubach *Pro Des* Philip Harrison *Ed* Clive Barrett and Sylvain Lebel *M* Normand Corbeil; songs performed by The Crystal Method, BT, 3rd Strike, etc *Costumes* Maria Schicker

MDP Worldwide / Diamant Cohen Prods / Apollomedia / Carousel Picture Co-UIP
93 mins. UK/Germany/Luxembourg. 2002.
Rel: 16 May 2003. Cert 12A.

The Eye ★★

(*Jian gui / Khon hen phi*)
Mun has been blind since the age of two but is exposed to a brave new world when a cornea transplant restores her vision. She's also exposed, unfortunately, to ghostly apparitions and premonitions of disaster, having picked up a form of second sight from the eyes' previous owner... Asian filmmakers' recent dominance of horror cinema springs a major leak with *The Eye*, a derivative concoction whipped up by the Pang Brothers of *Bangkok Dangerous* fame. The basic premise is lifted from that old sci-fi/horror warhorse, *The Hands of Orlac*, while an apocalyptic ending, featuring lots of gratuitously roasted motorists, is reminiscent of last year's *The Mothman Prophecies*. The elliptical editing impedes any real build-up of excitement, the score is bizarrely schizophrenic, a subplot involving a terminally ill little girl is saccharine in the extreme, and the shadowy harbingers of death look like 'street theatre' mime artists. And, to make matters worse, the film's single moment of real imaginative power is entirely blown by the poster tag-line. And since Metro Tartan didn't mind giving the game away, why should we? It reads: "What if the reflection you see is not yours... ?" JR

• *Mun* Angelica Lee *Dr Wah* Lawrence Chou *Ling* Chutcha Rujinanon *Yingying* Yut Lai So *Yee* Candy Lo *Mun's grandmother* Yin Ping Ko *Dr Eak* Pierre Png *Dr Lo* Edmund Chen *Mr Ching* Wai-Ho Yung
• *Dir / Scr / Ed* Oxide Pang, Danny Pang *Co-Scr* Jo Jo Yuet-chun Hui *Pro* Peter Ho-Sun Chan, Lawrence Cheng *Ph* Decha Srimantra *Art Dir* Simon So *M* Orange Music

Applause Pictures / Fortissimo Film Sales / Premier PR / Raintree Pictures Pte Ltd / Metro Tartan
99 mins. Hong Kong/Thailand/Singapore 2002.
Rel: 27 September 2002. Cert 15.

Far from Heaven ★★★★

This fifties-style melodrama made in homage to Douglas Sirk by the talented Todd Haynes both evokes the past and comments on the present. A Connecticut housewife (Julianne Moore) finds her life shaken twice over, first by the discovery that her husband (Dennis Quaid) is gay and then by falling in love with a black man (Dennis Haysbert), the son of her gardener. With a contemporary audience in mind, the issues of adultery and class are emphasised less than racism and homophobia. This precise and affectionate pastiche captures genuine emotion while commenting by implication on those two key issues. The audience is encouraged to ponder the degree of progress in both areas, but those still prejudiced are invited to recognise the folly of their ways. Not a major work, perhaps, but admirably stylish and effective. MS

• *Cathy Whitaker* Julianne Moore *Frank Whitaker* Dennis Quaid *Raymond Deagan* Dennis Haysbert *Eleanor Fine* Patricia Clarkson *Sybil* Viola Davis *Dr Bowman* James Rebhorn
• *Dir / Scr* Todd Haynes *Ph* Edward Lachman *Ed* James Lyons *M* Elmer Bernstein *Pro Des* Mark Friedberg *Costumes* Sandy Powell *Pro* Christine Vachon, Jody Patton

Clear Blue Sky Productions / John Wells Productions / Killer Films / Section Eight Ltd. / TF1 International / USA Films / Vulcan Productions / Entertainment
107 mins. US/France 2002. Rel: 7 March 2003. Cert 12A.

Above: Julianne Moore in Toff Haynes' retro-classic *Far from Heaven* (from Entertainment)

Fausto 5.0 ★★★★

Although presented by the Catalan theatre company, La Fura dels Baus, this contemporary variation on Goethe's *Faust* is very cinematic. It takes as its Faust figure a surgeon (Miguel Ángel Solà) and as his Mephistopheles a former patient (Eduard Fernández) who had been diagnosed as a terminal case but appears to have lived to refute that notion. Subdued colouring, spot-on casting and special attention to the soundtrack all contribute to an atmospheric, unsettling movie which, in addition to its stated inspiration, comes across as equally indebted to *Dr Jekyll and Mr Hyde.* Furthermore, in a modern context we are encouraged to ask if the devil, who releases in Dr Fausto the sexual desires he has repressed, is not in many ways a benefactor in disguise. Perhaps too many questions remain hanging in the air, but this is a highly original offering that constantly grips. MS

• *Julia* Najwa Nimri *Margarita* Raquel González *Santos Vella* Eduard Fernández *Dr Fausto* Miguel Ángel Solá
• *Dir* Álex Ollé, Isidro Ortiz, Carlos Padrisa *Scr* Fernando León de Aranda *Pro* Eduardo Campoy *Ass Pro* Thomas Spieker, Fernando Martín Sanz *Pro* Ramón Vidal *M* Josep Sanou Ph Pedro del Rey *Ed* Manel G. Frasquiel

CARTEL (Creativos Asociados de Radio y Televisión) SA / Fausto Producciones Cinematográficas / Programme Media de L'Union Europeene / TV 3 / Mephisto Films/ Soda Pictures
94 mins. Spain 2001. Rel: 6 June 2003. Cert 18.

Feardotcom ★

This dizzyingly unfocused horror flick about a homicidal website crosses the line between fear and absurdity like a refugee train on overdrive, bearing with it the not-usually-inept Stephen Dorff, Natascha McElhone and Stephen Rea. On the other hand, Udo Kier (playing someone called Polidori, just to amuse the more literate horror fans) has some experience with crushingly awful horror flicks – 1974's *Blood for Dracula*, to name but one, though that was at least *meant* to be absurd. As for the rest, it is a real shame that what might have been an intelligent, mean little chiller has sunk itself under the weight of gratuitous special effects and plainly ridiculous dialogue. AK

• *Detective Mike Reilly* Stephen Dorff *Terry Huston* Natascha McElhone *Alistair Pratt, 'The Doctor'* Stephen Rea *Polidori* Udo Kier *Denise* Amelia Curtis *Styles* Jeffrey Combs
• *Dir* William Malone *Scr* Josephine Coyle, story by Moshe Diamant *Pro* Moshe Diamant, Limor Diamant *Ph* Christian Sebaldt *Ed* Alan Strachan *M* Nicholas Pike *Pro Des* Jérôme Latour

ApolloMedia / Carousel Picture Company SA / DoRo Fiction Film GmbH / Fear.Com Productions Ltd / Film Fund Luxembourg / Filmyard Underwaterdeco / Franchise Pictures / Luxembourg Film Fund / MDP Worldwide / Milagro Films / Columbia Tristar
101 mins. UK/Germany/Luxembourg/USA 2002. Rel: 27 June 2003. Cert 18.

Le Fils ★★★★

(*The Son*)

The Belgian brothers Jean-Pierre and Luc Dardenne make films that eschew plot highlights and move at a slow pace. Consequently their work will never appeal to all, and this film's predecessor, *Rosetta*, didn't appeal to me. But here I was held by their unhurried revelation of a carpenter's adjustment to the death of his young child, not least through coming to terms with the fact that the youth responsible for causing this death is a human being and not a monster. Some will be unable to adjust to it but, if you are attuned to a Bressonian drama implicitly religious in nature, you should admire *The Son*. Its ending must be the most abrupt in cinema history, but it comes just when the film has made its point. Lead actor Olivier Gourmet is splendid and this is a work of cast-iron integrity. MS

• *Olivier* Olivier Gourmet *Francis* Morgan Marinne *Magali* Isabella Soupart *Omar* Nassim Hassaïni *Raoul* Kevin Leroy *Steve* Félicien Pitsaer *Philippo* Rémy Renaud *training centre director* Annette Closset
• *Dir / Pro / Scr* Jean-Pierre Dardenne, Luc Dardenne *Co Pro* Denis Freyd *Ph* Alain Marcoen *Ed* Marie-Hélène Dozo *Pro Des* Igor Gabriel *Costume* Monic Parelle

Archipel Films / Les Films du Fleuve / Radio Télévision Belge Francofone / Artificial Eye
103 mins. Belgium/France 2002.
Rel: 14 March 2003.
Cert 12A.

Right: A J Cook and Ali Larter face death together in *Final Destination 2* (from Entertainment)

Final Destination 2 ★★★½

Heading out of town for an end-of-school road trip with a carload of mates, Kimberly Corman has a truly horrifying vision of their impending deaths in a massive wreck. She tries to avoid the accident and save the lives of her friends as well as everyone else destined for the pile-up, but with mixed results. It seems that Death has a plan and doesn't like it altered… *Final Destination 2* works on many levels and almost all of them are enjoyable. First and foremost, it is grim, with violence so graphic that it's almost hypnotic. You *know* they're all going to die. You're just not sure how. And that's where the suspense lies… and, bizarrely, the fun. Starting out as a harrowing piece of dynamic horror, the story gradually becomes an insightful parody of its own genre. A brilliant piece of black humour, it plays with you and makes you laugh even while it terrifies and appalls you. SWM

• *Clear Rivers* Ali Larter *Kimberly Corman* A J Cook *Thomas Burke* Michael Landes *Eugene Dix* T C Carson *Rory* Jonathan Cherry *Kat* Keegan Connor Tracy
• *Dir* David R Ellis *Scr* J Mackye Gruber, Eric Bress, story by Gruber, Bress and Jeffrey Reddick *Ph* Gary Capo *Ed* Eric Sears *M* Alison Freebairn-Smith (songs), Shirley Walker *Pro Des* Michael Bolton *Pro* Warren Zide, Craig Perry *Ex Pro* Richard Brener, Toby Emmerich, Matt Moore, Jeffrey Reddick

New Line Cinema / Zide-Perry Productions / Entertainment
90 mins. US 2002. Rel: 7 February 2003. Cert 15.

Fogbound ★

Three friends go on holiday and are lost in a fog, which is a handy analogy for what happened to the audience during this dim and plodding film. The three characters involved are a couple, Ann (Orla Brady) and Leo (Ben Daniels), and their friend Ben (Luke Perry). As the tensions in the car rise, the film suddenly loses all narrative sense in its flashing references to a previous 18th century life that

Leo reckons he had, where he is an aristocratic duke about to murder two children. Far too odd, and indeed fogged up. AK

• *Bob* Luke Perry *Leo* Ben Daniels *Ann* Orla Brady *Dr Duff* Jeroen Krabbé *Gloria* Ali Hames *Shiny* Meg Kubota
• *Dir* Ate de Jong *Scr* de Jong, Michael Lally *Pro* de Jong, Angela Roessel *M* Frank Fitzpatrick *Ph* Edwin Roodhart *Pro Des* Ben van Os

InterMedia Film Equities Ltd / Meespierson Film CV / Mulholland Pictures BV / Blue Dolphin
97 mins. Netherlands/UK 2002. Rel: 4 April 2003. Cert 15.

Frailty ★★★★

Like *The Usual Suspects*, this is a tale, reliable or not, told in flashback as an FBI agent (Powers Booth) is offered the solution to a series of unsolved murders by the killer's brother (Matthew McConnaughey). This takes us back to the childhood of the two siblings, when their widowed father (Bill Paxton, also making an auspicious debut as director) revealed that the family had been chosen by God to eliminate those innocent-looking people who were really demons threatening creation. The plot-line may occasionally seem contrived but the piece is very well written and relies for its power not on gore but on menace atmospherically conveyed. Twists in the tale are to be expected but instead of going over the top they are satisfyingly in keeping. MS

• *Dad Meiks* Bill Paxton *Fenton Meiks* Matthew McConaughey *young Fenton Meiks* Matt O'Leary *Adam Meiks* Levi Kreis *young Adam Meiks* Jeremy Sumpter *Agent Wesley Doyle* Powers Boothe *Angel* Rebecca Tilney *Sheriff Smalls* Luke Askew
• *Dir* Bill Paxton *Scr* Brent Hanley *Ph* Bill Butler *Ed* Arnold Glassman *M* Brian Tyler *Art Dir* Nelson Coates and Kevin Cozen *Pro* David Kirshner, David Blocker, Corey Sienega

American Entertainment / Cinedelta / Cinerenta Medienbeteiligungs KG / David Kirschner Productions / UIP
99 mins. US 2002. Rel: 6 September 2002. Cert 15.

Frida ★★★½

Very much a personal project of Salma Hayek, who is both star and producer, this is a biopic about the Mexican painter Frida Kahlo. The film attempts to cover her career as an artist, various political issues and Frida's bisexual love life (25 years with the painter Diego Rivera and an affair with the exiled Trotsky included). Julie Taymor directs and everyone means well, but good scenes co-exist with Hollywood touches and arty flourishes and the film is only half successful. The most memorable performances come from Alfred Molina as Diego Rivera – his best portrayal to date – and from Roger Rees as Frida's father. MS

• *Frida Kahlo* Salma Hayek *Diego Rivera* Alfred Molina *Leon Trotsky* Geoffrey Rush *Tina Modotti* Ashley Judd *David Alfaro Siqueiros* Antonio Banderas *Nelson Rockefeller* Edward Norton *Lupe Marin* Valeria Golino *Cristina Kahlo* Mia Maestro *Guillermo Kahlo* Roger Rees *Matilde Kahlo* Patricia Reyes Spindola *Alejandro Gómez Arias* Diego Luna

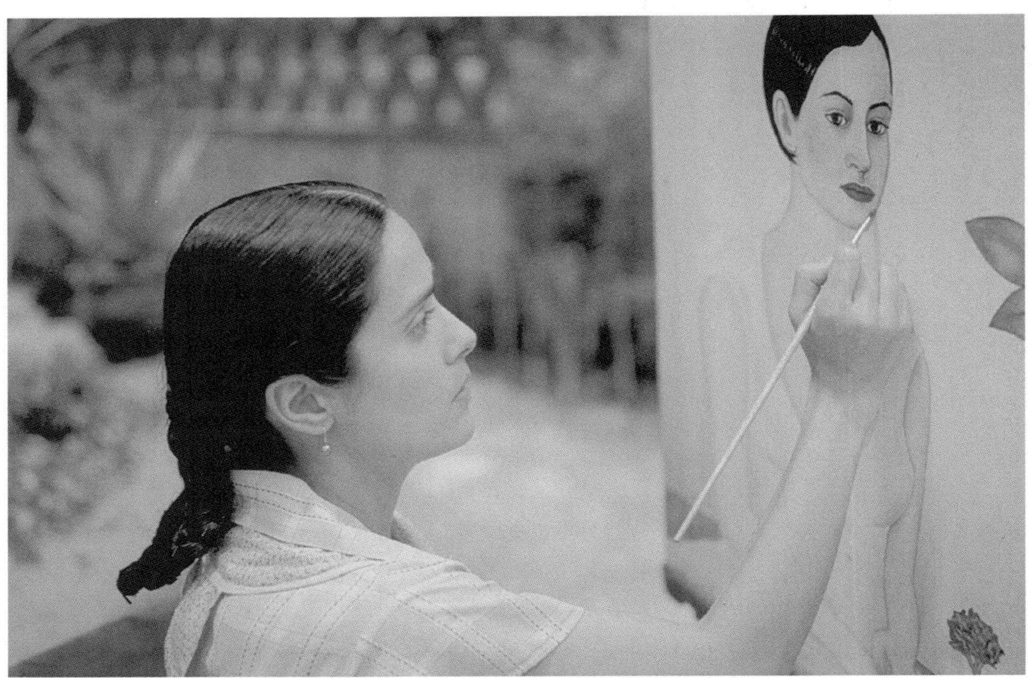

Left: Salma Hayek in the title role of her impassioned biopic *Frida* (from Buena Vista)

Gracie Saffron Burrows
• *Dir* Julie Taymor *Scr* Clancy Sigal, Diane Lake, Gregory Nava, Anna Thomas, based on a book by Hayden Herrera *Ph* Rodrigo Prieto *Ed* Françoise Bonnot *M* Elliot Goldenthal *Pro Des* Felipe Fernández del Paso *Pro* Sarah Green, Hayek, Jay Polstein, Lizz Speed, Nancy Hardin, Lindsay Flickinger, Roberto Sneider *Set Decoration* Hannia Robledo *Costumes* Julie Weiss

Handprint Entertainment / Lions Gate Films Inc. / Miramax Films / Trimark Pictures / Ventanarosa Productions / Buena Vista
122 mins. US 2002. Rel: 13 February 2003. Cert 15.

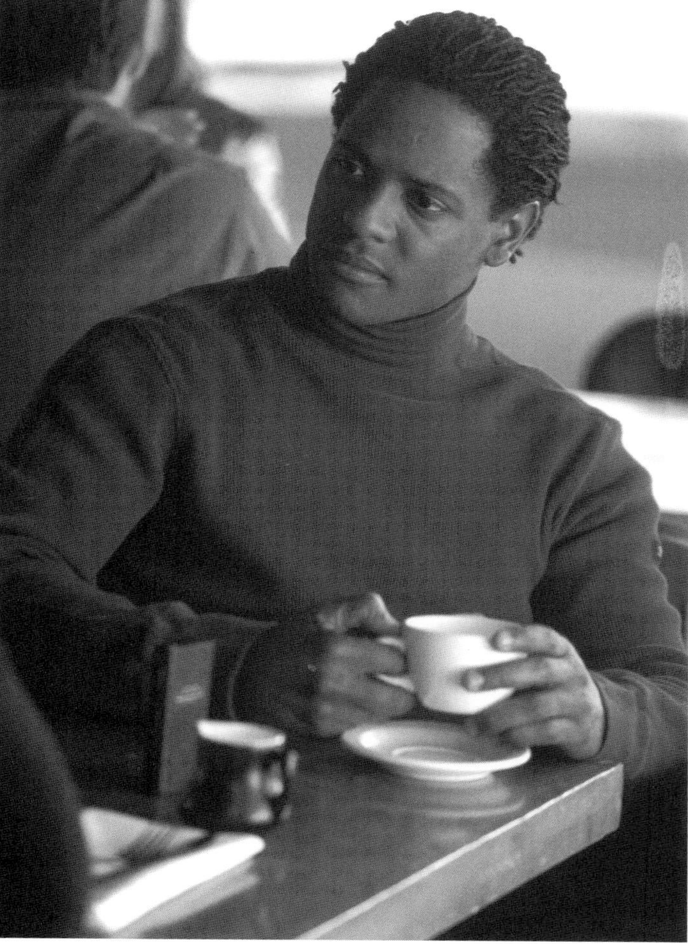

Above: Blair Underwood chills out on Soderbergh's uncharacteristically uncool *Full Frontal* (from Buena Vista)

Full Frontal ★½

When is a film not a film? When it's a film-within-a-film-within-a-film that winds itself so far up its own backside that it emerges as a home movie with irritable bowel syndrome. Having reaped universal acclaim with *Erin Brockovich*, *Traffic* and *Ocean's Eleven*, director Steven Soderbergh has opted for a spot of experimental game-playing. Recruiting actors he has previously worked with (and several others dazzled by his success), Soderbergh has concocted a series of vignettes shot on video. Largely improvised and only loosely connected, these sketches amount to little more than acerbic snapshots of middle-class Americans either directly or indirectly involved with showbusiness. While the smug, pretentious and navel-gazing self-indulgence of the film is bad enough, its total lack of cohesion is infuriating. As a sort of in-joke, the first film-within-a-film is shot on celluloid in a facetious attempt to show that the cinema can seem more real than life itself. The performances are all fine but the characters are so insular and shallow that you cannot help but despise them. JC-W

• *Gus* David Duchovny *Hitler* Nicky Katt *Lee* Catherine Keener *Linda* Mary McCormack *Carl* David Hyde Pierce *Francesca/Catherine* Julia Roberts *Calvin/Nicholas* Blair Underwood *Sam Osborne* Brad Rowe *with* Enrico Colantoni, Erika Alexander, Tracy Vilar, Brandon Keener, Jeff Garlin, David Fincher, Jerry Weintraub, Sandra Oh, Mike Malone, Cynthia Gibb, Brad Pitt, Terence Stamp
• *Dir* Steven Soderbergh *Pro* Scott Kramer and Gregory Jacobs *Scr* Coleman Hough, *Ph* Peter Andrews *Ed* Sarah Flack *Costumes* supplied by the cast

Miramax-Buena Vista International.
100 mins. USA 2002. Rel: 23 May 2003. Cert 18.

Fulltime Killer ★½

(*Chuen jik sat su*)
An *Assassins* style duel between two hitmen that spans the capitals of South East Asia, *Fulltime Killer* suffers from a fumbling inability to blend the knowing irony of its protagonists' cinematic references with its somber fidelity to the neo-cool aesthetic of the noir gangster thriller. Baffling motivations, and mutually unconsummated romances with profoundly fickle Gigi, froth the rivalry between Tok and O into an epic soufflé of gunfights and peacockery, leading to the twist-in-the-tale ending that collapses the entire confection. AK

• *Tok* Andy Lau *O* Takashi Sorimachi *Lee* Simon Yam *Chin* Kelly Lin *Gigi* Cherrie Ying *Fat Ice* Suet Lam *C7* Teddy Lin
• *Dir* Johnny To, Ka-Fai Wai *Scr* Joey O'Bryan, Ka-Fai Wai, based on the novel by Ho Cheung Ping *Pro* Andy Lau, Johnny To, Ka-Fai Wai *M* Alex Khaskin, Dave Klotz, Guy Zerafa *Ph* Siu-keung Cheng *Ed* David M Richardson *Pro Des* Silver Cheung, Jerome Fung

Milky Way Image Co. Ltd. / Teamwork Productions Ltd / Metro Tartan
100 mins. HK 2001. Rel: 27 June 2003. Cert 18.

G

Gangs of New York ★★★½

This is a terrific piece of film-making by Martin Scorsese. He reconstructs the New York of the mid-nineteenth century to reveal that the famous melting pot, far from symbolising a welcoming land of opportunity for all, was a city of squalor and violence dominated by rival factions. Technically the film is superb, but its personal storyline – son seeks to avenge his father's killing while falling for the killer's ex-mistress – is, as scripted, banal. Consequently, the historical overview, presented with all the fire and passion that Eisenstein brought to his silent classics, far outshines everything else, including the stars, Leonardo DiCaprio and Cameron Diaz. The one exception to this is the justly acclaimed performance of Daniel Day-Lewis, a remarkable presence as the main villain of the piece. MS

• *Amsterdam Vallon* Leonardo DiCaprio *Bill 'the Butcher' Cutting* Daniel Day-Lewis *Jenny Everdeane* Cameron Diaz *Priest Vallon* Liam Neeson *Boss Tweed* Jim Broadbent *Happy Jack* John C Reilly *Johnny* Henry Thomas *Monk McGinn* Brendan Gleeson
• *Dir* Martin Scorsese *Scr* Jay Cocks, Steven Zaillian, Kenneth Lonergan, based on a story by Cocks *Ph* Michael Ballhaus *Ed* Thelma Schoonmaker *M* Howard Shore *Pro Des* Dante Ferretti *Pro* Alberto Grimaldi, Harvey Weinstein

Cappa Production / Incorporated Television Company / Initial Entertainment Group / Miramax Films / P.E.A. Films / Q&Q Medien GmbH / Splendid Medien AG / Entertainment
168 mins. USA/Germany/Italy/UK/Netherlands 2002.
Rel: 9 January 2003.
Cert 18.

Above: Daniel Day-Lewis as the terrifying Bill 'the Butcher' Cutting in Scorcese's epic *Gangs of New York* (from Entertainment)

Gate to Avalon

See *Avalon*

Ghost Ship ★

A macho salvage crew comes upon a legendary find in the Antonia Graza, an Italian luxury liner lost for 40 years which suddenly appears on the cold Bering Seas. Their euphoria is literally short-lived as the grave secrets of the ship's demise rise up to confront the would-be profiteers... For all its atmospheric CG magnificence, *Ghost Ship*'s superb ly orchestrated kill scenes merely highlight the miserable inadequacies of the script. The clichéd dialogue is thoroughly painful in this glossy horror flick and retards any chance of its otherwise clever shocks building to a proper crescendo. One can only speculate about the behind-the-scenes preproduction fiascos that resulted in such rubbish from a crew ridiculously top-heavy with 'name' producers.
In a postmodern punchline, Gabriel Byrne wears a gaunt and haunted expression throughout, as if

apprehensive about a career lumbered with titles like *End of Days*, *Stigmata* and now this. AK

• *Maureen Epps* Julianna Margulies *Dodge* Ron Eldard *Ferriman* Desmond Harrington *Greer* Isaiah Washington *Murphy* Gabriel Byrne *Santos* Alex Dimitriades *Munder* Karl Urban *Katie* Emily Browning *Francesca* Francesca Rettondini *Second Officer* Cameron Watt
• *Dir* Steve Beck *Pro* Robert Zemeckis, Joel Silver, Mark Hanlon, John Pogue, Gilbert Adler *Ex Pro* Zemeckis, Silver, Gil Adler, Steve Richards, Bruce Berman *Scr* Hanlon, Pogue *Co Pro* Richard Mirisch *M* John Frizzell *Ed* Rodger Barton *Ph* Gale Tattersall *Ass Pro* Steve Jones *Pro Des* Graham 'Grace' Walker

Dark Castle Entertainment / Ghost Ship Films Pty Ltd / NPV Entertainment / Village Roadshow Productions / Warner Bros
90 mins. US 2002. Rel: 24 January 2003. Cert 18.

The Good Thief ★★★

From a filmmaker as distinguished as Neil Jordan, this heist movie is a disappointment. It may derive from Jean-Pierre Melville's *Bob le flambeur* of 1956 but, since that film was never released here, it has to stand on its own feet. In practice, it totters, despite the central presence of Nick Nolte as a gambler and crook on the Riviera planning a robbery under the eye of a suspicious cop (Tchéky Karyo). Compare it with the recently reissued *Rififi*, every inch a classic, or the modern, relaxed style of Soderbergh's remake of *Ocean's 11* and this seems routine, not really bad but definitely one heist movie too many. On the credit side, the colour design is striking and Chris Menges' photography is excellent as ever. Ralph Fiennes supplies a neat cameo and is credited as Fine Art Advisor. MS

• *Bob Montagnet* Nick Nolte *Roger* Tcheky Karyo *Paulo* Saïd Taghmaoui *Anne* Nutsa Kukhianidze *Raoul* Gerard Darmon *Remi* Marc Lavoine *Yvonne* Patricia Kell *Vladimir* Emir Kusturica *Albert* Mark Polish *Bertram* Mike Polish *Tony Angel* Ralph Fiennes *with* Warren Zavatta, Nicolas Dromard, Sarah Bridges.
• *Dir / Scr* Neil Jordan *Pro* Stephen Woolley and Seaton McLean *Ex Pro* Jordan, Kristin Harms and Thierry De Navacelle *Co Pro* Tracey Seaward *Ph* Chris Menges *Pro Des* Anthony Pratt *Ed* Tony Lawson *M* Elliot Goldenthal *Costumes* Penny Rose

Alliance Atlantis / TNVO Sari / Double Down Prods / Metropolitan Film Prods / Stephen Woolley / John Wells-Momentum Pictures
108 mins. France/UK/Ireland 2002.
Rel: 7 March 2003. Cert 15.

Goyangileul butaghae

See *Take Care of My Cat*

Grateful Dawg ★★★½

This is a heartfelt documentary made by Gillian Grisman about the close friendship her father, mandolin and banjo player David Grisman, shared with the late Jerry Garcia (who died in 1995, aged 53), the lead guitarist of the cult rock group The Grateful Dead. Like the Dead, the film slides quite purposefully away from the conventions of commercial media, presenting the relationship they shared as a kind of personal memoir, via old home videos, photographs, interviews and privately collected concert footage. And what music! Not nearly as flashy or politically loaded as Wim Wenders' *Buena Vista Social Club*, nor astriumphalist as *Down From the Mountain*, the greatest pleasure to be had from *Grateful Dawg* is the gentle intimacy it offers with its subjects, and their all-important music. AK

• *As themselves: Jerry Garcia, David Grisman, Joe Craven, Ricky Jay, Jim Kerwin*
• *Ex Pro* Craig Miller, David Grisman *Dir Pro* Gillian Grisman *Ed* Susan Baron *Ph* Rand Crook, Jessie Block *M* David Grisman, Jerry Garcia

11th Hour Productions & Entertainment Inc / Acoustic Disc / Columbia TriStar
81 mins. US 2000. Rel: 13 December 2002. Cert 12A.

A Guy Thing ★★

After a drunken blitz at his stag party, Paul wakes up to Karen, the 'tiki-girl' stripper from the night before. He assumes nobody will ever know of his supposed indiscretion, until he discovers that Karen is his fiancée's cousin. To further complicate matters, Karen's psychotically jealous ex embarks on a terror campaign and the more Paul spends time with Karen, the less he thinks he is ready to tie to knot. *A Guy Thing* takes on the usual stereotypes about male insecurities and marital commitment to banal effect. Jason Lee understudies the young John Cusack, while Julia Stiles and Selma Blair coast through a script so formulaic it might have been done on a calculator. AK

• *Paul* Jason Lee *Becky* Julia Stiles *Karen* Selma Blair *Ken* James Brolin *Jim* Shawn Hatosy *Sandra* Diana Scarwid *Dorothy* Julie Hagerty *Aunt Budge* Jackie Burroughs
• *Dir* Chris Koch *Scr* Greg Glienna, Pete Schwaba, Matt Tarses and Bill Wrubel *Ph* Robbie Greenberg *Ed* David Moritz *M* Mark Mothersbaugh *Pro Des* Dan Davis *Pro* David Ladd, David Nicksay

David Ladd Films / Metro-Goldwyn-Mayer Pictures / 20th Century Fox
102 mins. USA 2002. Rel: 13 June 2003. Cert 12A.

Hable con ella
See *Talk to Her*

Hahesdar
See *Time of Favour*

Half Past Dead ★½
When Steven Seagal kicks butt these days, he looks more like Marlon Brando than a martial arts master. Here, the spiritual grizzly plays an undercover FBI agent who happens to be stationed in the newly refurbished, hi-tech penal facility of Alcatraz. This is handy, because minutes before an inmate is to be executed in a state-of-the-art chamber (complete with adaptable backdrop) a team of Uzi-toting commandos break into the fortress to kidnap the condemned man. To retain an iota of street credibility, Seagal surrounds himself with badd-ass rappers (Ja Rule, Kurupt), but cannot save this shambles from looking like anything but a computer-generated video game. And the dialogue stinks (Nia Peeples: "I'm second-in-command and queen bitch of the universe"). JC-W

• *Sascha Petrosevitch* Steven Seagal *Donny/49er One* Morris Chestnut *Nick Frazier* Ja Rule *49er Six* Nia Peeples *Twitch* Kurupt *El Fuego* Tony Plana *Little Joe* Michael 'Bear' Taliferro *Williams* Claudia Christian *Jane McPherson* Linda Thorson *Lester* Bruce Weitz, and (uncredited) *Sonny Eckvall* Richard Bremmer and *SWAT captain* Don Michael Paul
• *Dir / Scr* Don Michael Paul *Pro* Andrew Stevens, Elie Samaha and Steven Seagal *Ex Pro* Christopher Eberts, Uwe Schott, Randall Emmett and George Furla *Ph* Mike Slovis *Pro Des* Albrecht Konrad *Ed* Vanick Moradian *M* Tyler Bates; songs performed by Ja Rule, DMX, Santana, etc *Costumes* Barbara Jager *Fight choreography* Xin Xin Xiong

Screen Gems / Franchise Pictures / Modern Media Filmproduktions-Columbia TriStar
98 mins. USA 2000. Rel: 2 May 2003. Cert 15.

Halloween Resurrection ★★
A group of kids take part in a reality TV show orchestrated by a hip-hop impresario for a chance to win a big cash payout. All they have to do is survive an entire night in the childhood home of the notoriously bloodthirsty Michael Myers… A heavy dose of reality-TV stylistics are used to cover up the redundancy of plot or intellect in the long line of *Halloween* films. It is kitsch entertainment value,

Below: The horror on Jamie Lee Curtis' face is real as she winds up in *Halloween Resurrection* (from Buena Vista)

and very little else, that continues to give the franchise a reason to live (again), a fact perhaps recognised in the opening sequence, which finally allows poor Jamie Lee Curtis to put this career demon to rest. AK

• *Laurie Strode* Jamie Lee Curtis *Michael Myers* Brad Loree *Freddie Harris* Busta Rhymes *Sara Moyer* Bianca Kajlich *Bill* Thomas Ian Nicholas *Myles* Ryan Merriman *Rudy* Sean Patrick Thomas *Nora* Tyra Banks • *Dir* Rick Rosenthal *Scr* Larry Brand, Sean Hood, based on characters created by Debra Hill and John Carpenter *Ph* David Geddes *Ed* Robert A Ferretti *M* Danny Lux, with *Halloween* theme by John Carpenter *Pro Des* Troy Hansen *Pro* Paul Freeman

Dimension Films / Nightfall Productions / Trancas International Films Inc / Buena Vista
89 mins. US 2002. Rel: 25 October 2002. Cert 15.

The Happiness of the Katakuris ★★★★

From horror director Miike Takashi comes this extraordinary Japanese work which, fusing black comedy and musical numbers, is really an allegory about the nature of life. It shows a family increasingly united in their desperate attempts to make a success of running a rural guest house, despite the fact that visitors, few in number, tend to end up dead (a fact to be hidden if the business is to prosper). The admirable cast play it absolutely straight. This might have been a deadpan method of making the humour even more telling, but instead it serves to downplay the kitsch element and to make this weird mix function as a comment on surviving whatever life throws at you. Where Ozon's *8 Women* was a light-hearted frolic adding songs to a whodunit, this in contrast emerges as a view of life as it is. It worked for me but it's so stylised and bizarre that it's clearly a specialised taste. MS

• *Masao Katakuri* Kenji Sawada *Terue Katakuri* Keiko Matsuzaka *Masayuki Katakuri* Shinji Takeda *Shizue Katakuri* Naomi Nishida *Jinpei Katakuri* Tetsuro Tanba *Miyake, the policeman* Naoto Takenaka • *Dir* Takashi Miike *Pro* Tetsuo Sasho and Hirotsugu Yoshida *Scr* Kikumi Yamagishi *Ph* Akio Nomura *Ed* Taiji Shimamura *M* Koji Makaino and Koji Endo *Visual effects* Misako Saka *Choreography* Ryohei Kondo

Metro Tartan
113 mins. Japan 2001. Rel: 16 May 2003. Cert. 15.

Happy Times ★★½

(*Xingfu Shiguang*)

Intended as a tragi-comic heart-warming humanitarian fable, this film is sad confirmation that the Chinese director of *Raise The Red Lantern*, Zhang Yimou, has lost his way. As sentimental and old-fashioned as Chaplin at his worst, it traces the attempts of an elderly bachelor to find a wife. That the endeavour yields something akin to a father/daughter relationship could be touching, but not when the tone is so artificial and the story contrived and phoney to a degree. Newcomer Dong Jie is well cast and appealing as the girl and that is some compensation, but nothing can save material as inept as this. It's well meant, but it simply won't do. MS

• *Old Zhao* Zhao Benshan *Wu Ying* Dong Jie *Chunky mama* Dong Lihua *Little Fu* Fu Biao *Old Li* Li Xuejian *Oxhead* Niu Ben • *Dir* Zhang Yimou *Scr* Guizi, based on the novella *Shifu, You'll Do Anything for a Laugh* by Mo Yan *Ed* Zhai Ru *Ex Pro* Edward R Pressman, Terence Malick, Wang Wei, Yang Qinglong, Zhang Weiping *Pro* Zhao Yu *Ph* Hou Yong *Pro Des* Cao Jiuping *M* San Bao

Guangxi Film Studio / Zhuhai Zhenrong / Fox
97 mins. China 2000. Rel: 27 September 2002. Cert PG.

Harry Potter and the Chamber of Secrets ★★★

Hogwarts becomes a dangerous place for Harry and his friends as a spate of mysterious attacks casts suspicion on their old friend Hagrid, ultimately forcing Professor Dumbledore to resign when his guarantee of Hagrid's innocence is tested. But thanks to a dangerously helpful house elf and a strange voice in his head, Harry knows something sinister is a-brewing, and it is up to him, Hermione and Ron to work out who the real villain is. The answer, (un)naturally, lies in the Chamber of Secrets...
The second film of J K Rowling's much-loved saga shows Harry growing into the hero he is meant to be. Chris Columbus plays it far too safe, putting very little into the film that wasn't already in the books, except for one highly incongruous hint of romance. The special effects are exciting and reassuringly child-friendly (even the most sinister monsters come with metaphorically blunted fangs and comical expressions) and the feel is generally that of an adventure where all will come out right in the end. AK

• *Harry Potter* Daniel Radcliffe *Ron Weasley* Rupert Grint *Hermione Granger* Emma Watson *Draco Malfoy* Tom Felton *Gilderoy Lockhart* Kenneth Branagh *Nearly Headless Nick* John Cleese *Rubeus Hagrid* Robbie Coltrane *Professor Flitwick* Warwick Davis *Vernon Dirsley* Richard Griffiths *Prof Albus Dumbledore* Richard Harris *Lucius Malfoy* Jason Isaacs *Prof Severus Snape* Alan Rickman *Petunia Dursley* Fiona Shaw *Prof Minerva MacGonagall* Maggie Smith *Molly Weasley* Julie Walters *Moaning*

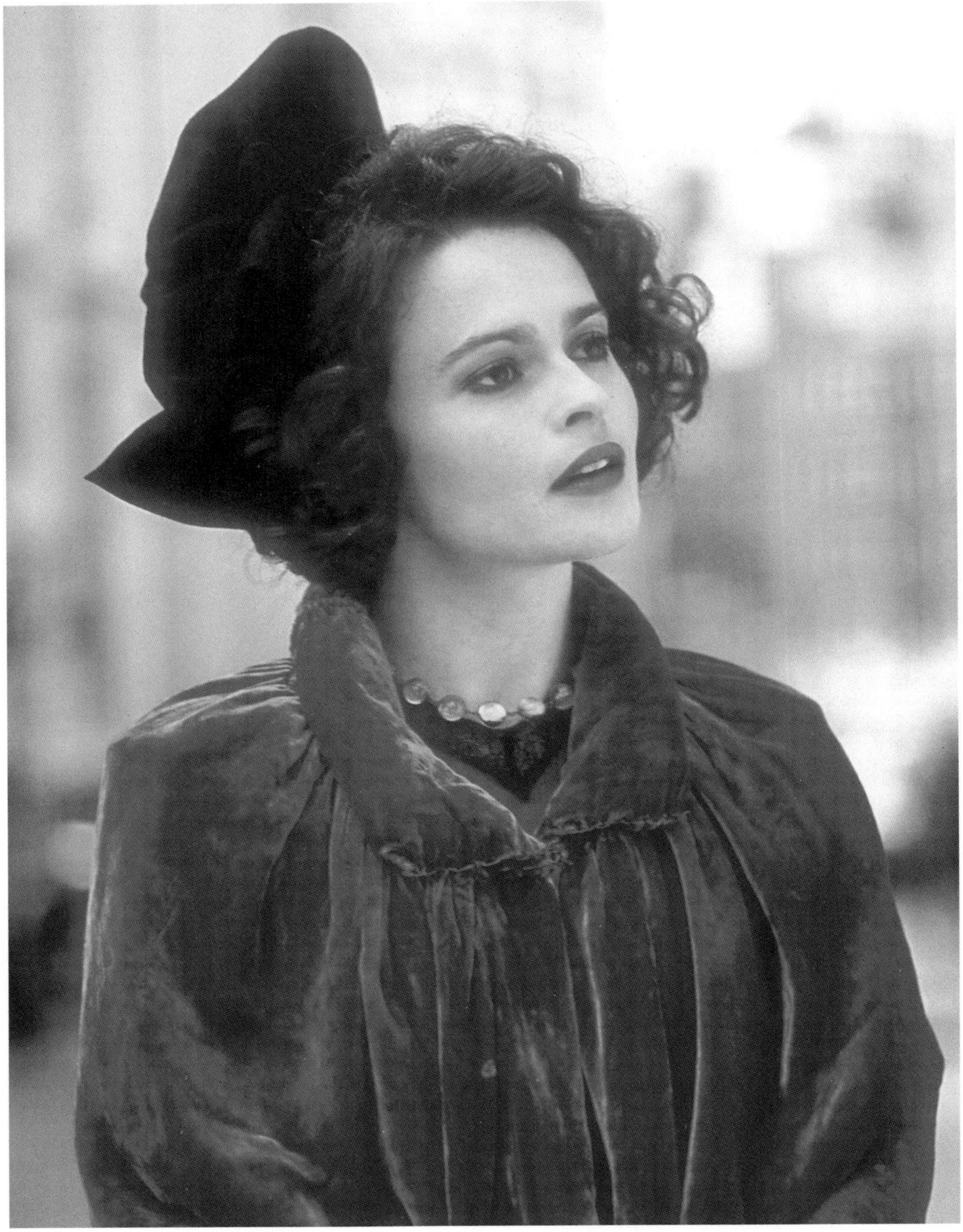

Left: Even Helena Bonham Carter's queer Bohemian minx can't lift *The Heart of Me* (from Pathé)

Myrtle Shirley Henderson
• *Dir* Chris Columbus *Scr* Steve Kloves, based on the novel by J K Rowling *Ph* Roger Pratt *Ed* Peter Honess *M* John Williams, William Ross *Pro Des* Stuart Craig *Pro* David Heyman *Set Decoration* Stephanie McMillan *Costumes* Lindy Hemming

1492 Pictures / Heyday Films / MIRACLE Productions / Warner Bros
160 mins. US/UK 2002. Rel: 15 November 2002. Cert PG.

The Heart of Me ★★★

This film version of Rosamond Lehmann's 1953 novel *The Echoing Grove* is well intentioned but unimpressive despite its talented cast (Eleanor Bron stands out in a supporting role). Uneasily structured as it jumps around in time, it tells a story that covers the period from 1934 to 1946 and concentrates on the relationship between two sisters. The domesticated Madeleine is very different from the more Bohemian Dinah, who has a passionate affair with her brother-in-law Rickie. The non-judgmental narrative saves the film from being old-fashioned in tone, but the script is characterless, leaving many elements unconvincing. The music score is ill-judged, too, and a quotation from William Blake is rendered trite by over-use. MS

• *Dinah Burkett* Helena Bonham Carter *Madeleine Masters* Olivia Williams *Rickie Masters* Paul Bettany *Mrs Burkett* Eleanor Bron *Anthony* Luke Newberry *Jack* Tom Ward *Betty* Gillian Hanna *Charles* Andrew Havill *Bridie* Alison Reid *with* Kathryn Tennant-Maw, Rebecca Charles, Rosie Bonham Carter
• *Dir* Thaddeus O'Sullivan *Pro* Martin Pope *Ex Pro* David M Thompson, Tracey Scoffield, Steve Christian, Keith Evans, Paul Federbush and Sebnem Askin *Scr* Lucinda Coxon *Ph* Gyula Pados *Pro Des* Michael Carlin *Ed* Alex Mackie *M* Nicholas Hooper; 'Heart and Soul' sung by Helena Bonham Carter *Costumes* Sheena Napier

BBC Films / Take 3 / Isle of Man Film Commission / Pandora-Pathé
96 mins. UK 2002. Rel: 2 May 2003. Cert 15.

Below Michael Sheen and travelling companion in the underachieving road movie *Heartlands* (from Buena Vista)

Heartlands ★★

Considering the talent invested in this little film, you wonder where it all went wrong. From the director of *East is East* (O'Donnell) and the writer of the critically acclaimed *TwentyFourSeven* and *A Room for Romeo Brass* (Fraser), not to mention such heavyweight producers as Michael Winterbottom, Andrew Macdonald and Duncan Kenworthy, *Heartlands* is a production truly blessed. It's also got a wonderful soundtrack, with engaging songs from Kate Rusby and John McCusker, and some glorious photography of the Peak District. The story of a non-entity who pursues his wayward wife to Blackpool, the film strives for a poetic melancholy but ends up as a series of underwhelming vignettes. The main problem is that we don't care for Colin, partly because he's called Colin and partly because he's in dire need of a hairstylist. Michael Sheen gives a reasonable impression of a toned-down Rowan Atkinson, but cannot find the heart and soul of this lamentable protagonist. JC-W

• *Colin* Michael Sheen *Ron* Mark Addy *Sandra* Jane Robbins *Geoff* Jim Carter *Mandy* Ruth Jones *Zippy* Paul Shane *Ian* Mark Strong *Sarah* Phillipa Peak *Janet* Celia Imrie *Ebony* Jade Rhodes *with* Kate Rusby and Eric Bristow (as themselves)
• *Dir* Damien O'Donnell *Pro* Richard Jobson and Gina Carter *Ex Pro* Andrew Eaton, Michael Winterbottom, Duncan Kenworthy and Andrew Macdonald *Scr* Paul Fraser *Ph* Alwin Kuchler *Pro Des* Tom Conroy *Ed* Fran Parker *M* John McCusker; songs performed by Kate Rusby *Costumes* Natalie Ward.

Miramax / Vestry Films / Revolution Films / DNA Films-Buena Vista International
91 mins UK/USA 2002. Rel: 27 April 2003. Cert 12A.

He Loves Me, He Loves Me Not ★★

(À la folie pas du tout)

Paris, the present. Angélique is blissfully in love with Loïc, a married doctor whom she believes will leave his wife for her. She bombards him with love trinkets to memorialise their liaisons, but when they are rejected without explanation she refuses to recognise that their affair is over, instigating a tragic end... Suddenly, the film rewinds to the beginning, and the entire romance is played from Loïc's perspective, revealing a warped psychosis behind Angélique's behaviour. Clever on paper, the film does not quite deliver with its looking-glass twist on *Fatal Attraction.* The collision of the blushingly romantic with the darkly insane may be symbolic of something important, but retards the emotional connection we need to have with the almost-lovers' predicament. AK

• *Angélique* Audrey Tautou *Loïc* Samuel Le Bihan *Rachel* Isabelle Carré *David* Clement Sibony *Héloïse* Sophie Guillemin
• *Dir* Laetitia Colombani *Scr* Colombani, Caroline Thivel *Ph* Pierre Aim *Ed* Véronique Parnet *M* Jérôme Coullet *Pro Des* Jean-Marc Kerdelhue *Pro* Charles Gasso

Cofimage 12 / TF1 Films Productions / TPS Cinéma / Téléma / Optimum
95 mins. France 2002. Rel: 22 November 2002. Cert 12A.

Heaven ★★★

Turin, the present. Phillipa places a bomb in the office of the drug lord who killed her husband, but kills four innocents instead. Arrested for terrorism, she is facing the death penalty until junior officer Fillipo falls for Phillipa and they uncover a conspiracy within the police force. Together they engineer her escape... *Heaven* reunites Blanchett and Ribisi, who were last together in *The Gift*. Blanchett is riveting as usual, while Ribisi is lukewarm. It also represents Tom Tykwer's mainstream debut. However, being his first un-self-scripted film (taking on an unfinished project by the late, great Krzysztof Kieslowski), he appears to compensate by overusing various trademark motifs: God's-eye views, clocks counting down, instant love affairs, and panoramic landscape abstractions. His auteur-branding weighs down what could have been an exciting thriller starring a pair of uniquely conceived protagonists (which we know Tykwer can do, cf *Princess and the Warrior*), resulting in a fudged opportunity. AK

• *Phillipa* Cate Blanchett *Filippo* Giovanni Ribisi *Filippo's father* Remo Girone *Regina* Stefania Rocca *Ariel* Alessandro Sperduti *Major Pini* Pini Mattia • *Dir* Tom Tykwer *Scr* Krzysztof Kieslowski, Krzysztof Piesiewicz *Pro* Maria Kopf, Stefan Ardnt, Manuela Stehr *Ex Pro* Anthony Minghella *Ph* Frank Griebe *M* Arvo Part *Pro Des* Uli Hanisch *Sound* Wolfgang Schukrafft *Ed* Mathilde Bonnefoy

Mirage Enterprises / Miramax Films / Noé Productions / Star Edizioni Cinematografiche / X-Filme Creative Pool / Buena Vista
97 mins. Germany/Italy/France/UK 2002.
Rel: 9 August 2002. Cert PG.

Hejar ★★★½

Unsophisticated but sincere, this Turkish feature reflects on tensions in that country through the tale of a retired judge in Istanbul. His humanity is stirred when fate puts him in the position of looking after the eponymous Hejar, a five-year-old Kurdish orphan whose grandfather might or might not be able to provide a home. Well acted (not least by Fusun Demirel as the judge's housekeeper), this humane film was strong enough politically to be banned in its own country. But as cinema it has to be said that the film is over-long, sometimes sentimental and burdened by an unnecessary subplot about a widow with her eye on the judge. But, though far from faultless, it certainly has its heart in the right place. MS

• *Rifat Bey* Sükran Güngör *Hejar* Dilan Erçetin *Sakine* Füsun Demirel *Müzeyyen Hanim* Yildiz Kenter *Abdulkadir Evdo Emmi* _smail Hakki Sen • *Dir / Scr / Pro* Handan Ipekçi *Ph* Erdal Kahraman *Ed* Nikos Kanakis *Pro Des* Mustafa Ziya Ulkenciler, Natali Yares *M* Serdar Yalcin, Mazlum Cimen *Ex Pro* Sahin Alparslan

Yeni Yapim Film / Hyperion / Focus Film / Tivoli Filmproductions / Rio Cinema Distribution
119 mins. Turkey/Greece/Hungary 2000.
Rel: 7 February 2003. Cert PG.

Hey, Arnold! The Movie ★★

A straight rip from the incomprehensibly popular Nickelodeon Channel children's cartoon series, this movie could be seen (by someone keen to intellectualise it) as a desperate attempt by the marginalised American left to influence a future generation of voters with a story that pits an industrialist Ronald Reagan soundalike, Mr Scheck, against the oblong-headed Arnold and his playground pals. Their only hope of stopping Scheck's monolithic mall-development from swallowing up their nostalgia-drenched neighbourhood is to hunt down a document that will prove its historical status. Various thin homages to famous Hollywood action movies are thrown in to prolong the wait until Arnold's eventual, fuzzy-hearted triumph. AK

• *voices: Arnold* Spencer Klein *Helga/Deep Voice* Francesca Marie Smith *Gerald/Rasta Guy* Jamil Smith *Grandpa/Nick Vermicelli* Dan Castellaneta *Grandma/Mayor Dixie/Red* Tress MacNeille *Scheck* Paul Sorvino *Bridget* Jennifer Jason Leigh *Coroner* Christopher Lloyd *Big Bob/Head of Security* Maurice LaMarche *Mr Bailey* Vincent Schiavelli • *Dir* Tuck Tucker *Scr* Craig Bartlett and Steve Viksten, based on characters created by Bartlett *Animation directors* Christine Kolosov and Frank Weiss *Ed* Christopher Hink *M* Jim Lang *Pro Des* Guy Vasilovich *Pro* Albie Hecht and Bartlett

Nickelodeon Animation Studios / Nickelodeon Movies / Snee-Oosh Productions / Viacom Productions Inc / UIP
76 mins. US 2002. Rel: 20 December 2002. Cert U.

High Crimes ★★

A powerful attorney is dragged into a high-level conspiracy when her husband's military history catches up with him and puts him in a court martial, accused of massacring innocent villagers... Starring Ashley Judd and Jim Caviezel as the wife and husband, with Morgan Freeman as the maverick army lawyer who helps defend the charges, *High Crimes* races through its plot twists in rigid adherence to courtroom drama convention. Caviezel is outstanding as usual, playing wounded innocence to perfection and then switching form with total conviction. Less persuasive are Judd, who never quite inhabits her role, and Freeman, apparently locked on autopilot. The achingly neat Hollywood ending gives up the hint of originality and will leave most audiences casting about for a reason to care about who really did what to whom. AK

• *Claire Kubik* Ashley Judd *Grimes* Morgan Freeman *Tom Kubik* Jim Caviezel *Embry* Adam Scott *Major Hernandez* Juan Carlos Hernández *Jackie* Amanda Peet *Brigadier General Marks* Bruce Davison *Mullins* Tom Bower

• *Dir* Carl Franklin *Scr* Yuri Zeltser, Cary Bickley, based on the novel by Joseph Finder *Ph* Theo Van de Sande *Ed* Carole Kravetz-Aykanian *M* Graeme Revell *Pro Des* Paul Peters *Pro* Arnon Milchan, Janet Yang, Jesse B' Franklin

Epsilon Motion Pictures / Manifest Film Co / Monarch Pictures / New Regency Pictures / Regency Enterprises / 20th Century Fox
115 mins. US 2002. Rel: 25 October 2002. Cert 12A.

Hijack Stories ★★★½

Sox is a good-looking actor from a wealthy South African family. Fancying himself an aspiring star in the mould of Wesley Snipes, he auditions for the part of a gangster in a TV series. But Sox is something of an anomaly. He is ostracised from the black community for his middle-class upbringing, yet is lumped together with the ghetto class by the whites. However, to better understand the character he will play, he calls on a childhood friend, an underworld figure in Soweto, to help him adopt the mannerisms of a real gangster. Of course, Sox is letting himself in for some major life lessons... A vivid and entertaining look at the underbelly of Soweto life, *Hijack Stories* manages to tackle a number of pertinent issues in an accessible and compelling way. Indeed, the film makes its points with some force, but never at the expense of its plausibility, excitement or even its generous sense of humour. A minor gem. JC-W

• *Sox* Tony Kgoroge *Zama* Rapulana Seiphemo *Fly* Percey Matsemala *Joe* Makhaola Ndebele *Grace* Moshida Motsmegwa *Nicky* Emily McArthur *Bra Dan* Owen Sejake *Kenneth* Harrold 'Speedy' Matlhabo *Steve* George Lamola *casting director* Robert Whitehead
• *Dir* Oliver Schmitz *Pro* Christopher Meyer-Wiel *Co Pro* Nadine Marsh Edwards *Ass Pro* Marc Sillam and Michael Markovitz *Scr* Schmitz, from a story by Schmitz and Lesego Rampolokeng *Ph* Michel Amathieu *Pro Des* Carmel Collins *Ed* Schmitz and Derek Trigg *M* Martin Todsharow *Costumes* Nadia Kruger *Choreography* Robyn Oblin *Sound* Marcel Spisak

Christoph Meyer-Wiel / Philippe Guez / Schlemmer Film / Septième Prods / Xenos Pictures / Paradis Films / British Screen / BskyB-Momentum
90 mins. Germany/UK/France 2000. Rel: 19 July 2002. Cert 15.

El hijo de la novia

See *Son of the Bride*

His Secret Life ★★★★

(*Tableau de famille / Le fate ignoranti*)
Rome today. When attempting to come to terms with the sudden death of her husband, Antonia (the excellent Margherita Buy) is surprised to come across evidence of his infidelity and even more shaken to discover that the husband's hidden relationship had been with a man. As told with real human feeling by Ferzan Ozpetek, this over-episodic lesson in accepting the lifestyles of others is appealing, without quite equalling the impact of Ozpetek's first feature, ***Hamam – The Turkish Bath.*** It leaves one pondering the fact that platonic love, however strong, can rarely result in a decision to share lives, whereas the sexual urge, however quickly it may falter, does invite that response. The film's portrayal of a gay milieu is one of the most authentic yet captured on film. MS

• *Antonia* Margherita Buy *Michele* Stefano Accorsi *Serra* Serra Yilmaz *Massimo* Andrea Renzi *Ernesto* Gabriel Garko *Veronica* Erica Blanc
• *Dir* Ferzan Ozpetek *Scr* Gianni Romoli and Ozpetek *Ph* Pasquale Mari *Ed* Patrizio Marone *M* Andrea Guerra *Pro* Tilde Corsi and Romoli

Les Films Balenciaga / R&C Produzioni / Peccadillo Pictures
109 mins. France/Italy 2001. Rel: 25 April 2003. Cert 15.

Hoffman

See *Max*

Honogurai Mizu No Soko Kara

See *Dark Water*

Hope Springs ★★½

Based on a novel by Charles Webb, who wrote *The Graduate*, this finds Britain's Mark Herman (*Brassed Off, Little Voice*) writing and directing his first Hollywood movie. It's a modest romantic comedy and it centres on an artist (Colin Firth), the fiancée he wrongly believes to have thrown him over (Minnie Driver) and the American girl (Heather Graham) whom he encounters in the small New England town of Hope. The decent cast are flawed by the silliness of the script, and it's but a pale shadow of last year's *Serendipity*, in which another British director working in America, Peter Chelsom, illustrated perfectly how this kind of film can be made lightweight but engaging. This one is way off-target. MS

• *Colin* Colin Firth *Vera* Minnie Driver *Mandy* Heather Graham *Mayor Doug* Oliver Platt *Joanie* Mary Steenburgen
• *Dir* Mark Herman *Scr* Herman, based on the novel *New Cardiff* by Charles Webb *Pro* Uri Fruchtmann, Barnaby Thompson *M* John Altman *Ph* Ashley Rowe *Ed* Michael Ellis *Pro Des* Don Taylor, Kelvin Humenny

Buena Vista Pictures / Fragile Films / Mumbo Jumbo Productions / Prominent Features / Scala Films / Touchstone Pictures / Buena Vista
92 mins. UK/US 2003. Rel: 9 May 2003. Cert 12A.

The Hot Chick ★

A pair of magical earrings transport an über-cheerleader into the body of a hairy middle-aged goon, and vice versa... Welcome to the tasteless porridge that is Rob Schneider's *Tootsie*-fantasy gone awfully awry. Packed so full of cheap shots at the stereotypical movie experience of American high-school, there is precious little to really enjoy apart from the very occasional guffaw when Schneider eases off the stupid pedal and comes up with something genuinely risqué. The usual band of Adam Sandler's hangers-on are in evidence, ploughing through the random gags that trademark their films. AK

• *Clive Maxtone/Jessica Spencer* Rob Schneider *April Thomas* Anna Faris *Billy* Matthew Lawrence *Jake* Eric Christian Olsen *Stan Thomas* Robert Davi *Melora Hardin* Carol Spencer *Lulu* Alexandra Holden *Jessica Spencer/Clive Maxtone* Rachel McAdams *Keecia 'Ling-Ling' Jackson* Maritza Murray *Mrs Thomas* Fay Hauser *Keecia's Korean mother* Jodi Long
• *Dir* Tom Brady *Scr* Brady, Rob Schneider *Ph* Tim Suhrstedt *Ed* Peck Prior *M* John Debney *Pro Des* Marc Fisichella *Pro* John Schneider, Carr D'Angelo

Happy Madison / Touchstone Pictures / Walt Disney Pictures / Buena Vista
104 mins. US 2002. Rel: 23 May 2003. Cert 12A.

The Hours ★★★★½

This is David Hare's adaptation of Michael Cunningham's novel, which took Virginia Woolf's *Mrs Dalloway* as its model and inspiration. It follows the original novel in capturing the essence of a woman's life through the minutiae of one day in her existence, but expands that notion by applying it to three women seen in interweaving narratives. One deals with Woolf herself (Nicole Kidman). A second features a housewife in fifties LA (Julianne Moore), who is reading about Clarissa Dalloway. The third, set in contemporary New York, is an affectionate pastiche which playfully redistributes Woolf's material, but remains serious at heart as its Clarissa (Meryl Streep) confronts the anguish of life. Brilliant performances all round, superb direction by Stephen Daldry and fine music by Philip Glass, but there is one flaw. Subtle parallels hold the stories together but more direct connections (revealed towards the close) conflict with Woolf's style. MS

• *Clarissa Vaughan* Meryl Streep *Laura Brown* Julianne Moore *Virginia Woolf* Nicole Kidman *Richard Brown* Ed Harris *Kitty Barlowe* Toni Colette *Julia Vaughan* Claire Danes *Louis Waters* Jeff Daniels *Leonard Woolf* Stephen Dillane *Sally Lester* Allison Janney *Dan Brown* John C Reilly *Vanessa Bell*

Below: Nicole Kidman transforms herself into Virginia Woolf in the subtle and complex *The Hours* (from Buena Vista)

Miranda Richardson *Quentin Bell* George Loftus *Julian Bell* Charley Ramm *Angelica Bell* Sophie Wyburd *Lottie Hope* Lyndsay Marshal *Nelly Boxall* Linda Bassett *Barbara* Eileen Atkins
• *Dir* Stephen Daldry *Pro* Robert Fox, Scott Rudin *Scr* David Hare, from the novel by Michael Cunningham *Ph* Seamus McGarvey *Ed* Peter Boyle *Pro Des* Maria Djurkovic *M* Philip Glass

Miramax / Scott Rudin Productions / Buena Vista
114 mins. US 2002. Rel: 14 February 2003. Cert 12A.

How to Lose a Guy in 10 Days ★★★

Andie is a Pulitzer wannabe but is stuck as the 'How To' columnist on a shallow glossy. Ben, meanwhile, is a hotshot ad-man who bets his boss that he knows what women really want. If he can prove it by making a girl fall for him, he wins a lucrative diamond campaign. By a twist of a scriptwriter's pen, Andie and Ben end up vying for each other's affections – the only catch being that Andie plans to 'lose' Ben with clichéd bad-dating behaviour as a research project for her column... A polished date flick that benefits from Kate Hudson's innate sweetness, this romcom rises above the usual dross with an edge that may perhaps be credited to the involvement of Burr Steers (writer/director of the brilliantly nihilistic *Igby Goes Down*) in a script that gives the old mating game a good jab in the ribs. AK
• *Andie Anderson* Kate Hudson *Ben Barry* Matthew McConaughey *Tony* Adam Goldberg *Spears* Michael Michele *Green* Shalom Harlow *Lana* Bebe Neuwirth *Phillip Warren* Robert Klein *Michelle* Kathryn Hahn *Thayer* Thomas Lennon *Jeannie* Annie Parisse
• *Dir* Donald Petrie *Scr* Kristen Buckley, Brian Regan, Burr Steers, based on the book by Michelle Alexander and Jeannie Long *Ph* John Bailey *Ed* Debra Neil-Fisher *Pro Des* Thérèse DePrez *Pro* Lynda Obst, Robert Evans, Christine Peters

Lynda Obst Productions / Moviemakers Productions / Robert Evans Company / UIP
115 mins. US/Germany 2003. Rel: 18 April 2003. Cert 12A.

L'Homme du train ★★★½

Set in a French provincial town, Patrice Laconte's latest is perfectly cast. Jean Rochefort plays a retired teacher, a widower who relishes the chance to talk when he puts up a visitor who has found the local hotel to be closed. Surprisingly he's not deterred to discover that the rather silent but sympathetic stranger (Johnny Hallyday) is a criminal planning a robbery. But then the teacher has always dreamed of a life of excitement, just as the crook has fantasised about being respectable. Humour and drama merge

Below: Matthew McConaughey and Kate Hudson rerun the battle of the sexes in *How to Lose a Guy in 10 Days* (from UIP)

to telling effect and *L'Homme du train* would be a fine film but for the disastrous final minutes when a kind of surreal fantasy at odds with everything that has gone before ruins the effect. MS

• *Milan* Johnny Hallyday *Manesquier* Jean Rochefort *Sadko* Pascal Parmentier
• *Dir* Patrice Leconte *Scr* Claude Klotz *Ph* Jean-Marie Dreujou *Ed* Joëlle Hache *M* Pascal Estève *Pro Des* Ivan Maussion *Pro* Philippe Carcassonne

Canal+ / Ciné B / Cinéma Parisien / Eurimages / FCC / Film Council / La Sofica / Sofinergie 5 / Media Suits / Natexis Banques Populaires Images 2 / Pandora Filmproduktion GmbH / Rhône-Alpes Cinéma / Tubedale Films / Zoulou Films
90 mins. France/Germany/UK 2002.
Rel: 21 March 2003. Cert. 12A.

Huit femmes

See *8 Women*

Hundstage

See *Dog Days*

The Hunted ★½

How many times can that fine, Oscar-winning actor Tommy Lee Jones recycle the same character? Having supplied his edgy gravitas to the part of the dogged US Marshal Sam Gerard in *The Fugitive* (for which he won an Academy Award), Jones reprised the role in the sloppy and silly *U.S. Marshals*. A year later, in *Double Jeopardy*, he portrayed a dogged parole officer chasing Ashley Judd all over the US. And here he's a seasoned Special Forces trainer tracking an unhinged former pupil through woodland and urban terrain. Relentlessly violent and one-dimensional, the film is remarkable for Jones' laziness (he was paid $17m, so why should he care?) and Del Toro's craziness. FYI: The late Johnny Cash provides the film's emotional message by rasping the opening song, 'Highway 61 Revisited' (by Bob Dylan), and ends the movie with his recent classic 'The Man Comes Around'. CB

• *Lt Bonham* Tommy Lee Jones *Aaron Hallam* Benicio Del Toro *Abby Durrell* Connie Nielsen *Irene* Leslie Stefanson *Ted Chenoweth* John Finn *with* José Zuniga, Ron Canada, Mark Pellegrino, Lonny Chapman, Rex Linn, Eddie Velez.
• *Dir* William Friedkin *Pro* Ricardo Mestres and James Jacks *Ex Pro* David Griffiths Peter Griffiths, Marcus Viscidi and Sean Daniel *Co Pro* Art Montersatelli *Scr* David Griffiths, Peter Griffiths and Art Monterastelli *Ph* Caleb Deschanel *Pro Des* William Cruse *Ed* Augie Hess *M* Brian Tyler *Costumes* Gloria Gresham

Paramount / Lakeshore Entertainment / Alphaville-Helkon SK
94 mins. USA 2003. Rel: 6 June 2003.
Cert 15.

Above: Jean Rochefort and Johnny Hallyday trade places in *L'homme du train* (from Canal+)

I

Above: Rose Byrne and Henry Thomas in *I Capture the Castle* (from Momentum)

I Capture the Castle ★★

A once-famous, now-blocked writer and his Bohemian family live in harmonious poverty in their crumbling castle until the arrival of their young and wealthy American landlords sparks the first blush of love for the two daughters. The Yanks are themselves a mismatched pair of reunited brothers and provide a juicy choice between the city sophisticate and the Californian cowboy. Naturally, neither of the girls can decide which one to fall in love with... Aptly mannered and beautifully shot, this adaptation of Dodie Smith's novel nevertheless neglects to adequately 'bitter' the 'sweet'. Without the dramatic anchors to put necessary substance into the domestic tragedies, the film is a mere antique box of girlish fantasies, comic episodes and syrupy sentiment. Even the final confrontation between dreamy daughter and imperious father feels like strained, genteel comedy instead of the proclamation of feminine maturity it was presumably meant to be. AK

• *Simon Cotton* Henry Thomas *Neil Cotton* Marc Blucas *Rose Mortmain* Rose Byrne *Cassandra Mortmain* Romola Garai *James Mortmain* Bill Nighy *Topaz Mortmain* Tara Fitzgerald *Stephen Colley* Henry Cavill *Mrs Cotton* Sinead Cusack *Thomas* Joe Sowerbutts

• *Dir* Tim Fywell *Scr* Heidi Thomas, based on the novel by Dodie Smith *Ph* Richard Greatrex *Ed* Roy Sharman *M* Dario Marianelli *Pro Des* John-Paul Kelly *Pro* David Parfitt, Anant Singh, David M Thompson

50 Cannon Entertainment / BBC / Distant Horizons / Icon / Isle of Man Film Commission / Perpetual Motion / Take 3 Partnership / Trademark Films / Momentum Pictures
113 mins. UK 2003. Rel: 9 May 2003. Cert 12A.

I Spy ★★½

When the prototype fighter plane Switchblade is stolen by notorious arms dealer Arnold Gundars (Malcolm McDowell), inexperienced US spy Alex Scott (Owen Wilson) is tagged to retrieve it. Teamed up with civilian boxing pro Kelly Robinson (Eddie Murphy), Scott also gets help from Special Agent Rachel Wright (Famke Janssen), the object of his unrequited love. *Dr Dolittle* director and actor reunite to resurrect another television series on the big screen. Unfortunately, Betty Thomas couldn't capture the same lightning in a bottle that she managed with *The Brady Bunch Movie.* While the chemistry between Wilson and Murphy is fine, there simply aren't enough funny moments to make this a comedy and too few genuine twists to make it

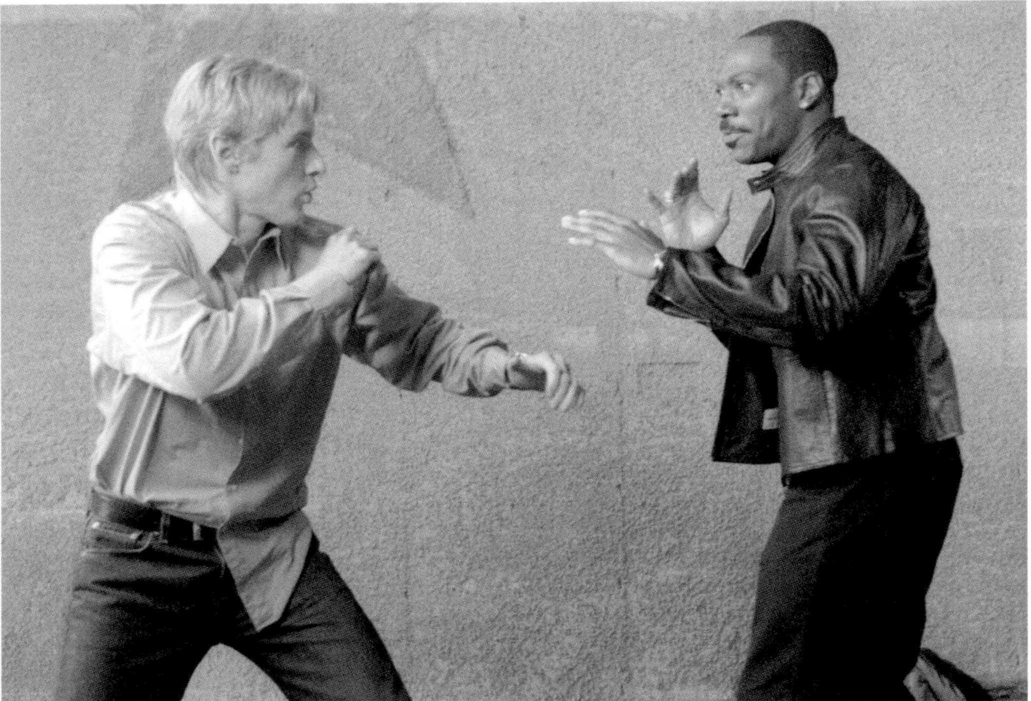

Left: Perhaps Owen Wilson and Eddie Murphy blame each other for *I Spy* (from Columbia Tristar)

a thriller. Instead, it meanders its way through a few action sequences and has its share of charming moments, but lacks real zing. SWM

• *Kelly Robinson* Eddie Murphy *Alex Scott* Owen Wilson *Special Agent Rachel Wright* Famke Janssen *Arnold Gundars* Malcolm McDowell *Carlos* Gary Cole *McIntyre* Bill Mondy *Jerry* Phill Lewis
• *Dir* Betty Thomas *Scr* Marianne Wibberley, Cormac Wibberley, Jay Scherick, David Ronn, from a story by Marianne and Cormac Wibberley *Ph* Oliver Wood *Ed* Peter Teschner *M* Richard Gibbs *Pro Des* Marcia Hinds-Johnson *Pro* Jenno Topping, Thomas, Mario Kassar, Andy Vajna

C-2 Pictures / Columbia Pictures Corporation / Sheldon Leonard Productions / Tall Trees Productions / Columbia Tristar
97 mins. US 2002. Rel: 24 January 2003. Cert 12A.

Identity ★★★★

This and *Frailty* are the best Hollywood thrillers of the year. Cleverly written and well paced by director James Mangold, *Identity* sets up unease from the start as an unseen accused killer is questioned by a psychiatrist (Alfred Molina). Before long we are witnessing a series of murders during one wild and stormy night at a motel – all of which amounts to knowing variations on *Ten Little Indians*, *Psycho* and even *The Three Faces of Eve*. Excellent cast, great set design and a welcome succinctness (so that we don't have time to ask too many questions) render this an entertaining thriller, one that right down to the handling of its outrageous surprise twist shows much competence and good judgment. Have fun. MS

• *Ed* John Cusack *Rhodes* Ray Liotta *Paris* Amanda Peet *Larry* John Hawkes *doctor* Alfred Molina *Ginny* Clea DuVall *George York* John C McGinley *Lou* William Lee Scott *Robert Maine* Jake Busey *Caroline Suzanne* Rebecca DeMornay *Malcolm Rivers* Pruitt Taylor Vince
• *Dir* James Mangold *Scr* Michael Cooney *Ph* Phedon Papamichael *Ed* David Brenner *M* Alan Silvestri *Pro Des* Mark Friedberg *Pro* Cathy Konrad

Columbia Pictures Corporation / Konrad Pictures / Columbia TriStar
90 mins. US 2003. Rel: 13 June 2003. Cert 15.

Igby Goes Down ★★★

In recent years such works as *Donnie Darko* and *Ghost World* have made distinguished additions to the genre epitomised most famously by J D Salinger's *The Catcher in the Rye*: works centred on a young, misunderstood rebel more genuine and sensitive than those around him. Seventeen-year-old Igby in this directorial debut by Burr Steers is just such a hero, and Kieran Culkin plays him splendidly. But if affluent intellectual New Yorkers convincingly exist in their own world in the films of Whit Stillman, Steers as writer muddies the waters. He injects chunks of black comedy and an element of camp grotesquery reminiscent of John Waters (not least in the portrait of a mother from hell, played by Susan Sarandon). The artificiality and the conflicting tones all too often throw this film off course, but Culkin does manage some amazing rescue work and achieves moments of truth. MS

• *Jason 'Igby' Slocumb Jr* Kieran Culkin *Sookie Sapperstein* Claire Danes *D H Banes* Jeff Goldblum *Russel* Jared Harris *Rachel* Amanda Peet *Oliver Slocumb* Ryan Phillippe *Jason Slocumb* Bill Pullman *Mimi Slocumb* Susan Sarandon
• *Dir / Scr* Burr Steers *Ph* Wedigo von Schultzendorff *Ed* William Anderson *M* Uwe Fahrenkrog-Peterson *Pro Des* Kevin Thompson *Pro* Marco Weber, Lisa Tornell

Atlantic Streamline / Crossroads Films / Igby Productions Inc / Optimum Releasing
98 mins. US 2002. 13 June 2003. Cert 15.

I'll Be There ★½

Old time rock 'n' roll and the angelic voice of Charlotte Church collide in a remote Welsh village in this insipid British confection. The idea of rock music permeating a small rural community is not without its interest, but it fails to take off under the leaden direction of Craig Ferguson. Ferguson, who starred in and co-wrote the amusing and lively comedies *The Big Tease* and *Saving Grace*, plays a hard-drinking, washed-up rock star whose wild antics land him back in the media spotlight and a psychiatric ward. There, he's confronted by a former lover and the teenage daughter he never knew he had. As the latter, Charlotte Church (in her film debut) looks ill at ease in front of the camera, although she's nowhere near as embarrassing as Joss Ackland as a bloated 70-year-old rock singer. Ferguson himself fails to convince us that he's anything more than an actor playing a rock star, while the rest of the cast are equally unconvincing. JC-W

• *Paul Kerr* Craig Ferguson *Rebecca* Jemma Redgrave *Olivia* Charlotte Church *Evil Edmonds* Joss Ackland *Digger McQuade* Ralph Brown *Graham* Ian McNeice *Dr Bridget* Imelda Staunton *Sam Gervasi* Anthony Head *Gordano* Stephan Noonan *Mary* Marion Bailey *Ivor* Tom Ellis
• *Dir* Craig Ferguson *Pro* James G Robinson *Ex Pro* Guy McElwaine *Co Pro* David C Robinson and Wayne Morris *Scr* Ferguson and Philip McGrade *Ph* Ian Wilson *Pro Des* Tim Harvey *Ed* Sheldon Kahn *M* Trevor Jones *Costumes* Stephanie Collie

Warner / Morgan Creek / Immortal Entertainment-Warner
104 mins. UK/USA 2003. Rel: 13 June 2003. Cert 12A.

In the Name of Buddha ★★★½

This long, impassioned film from Sri Lanka is a powerful anti-war statement, albeit one couched in terms akin to Bollywood while also emphasising the horror. It takes the story of one family to show the suffering of the Tamils over nearly two decades and presents itself openly as a plea for peace. However, it takes somebody more familiar than I with the tragic facts of this recent history to know whether or not the film shows (not least in its attitude to India) a proper impartiality. There are moments of sentimentality and the idiom, with its use of music and song, is alien to us. But, if you accept the style for what it is, you are left with a film which, sometimes echoing Russian cinema of the twenties, sustains its epic length of almost two and a half hours. MS

• *Siva* Shiju *Geetha* Soniya *Leader* Jyothi Lal *Mikara* Amit *Doctor* Jayasurya
• *Dir / Scr* Rajesh Touchriver, from a story by Sai George *Pro* K Shanmughathas, Sai George *Ph* Jain Joseph Rajaratnam *Ed* Ranjan Abraham *Pro Des* Sunil Baba *M* Rajamani

Da'Sai Films / Sai Ann Films / Miracle Communications
146 mins. Sri Lanka 2002. Rel: 16 May 2003

In This World ★★★★

Taking a tip from the quasi-documentary style to be found in so many Iranian masterpieces, Michael Winterbottom here offers a deeply compassionate study of two refugee Afghan youths. They set out from a camp in Pakistan hoping to reach London, and the film's aim – like that of the Oscar-winning *Journey of Hope* (1990) – is to make the audience identify with the plight of these illegal immigrants. A few stylised flourishes seem to belong to a different film, but what counts is that this is a warmly sympathetic yet unsentimental human document. Although in essence it may reprise the themes of that earlier film, the detail and the locations provide a topical flavour. The non-professional players are wholly convincing and, even if *Wonderland* remains Winterbottom's finest achievement to date, this is a thoroughly commendable work. Although technically a British film, it is largely sub-titled, thus adding to the sense of authenticity. MS

• *as themselves* Jamal Udin Torabi, Enayatullah *travel agent* Imran Paracha *Enayat's brother* Hiddayatullah *Enayat's father* Jamau *Enayat's uncle* Wakeel Khan *Enayat's uncle* Lal Zarin *Jamal's older brother* Mirwais Torabi *money changer* Ahsan Raza *groom* Abdul Ahmad *Jamal's younger brother* Amanullah Torabi
• *Dir* Michael Winterbottom *Scr* Tony Grisoni *Ex Pro* Chris Auty David M Thompson *Pro* Andrew Eaton, Anita Overland *Co Pro* Behrooz Hashemian *Ass Pro* Fiona Neilson *M* Dario Marianelli *Ph* Marcel Zyskind *Ed* Peter Christelis

BBC / Film Council / Revolution Films / The Film Consortium / The Works / ICA Projects
90 mins. UK 2003. Rel: 28 March 2003. Cert 15.

Innocence ★★★★½

The Australian-based writer/director Paul Cox re-emerges with this wonderful study of love rekindled in old age. Two youngsters, Claire and Andreas, fall in love but are destined to go different ways in life. However, when Andreas (Charles Tingwell) is a widower in his seventies, he encounters Claire (Julia Blake) once again. She is married to John (Terry Norris), but that relationship has sunk into routine and for both Claire and Andreas their reunion ignites a passion capable of making their lives meaningful again. Although beautifully sensitive, the film is not flawless – the last stages of the narrative have uneasy moments and the youthful lovers are stereotypes – but, even so, it's not to be missed. In particular Julia Blake's performance is luminous, one of the very best seen this year. There's also a lovely characterisation from Marta Dusseldorp as Andreas' understanding daughter. MS

• *Claire* Julia Blake *Andreas* Charles Tingwell *John* Terry Norris *David* Robert Menzies and *Monique* Marta Dusseldorp
• *Dir / Scr* Paul Cox *Ph* Tony Clark *Ed* Simon Whitington *M* Paul Grabowsky *Pro Des* Tony Cronin *Pro* Paul Cox and Mark Patterson

CinéTé / Film Victoria / Fireworks Pictures / Het Fonds in Vladderen / Illumination Films / International Film Festival Ghent / New Oz Productions / Showtime Australia / South Australian Film Corporation / Strand / Capers Matcine
95 mins. Australia/Belgium 2000. Rel: 9 January 2003. Cert 12A.

Insomnia ★★★½

Infamous detective Will Dormer and his partner are sent to Alaska to help with a murder case as a kind of punishment. Disoriented by the perpetual sun of the Alaskan summer, Will makes a mistake in his otherwise surefooted hunt for the murderer, an oddball crime novelist played with astounding intensity by Robin Williams. Suddenly, the tables are turned and the positions of hunter and prey are blurred... Christopher Nolan's remake of Erik Skjoldbjaerg's Swedish original could have been a tragedy of Hollywood style over European substance. However, it plays with such pulsating confidence that it succeeds in spite of a comatose Al Pacino in 'burnt-out cop' mode. There is a lot of arty pretension for what is essentially a character-driven suspense thriller, but the stunning visuals and gripping performances keep the story on track. AK

• *Will Dormer* Al Pacino *Walter Finch* Robin Williams *Ellie Burr* Hilary Swank *Rachel Clement* Maura Tierney *Hap Eckhart* Martin Donovan *Fred Duggar* Nicky Katt *Chief Nyback* Paul Dooley
• *Dir* Christopher Nolan *Scr* Hillary Seitz, based on the film directed by Erik Skjoldbjaerg, written by

Below: Al Pacino as a burnt out detective in Christopher Nolan's *Insomnia* (from Buena Vista)

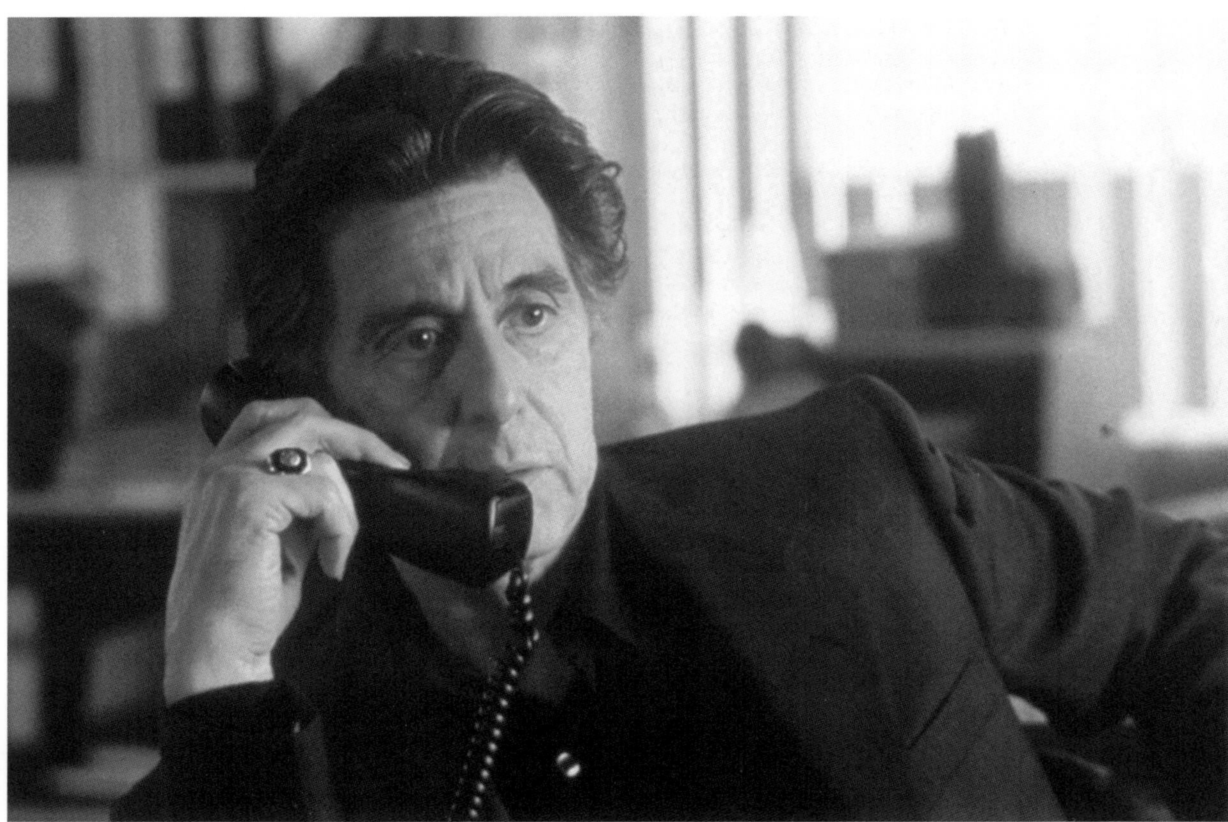

Nikolaj Frobenius and Skjoldbjaerg *Ph* Wally Pfister *Ed* Dody Dorn *M* David Julyan *Pro Des* Nathan Crowley *Pro* Broderick Johnson, Andrew A Kosove, Paul Junger Witt, Edward L McDonnell

Alcon Entertainment / Insomnia Productions / Section Eight Ltd / Summit Entertainment / Witt-Thomas Productions / Buena Vista
118 mins. US 2002. Rel: 30 August 2002. Cert 15.

Intacto ★★★½

Set on Tenerife, this debut feature by Juan Carlos Fresnadillo is intriguing yet over-shadowed by *Abre los ojos* (Open Your Eyes, 1997), with which it shares a producer. It blends a mystery thriller with concepts related to luck, its importance and its acquisition. *Intacto* is the story of how a plane crash survivor (the appealing Leonardo Sbaraglia) becomes caught up in the vengeance planned by a protégé (Eusebio Poncela) for the mentor who turned against him (the ever-authoritative Max von Sydow). The metaphysical element provides novelty rather than depth, and the audience is left hanging on uneasily instead of finding the mystification within the complex plot agreeable. References to the Holocaust, instead of adding weight, seem somewhat tasteless, but for all that it's by no means uninteresting. MS

• *Tomás* Leonardo Sbaraglia *Federico* Eusebio Poncela *Sara* Mónica López *Alejandro (bullfighter)* Antonio Dechent *Samuel* Max von Sydow *Horacio* Guillermo Toledo *Marido Sara* Alber Ponte *Hija Sara* Andrea San Vicente Momentum
• *Ass Pro* Ghislain Barrois, Ignacio Salazar *Exec Pro* Fernando Bovaira, Enrique López Lavigne *Pro* Sebastián Álvarez *M* Lucio Godoy *Ph* Xavi Giménez *Ed* Nacho Ruiz Capillas *Pro Des* César Macarrón

Canal+ España / Gestevisión Telecinco SA / Sociedad General de Cine / Telecinco / Tenerife Film Commission / Momentum
108 mins. Spain 2001. Rel: 11 April 2003. Cert 15.

O invasor

See *The Trepasser*

Irréversible ★★★★½

Notoriously controversial, this Paris-set drama tells its story backwards but never confusingly. Starting with a night-time killing in a gay club, it reverses step by step until we discover that the killer (Vincent Cassel) had acted in an attempt to avenge the exceedingly violent rape of the woman he loves (Monica Bellucci), who, at the start of the day, could never have guessed the fate awaiting her through being in the wrong place at the wrong time. A shattering experience, *Irréversible* is a genuine work of art which can only be fully assessed when the beautifully judged scene of early morning lovemaking near the close underlines the fragility of happiness and of life itself in the contemporary world. But the hysteria of the opening and the unnecessary final scene (after an affecting plot surprise) can reasonably be criticised. Not being a censor, I leave aside my fear that the rape and murder scenes could be dangerous if viewed by unbalanced persons. MS

• *Alex* Monica Bellucci *Marcus* Vincent Cassel *Pierre* Albert Dupontel *Le Tenia* Jo Prestia *Philippe* Philippe Nahon
• *Dir / Scr / Ed* Gaspar Noé *Ph* Noé, Benoît Debie *M* Thomas Bangalter *Pro Des* Alain Juteau *Pro* Richard Grandpierre, Christophe Rossignon

120 Films / Eskwad / Grandpierre / Les Cinémas de la Zone / Nord-Ouest Productions / Rossignon / Studio Canal / Metro Tartan
97 mins. France 2002. Rel: 31 January 2003. Cert 18.

Ivansxtc ★★★★

Tolstoy's *Death of Ivan Illych* is transformed into this scathing critique of Hollywood's warped aesthetics. Bernard Rose was moved by the true story of Jay Moloney, his one-time agent who was once the the head of the super agency CAA, only to fade into obscurity two years later. On the day *Ivansxtc* wrapped, Rose discovered that Jay had committed suicide. Shot on high-def digital cameras, the textural coarseness fits the story's seedy tone. Hollywood comes across as a soulless Gomorrah, populated by smiling ghouls and cokehead bimbos. A micro-budget of $500,000 meant that most of the supporting cast are friends and family of the filmmakers, which goes some way to explaining the B-list cameos and pretty uneven performances. Danny Houston, however, is riveting and plays out the film's themes of 'Art versus Commerce' and the fear of death with profound sensitivity. The glittering backdrop of the movie business resembles nothing so much as a culture in terminal decline, selling an image of beauty and compassion to the world while appreciating neither at home. AK

• *Ivan Beckman* Danny Huston *Don West* Peter Weller *Joe* Jay Itzkowitz *Charlotte White* Lisa Enos *Margaret Mead* Lisa Henson *Lloyd Hall* Hal Lieberman *Danny McTeague* James Merendino *Barry Oaks* Adam Krentzman and *Ted Zimblest* Dan Ireland
• *Dir* Bernard Rose *Scr* Rose, Lisa Enos, based on the novel *The Death of Ivan Illyich* by Tolstoy *Ph* Rose and Ron Forsythe *Pro* Enos

Alternative Investments of Michigan / Enos/ Rose / Rhino Films / Metro Tartan
92 mins. US 2002. Rel: 19 July 2002. Cert 18.

J

Left: Chief prankster Johnny Knoxville gets a different kind of boob job in *Jackass: The Movie* (from UIP)

Jackass: The Movie ★★★★

Bless the accountants at MTV, who obviously have more money than sense. Signing a big cheque to Johnny Knoxville's mentally unstable crew with the proviso "Don't kill anybody" appears to have been the extent of their involvement. The result is a tasteless, compulsive, homoerotic, masochistic, possibly criminal, completely satisfying train-wreck of a movie. They dance with alligators, they poop in plumbing stores, they swim in sewage recycling plants, they show no respect whatsoever to anyone or anything. Even their cameraman couldn't keep up, his nerve collapsing at the Let's Give Ourselves Intimate Papercuts Party. AK

• *as themselves* Johnny Knoxville, Bam Margera, Chris Pontius, Steve-O, Dave England, Ryan Dunn, Jason 'Wee-Man' Acuna, Preston Lacy and Ehren McGehey, Spike Jonze.
• ***Dir*** Jeff Tremaine ***Ph*** Dimitry Elyashkevich ***Pro*** Tremaine, Spike Jonze and Johnny Knoxville ***Ed*** Liz Ewart, Mark Hansen, Kristine Young

Dickhouse Productions / Lynch Siderow Productions Inc / MTV Films / Paramount Pictures / UIP
85 mins. US 2002. Rel: 28 February 2003. Cert 18.

Japon ★★★★½

Set in Mexico, Carlos Reygadas' first feature is an

astounding work. It's not perfect (the pacing is misjudged towards the close and the finale is just too much of a set-piece to be completely satisfactory), but we are still aware of a highly original talent at work. The compositions in Scope are magnificent, as is the use of music. This is a visionary film showing an urban man in the countryside pondering suicide but becoming reconciled to life. Despite the soundtrack's use of the St Matthew Passion, it plays less as a religious drama than as an exploration of what the natural world has to offer (the grandeur of canyons matched by the tenderness of sex). It's demanding but genuinely extraordinary and worthwhile, as it moves from being a study of a man welcoming death to a lament for the loss of a life. MS

• *the man* Alejandro Ferretis *Ascen* Magdalena Flores *Sabina* Yolanda Villa *Juan Luis* Martín Serrano *the judge* Rolando Hernández *the singer* Bernabe Pérez *Fernando* Fernando Benítez *the hunter* Carlo Reygadas Barquín
• *Dir / Scr / Pro* Carlos Reygadas *Ph* Diego Martinez Vignatti *Ed* Daniel Melguizo, Carlos Serrano, David Torres *Pro Des* Alejandro Reygadas

Hubert Bals Fund / Instituto Mexicano de Cinematografía / Mantarraya Producciones / No Dream Cinema / Solaris Film / Artificial Eye
133 mins. Mexico/Spain 2002. Rel: 21 February 2003. Cert 18.

Jason X ★★½

In the 25th century, a group of teens on a field trip to the now uninhabitable Earth discover the cryogenically preserved remains of a young woman and a hockey-masked, machete-toting misanthrope in the old government's subterranean Crystal Lake complex. After bringing the two bodies back with them to their ship, they use medical nanotechnology to repair the woman while a thawed Jason springs back to murderous life all on his own. Enter the chaperoning Marines, brandishing hi-tech weapons that make short work of the seemingly unstoppable Jason. Alone in the sick bay, however, the medical nanites rebuild Jason using both the organic and inorganic materials on hand. The new and improved cyborg Jason sets about doing what he does best, ie, killing everyone on board... This is so hokey it's actually fun, with the filmmakers taking jabs at the *Friday the 13th* franchise's own cliché-riddled legacy. Nor will it disappoint Jason devotees. SWM

• *Jason Voorhees/Uber-Jason* Kane Hodder *Rowan* Lexa Doig *KAY-EM 14* Lisa Ryder *Tsunaron* Chuck Campbell *Professor Lowe* Jonathan Potts *Sgt Brodski* Peter Mensah *Janessa* Melyssa Ade *Waylander* Derwin Jordan
• *Dir* Jim Isaac *Pro* Noel Cunningham *Ex Pro* Sean S Cunningham, Isaac *Scr* Todd Farmer *Ph* Derick Underschultz *Ed* David Handman *M* Harry Manfredini *Pro Des* John Dondertman, James Oswald

Crystal Lake Entertainment Inc / Friday X Productions / New Line Cinema / Entertainment
91 mins. US 2002. Rel: 19 July 2002. Cert 15.

Joe Somebody ★★

Dumped on the shelf for 12 months, this was meant to be a perfectly agreeable diversion spotlighting the comedic appeal of Tim Allen. Here, Allen plays Joe Scheffer, a milquetoast Everyman stuck in a mindless job working for a pharmaceuticals company. Then, when a co-worker humiliates Joe in front of his daughter, he demands satisfaction and redefines himself. This was not a box-office success in the US (which may explain its belated release here), but it does have the occasional deft comic touch. You could do worse: you could see Allen in his other December release, *The Santa Clause 2*. CB

• *Joe Scheffer* Tim Allen *Meg Harper* Julie Bowen *Callie Scheffer* Kelly Lynch *Natalie Scheffer* Hayden Panettiere *Chuck Scarett* Jim Belushi *Jeremy* Greg Germann *Pat Chilcutt* Robert Joy *Mark McKinney* Patrick Warburton
• *Dir* John Pasquin *Pro* Arnold Kopelson, Anne Kopelson, Matthew Gross, Ken Atchity and Brian Reilly *Ex Pro* Arnon Milchan, Chi-Li Wong and William W Wilson III *Scr* John Scott Shepherd *Ph* Daryn Okada *Pro Des* Jackson De Govia *Ed* David Finfer *M* George S Clinton *Costumes* Lou Eyrich and Kathy O'Rear

Fox 2000 Pictures / Regency Enterprises / Kopelson Enterprises-Fox
98 mins. USA 2001. Rel: 29 November 2002. Cert PG.

Johnny English ★★½

'Mr Bean goes to MI5' is the basic set-up of this moderately entertaining conga line of Bond-inspired send-ups. (Curious, really, that it was co-written by the same team behind the current crop of 007 flicks.) Rowan Atkinson plays Johnny English a frustrated desk jockey who gets his chance at active duty when the entire '00' force is suddenly deicmated. Full of his imagined potential, he botches up the spy-schtick with wonderful predictability, with only the unacknowledged efforts of his faithful sidekick, Bough, to keep him on track. Nothing is done in moderation as the team play fast-and-loose with the secret agent genre, with Malkovich giving an especially inflated interpretation of the megalomaniac Bond villain. AK

• *Johnny English* Rowan Atkinson *Lorna Campbell* Natalie Imbruglia *Bough* Ben Miller *Pascal Sauvage*

Left: Rowan Atkinson is all fingers and thumbs in Peter Howitt's *Johnny English* (from UIP)

John Malkovich *Pegasus* Tim Pigott-Smith *Prime Minister* Kevin McNally *Archbishop of Canterbury* Oliver Ford Davies *Vendetta* Douglas McFerran • *Dir* Peter Howitt *Scr* Neal Purvis, Robert Wade, William Davies *Ph* Remi Adefarasin *Ed* Robin Sales *M* Edward Shearmur *Pro Des* Chris Seagers *Pro* Tim Bevan, Eric Fellner, Mark Huffam

Rogue Male Films Ltd. / Working Title Films / UIP
87 mins. UK 2003. Rel: 11 April 2003

Just Married ★★½

LA, Switzerland and Italy; the present. When Tom throws a wayward football into the pretty head of Sarah McNerny, the two kids from distant ends of LA society fall truly, madly and deeply in love. The question is, is love enough? Especially when they find themselves locked together in a room marked 'Honeymoon From Hell'... This disposable romcom overcomes its deeply formulaic roots thanks to the genuine electricity between the leads (who, in traditional Hollywood fashion, became involved for real after filming) and a script that seasons their kooky sitcom sequences with just enough genuine feeling. AK

• *Tom Leezak* Ashton Kutcher *Sarah McNerny* Brittany Murphy *Peter Prentiss* Christian Kane *Mr McNerny* David Rasche *Kyle* David Moscow *Lauren McNerny* Monét Mazur
• *Dir* Shawn Levy *Scr* Sam Harper *Ph* Jonathan Brown *Ed* Don Zimmerman, Scott Hill *M* Christophe Beck *Pro Des* Nina Ruscio *Pro* Robert Simonds

Twentieth Century Fox / Mediastream 1. Productions / Robert Simonds Productions / Fox
94 mins. US/Germany 2002. Rel: 21 March 2003. Cert 12A.

Juwanna Mann ★★

... or *Tootsie* goes to the hoop! When NBA hotshot Jamal Jeffries blows his career, he slaps on some make-up and fake boobs to take on the WNBA. Sporadically funny, particularly when the gender-jostling jokes are least subtle, the flick fails to make enough of the gleeful enthusiasm Miguel A Nuñez Jr was clearly willing to put into playing a panto transsexual. The film ultimately stays true to *Tootsie* mould with happy endings all round, making one wonder if it isn't about time the subgenre crystallised by *Some Like it Hot* had the good grace to die out. AK

• *Jamal Jeffries/Juwanna* Mann Miguel A Nuñez Jr *Michelle Langford* Vivica A Fox *Puff Smokey Smoke* Tommy Davidson *Lorne Daniels* Kevin Pollack *Romeo* Ginuwine *Latisha Jansen* Kim Wayans *Tina Parker* Kimberly Jones (credited as Lil' Kim) *Coach Rivers* Annie Corley *Tammi Reiss* Vickie Sanchez *Heather Quella* Magda Rowonowitch
• *Dir Jesse Vaughan Scr Bradley Allenstein, Carol Leifer, Chuck Martin Pro Bill Gerber, Steve Oedekerk, James G Robinson Ex Pro Ralph Singleton, Jonathan A Zimbert Co Pro Kia Jam Ed Justin Green Pro Des Eve Cauley Ph Reynaldo Villalobos*

Morgan Creek / Warner Bros
91 mins. US 2002. Rel: 4 October 2002. Cert 12A.

K-19: The Widowmaker ★★

Harrison Ford is Captain Aleksei Vostirikov, in charge of the Soviet nuclear submarine K-19 on its maiden voyage. At the height of the Cold War, his first exercise is one in brinkmanship, intended to strike fear into the West with an uncomfortably proximate missile test. But his patriotism locks horns with his XO Mikhail Polenin's pragmatism, who tersely points out that the craft is barely fit for active duty. Vostirikov bluntly tempts the fates, who strike the K-19 with a deadly malfunction that forces its young crew into heroic sacrifices to prevent a nuclear war... A glimpse of the good movie this could have been is provided by a scene where the doomed crew surface to play football on the Arctic pack ice. For some minutes, we see them as comrades, alive in the moment and human. Everywhere else, they're shown stripped of authenticity in a highly processed 'historical' thriller, clogged with forced dramatics and grim-faced pouting. AK

• *Aleksei Vostrikov* Harrison Ford *Mikhail Polenin* Liam Neeson *Vadim* Peter Sarsgaard *Dmitri* Sam Spruell *Kuryshev* Peter Stebbings *Pavel* Christian Camargo *Lapinsh* Roman Podhora *Vasily* Sam Redford *Demichev* Steve Nicolson *Suslov* Ravil Isyanov *Partonov* Tim Woodward *Kornilov* Lex Shrapnel *Leonid* Shaun Benson Anton *Kristen Holden-Reid Sergei* Dmitry Chepovetsky *Kiklidze* Christopher Redman *Maxim* Tygh Runyan Marshal Zelentsov *Josh Ackland* Admiral Bratyeev *John Shrapnel* Konstantin *George Anton* Anatoly *James Ginty Kuryshev* Peter Stebbings *Pavel* Christian Camargo
• *Dir / Pro* Kathryn Bigelow *Scr* Christopher Kyle, based on the story by Louis Nowra *Ph* Jeff Cronenweth *Ed* Walter Murch *M* Klaus Badelt *Pro Des* Karl Juliusson, Michael Novotny

First Light Production / IMF Internationale Medien und Film / InterMedia Film Equities Ltd. / National Geographic Society / New Regency Pictures / Palomar Productions / UIP
138 mins. US/UK/Germany 2002. Rel: 25 October 2002. Cert 12A.

Kangaroo Jack ★★★

A kangaroo runs off with New York mob money that Charlie and Louis were meant to deliver to an Australian hitman. Cue a bickering scamper for the cash, with a beautiful veterinarian in tow to guide them across the Aussie outback. All they need is for the mob and the hitman to believe they've done a runner with the cash... Gratifyingly well done for what must have been an insane pitch, this family adventure is a gag-a-minute, laugh-out-loud comic adventure that promises to please anyone. The basic idea is so ludicrous that even the clichéd fish-out-of-water gags about 'Yanks in Oz' feel fresher than they have a right to, while Walken's turn as a ruthless mobster obsessed with improving his vocabulary is worth the ticket price alone. And who can dislike a movie that features a band of beat-rapping, breakdancing marsupials? AK

• *Charlie Carbone* Jerry O'Connell *Louis Booker* Anthony Anderson *Jessie* Estella Warren *Frankie Lombardo* Michael Shannon *Blue* Bill Hunter *Sal Maggio* Christopher Walken *Mr Smith* Marton Csokas *Mr Jimmy* David Ngoombujarra
• *Dir* David McNally *Scr* Steve Bing, Scott Rosenberg, based on a story by Bing and Barry O'Brien *Ph* Peter Menzies Jr *Ed* John Murray, William Goldenberg, Jim May *M* Trevor Rabin *Pro Des* George Liddle *Pro* Jerry Bruckheimer

Castle Rock Entertainment / Jerry Bruckheimer Films / Warner Bros
89 mins. US 2003. Rel: 16 May 2003. Cert PG.

The King is Dancing ★★★½

(*Le Roi danse*)

Clearly an attempt to repeat the success of 1994's *Farinelli*, Gérard Corbiau's latest period drama again turns to history for a work blending classical music (the central character is the composer Lully), drama, spectacle and a touch of sex to spice it up. A central thread is Lully's standing with Louis XIV before and after the latter became king. Struggles for power in the French court are interwoven with the amorous exploits of the married but bisexual composer, while his relationship with the king echoes the Falstaff/Hal theme as elaborated by Shakespeare. But here the material is episodic and not unlike a period soap opera. Those content to accept this limitation (and it *is* a limitation) will find the film handled opulently and with confidence, well justifying the use of the Scope format. MS

• *Louis XIV* Benoît Magimel *Lully* Boris Terral *Molière* Tchéky Karyo *Anne d'Autriche* Colette Emmanuelle *Madeleine* Cécile Bois *Julie* Claire Keim *Cambert* Johan Leysen *Conti* Idwig Stephane
• *Dir* Gérard Corbiau *Pro* Dominique Janne *Ass Pro* Stéphane Moatti *Scr* Andrée Corbiau, Gerard Corbiau, Eve de Castro and Didier Decoin, from *Lully ou le musicien du soleil* by Philippe Beaussant *Ph* Gérard Simon *Ed* Philippe Ravoet, Ludo Troch *Pro Des* Hubert Pouille *Costume* Olivier Bériot

France 2 Cinema / K-Dance / K-Star / K2 SA / Canal + / MMC Independent GmbH / RTL / Tvi / Cinefrance
115 mins. France/Germany/Belgium 2002. Rel: 5 July 2002. Cert 15.

Knafayim Shvurot

See *Broken Wings*

Kaante

See *Thorns*

Laissez-passer

See *Safe Conduct*

Lantana ★★★

Leon Zat is the cop in charge of a murder investigation, an unremarkable assignment until he discovers the body belongs to his wife's therapist. As he probes further into the lives of various potential suspects, he comes to reflect obliquely upon his own life, while the audience receives a good, hard look at the dynamics underpinning three very different marriages. *Lantana's* title is a metaphorical reference to a thorny Australian bush weed whose bright flowers adorn a rough growth. The film opens in the style of a neo-noir mystery with a low pan onto a broken body embedded in the undergrowth. However, its true ambition is a forensic sketch of the relationships which either choke or blossom in the humidity of a parochial Australian town. The acting is first-rate but the narrative is sometimes too involved to maintain the interest of anyone not already partial to heavy drama. AK

• *Leon* Anthony LaPaglia *John* Geoffrey Rush *Valerie* Barbara Hershey *Sonja* Kerry Armstrong *Jane* Rachael Blake *Patrick* Peter Phelps
• *Dir* Ray Lawrence *Scr* Andrew Bovell, based on his stage play *Speaking in Tongues Ph* Mandy Walker *Ed* Karl Sodersten *M* Paul Kelly *Pro Des* Kim Buddee *Pro* Jan Chapman

Australian Film Finance Corporation / Beyond Films / Jan Chapman Productions / MBP (Germany) / New South Wales Film & Television Office / Winchester Films
121 mins. Australia 2001. Rel: 16 August 2002. Cert 15.

The Last Great Wilderness ★★½

Young Adam, an autumn 2003 release, is all set to reveal David Mackenzie as a major talent. This earlier offering also contains hints of his quality in its visuals and technical fluency, but the material is such a mish-mash that the elements never cohere. In part a road movie set mainly in Scotland, it starts off echoing Aki Kaurismäki but ends up borrowing from *The Wicker Man*. Between times, scenes set in a retreat for trauma victims miss out on any intended menace, and, despite being touched on unexpectedly, the issue of sexuality fails to generate any pertinent comment. However, the two male leads, portraying strangers who meet, join up and become friends against the odds, play well together. Sadly, though, there's no credibility here and consequently little interest, despite this being a personal venture for Mackenzie, whose brother Alastair is the star. MS

• *Charlie* Alastair Mackenzie *Vicente* Jonny Phillips *Magnus* Ewan Stewart *Ruaridh* David Hayman *Claire* Victoria Smurfit *Morag* Louise Irwin *Flora* Jane Stenson *Paul* John Comerford
• *Dir* David Mackenzie *Pro* Gillian Berrie *Co Pro* Simon Cull *Scr* Michael Tait, Alastair Mackenzie, David Mackenzie *Ph* Simon Dennis *Ed* Jake Roberts *Pro Des* Tom Sayer *Art Dir* Laurel Wear *M* The Pastels

Monkey Puzzle / Scottish Screen / Serious Facilities / Sigma Films Ltd / Zentropa Entertainments / Feature Film Company
95 mins. UK/Denmark 2002. Rel: 9 May 2003. Cert 18.

L.I.E. ★★★★

This brave film by Michael Cuesta uses a New York setting – the title refers to the Long Island Expressway – to tell a story designed to challenge unconsidered attitudes about paedophiles. While starting to investigate his own sexuality, 15-year-old Howie (promising Paul Franklin Dano) finds a kindly surrogate father figure in Big John (the excellent Brian Cox), a man sexually attracted to teenage boys. By avoiding didacticism and treating the characters as complex human beings, the film effectively challenges the simplifications of press hate campaigns that portray paedophiles only as monsters. The film's one weakness is its too obviously set-up dramatic ending, but it's a piece which, far from telling you what to think, invites the audience to ponder what they have seen. That's doubtless why what could sound like sleazy exploitation has justly received wide acclaim. MS

• *Big John Harrigan* Brian Cox *Howie Blitzer* Paul Franklin Dano *Gary Terrio* Billy Kay *Marty Blitzer* Bruce Altman *Kevin Cole* James Costa *Brian* Tony Donnelly *Scott* Walter Masterson *guidance counsellor* Marcia DeBonis and *Marty's lawyer* Adam LeFevre
• *Dir* Michael Cuesta *Scr* Stephen M Ryder, Michael Cuesta, Gerald Cuesta *Ph* Romeo Tirone *Ed* Eric Carlson, Kane Platt *M* Mark Wike, Pierre Földes *Pro Des* Elise Bennett *Pro* René Bastian, Linda Moran, Michael Cuesta

Alter Ego Entertainment / Belladonna Productions LLC / Metro Tartan
108 mins. US 2001. Rel: 29 November 2002. Cert 18.

The Life of David Gale ★★½

Alan Parker's latest starts out as though its story of a journalist (Kate Winslet) summoned to interview a convicted murderer, David Gale (Kevin Spacey), will provide a powerful drama and comment tellingly on the retention of the death penalty in such states as Texas. But, as the tale proceeds and becomes ever more convoluted, we realise that the material is hokum. This extends to the portrayal of a woman obsessed with the need to challenge capital punishment, a role so poorly written that it wastes the excellent Laura Linney. There are distant echoes

Above: Kevin Spacey ponders the old half-full/half-empty question in Alan Parker's *The Life of David Gale* (from UIP)

of Fritz Lang's 1956 thriller *Beyond a Reasonable Doubt*: that too was hokum, but enjoyable because unpretentious and dispatched in a swift 80 minutes. This film takes much longer – 50 minutes longer, in fact – thereby giving us plenty of time in which to realise what nonsense it is. The movie is helped by its talented cast, but they certainly can't save it. MS

• *Bitsey Bloom* Kate Winslet *Barbara Kreuster* Cleo King *A J Roberts* Constance Jones *David Gale* Kevin Spacey *Constance Harraway* Laura Linney *Joe Mullarkey* Lee Ritchey *Zack Stemmons* Gabriel Mann *Dusty Wright* Matt Craven *motel waitress* Brandy Little *Margie* Cindy Waite
• *Dir* Alan Parker *Pro* Nicholas Cage, Parker *Co Pro* Lisa Moran *Ph* Michael Seresin *Ed* Gerry Hambling *Pro Des* Geoffrey Kirkland *M Alex Parker, Jake Parker*

Dirty Hands Productions / InterMedia Film Equities Ltd / Mikona Productions GmbH / Saturn Films / UIP 130 mins. US/Germany 2002. Rel: 14 March 2003. Cert 15.

Life or Something Like It ★★

Seattle; today. Lanie Kerrigan has everything a gal could want: great hair, spectacular teeth, a high-profile job as a star TV reporter and a famous, wealthy, studly boyfriend. But then she's worked hard for her position in high society and plans her life down to the last wrinkle-free wrinkle. Then a bum on the street predicts that she has just five days to live. When his other predictions come true, Lanie begins to question the real value of her perfect life... Few actresses would find it easier to play perfect than Angelina Jolie and, after her string of performances as a one-dimensional ass-kicker, it's fun to see her play a one-dimensional cupcake. However, the film's lack of credibility and slick, thin veneer prevents it from connecting on any emotional level, in spite of its attempts to tackle such weighty issues as destiny, kismet and transcendentalism. Bergman would be appalled. CB

• *Lanie Kerrigan* Angelina Jolie *Pete* Edward Burns *Prophet Jack* Tony Shalhoub *Cal* Christian Kane *Andrea* Melissa Errico *Lanie's father* James Gammon *Deborah Connors* Stockard Channing *with* Lisa Thornhill, Greg Itzin, Max Baker
• *Dir* Stephen Herek *Pro* Arnon Milchan, John Davis, Chi-Li Wong and Toby Jaffe *Ex Pro* Ric Kidney, Ken Atchity and Teddy Zee *Scr* John Scott Shepherd and Dana Stevens

Twentieth Century Fox / Regency Enterprises / Davis Entertainment-Fox 103 mins. USA 2002. Rel: 28 March 2003. Cert 12A.

Lighthouse ★★

An unusually high number of British-made horror movies have come out this year, though a return to the time when Britain was considered the world leader in dispensing screen chills seems unlikely. This one, for example, was made back in 1998 and was consigned to US video (retitled *Dead of Night*) long before scraping a UK theatrical release as stablemate to an uncensored print of *The Evil Dead*. ("Twice the Horror … All the Fear! The Return of the Horror Double Bill," screamed the ads.) The claustrophobic set-up is familiar stuff: when a prison ship founders, its motley crew of convicts and warders find themselves clinging to the titular beacon while merciless serial killer Leo Rook lops off heads right and left. Impenetrably murky and shriekingly scored, the film is distinguished by a highly accomplished suspense set-piece located in a men's lavatory, where Paul Brooke's demise is precipitated by a troublesome aerosol can. Otherwise, fans of British horror (by necessity a nostalgic lot) will probably prefer to stick with 1971's rather similar *Tower of Evil*. JR

• *Richard Spader* James Purefoy *Dr Kirsty McCloud* Rachel Shelley *Leo Rook* Christopher Adamson *Capt Campbell* Paul Brooke *Ian Goslet* Don Warrington *O'Neil* Chris Dunne *Weevil* Bob Goody *Spoons* Pat Kelman *Hopkins* Peter McCabe *Brownlow* Norman Mitchell
• *Dir / Scr* Simon Hunter *Pro* Tim Dennison, Mark Leake *Co Pro* Peta Inglesent *Ph* Tony Imi *Ed* Paul Green *Pro Des* Simon Bowles *Art Dir* Christian Huband *M* Debbie Wiseman

Arts Council / British Screen / Tungsten Pictures / Winchester Films / Feature Film Company
95 mins. GB 1999. Rel: 17 July 2002. Cert 15.

Like Mike ★★½

LA, the present. Calvin Cambridge is a basketball-crazy orphan who makes a wish to be 'like Mike', meaning 'like Michael Jordan'. Lightning strikes a pair of beat-up sneakers donated to the orphanage, imbuing the shoes with magical powers. These bring Calvin to the attention of the Los Angeles Knights when he embarrasses their star player one-on-one. He becomes the new team star, but along the way realises what he really wants is a family. Will the magic in the shoes help him find one? Firmly a 'Life Lessons Through Sports' wish-fulfilment fantasy, *Like Mike* comes complete with cut-out villains and umpteen scenes featuring kids saving the day on their scooters. While its kid rap star L'il Bow Wow has personality enough to overcome his lack of acting experience, he cannot quite carry off the dramatic moments as convincingly as his co-star Jonathon Lipnicki, who quietly steals every scene he's in. AK

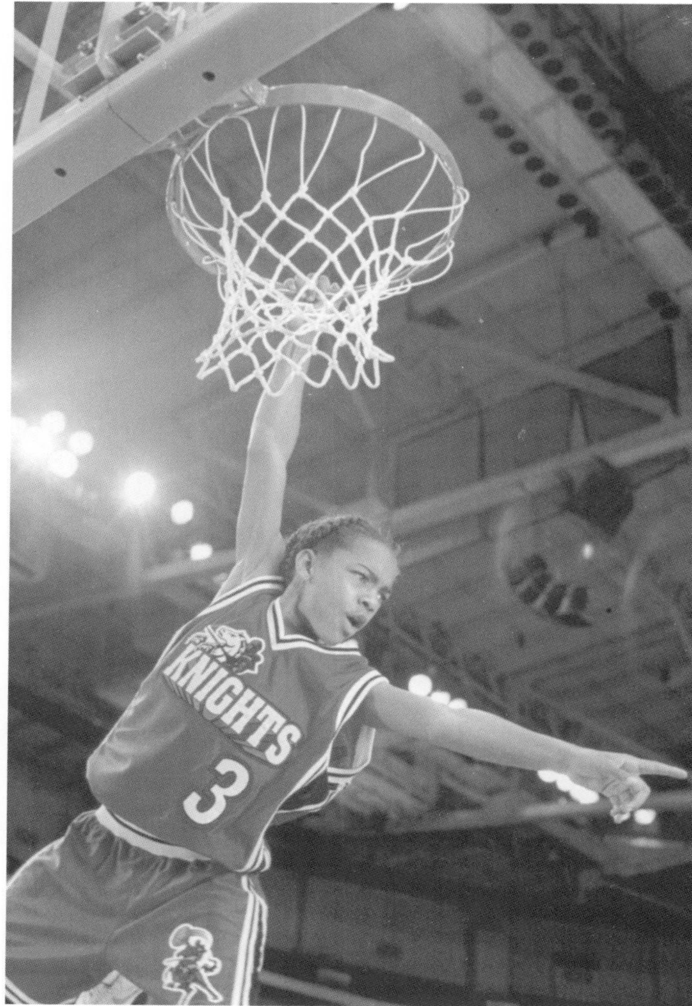

Above: L'il Bow Wow fills Michael Jordan's shoes in *Like Mike* (from Fox)

• *Calvin Coolidge* L'il Bow Wow *Tracey Reynolds* Morris Chestnut *Murph* Jonathan Lipnicki *Reg Stevens* Brenda Song *Ox* Jesse Plemons *Marlon* Julius Charles Ritter *Stan Bittleman* Crispin Glover *Sister Theresa* Anne Meara *Coach Wagner* Robert Forster *Frank Bernard* Eugene Levy *Marvin Joad* Roger W Morrissey
• *Dir* John Schultz *Scr* Michael Elliot, Jordan Moffet *Ph* Shawn Maurer *Ed* Peter Berger, John Pace *M* Richard Gibbs *Pro Des* Arlan Jay Vetter *Pro* Barry Josephson, Peter Heller

Twentieth Century Fox / Heller Highwater Productions / Josephson Entertainment / Like Mike Productions / NBA Entertainment / Fox
100 mins. US 2002. Rel: 13 December 2002. Cert PG.

Lilo & Stitch ★★★½

After a trailer campaign featuring a tiny blue-skinned alien monster destroying the sets of other Disney classics like *Beauty & the Beast* and *Aladdin*, the suggestion was that Disney might be doing a *Shrek*, satirising its own genre. But *Lilo & Stitch* is not the subversive exercise it hints at being. It's the story of how the alien Stitch escapes to idyllic Hawaii, where his destructive instincts are frustrated by an absence of tall buildings, snarling highways and flimsy suspension bridges. Little orphan Lilo adopts the pint-sized Godzilla and they find their turbulent personalities match one another. Meanwhile, Stitch's alien jailers have sent a team to recapture their blue ball of destruction. The film then droops into the easy sentimentality you expect from Disney, extolling the virtues of family as people obliged to take you in, no matter what. For the benefit of the cynical, the cloying sweetness is intermittently relieved by Elvis-inspired musical interludes and the usual array of cute and clever jokes. AK

• Voices: *Stitch* Chris Sanders *Lilo* Daveigh Chase *Nani* Tia Carrere *Cobra Bubbles* Ving Rhames *Jumba* David Ogden Stiers *Pleakley* Kevin McDonald *David Kawena* Jason Scott Lee *Grand Councilwoman* Zoe Caldwell *Captain Gantu* Kevin Michael Richardson *Hula teacher* Kunewa Mook
• *Dir / Scr* Chris Sanders, Dean Deblois *Ed* Darren Holmes *M* Alan Silvestri, with songs performed by Mark Keali'i Ho'omalu, Wynonna Judd and Elvis Presley *Pro Des* Paul Felix, Ric Sluiter

Walt Disney Animation / Walt Disney Pictures / Walt Disney Television Animation / Buena Vista
85 mins. US 2002. Rel: 4 October 2002. Cert U.

Lily 4-Ever ★★★

Sweden's Lukas Moodysson tells an uncompromisingly bleak story here. Her mother abandons 16-year-old Lilya (rivetingly played by Oksana Akinshina), a girl who never knew her father, in Tallinn. With a victimised boy as her only close companion, she soon decides to risk all when she falls for a man who offers her a home in Sweden. The gritty realism of this tale, not without echoes of Fellini's *Nights of Cabiria*, leads to an exposé of prostitution rings that fasten on illegal immigrants. The film promises to be harsh but brilliant until, after the first two thirds, it suddenly adds a whimsical mystical element wholly inappropriate to everything that has preceded it. This ruins a film with many remarkable qualities. MS

• *Lilya* Oksana Akinshina *Lilya's mother* Ljubov Agapova *Volodya* Artiom Bogucharskij *Natasha* Elina Beninson *Aunt Anna* Lilia Shinkareva *Andrei* Pavel Ponomarev *Witek* Tomas Neumann
• *Dir / Scr* Lukas Moodysson *Ph* Ulf Brantas *Ed* Michal Leszczylowski *M* Nathan Larson *Pro Des* Josefin Asberg *Pro* Lars Jonsson

Det Danske Filminstitut / Film i Väst / Memfis Film Rights / Nordisk Film & TV Fond / Svenska Filminstitutet / Sveriges Television / Zentropa Entertainments / Metrodome
109 mins. Denmark/Sweden 2001.
Rel: 25 April 2003. Cert 18.

Live Forever ★★★

John Dower, the man behind this energetic and utterly disrespectful history of the Britpop phenomenon of the 1990s, admits the only reason Noel Gallagher from Oasis agreed to be interviewed was that the production company behind *Live Forever* had won an Oscar for *One Day in September*. Good for him, because we'd otherwise be denied this frenetic and subtly intelligent tour of a fleeting age of glorious British achievement – and inglorious celebrity behaviour – guided by the people who were actually there. (Including, in no order of importance,

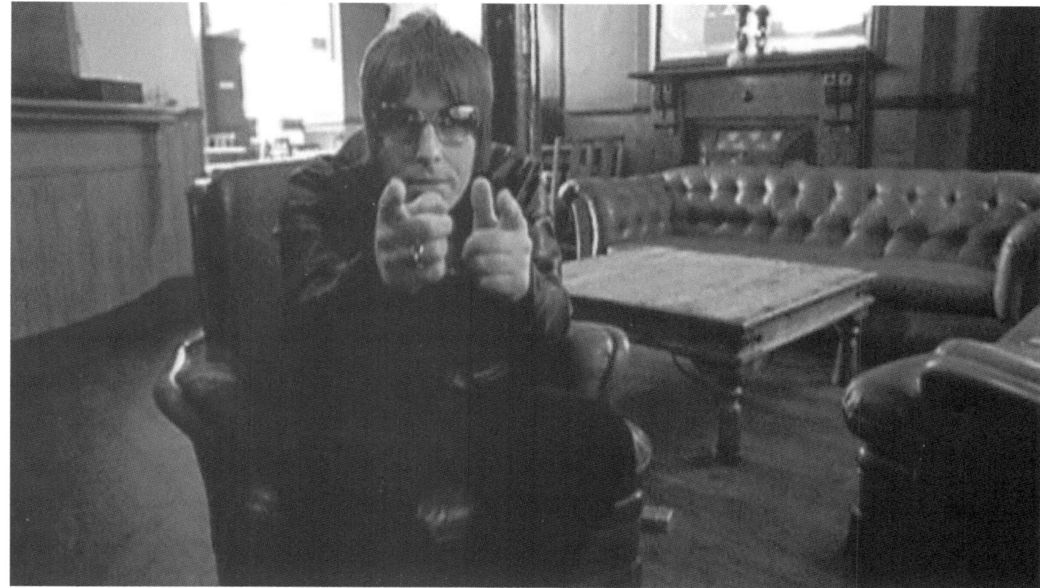

Right: Oasis front man Liam Gallagher in the revealing documentary *Live Forever* (from Helkon)

the Gallagher brothers, Jarvis Cocker, Damon Albarn and Peter Mandelson. No, I don't know what Mandy is doing in there, either.) It's a fun trip that only confirms how blissfully insubstantial the so-called phenomenon was, and it makes a wonderful partner to *24-Hour Party People*. AK

• *with* Noel Gallagher, Liam Gallagher, Jarvis Cocker, Damon Albarn, Louise Wener
• *Dir / Scr* John Dower *Pro* John Battsek

Passion Pictures / Helkon SK
86 mins. UK 2003. Rel: 7 March 2003. Cert 15.

The Lord of the Rings: The Two Towers ★★★½

The middle chapter of Peter Jackson's monumental version of Tolkien's saga sees the Fellowship split into three groups, with Frodo and Sam being led into Mordor by Gollum while Aragorn, Legolas and Gimli follow the trail of Pippin and Merry. It ranges over more of the magnificent Middle-Earth landscape, which is as much a character in the drama as anyone else. The story develops at a rushed pace, unsurprising considering the amount of ground it has to cover, but it's ultimately unsatisfying despite all the excitement. There are dramatic moments aplenty that stay true to the heroic style of the book, but the sheer bulk of the story refuses to fit gracefully within the constraints of even a three-hour film. It might have been better for Jackson to have made a series of six films instead of awaiting the DVD release to show the extended (and inevitably more sensible) edit. The original release is therefore relegated almost to a work in progress, albeit one boasting the most impressive panoramas and mass battle scenes in cinematic history. AK

• *Frodo Baggins* Elijah Wood *Gandalf* Ian McKellen *Arwen* Liv Tyler *Aragorn* Viggo Mortensen *Samwise 'Sam' Gamgee* Sean Astin *Galadriel* Cate Blanchett *Gimli/voice of Treebeard* John Rhys-Davies *Théoden* Bernard Hill *Saruman* Christopher Lee *Peregrin 'Pippin' Took* Billy Boyd *Meriadoc 'Merry' Brandybuck* Dominic Monaghan *Legolas* Orlando Bloom *Elrond* Hugo Weaving *Eowyn* Miranda Otto *Faramir* David Wenham *Grima Wormtongue* Brad Dourif *voice of Smaegol/Gollum* Andy Serkis *Eomer* Karl Urban and

Below: John Rhys-Davies and Orlando Bloom (on the white horse) prepare for battle in Peter Jackson's *The Lord of the Rings: The Two Towers* (from Entertainment)

Haldir Craig Parker
• *Dir* Peter Jackson *Scr* Fran Walsh, Philippa Boyens, Stephen Sinclair and Jackson, based on the book by J R R Tolkien *Ph* Andrew Lesnie *Ed* Michael Horton and Jabez Olssen *M* Howard Shore *Pro Des* Grant Major *Special make-up, creatures, armour and miniatures* WETA Workshops, Richard Taylor, Ngila Dickson *Visual effects supervisor* Jim Rygiel *Pro* Barrie M Osborne, Walsh and Jackson

New Line Cinema / The Saul Zaentz Company / Tolkien Enterprises / WingNut Films / Entertainment
179 mins. US / NZ 2002. Rel: 20 December 2002. Cert 12A.

Lost in La Mancha ★★★★★

Terry Gilliam's admirers will be delighted that his aborted attempt to make a film based on *Don Quixote* has at least yielded this feature-length documentary. It's a fascinating account of what went wrong, from catastrophic weather conditions on location to the illness of lead actor Jean Rochefort just after shooting started. Although it would be possible to have taken a different approach (the film includes a comment on a Gilliam shoot being chaotic but it never investigates whether the filmmaker's decisions contributed to the fiasco), this record of events combines candour with sympathy for Gilliam's plight. We are left admiring Gilliam's stubborn courage as he declares that this is a trailer for a film which may yet be made. Meanwhile, he's lucky to have in Keith Fulton and Louis Pepe filmmakers whose skills shine out in this beautifully made documentary. MS

• *narrator* Jeff Bridges *themselves* Bernard Bouix, René Cleitman, Johnny Depp, José Luis Escolar, Benjamín Fernández , Terry Gilliam, Tony Grisoni, Vanessa Paradis, Philip A Patterson, Nicola Pecorini, Gabriella Pescucci, Jean Rochefort
• *Dir / Scr* Keith Fulton, Louis Pepe *Ph* Pepe *Ed* Jacob Bricca *M* Miriam Cutler *Pro* Lucy Darwin *Pro Des* Benjamín Fernández

Eastcroft Productions / Low Key Productions / Quixote Films Limited / Optimum
93 mins. UK/US 2002. Rel: 2 August 2002. Cert U.

Love Liza ★★

This directorial debut by actor Todd Louiso begins promisingly but the misjudgments in Gordy Hoffman's screenplay soon become evident. In *The Son's Room*, another study in grieving, we were introduced to the family concerned prior to the sudden death that left them pole-axed. Not so here, so there's less reason to identify with the bereaved widower Wilson, well played though he is by the writer's brother Philip Seymour Hoffman. Wilson's wild, erratic behaviour is credible, but often tiresome too. The longer the film goes on, the less we care for this character. Occasional comic touches fail to alleviate the gloom and, although it lasts only 90 minutes, the movie comes to seem interminable, A letter from the late Liza opened only at the film's close leaves her suicide unexplained, thereby adding to our dissatisfaction. MS

• *Wilson Joel* Philip Seymour Hoffman *Mary Ann Bankhead* Kathy Bates *Denny* Jack Kehler *Maura Haas* Sarah Koskoff *Tom Bailey* Stephen Tobolowsky *Brenda* Erika Alexander
• *Dir* Todd Louiso *Scr* Gordy Hoffman *Ph* Lisa Rinzler *Ed* Anne Stein Katz *M* Jim O'Rourke *Pro Des* Stephen Beatrice *Pro* Ruth Charny, Chris Hanley, Jeff Roda, Fernando Sulichin

Blacklist Films / Kinowelt Filmproduktion / Muse Productions / Studio Canal / Wild Bunch / Columbia Tristar
90 mins. US/France/Germany 2002. Rel: 31 January 2003. Cert 15.

Lovely & Amazing ★★★

Nicole Holofcener's follow-up to *Walking & Talking* depicts a mother suffering the trials of her four desperately neurotic daughters, including an eight-year old adoptee who yearns for white skin and straight hair, just like her mommy. Stuffed with character, moderately witty but hopelessly scattered, the film falls a little short of the funny, idiosyncratic study of maturing women it wants to be. Elizabeth complains of her boyfriend, "He doesn't have the patience for my insecurities." Neither, unfortunately, do we. Granted there are some, well, lovely and amazing scenes, as when Elizabeth forces a fellow actor (played by Dermot Mulroney) to analyse her naked body. He thinks it's a trap, but she needs it to subdue her neuroses. The best performance, however, is a subtle one from Jake Gyllenhaal in a supporting role. AK

• *Michelle Marks* Catherine Keener *Jane Marks* Brenda Blethyn *Elizabeth Marks* Emily Mortimer *Annie Marks* Raven Goodwin *Kevin McCabe* Dermot Mulroney *Jordan* Jake Gyllenhaal *Bill* Clark Gregg *Paul* James Le Gross
• *Dir / Scr* Nicole Holofcener *Pro* Anthony Bregman, Eric d'Arbeloff, Ted Hope *Ph* Harlan Bosmajian *Ed* Rob Frazen *M* Craig Richey *Pro Des* Devorah Herbert

Blow Up Pictures / Good Machine / Roadside Attractions / Metrodome
91 mins. US 2001. Rel: 2 August 2002. Cert 15.

Lundi matin

See *Monday Morning*

M

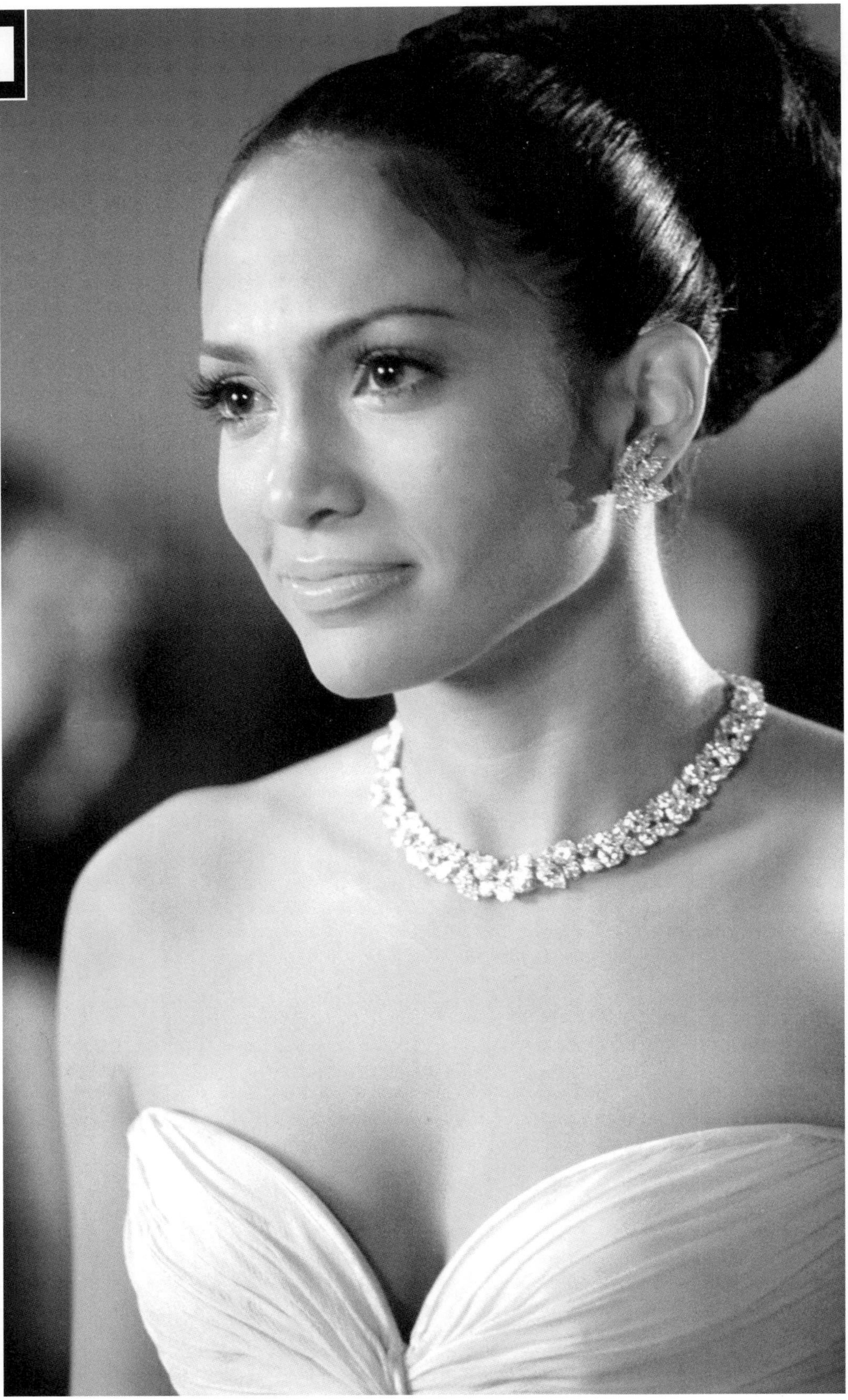

Left: J-Lo is chamber-made in Wayne Wang's *Maid in Manhattan* (from Columbia Tristar)

Ma Femme est une actrice

See *My Wife is an Actress*

The Magdalene Sisters ★★★★½

A timely release in a year that has seen the Catholic church dogged by scandal and controversy, Peter Mullan's deeply unsettling story based on the thousands of Irish girls sentenced to reforming workhouses (for 'sins' such as being an unmarried mother, a victim of rape, or just too pretty) is an unflinching indictment of the Catholic church in Ireland. The film follows three girls, Margaret, Rose and Bernadette, who are interned at the convent on the same day. They are swiftly introduced to the profoundly oppressive atmosphere that convent head Sister Bridget enforces with the pious efficiency of a Nazi prison warden. Displaying breathtaking directorial confidence, Mullan swiftly moves on to portraying the individual dramas and escalates the horrors of the system. The camera-work is gritty and lucid, the acting impassioned, and the screenplay profoundly affecting. Were it not for a rhythmic unsteadiness in the final act – a hesitance, perhaps, about whether things ought to end well or not – it would have been a rough masterpiece. AK

• *Margaret* Anne-Marie Duff *Patricia Rose* Dorothy Duffy *Bernadette* Nora-Jane Noone *Crispina* Eileen Walsh *Sister Bridget* Geraldine McEwan
• *Dir / Scr* Peter Mullan *Ph* Nigel Willoughby *Ed* Colin Monie *M* Craig Armstrong *Pro* Frances Higson *Pro Des* Mark Leese *Costumes* Trisha Biggar

Bórd Scannán na hÉireann / Element Films / Film Council / PFP Films Ltd / Scottish Screen / Temple Films / Momentum Pictures
119 mins. UK/Ireland 2002. Rel: 21 February 2003. Cert 15.

Maid in Manhattan ★★

Unassuming Marisa Ventura is forced to masquerade as a socialite when she is caught in a 'borrowed' Dolce & Gabbana suit by the dashing Senator Christopher Marshall. Her son manoeuvres his mother into a Cinderella romance, with a twist that has the ugly sisters and evil stepmother blended into Marisa's real mother, who is a cancer in Marisa's self-esteem... With Wayne Wang directing and Ralph Fiennes taking the romantic lead, this could have been a corker. But the script is bland and predictable, while a warm beer promises more excitement than the clinches between Ms Lopez and Mr Fiennes. Honourable mention goes to Stanley Tucci, whose cameos almost (but don't quite) justify this messy confection. AK

• *Marisa Ventura* Jennifer Lopez *Christopher Marshall* Ralph Fiennes *Caroline Lane* Natasha Richardson *Jerry Siegel* Stanley Tucci *Ty Ventura* Tyler Garcia Posey *Paula Burns* Frances Conroy *John Bextrum* Chris Eigeman *Stephanie Kehoe* Marissa Matrone *Rachel Hoffberg* Amy Sedaris *Veronica Ventura* Priscilla Lopez *Lionel Bloch* Bob Hoskins
• *Dir* Wayne Wang *Scr* Kevin Wade, based on a story by Edmond Dantes *Ph* Karl Walter Lindenlaub *Ed* Craig McKay *M* Alan Silvestri *Pro Des* Jane Musky *Pro* Elaine Goldsmith-Thomas, Deborah Schindler and Paul Schiff

Hughes Entertainment / Red Om Films / Revolution Studios / Shoelace Productions / Columbia Tristar
105 mins. US 2003. Rel: 7 March 2003. Cert PG.

A Man Apart ★

A good thing for Hollywood's new action hero, Vin Diesel, that his career is built on his karate chops, not his acting chops, because if this terrible cop-goes-renegade mess is anything to go by, his beef is all he has going for him. As Sean Vetter, a DEA agent hunting 'Ed Diablo', the mob boss who killed his wife, Diesel broods and barks with all the conviction of a kindergarten bully, an impression confirmed by the babyish morality he spouts periodically, with an amazingly straight face. If he hadn't taken this role, it would surely have gone to Steven Seagal, who really owns the copyright to this kind of story. AK

• *Sean Vetter* Vin Diesel *Demetrius Hicks* Larenz Tate *Hollywood Jack Slayton, aka Diablo* Timothy Olyphant *Guillermo 'Memo' Lucero* Geno Silva *Stacy Vetter* Jacqueline Obradors *Ty Frost* Steve Eastin *Mateo Santos* Juan Fernandez *Pomona Joe* Jeff Kober
• *Dir* F Gary Gray *Pro* Tucker Tooley, Vincent Newman, Joseph Nittolo, Vin Diesel *Ex Pro* Robert J Degus *Scr* Christian Gudegast, Paul Scheuring *Ph* Jack N Green *Ed* Bob Brown, William Hoy *Costumes* Shawn Barton. *Music* Anne Dudley *Pro Des* Ida Random, Tom Reta

Avery Pix / Newman / Tooley Films / Entertainment
109 mins. US 2001. Rel: 4 April 2003. Cert 18.

The Man Without a Past ★★½

The eponymous hero of Aki Kaurismäki's latest tragi-comedy is attacked by muggers on arriving in Helsinki and taken to hospital, where he is pronounced dead. Without any explanation, the bandaged man promptly rises from his bed and walks out of the hospital unchallenged. Kaurismäki's films often suggest fables, but, if we are to be touched by his lonely characters and made to share their hopes, there needs to be more credibility than is offered here. The deadpan humour remains intact, but it too is undermined because the leading actor, Markku Peltona, lacks the underlying appeal of his predecessors, Kari Väänänen and the late Matti Pellonpää. The more experienced Kati Outinen plays the Salvation Army loner who falls for the amnesiac hero but she too is constricted by Kaurismäki's screenplay. Not a patch on his *Drifting Clouds* of 1996. MS

• *M* Markku Peltola *Irma* Kati Outinen *Nieminen* Juhani Niemela *Kaisa Nieminen* Kaija Pakarinen *Anttila* Sakari Kuosmanen *flea market manager* Annikki Tahti *the Salvation Army Band* Marko Haavisto, Poutahaukat *Hannibal* Tahti
• *Dir / Scr / Pro* Aki Kaurismäki *Ph* Timo Salminen *Ed* Timo Linnasalo *Pro Des* Markku Patila, Jukka Salmi

Bavaria Film / Pandora Filmproduktion GmbH / Pyramide Productions / Sputnik Oy / Yleisradio / ICA Projects
97 mins. Finland/Germany/France 2002. Rel: 24 January 2003. Cert 12A.

The Matrix Reloaded ★★★

The middle chapter of the Wachowski Brothers' sci-fi trilogy arrived to worldwide fanfare and queues around the block. Unfortunately, it left most of us feeling that somehow, in a movie nearly three hours long, we were shortchanged. Haunted by premonitions of Trinity's death and worshipped by some as a latterday Jesus, Neo has to unravel his destiny while doing battle with a Mr Smith, who is able to endlessly copy himself. Outside the Matrix, the human fortress of Zion is threatened by an overwhelming attack, which Morpheus believes can be halted if Neo fulfils the prophecies... Visually arresting, the film could have done with far less portentous dialogue and mystic existentialism and more of the cool stuff we love (the costumes alone are almost worth the admission price). The special effects are a cut above anything else to date, and when it does come alive, it really rocks. But... apologies to the Wachowskis... this should have been better.
FYI: The cinema release was partnered by a DVD release of animated films based on the world of the Matrix called *The Animatrix*, a computer game called *Enter The Matrix* and an IMAX version released on 6 June 2003. AK

• *Neo* Keanu Reeves *Morpheus* Laurence Fishburne *Trinity* Carrie-Anne Moss *Agent Smith* Hugo Weaving *Niobe* Jada Pinkett Smith *the Oracle* Gloria Foster *Persephone* Monica Bellucci *Zee* Nona Gay *Keymaker* Randall Duk Kim *Commander Lock* Harry Lennix *Link* Harold Perrineau *Twin #2* Adrian Rayment *Twin #1* Neil Rayment *The Architect* Helmut Bakaitis *Seraph* Colin Chu Sing Nai *Bane* Ian Bliss *The Keymaker* Randall Duk Kim *Merovingian* Lambert Wilson *Councillor Harmann* Anthony Zerbe
• *Dir / Scr* Wachowski Brothers *Pro* Joel Silver *Ph* Bill Pope *Ed* Zach Staenberg *M* Don Davis Rob Dougan, Scott Humphrey, Marilyn Manson, Paul Oakenfold, P.O.D., Sonny Sandoval, Ben Watkins, Rob Zombie *Pro Des* Owen Paterson *Art Direction* Hugh Bateup, Jules Cook, Mark W Mansbridge, Catherine Mansill, Charlie Revai *Set Decoration* Brian Dusting, Ronald R Reiss *Costumes* Kym Barrett *Visual Effects Supervisor* John Gaeta *Action choreographer* Woo-ping Yuen

NPV Entertainment / Silver Pictures / Village Roadshow Productions / Warner Bros
138 mins. US 2003. Rel: 23 May 2003. Cert 15.

Max ★★

The notion behind this film is intriguing: to show how an insignificant corporal living in Munich in 1918 might have had a very different future had he found acceptance as an artist. The point is that the corporal was Adolf Hitler, and Noah Taylor has a good shot at creating a seeming nonentity while also enabling us to believe that this man could grow into the monster known to history. But, if the idea is promising, the execution is dire. The use of English dialogue makes this a Europudding, and the bathetic screenplay fatally puts too much emphasis on the fictional character of an art dealer named Max (John Cusack), who needs to be much more interesting if he is to justify his central role. Subsidiary characters are underdeveloped, which may be due to cuts; Janet Suzman, for example, is barely glimpsed. A huge disappointment. MS

• *Max Rothman* John Cusack *Adolf Hitler* Noah Taylor *Liselore Von Peltz* Leelee Sobieski *Nina Rothman* Molly Parker *Captain Mayr* Ulrich Thomsen
• *Dir / Scr* Menno Meyjes *Ph* Lajos Koltai *Ed* Chris Wyatt *M* Dan Jones *Pro Des* Ben Van Os *Pro* Andras Hamori

Aconit Pictures / Alliance Atlantis Communications / Bioskop Film / Film Council / H20 Motion Pictures / Natural Nylon II / Pathé
108 mins. Canada / Germany / Hungary / UK 2002. Rel: 20 June 2003. Cert 15.

Men in Black II ★★½

(aka *MIB2*)
Beyond the improbable technology – the amazingly cool 'flashy thing', aka Memory Neuralyzer, and those fantastic guns built like mutant trombones – the first *MIB* had charm. The chemistry between Will Smith's hip young urban jock and Tommy Lee Jones' Texan veteran, however, has fizzled. The sequel has clearly been buffed up with a bigger budget and better CG, but delivers only déjà vu thanks to a trailer campaign that revealed just about everything. The baddies are also a letdown, with Lara Flynn

Boyle playing Serleena (in case you care, she's a Medusa-like shape-changer come to Earth to find an artefact called the Light of Zartha) and MTV's *Jackass* host Johnny Knoxville as a two-headed sidekick. It's up to Jay to somehow unlock Kay's wiped memory banks if they are to find the Light of Zartha before Serleena does and – in between the wisecracks – save the world. Again. AK

• *Jay* Will Smith *Kay* Tommy Lee Jones *Zed* Rip Torn *Serleena* Lara Flynn Boyle *Jeebs* Tony Shalhoub *Laura Vasquez* Rosario Dawson *Scrad/ Chad* Johnny Knoxville *Agent Tee* Patrick Warburton *Agent M* Michael Jackson
• *Dir* Barry Sonnenfeld *Scr* Robert Gordon, Barry Fanaro, based on a story from the Malibu Comic by Lowell Cunningham *Ph* Greg Gardiner *Ed* Steven Weisberg, Richard Pearson *M* Danny Elfman *Pro Des* Bo Welch *Make-up* Rick Baker *Pro* Walter F Parkes, Laurie MacDonald

Amblin Entertainment / Columbia Pictures Corporation / MacDonald-Parkes / Columbia Tristar
88 mins. US 2002. Rel: 2 August 2002. Cert PG.

Minor Mishaps ★★★★

(*Små ulykker*)

Copenhagen, today. The sudden death of his wife puts John – an elderly hospital porter with a robust sense of humour and a weak heart – and his dysfunctional family into turmoil. The unspoken lynchpin of their family, the wife's death sparks off a series of domestic traumas that threaten to tear the family apart. Every sort of mishap, from infidelity to desertion, heart attacks to accusations of incest, surface suddenly to torment their lives. An homage to Mike Leigh, *Minor Mishaps* is a wonderful film of rare sensitivity and bittersweet beauty. Largely improvised, the film is a collage of over 80 hours of footage that nevertheless flows with astonishing congruence. And whether it is Eva the arty coot or Marianne the bundle of insecurities, each character is a perfectly unique invention. Director Annette K Olesen delivers scene after scene of profound emotion and piercing humour in a little world peopled by fresh characters without a clichéd bone in their bodies. That alone makes *Minor Mishaps* a true gem. AK

• *John* Jorgen Kiil *Marianne* Maria Wurgler Rich *Tom* Henrik Prip *Soren* Jesper Christensen *Eva* Jannie Faurschou *Hanne* Keran-Lise Mynster *Lisbeth* Julie Wieth *Peter* Heine Ankerdal *Pelle* Kristian Leth *Ellen* Tina Gylling
• *Dir* Annette K Olesen *Scr* Kim Fupz Aakeson *Ph* Morten Soborg *Ed* Nikolaj Monberg *Line Pro* Karen Bentzon *M* Jeppe Kaas *Ex Pro* Peter Aalbæk Jensen.

Zentropa Entertianment S6 / TV2 / The Danish Film Institute / Artificial Eye
109 mins. Denmark/Sweden 2002.
Rel: 20 September 2002. Cert 15.

Minority Report ★★★★

Washington DC, 2054. A system which uses a trio of psychics to predict crimes before they happen claims infallibility, and has a champion in the shape of Chief John Anderton, a man driven by the loss of his young son. However, when the psychic 'pre-cogs' predict a murder that Anderton will apparently commit, his faith in the system is swept away in a rising flood of paranoia. He goes renegade and hunts for clues that will prove his 'future' innocence, but it seems that his destiny lies on a road that may not have an exit... Steven Spielberg teams up with Tom Cruise to produce perhaps the most convincing sci-fi dystopia since *Blade Runner*, another film whose premise was lifted from the fevered pen of Phillip K Dick. Dressed up with thoroughly convincing hi-tech artefacts, the film moves swiftly enough to gloss over its inevitable illogicalities while delivering some potent action sequences and seamless special effects work. On reflection, however, the ideas it develops about culpability and determinism are less intriguing than they at first appear, though that might not matter considering the luxuriously detailed vision of the future that backgrounds the entire film. AK

• *John Anderton* Tom Cruise *Danny Witwer* Colin Farrell *Agatha* Samantha Morton *Lamar Burgess* Max von Sydow *Lara Clarke Anderton* Kathryn Morris *Gordon Fletcher* Neal McDonough *Gideon* Tim Blake Nelson *Dr Solomon Eddie* Peter Stormare *Rufus Riley* Jason Antoon *Iris Hineman* Lois Smith *Leo F Crow* Mike Binder
• *Dir* Steven Spielberg *Scr* Scott Frank, Jon Cohen, based on the short story by Philip K Dick *Ph* Janusz Kaminski *Ed* Michael Kahn *M* John Williams *Pro Des* Alex McDowell *Pro* Gerald R Molen, Bonnie Curtis, Walter F Parkes, Jan de Bont *Costumes* Deborah Lynn Scott

20th Century Fox / Amblin Entertainment / Blue Tulip / Cruise-Wagner Productions / DreamWorks SKG / Fox
145 mins. US 2002. Rel: 5 July 2002. Cert 12A.

Monday Morning ★★

(*Lundi matin*)

Otar Iosseliani's languid ballet of symbols masquerading as a French Everyman's mid-life road trip to Italy is conceitedly and consciously boring. The surface layer is ostensibly about Vincent escaping the mundanities of his life as a factory welder and unappreciated husband by taking a trip to Venice to indulge his artistic aspirations. His family takes no emotional notice of his departure; whenever the film cuts to them, they are absorbed in their own private and studiously inconsequential dramas. Vincent himself accomplishes very little during his trip, and his adventures don't amount to very much. Fine, then, if the film is meant to exhibit the spiritual vacuum its characters live in. But this is the epitome of the kind of arthouse film where nothing happens and we are all supposed to be impressed. AK

• *Vincent* Jacques Bidou *la femme de Vincent* Anne Kravz-Tarnavsky *la mère de Vincent* Narda Blanchet *le père de Vincent* Radslav Kinski *Nicolas, l'aîné de Vincent* Dato Tarielashvili-Iosseliani *Gaston, le cadet de Vincent* Adrien Pachod *Michel, le voisin* Pascal Chanal
• *Dir / Scr / Ed* Otar Iosseliani *Pro* Roberto Cicutto, Martine Marignac, Luigi Musini, Maurice Tinchant *M* Nicholas Zourabichvili *Ph* William Lubtchansky *Pro Des* Emmanuel de Chauvigny

Centre National de la Cinématographie / Cofimage 12 / Gimages 4 / Le Studio Canal+ / Mikado Films / Pierre Grisé Productions / Rhône-Alpes Cinéma / Artificial Eye
128 mins. France/Italy 2002. Rel: 6 December 2002. Cert PG.

Mon-Rak Transistor ★½

(aka *Transistor Love Story*)
This awful film from Thailand shares a producer with 2001's delightfully kitsch *Tears of the Black Tiger*, but the writer/director of that film was not involved. The cast is passable, the colour photography capable – but that's all that can be said on the plus side. In a tone more straight than camp, the film tells ineptly the story of a would-be pop singer who deserts the wife he has wooed despite parental opposition. He attains belated success in a band but ends up in jail. This is after resisting homosexual advances, causing a death and suffering as a cane-cutter under an evil overseer. Topping this concoction, there's a grossly sentimental ending – all this with no reality to make us care, no sense of parody to provide fun and no star charisma to compensate. It looks like a third-rate movie of the 1960s and is no more entertaining. MS

• *Phaen* Supakorn Kitsuwon *Sadaw* Siriyakorn Pukkavesh *Yhord* Black Phomtong *Suwat* Somlek Sakdikul *Dao* Porntip Papanai *Siew* Ampon Rattanawong *Sadaw's father* Prasit Wongrakthai *old prison guard* Chartchai Hamnuansak
• *Dir / Scr* Pen-Ek Ratanaruang *Pro* Duangkamol Limcharoen, Nonzee Nimibutr *Ex Pro* Charoen Iamphungporn *Ph* Chankit Chamniwikaipong *Ed* Patamanadda Yukol *Pro Des* Saksiri Chantarangsri *M* Amornbhong Methakunavudh, Chartchai Pongprapapan

Cinemasia / ICA
115 mins. Thailand 2001. Rel: 6 June 2003. Cert 15.

Moonlight Mile ★★½

New England in the 1970s. Jake Gyllenhaal plays Joe, who, following the sudden death of his fiancée, finds himself supporting the girl's parents and treated as though he were their son-in-law. Ironically, they are unaware that the engagement had just been broken off and complications ensue when he falls for a local girl (Ellen Pompeo)... For two-thirds of the time, a feeling of contrivance, particularly in the dialogue, is countered by the acting; Dustin Hoffman and Susan Sarandon are the parents and Hoffman gives his best performance for years. But in the last third a totally implausible and sentimental courtroom scene finally sinks the picture. What had been inferior to, say, *The Son's Room* or *In the Bedroom* ends up being downright bad by any standards. MS

• *Joe Nast* Jake Gyllenhaal *Ben Floss* Dustin Hoffman *Jojo Floss* Susan Sarandon *Berti Knox* Ellen Pompeo *Cheryl* Aleksia Landeau *Rabbi* Richard Messing *Cantor* Lev Friedman *Mona Camp* Holly Hunter *Mike Muleahey* Dabney Coleman
• *Dir / Scr* Brad Silberling *Ph* Phedon Papamichael *Ed* Lisa Zeno Churgin *M* Mark Isham *Pro Des* Missy Stewart *Pro* Mark Johnson, Silberling

Gran Via / Hyde Park Entertainment / Punch Productions Inc / Reveal Entertainment / Touchstone Pictures / Buena Vista
116 mins. US 2002. Rel: 21 February 2003. Cert 15.

Morvern Callar ★★★★

Despite having such a singular name, Morvern Callar is a nondescript Scots lass who, having discovered her boyfriend dead in her bathroom under blinking Christmas lights, goes slightly mad. Lying to friends that he's away on a trip and sleeping with his corpse, she then buries him in a secret, though visually exhilarating, non-ceremony and goes on a wild holiday to Spain on his credit cards. But when the unpublished novel he left her (which she disingenuously puts her own name on) is enthusiastically picked up by a London publisher, she is given the opportunity to completely reinvent herself to fit her fantasies... Samantha Morton is utterly enthralling in the title role, gracing her frankly unlikeable character with a sublime humanity that holds our attention throughout the languid and mostly uneventful narrative. Lynne Ramsay's adaptation of cult writer Alan Warner's novel stays true to the punk-beat lyricism of the original text while adding her own brand of vivid, voluptuous emptiness. AK

• *Morvern Callar* Samantha Morton *Lanna* Kathleen McDermott *boy in Room 1022* Raife Patrick Burchell *Dazzer* Dan Cadan *Sheila Tequila* Carolyn Calder *Tom Boddington* Jim Wilson *Susan* Dolly Wells

Couris Jean Ruby Milton *Vanessa* Linda McGuire • *Dir* Lynne Ramsay *Scr* Liana Dognini and Ramsay, based on the novel by Alan Warner *Ph* Alwin H Kuchler *Ed* Lucia Zucchetti *M* Andrew Cannon *Pro Des* Jane Morton *Pro* George Faber, Charles Pattinson and Robyn Slovo

Company Pictures / Momentum
97 mins. UK 2002. Rel 1 November 2002. Cert 15.

The Most Fertile Man in Ireland ★

While dispensing scientific data on the one hand (we are told that hamsters are now three times more fertile than the human male), this lowbrow comedy doesn't make a lot of sense. Our gormless hero, a 24-year-old virgin with sperm like "tadpoles on speed," is raped while asleep by an opportunistic would-be mother. True, Eamonn Manley (ha ha – funny name, that) can get it up in his sleep, although this limp comedy never shows us how. In fact, a sex comedy without any sex or humour is a bit of a cheek. It doesn't matter how many times Eamonn falls over, or how much music swells on the soundtrack, the laughs won't come. Part of the problem is the script (it's not funny), another is the direction (everybody speaks like they're reading jokes from a cracker), and another is the artless performance of Kris Marshall, who is neither credible as an actor nor talented as a physical comedian. JC-W

• *Eamon Manley* Kris Marshall *Billy Wilson* James Nesbitt *Rosie* Kathy Kiera Clarke *Millicent* Bronagh Gallagher *Mr Manley* Kenneth Cranham *Mary Mallory* Tara Lynne O'Neill *Maeve* Pauline McLynn *Raymond* Marc O'Shea *Dr Johnson* Toyah Willcox
• *Dir* Dudi Appleton *Pro* David Collins *Ex Pro* Rod Stoneman *Scr* Jim Keeble *Ph* Ronan Fox *Pro Des* Tom Conroy *Ed* Emer Reynolds *M* James Johnston *Costumes* Eimer Ní Mhaoldomhnaigh

Bord Scannán na hÉireann / The Irish Film Board / Samson Films-Rock City
94 mins. Ireland/Northern Ireland 2002. Rel: 20 June 2003. Cert 15.

Mostly Martha ★★★½

Quite splendidly performed by its leading players, Martina Gedeck and Sergio Castellitto, this is a tragi-comedy which, as with the superior *Italian for Beginners*, turns into a feel-good movie. Gedeck is the workaholic Martha, famed as Hamburg's best chef but whose life is turned upside down when her sister's sudden death results in her having to look after her eight-year-old niece (able Maxine Foreste). Castellitto is the Italian who becomes Martha's rival in the kitchen, but the players lose out to storytelling that turns increasingly unlikely and contrived. It is all too evident that the film has sacrificed credibility in the interests of milking the audience's emotions. There's talk of a Hollywood remake, but by the end you feel that you are watching it already – except that this cast won't be equalled. Original title: *Bella Martha*. MS

• *Martha Klein* Martina Gedeck *Mario* Sergio Castellitto *Lina* Maxime Foerste *Frida* Sibylle Canonica *Lea* Katja Studt *Jan* Oliver Broumis *therapist* August Zirner *Sam Thalberg* Ulrich Thomsen
• *Dir / Scr* Sandra Nettelbeck *Pro* Christoph Friedel, Karl Baumgartner *Ph* Michael Bertl *Pro Des* Thomas Freudenthal *M* Manfred Eicher *Food Des* Rocco Dressel

Bavaria Film / Kinowelt Filmproduktion / Palomar / Pandora Filmproduktion / Prisma Film / Rai Cinemafiction / SRG SSR idée suisse / Schweizer Fernsehen / Südwestdeutscher Rundfunk / T&C Film / Teleclub AG / Westdeutscher Rundfunk / arte / Österreichischer Rundfunk / Optimum Releasing
106 mins. Italy/Germany/Austria/Switzerland 2001. Rel: 16 May 2003. Cert PG.

Mr Deeds ★½

Frank Capra's *Mr Deeds Goes to Town* goes through the Adam Sandler cement-mixer to become so generic in so many ways that it might as well be a documentary on the convenience of clichés. As Longfellow Deeds, Sandler inherits a zillion-dollar company from an uncle and moves away from his cosy, hick-town existence into the big bad city. There, he becomes a target for Babe Bennett, a tabloid reporter who masquerades as a fellow hick-towner to get close to him, and Chuck Cedar, your typical bouffant-haired industrialist villain. Sandler then grinds through a series of sketches, some hilarious, the rest awesomely boring, before delivering a speech about small-town virtues and childhood dreams that remind several hundred stockholders where they last saw their conscience. When John Turturro's supporting role as a foot fetishist butler is the best thing about the film, you know you are watching a classy film ... not! AK

• *Longfellow Deeds* Adam Sandler *Babe Bennett* Winona Ryder *Chuck Cedar* Peter Gallagher *Mac McGrath* Jared Harris *Marty* Allen Covert *Cecil Anderson* Erick Avari *Emilio Lopez* John Turturro *Crazy Eyes* Steve Buscemi
• *Dir* Steven Brill *Scr* Tim Herlihy, adapted from *Mr Deeds Goes to Town* by Frank Capra and Robert Riskin, based on a story by Clarence Budington Kelland *Ph* Peter Lyons Collister *Ed* Jeff Gourson *M* Teddy Castellucci *Pro Des* Perry Andelin Blake *Pro* Sid Ganis and Jack Giarraputo

Happy Madison / Columbia Pictures / New Line Cinema

/ Out of the Blue Entertainment / Columbia Tristar
96 mins. US 2002. Rel: 1 November 2002. Cert 12A.

Mrs Caldicot's Cabbage War ★★★

It's easy to be snooty about this rather undistinguished film, but wrong for all that. Pauline Collins, a strong presence as ever, plays a widow who rouses her fellow inmates into rebellion when pushed into living in a rest home for the elderly. There's valid social comment beneath the sometimes rather banal comedy and, although it's unsophisticated in the extreme, the right audience will derive much pleasure from this film. Writing and direction could easily be improved, and the film clearly wins any award going for the year's least appealing title. Nevertheless, that title has meaning, covering both the revolt against the cabbage served regularly at meals and the importance of not treating old people in ways that make them degenerate into vegetables. MS

• *Thelma Caldicot* Pauline Collins *Derek* Peter Capaldi *Veronica* Anna Wilson-Jones *Audrey* Gwenllian Davies *Joyce* Sheila Reid *Leslie* Frank Mills *Bernard* Frank Middlemass
• *Dir* Ian Sharp *Scr* Malcolm Stone, based on the novel by Vernon Coleman *Pro* Andy Birmingham *M* Alan Lisk *Ph* Sue Gibson *Ed* Gerry Hambling *Pro Des* Malcolm Stone

Evolution / Arrow Films
110 mins. UK 2000. Rel: 31 January 2003. Cert 12.

My Big Fat Greek Wedding ★★★

The surprise hit of the year, this small-budget silver screen transposition of a one-woman stage show about minority marriage culture in Chicago grew into a word-of-mouth box-office moussaka. Toula is the Greek in question, scarred by cultural differences that might bother a Shaker community. That she feels so isolated in America for being Greek is a telling thing. Anyway, she grows up shy and cloistered, working in her father's Greek restaurant and suffering the joys of a large extended family. She then meets and falls in love with Michael Constantine, who is not Greek and therefore falls foul of her father's Old World prejudices. Funny and heartfelt, but with an oddly fabricated script, the film works in spite of its wooden narrative, thanks mostly to the hot Hellenic rhythms the cast bring to the olive-oiled table. AK

• *Toula* Nia Vardalos *Ian Miller* John Corbett *Gus* Michael Constantine *Maria* Lainie Kazan *Aunt Voula* Andrea Martin *Angelo* Joey Fatone *Nikki* Gia Carides *Nick* Louis Mandylor *Yia Yia* Bess Meisler *Hayley Miller* Fiona Reid *Rodney Miller* Bruce Gray *Mike* Ian Gomez *Paris* Arielle Sugarman
• *Dir* Joel Zwick *Scr* Nia Vardalos *Pro* Tom Hanks, Rita Wilson, Gary Goetzman *Ph* Jeffrey Jur *Ed* Heather Persons *Ex Pro* Steven Shareshian, Paul Brooks, Jim Milio, Norm Waitt, Mark Hufnail, Melissa Peltier *Pro Des* Gregory Keen *Ed* Mia Goldman *M* Alexander Janko, Chris Wilson

Big Wedding / Gold Circle Films / HBO / MPH Entertainment / Ontario Film Development Corporation / Playtone /Entertainment
95 mins. US/Canada 2002.
Rel 20 September 2002. Cert PG.

My Little Eye ★★★★

A huge advance on Marc Evans' earlier work, this psychological thriller invites us to share the experience of its five leading characters, who have agreed to live in an isolated house for six months. There's a large payment at the end of it if no one leaves, and meanwhile what they do is observed by cameras set up as for reality TV. We, the audience, share this viewpoint as tensions build, and it eventually transpires that one of the group is a murderer who has engineered this situation. This is hardly the scariest film of the year as the hype would have it, and as a take on reality TV notched up to murderous proportions the underrated *Series 7 – The Contenders* was superior. Nevertheless, this is ably written, acted and directed and will undoubtedly supply a suitably unsettling entertainment for those attracted. MS

• *Matt* Sean C W Johnson *Rex* Kristopher Lemche *Danny* Stephen O'Reilly *Emma* Laura Regan *Charlie* Jennifer Sky *Travis Patterson* Bradley Cooper *cop* Nick Mennell
• *Dir* Marc Evans *Scr* James Louis Watkins, David Hilton *Ph* Hubert Taczanowski *Ex Pro* Christopher Zimmer, Eric Fellner, Tim Bevan, Natascha Wharton, Alan Greenspan *Pro Des* Crispian Sallis *Ed* Marguerite Arnold *Pro* Jane Villiers, David Hilton, Jonathon Finn *M* Bias Postproduccion

Studio Canal / Universal Pictures / WT2 / Working Title Films / imX Communications Inc. / Momentum
95 mins. UK/USA/France/Canada 2002.
Rel: 4 October 2002. Cert 18.

My Wife is an Actress ★★

(*Ma Femme est une actrice*)

Yvan is a national sportscaster whose fame is overshadowed by his actress wife, Charlotte. Stopped on the street and bothered in restaurants, Yvan reckons himself something of a saint for his teeth-gritted tolerance. Until, that is, Charlotte goes off to London to shoot a film with a notorious English playboy and he starts to worry about whether actors do more than simply 'act' their love scenes. Presumably for contrast, a side plot has Yvan's sister in a running feud with her Gentile husband about

Above: Laura Regan and Jennifer Sky in Marc Evans' unsettling *My Little Eye* (from Momentum)

whether their soon-to-arrive son should be circumcised. The film deliberately blurs the line between art and life by retaining the first names of director/star Yvan Attal and his real-life celebrity spouse, Charlotte Gainsbourg. However, the desired effect is lost in Attal's cluttered and pedestrian script, that does little more than showcase the married leads. The result hovers in limbo, being neither a proper farce nor an intimate study of fame. AK

• *Charlotte* Charlotte Gainsbourg *Yvan* Yvan Attal *John* Terence Stamp *Nathalie* Noémie Lvovsky *Vincent* Laurent Bateau *Geraldine* Ludivine Sagnier *David* Keith Allen *Georges* Lionel Abelanski *Assistance Director* Jo McInne
• *Dir / Scr* Yvan Attal *Ph* Rémy Chevrin *Ed* Jennifer Auger *Pro Des* Katia Wyszkop *Pro* Claude Berri *M* Brad Mehldau

Centre National de la Cinématographie / Katharina / Le Studio Canal+ / Renn Productions / TF1 Films Productions / Pathé
95 mins. France 2001. Rel: 27 September 2002. Cert 15.

Narc ★★★★

This tough police procedural featuring a narcotics squad in Detroit comes close to being a classic of the genre, thanks to the skills of writer/director Joe Carnahan and some terrific acting, not least from Ray Liotta as a violent cop. Jason Patric appears as another member of the force seeking to rehabilitate himself after a botched arrest. This he hopes to do by being successful in investigating the murder of Liotta's partner. The strains and stresses of a cop's life are convincingly portrayed, but the second half of this powerful movie doesn't quite come off. This is because in its final stages the plot becomes too tricksy for its own good – a common fault today, when an excess of action is often favoured at the expense of credibility. MS

• *Nick Tellis* Jason Patric *Henry Oak* Ray Liotta *Darnell Beery* Busta Rhymes *Captain Cheevers* Chi McBride
• *Dir / Scr* Joe Carnahan *Ph* Alex Nepomniaschy *Ed* John Gilroy *M* Cliff Martinez *Pro Des* Greg Beale, Taavo Soodor *Pro* Diane Nabatoff, Ray Liotta, Michelle Grace, Julius R Nasso

Cruise-Wagner Productions / Cutting Edge Entertainment / Emmet Furla Films / Lions Gate Films / Narc LLC / Paramount Pictures / Splendid Pictures / Tiara Blu Films / UIP
105 mins. US 2003. Rel 7 February 2003. Cert 18.

National Lampoon's Van Wilder

See *Van Wilder: Party Liaison*

National Security ★

Martin Lawrence and Steve Zahn buffoon their way through this mind-numbingly clichéd buddy movie based on the adventures of two security guards who find themselves united against a shady conspiracy to steal 'special' beer barrels. Not even Zahn's characteristically snappy timing can survive Lawrence's mawkish mugging or the cripplingly ridiculous script, which trawls through the usual trappings of the genre in a lumpen mixture of lowest common denominators that can hardly be dignified with the word 'parody'. AK

• *Earl Montgomery* Martin Lawrence *Hank Rafferty* Steve Zahn *Detective Frank McDuff* Colm Feore *Lieutenant Washington* Bill Duke *Nash* Eric Roberts *Charlie Reed* Timothy Busfield
• *Dir* Douglas Dugan *Pro* Boby Newyer, Jeff Silver, Michael Green *Scr* Jay Scherick, David Ronn *Ph* Oliver Wood *Ed* Debra Neil-Fisher *Pro Des* Larry Fulton *M* Randy Edelman *Exec Pro* Moritz Borman, Guy East, Nigel Sinclair, Martin Lawrence *Co Pro* Andy Given, Scott Strauss, Sharon Dugan

Columbia Pictures Corporation / InterMedia Film Equities Ltd / Outlaw Productions / The Firm / Columbia Tristar
88 mins. US 2003. Rel: 21 March 2003. Cert 12A.

The New Guy ★★★½

Dizzy Harrison (the always empathetic D J Qualls) is a high-school geek who manages to get himself expelled in order to attend a new school where he can reinvent himself as cool dude Gil Harris. A wry Eddie Griffin plays jailbird Luther, who serves as Dizzy's imprisoned Henry Higgins. Of course, the plan sours when Dizzy is 'outed' by rivals in his new school. Our hero hooking up with the head cheerleader (yummy Eliza Dushku) and transforming his new school into a Utopian model forms the backbone of this unusually effective teen fantasy pic. The familiar message of being true to oneself rings especially true here with excellent, if familiar, characters and a few new, really funny, situations. And how perfect is casting Lyle Lovett as D J Qualls' dad? An unexpected treat. SWM

• *Dizzy Harrison/Gil Harris* D J Qualls *Danielle* Eliza Dushku *Nora* Zooey Deschanel *Bear* Lyle Lovett *Kirk* Jerod Mixon *Kiki Pierce* Illeana Douglas *Luther* Eddie Griffin *Ted* Kool Mo Dee *Warden* Henry Rollins *music store employee* Vanilla Ice *with* David Hasselhoff, Jerry O'Connell, Tommy Lee and Tony Hawk in ridiculous cameos
• *Dir* Ed Decter *Scr* David Kendall *Ph* Michael D O'Shea *Ed* David Rennie *M* Ralph Sall, Nick Glennie-Smith; song: Bowling for Soup *Pro Des* Dina Lipton *Pro* Gordon Gray, Mark Ciardi, Todd Garner

Bedlam Pictures / Frontier Pictures / Revolution Studios / Columbia Tristar
89 mins. US 2002. Rel: 20 September 2002. Cert 12A.

Nicholas Nickleby ★★★

Although thankfully closer to Dickens than the chosen publicity tag ("In Life's Journey, Love Will Play Its Part"), this classic adaptation by Douglas McGrath, who gave us *Emma*, is of very variable quality. Thanks to Jim Broadbent and Juliet Stevenson, the school-life cruelties of Dotheboys Hall come across strongly, and the scenes of theatre life work well enough in the unexpected hands of Nathan Lane and Dame Edna Everage (the latter making her debut in a straight role!). As in Dickens, romance fares less well, and there is miscasting; Jamie Bell's Smike proves that he's not a natural when playing one of life's victims and Christopher Plummer lacks the steel for the unscrupulous Ralph Nickleby. Very uneven, it undoubtedly leaves the 1947 movie by Alberto Cavalcanti as the adaptation with the true Dickensian flavour. MS

Right: Jamie Bell as Smike in Douglas McGrath's *Nicholas Nickleby* (from Fox)

• *Nicholas Nickleby* Charlie Hunnam *Smike* Jamie Bell *Wackford Squeers* Jim Broadbent *Newman Noggs* Tom Courtenay *Mr Folair* Alan Cumming *Mrs Crummles/Mr Leadville* Barry Humphries *Sir Mulberry Hawk* Edward Fox *Kate Nickleby* Romola Garai *Madeline Bray* Anne Hathaway *Vincent Crummles* Nathan Lane *Ralph Nickleby* Christopher Plummer *Charles Cheeryble* Timothy Spall *Mrs Squeers* Juliet Stevenson
• *Dir / Scr* Douglas McGrath, based on the novel by Charles Dickens *Ph* Dick Pope *Ed* Lesley Walker *M* Rachel Portman *Pro Des* Eve Stewart *Pro* Simon Channing-Williams, John N Hart Jr, Jeffrey Sharp *Costumes* Ruth Myers *Make-up* Sarah Monzani

Hart-Sharp Entertainment / Cloud Nine Films Ltd / Fox
132 mins. US/UK 2003. Rel: 27 June 2003. Cert PG.

Nine Queens ★★★½

(*Nueve Reinas*)
Buenos Aires, the present. Two grifters, an old hand and a young gun, join forces to run the con of their lives involving the legendary 'Nine Queens', a set of rare stamps worth millions. The question that plagues them, though, is how they can trust each other when they both lie for a living. Indisputably slick and coolly stylish, Fabián Bielinsky's remarkably prescient film (anticipating the latest meltdown in the Argentinian economy) is different from most films of the genre because the players are merely ciphers by comparison to the bigger con game of Argentinian politics. Perhaps we are to read into the regal centrepiece of the fraud the 'forged' sovereignty of the state. The most heartfelt speech in the film identifies practically the entire system as a fraud on the public. But the film doesn't trip over its politics and remembers its main duty to entertain, a job it does with frantic patter, delicious characters and a fabulously intricate plot that is never predictable. AK

• *Marcos* Ricardo Darín *Juan* Gastón Pauls *Valeria* Leticia Brédice *Federico* Tomás Fonzi *Vidal Gandolfo* Ignasi Abadal *Washington* Alejandro Awada *Berta* Elsa Berenguer *Stamp Expert* Leo Dyzen *Ramiro* Ricardo Díaz Mourelle *Berta's Lover* Carlos Falcone
• *Dir / Scr* Fabián Bielinsky *Ph* Marcelo Camorino *Ed* Sergio Zottola *M* César Lerner *Pro Des* Daniela Passalaqua *Pro* Cecilia Bossi

FX SOUND / Industrias Audiovisuales Argentinas / J.Z. & Asociados / Kodak Argentina / Naya Films / Patagonik Film Group / Optimum
114 mins. Argentina 2001. Rel: 12 July 2002. Cert 15.

Novocaine ★★

Steve Martin has apparently trademarked the scenario that dumps an orderly professional into circumstances that wreck his controlled existence to (sometimes) comic effect, demonstrating that in chaos lies a kind of freedom and joy. In this case, the stereotype in question is a dentist, the chaos comes in the form of a femme fatale who seduces him for access to his drug cabinet, and the comic effects are, sadly, absent. Ditto the freedom and joy. Marching along humourlessly to an excellent soundtrack, *Novocaine* starts off with the promise of edgy cool but wraps itself up so tightly in its neo-noir plot-knots that its title well describes the numbing effect it had on its rather small audiences. AK

• *Fred Sangster* Steve Martin *Jean Noble* Laura Dern *Susan* Helena Bonham Carter *Harlan Sangster* Elias Koteas *Duane* Scott Caan, with a cameo by Kevin Bacon
• *Dir / Scr* David Atkins, based on a story by Paul Felopulos and Atkins *Ph* Vilko Filac *Ed* Melody London *M* Steve Bartek, Danny Elfman *Pro Des* Sharon Seymour *Pro* Paul Mones, Daniel M Rosenberg

Artisan Entertainment / Numb Gums Productions / Momentum
94 mins. US 2001. Rel: 5 July 2002. Cert 15.

Nowhere in Africa ★★★★

Generally underrated by British critics, this Oscar-winning German film is a thoroughly engaging piece of popular cinema. It tells the story of a Jewish family who fled to Kenya in 1938 and traces their lives through the war years. That war, together with the Holocaust, provide what Satyajit Ray once described as a distant thunder. Nevertheless, as a German the husband is subjected to internment, and the varied treatment of the exiles by both whites and coloureds has its part in a tale told without longueurs despite a running time of 142 minutes. Central, however, are the childhood experiences of the daughter, akin to those of Stefanie Zweig on whose novel this film is based. The locations are admirably used and, if the music is occasionally misjudged, this is a wholly sympathetic film and particularly strong in its final, atmospheric post-war sequences. MS

• *Jettel Redlich* Juliane Kohler *Walter Redlich* Merab Ninidze *Suskind* Matthias Habich *Owuor* Sidede Onyulo *older Regina* Karoline Eckertz *younger Regina* Lea Kurka
• *Dir / Scr* Caroline Link, based on the novel by Stefanie Zweig *Ph* Gernot Roll *Ed* Patricia Rommel *M* Niki Reiser *Pro* Peter Herrmann

Bavaria Film / Constantin Film Produktion / MTM Cineteve / Optimum Releasing
141 mins. Germany 2001. Rel: 4 April 2003. Cert 15.

Nueve Reinas

See *Nine Queens*

O

O ★★½

Palmetto Grove Academy, Charleston, South Carolina; the present. Shakespeare not only had a knack for inventing a neat turn of phrase, he dreamed up some really good stories. However, by being cloaked in the elaborate word play of his imagining, many of these plots only worked within the limits of Shakespeare's poetic format. Here, the writer Brad Kaaya has taken the melodramatic conceit of ***Othello*** and placed it in the basketball milieu of a South Carolina high school. Replacing swords and daggers with guns and crowbars and introducing such high school elements as sport and steroids, Kaaya has wandered off the map. The result is that the film never feels fully connected to a contemporary reality, while the narrative twists smack of unconvincing melodrama. The actors do the best that they can under the circumstances – there is an interracial sex scene that wields considerable erotic potency – but the odds are stacked against them. JC-W

• *Odin James* Mekhi Phifer *Hugo Goulding* Josh Hartnett *Desi Brable* Julia Stiles *Michael Casio* Andrew Keegan *Emily* Rain Phoenix *Coach Duke Goulding* Martin Sheen *Dean Brable* John Heard *Roger* Elden Henson *Dell* Anthony 'AJ' Johnson *Brandy* Rachel Schumate *with* Chris Freihofer, Lisa Benavides, Christopher Jones
• *Dir* Tim Blake Nelson *Pro* Eric Gitter, Anthony Rhulen and Daniel L Fried *Ex Pro* Michael I Levy and William Shively *Co Pro* Lisa Gitter and Betsey Danbury *Scr* Brad Kaaya *Ph* Russell Lee Fine *Pro Des* Dina Goldman *Ed* Kate Sanford *M* Jeff Danna; Verdi; songs performed by Roscoe, Kurupt featuring Noreaga, Black Star, Crush, Sheeba Black, Spooks, and OutKast, *Costumes* Jill Ohanneson *Sound* Tom Myers.

Chickie the Cop / Daniel Fried Prods / Rhulen Entertainment / Sundance Institute-Buena Vista.
95 mins. USA 2001. Rel: 13 September 2002. Cert 15.

Old School ★★★½

Three thirty-something buddies regress to the best years of their lives when they start a new fraternity at Harrison University. But the street parties, KY jelly-wrestling and midnight streaking come to an ugly end when the evil dean closes them down. Can the boys and their new pledges get their fraternity back, or does prissy evil triumph? Wrapped inside this return to *Animal House* is a smart comment on the socialised habits that come with a job, a wife and being 'all grown up'. However, that should not detract from the hilariously entertaining spectacle of grown men behaving like teenaged idiots, especially when presented with the unrestrained gusto of 'Frank the Tank', who one-ups almost every comic turn with the definitive punchline. 'Dignity' is simply not in his college vocabulary. AK

• *Mitch* Luke Wilson *Frank* Will Ferrell *Beanie* Vince Vaughn *Pritchard* Jeremy Piven *Nicole* Ellen Pompeo *Heidi* Juliette Lewis *Lara* Leah Remini *Blue* Patrick Cranshaw *Marissa* Perrey Reeves *Darcie* Elisha Cuthbert *Mark* Craig Kilborn *Peppers* Seann William Scott *Gary, oral sex instructor* Andy Dick *themselves* Snoop Dogg, Warren G, Archbishop Don Magic Juan and James Carville
• *Dir* Todd Phillips *Scr* Phillips, Scot Armstrong, based on a story by Court Crandall, Phillips and Armstrong *Ph* Mark Irwin *Ed* Michael Jablow *M* Theodore Shapiro *Pro Des* Clark Hunter *Pro* Daniel Goldberg, Joe Medjuck, Phillips *Ex Pro* Ivan Reitman, Tom Pollock

DreamWorks SKG / The Montecito Picture Company / UIP
90 mins. US 2003. Rel: 9 May 2003. Cert 15.

Once Upon A Time in the Midlands ★★★★

Shane Meadows completes his Midlands trilogy with a uniquely off-centre comic romance about nice-but-limp garage owner Dek, who has to face his girlfriend's psychotic nutter of an ex, Jimmy, and overcome his own sense of inadequacy to win back his Shirley's respect. The cheeky homage to Sergio Leone also takes a swipe at the displaced Country & Western fans of Middle England, who dream of longhorns and wear their Stetsons to the line-dancing night at the bingo hall. A very strong cast made up of British film and TV veterans lifts the basic satire onto a cloud of high-grade soap opera enlightenment that cannot fail to amuse. AK

• *Jimmy* Robert Carlyle *Vanessa* Vanessa Feltz *Charlie* Ricky Tomlinson *Carol* Kathy Burke *Audience Guest* Vicki Patterson *Shirley* Shirley Henderson *Marlene* Finn Atkins *Donna* Kelly Thresher *Dek* Rhys Ifans *Donut* Andrew Shim *Emerson* Ryan Bruce *Lake* Eliot Otis Brown Walters *Jumbo* Anthony Strachan
• *Dir* Shane Meadows *Scr* Paul Fraser, Meadows *Pro* Andrea Calderwood *Line Pro* Claire Hunt *Ex Pro* Hanno Huth, Paul Trijbits, Paul Webster *Co Pro* Louise Knight, James Wilson *M* John Lunn *Ph* Brian Tufano *Ed* Peter Beston, Trevor Waite *Pro Des* Crispian Sallis

Big Arty / East Midlands Media Initiative / Film Council / Senator Film Produktion / Slate Films / FilmFour
104 mins. UK/Germany 2002. Rel: 6 September 2002. Cert 15.

The One and Only ★★

Take a kitchen fitter, a baby-mad wife, a randy Italian footballer and his fragile English Rose; mix

them together with various wild-eyed bids for 'character' eccentricity (namely a Neanderthal, a slapper and an airhead blonde); then force-fit onto the framework of a decent Danish romcom (Susanne Bier's *Den Eneste Ene*) and relocate 'oop North' for the crucial 'funny-accent' factor. That, in a nutshell, is *The One and Only*. There really isn't anything to say about the cheap laughs, the corny slapstick, the heavy mooning and the heavier caricatures, except that they work well enough provided you leave your artistic discrimination at the popcorn stand. And I haven't yet mentioned the racist running joke about the apparently unpronouncable name of an African orphan… AK

• *Neil* Richard Roxburgh *Stevie* Justine Waddell *Andrea* Jonathan Cake *Jenny* Aisling O'Sullivan *Stella* Patsy Kensit *Stan* Michael Hodgson *Sharon* Kerry Rolfe *Donna* Donna Air *Mgala* Angel Thomas
• *Dir* Simon Cellan Jones *Scr* Peter Flannery, based

Above: Jonathan Cake in Simon Cellan Jones' *The One and Only* (from Pathé)

on the Danish screenplay by Susanne Bier *Line Pro* Rosa Romero *Pro* Leslee Udwin *M* Gabriel Yared *Ph* Remi Adefarasin *Ed* Pia Di Ciaula *Pro Des* Zoe MacLeod *Ex Pro* Susanne Bier, François Ivernel, Cameron McCracken, Didier Sapaut *Ass Pro* Peter Mitchell

Assassin Films / Film Council / Pathé
91 mins. UK/France 2002. Rel: 21 February 2003. Cert 15.

One Hour Photo ★★★

Somewhere in deepest suburbia, the Yorkin family lives in nuclear bliss, unaware that their photographs provide Seymour 'Sy' Parrish, their one-hour photo developer, the fantasy family he never had. When he finds pictures that prove Will Yorkin is having an affair, it tips the fantasy into reality and Seymour sets out to save the family he doesn't have, with tragic results... Robin Williams is stunningly effective as Seymour Parrish in this fascinating psychological drama that disingenuously shifts sympathies between the stalker and the stalked. His emotions coil underneath his nervous expressions for the length of the film, snapping right on cue in the tense final act. Deeply disturbing thanks to its acutely tuned performances, it is nevertheless betrayed by a limp Hollywood ending which explains far too much, and then not very convincingly. AK

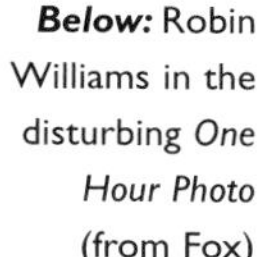

Below: Robin Williams in the disturbing *One Hour Photo* (from Fox)

• *Seymour Parrish* Robin Williams *Nina Yorkin* Connie Nielsen *Will Yorkin* Michael Vartan *Bill Owens* Gary Cole *Maya Burson* Erin Daniels *Detective Paul Outerbridge* Clark Gregg *repairman* Nick Searcy *Jakob Yorkin* Dylan Smith *Detective James Van Der Zee* Eriq La Salle
• *Dir / Scr* Mark Romanek *Ph* Jeff Cronenweth *Ed* Jeffrey Ford *M* Reinhold Heil, Johnny Klimek *Pro Des* Tom Foden *Pro* Christine Vachon, Pamela Koffler, Stan Wlodkowski

Catch 23 Entertainment / Killer Films / Laughlin Park Pictures / Madjak Films / Fox
96 mins. US 2002. Rel: 4 October 2002. Cert 15.

Open Hearts ★★★★½

(*Elsker dig for evigt*)

The first of Susanne Bier's films to be released here, this Danish movie observing the Dogme rules uses close work with hand-held cameras to absorb us in the lives of its characters. An unexpected incident links two couples, one starting out on life, having decided that their established bond is a sound basis for matrimony; the other settled and with a teenage daughter, yet less than secure in their marriage. How all four respond to life (and to the slings and arrows of outrageous fortune) makes for a totally believable drama in which we understand the actions, both

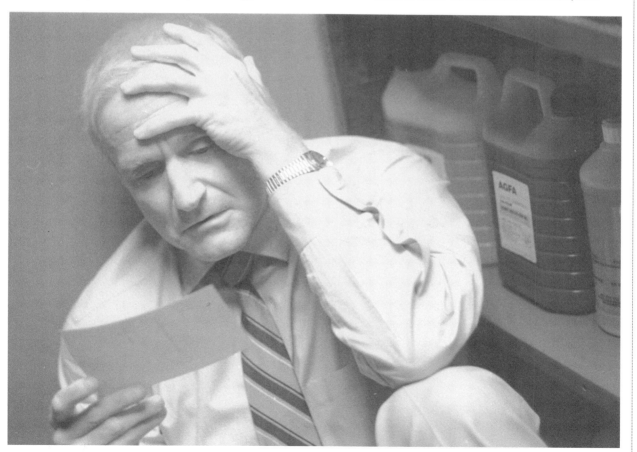

good and bad, of all four. *Open Hearts* doesn't provide its own perspective on human behaviour as did Liv Ullmann's *Faithless*, written by Ingmar Bergman, but the fact that it invites comparison with that masterpiece is high praise in itself. The cast is flawless. MS

• *Cecilie* Sonja Richter *Joachim* Nikolaj Lie Kaas *Niels* Mads Mikkelsen *Marie* Paprika Steen *Stine* Stine Bjerregaard *Hanne* Birthe Neumann *Finn* Niels Olsen *Thomsen* Ulf Pilgaard
• *Dir* Susanne Bier *Scr* Anders Thomas Jensen *Ph* Morten Soborg *Ed* Pernille Bech Christensen, Thomas Krag *M* Jesper Winge Leisner *Pro* Vibeke Windelov

Det Danske Filminstitut / Zentropa Entertainments / Icon
113 mins. Denmark 2002. Rel: 4 April 2003. Cert 15.

Orange County ★★

Shaun Brumder, a teenage surfer with literary ambitions, has his dreams of a Stanford education wrecked by an administrative error. He attempts to get into Stanford anyway, with disastrous help from his brother... Colin Hanks makes a passable lead in this genre soufflé, the kind of madcap jaunt that his dad Tom started his career with. However, when the mediocre script (Mike *Chuck & Buck* White really sold out cheaply here) is overloaded with a 'Who's Who' of 1980s comic celebrities, the whiff of nepotism intensifies into a pong. The discontinuity between the film's ambition and execution is epitomised by the finale, which shows Shaun shouting "I'm gonna go surfing!" and then sprinting excitedly into a flat sea. AK

• *Shaun Brumder* Colin Hanks *Ashley* Schuyler Fisk *Cindy Beugler* Catherine O'Hara *Bob Beugler* George Murdock *Lance Brumder* Jack Black *Lupe* Lillian Hurst *Bud Brumder* John Lithgow *Charlotte Cobb* Lily Tomlin *Marcus Skinner* Kevin Kline, *with* Chevy Chase, Harold Ramis and Ben Stiller (uncredited)
• *Dir* Jake Kasdan *Scr* Mike White *Ph* Greg Gardiner *Ed* Tara Timpone *M* Michael Andrews *Pro Des* Gary Frutkoff *Pro* Scott Rudin, Van Toffler, David Gale, Scott Aversano

MTV Films / Paramount Pictures / Scott Rudin Productions / UIP
82 mins. US 2002. Rel: 8 November 2002. Cert 12.

Our Father ★★★

(*Abouna*)
Visually this film is striking, and it also has the advantage of an unfamiliar setting: Chad, near the border with Cameroon. There's human appeal too in the story of two brothers, aged 15 and eight respectively, who miss their absent father and find life harsh when their mother deposits them in a Koranic school in the country. Unfortunately, all this potential is weakened by several unlikely incidents, inadequate dramatisation and the introduction into the plot of a glamorous mute girl wearing a golden dress that never gets dirtied. Even more seriously, the film is structurally misjudged – given the title, the missing father seems important even in his absence, but that side of the story is suddenly dropped in favour of a belatedly introduced subplot about the mother's health. For all the film's qualities, we eventually feel let down. MS

• *Tahir* Ahidjo Mahamet Moussa *Amine* Hamza Moctar Aguid *mother* Zara Haroun *mute girl* Mounira Khalil *father* Koulsy Lamko *Headmaster* Garba Issa
• *Dir / Scr* Mahamet Saleh Haroun *Ph* Abraham Haile Biru *Ed* Sarah Taouss Matton *M* Diego Mustapha N'Garade *Pro Des* Laurent Cavero *Pro* Guillaume de Seille

Commission Européenne / Duo Films / Goi-Goi Productions / Hubert Bals Fund / Ministry of Promotion and Development / Tele-Chad / arte France Cinéma / ICA Projects
84 mins. Chad / France 2002.
Rel: 22 November 2002. Cert n/a.

Below: Colin Hanks (right) sees the funny side in *Orange County* (from UIP)

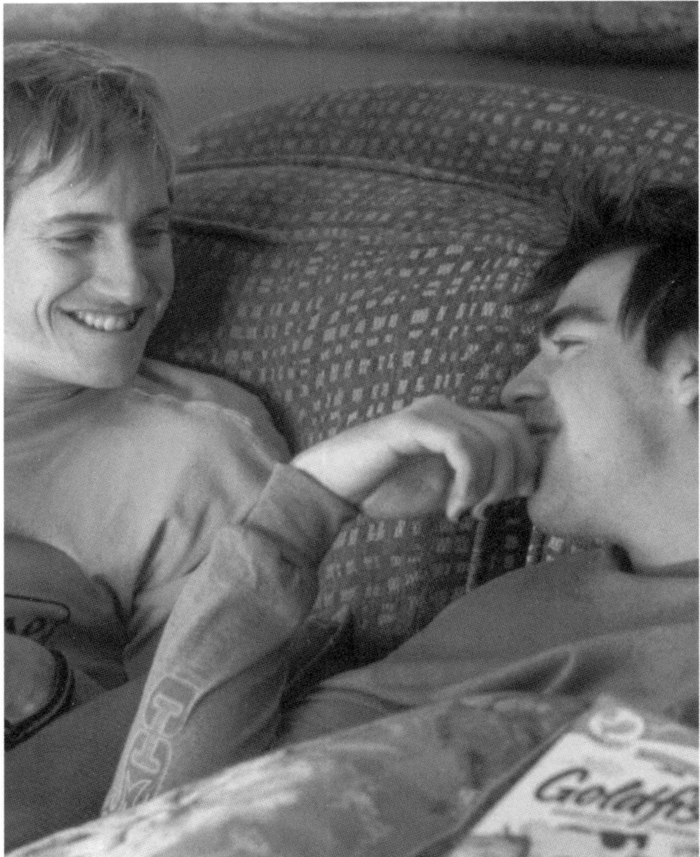

P

Perfume de violettas ★★★½

Subtitled *No One is Listening*, this is a sad little piece from Mexico centred on its tragic heroine, 15-year-old Yessica (Ximena Ayala). Ill-treated at school by bullying fellow pupils and teachers alike, she finds solace in friendship with a lonely girl in the same class, Miriam (Nancy Gutiérrez). But Miriam's mother is hostile and, when Yessica becomes a rape victim, lies are told which put the blame on her as a promiscuous girl. Director and co-writer Maryse Sistach is undoubtedly sincere and intends that the audience should be moved while finding social criticism in this grim tale. The film is well played and technically able but, by the time Sistach ends up adding yet another dark twist of fate, you feel that the film has lost its way by pushing its case to extremes. MS

• *Yessica* Ximena Ayala *Miriam* Nancy Gutiérrez *Alicia* Arcelia Ramírez *mamá de Yessica* María Rojo *Jorge* Luis Fernando Peña
• *Dir* Marisa Sistach *Scr* José Buil, Sistach *Pro* José Buil *M* Annette Fradera *Ph* Servando Gajá *Ed* Buil, Humberto Hernández *Pro Des* Guadalupe Sánchez, Soledad González *Costumes* Alejandra Dorantes

Centro de Capacitación Cinematográfica / Cnca / Filmoteca de la UNAM / Fondo para la Producción Cinematográfica de Calidad / Foprocine / Hubert Bals Fund / Instituto Mexicano de Cinematografía / John Simon Guggenheim Memorial Foundation / Palmera Films / Producciones Tragaluz / City Screen
88 mins. Mexico 2001. Rel: 9 January 2003. Cert 15.

Left: Colin Farrell finds it's not so good to talk in *Phone Booth* (from Fox)

Personal Velocity ★★½

A collection of vignettes about three very different women, each approaching some kind of life crisis or critical decision, this cinematic translation of a book of short stories by Arthur Miller's daughter (also Mrs Daniel Day-Lewis) tries to duplicate the eloquent simplicity of observation boasted by her original text. However, the lack of a clear guiding idea hampers the ability of the audience to connect with the lives artfully being sketched on screen. A hard one to love, but perhaps best watched with Miller's book on hand to lend depth to the pretty pictures and beautiful people. AK

• *narrator* John Ventimiglia *Delia* Kyra Sedgwick *May Wurtzle* Nicole Murphy *Greta* Parker Posey *Lee* Tim Guinee *Avram* Ron Liebman *Paula* Fairuza Balk *Vincent* Seth Gilliam
• *Dir / Scr* Rebecca Miller, based on her book of short stories *Ph* Ellen Kuras *Ed* Sabine Hoffman *M* Michael Rohatyn *Pro Des* Judy Becker *Pro* Lemore Syvan, Gary Winick, Alexis Alexanian

Blue Magic Pictures / Goldheart Pictures / IFC Productions / InDigEnt / Optimum Releasing
86 mins. USA 2003. Rel: 28 March 2003. Cert 15.

Phone Booth ★★½

Small-time PR hustler Stu Shephard unwittingly finds himself trapped in a busy Manhattan phone booth by a sniper who refuses to release him until he bares his soul and reveals himself as a weak impersonation of a human being. Interesting for the singularity of its premise (the entire drama, complete with SWAT teams, plays out on one city block) and the energy Colin Farrell puts into Stu (he's on screen for nearly the entire length of the film), *Phone Booth* nevertheless disintegrates rapidly after the halfway mark, when the sniper's demands balloon to preposterously neurotic levels and the cops become the embodiment of well-trained incompetence. AK

• *Stu Shepard* Colin Farrell *the caller* Kiefer Sutherland *Captain Ramsay* Forest Whitaker *Kelly Shepard* Radha Mitchell *Pamela McFadden* Katie Holmes *Felicia* Paula Jai Parker *Leon* John Enos III
• *Dir* Joel Schumacher *Scr* Larry Cohen *Ph* Matthew Libatique *Ed* Mark Stevens *M* Harry Gregson-Williams *Pro Des* Andrew Laws *Pro* Gil Netter, David Zucker

Fox 2000 Pictures / Zucker-Netter / 20th Century Fox
81 mins. US 2003. Rel: 18 April 2003. Cert 15.

Possession ★★½

A S Byatt's century-hopping literary romance is given an unexpectedly respectful treatment by Neil LaBute, a director infamous for his confrontational black comedies. But apart from some distracting casting (Gwyneth Paltrow pressing her cut-glass British accent into service again), LaBute translates the story – about two literary detectives who track down the lost love letters of a celebrated Victorian poet to his 'dark lady' – with an almost bland conformism. Ultimately, the results disappoint, mainly because the elemental richness required to bring a story this complicated to life – I count three romances, cut across two centuries, multi-layered and tied to a nest of contingent relationships – was in neither the director's nor scriptwriters' toolkits. What saves the film is the sense of earnest endeavour that persuades us to care just a little more than we should about how it all turns out. AK

• *Maud Bailey* Gwyneth Paltrow *Roland Michell* Aaron Eckhart *Randolph Ash* Jeremy Northam *Christabel LaMotte* Jennifer Ehle *Blanche Glover* Lena Headey *Ellen Ash* Holly Aird *Fergus Wolfe* Toby Stephens *Cropper* Trevor Eve *Blackadder* Tom Hickey.
• *Dir* Neil LaBute *Scr* David Henry Hwang, Laura Jones and LaBute, based on the novel by A S Byatt *Pro* Paula Weinstein and Barry Levinson *Ph* Jean Yves Escoffier *Ed* Claire Simpson *M* Gabriel Yared *Pro Des* Luciana Arrighi

Baltimore Spring Creek Productions / Contagious Films / Focus Features / USA Films / Warner Bros
102 mins. US 2002. Rel: 25 October 2002. Cert 12A.

Pot Luck ★★★★

(*L'auberge Espagnole*)

Shot two years ago, Cédric Klapisch's film is a Europudding which, just for once, converts that term into one of praise rather than abuse. It's not faultless and it's rather longer than it needs to be, but this is a movie that warms the heart and avoids sentimentality. A comedy set in Barcelona, it shows youngsters of several nationalities sharing accommodation to cut costs, and their relationships, sexual and otherwise, are central to the tale. Klapisch pokes fun at national stereotypes (a crass Brit is spot on) but he does so only to reveal how spending time together leads these people to appreciate how much they have in common. Audiences at festivals have acclaimed this film and one can see why. Audrey Tautou (pre-*Amèlie*) appears in a supporting role, but most appropriately the attractive cast play as a team. AK

• *Xavier* Romain Duris *Anne Sophie* Judith Godrèche *Martine* Audrey Tautou *Isabelle* Cécile de France *Wendy* Kelly Reilly
• *Dir / Scr* Cédric Klapisch *Ph* Dominique Colin *Ed* Francine Sandberg *M* Loïk Dury aka Kouz 1 *Pro Des* François Emmanuelli *Pro* Bruno Lévy

Bac Films / Ce Qui Me Meut Motion Pictures / France 2 Cinéma / Mate Films / Mate Producciones SA / Studio Canal / Vía Digital / Cinefrance
122 mins. France/Spain 2002. Rel: 9 May 2003. Cert 15.

The Powerpuff Girls ★★★

Craig McCracken and Charlie Bean bring their cult cartoon to the big screen with the same eye-popping panache of the television series. Brilliant but lonely Townsville scientist Professor Utonium gathers up all the ingredients to make the perfect little girl: sugar and spice and everything nice. When his sinister lab assistant, a monkey named Mojo Jojo, inadvertently adds the mysterious Chemical X to the mix, however, three super-powered little girls spring forth! Blossom, Bubbles and Buttercup have to learn how to cope with their powers, a town that (justifiably) fears them, and the machinations of Jojo in his own bid to conquer Townsville. The unique, whiz-bang style of the cartoon series doesn't lend itself well to this longer format, with some scenes dragging in an attempt to fill out the story. Still, the effort is appreciated and kids are sure to enjoy this prequel to the series they enjoy at home. SWM

• voices: *Blossom* Catherine Cavadini *Bubbles* Tara Strong *Buttercup* E G Daily *Mojo Jojo* Roger L Jackson *Professor Utonium* Tom Kane *Mayor/narrator/ Ka-Ching Ka-Ching* Tom Kenny
• *Dir* Craig McCracken *Scr* Charlie Bean, Lauren Faust, McCracken, Paul Rudish, Don Shank *Animation director* Genndy Tartakovsky *Ed* Rob DeSales *M* James L Venable *Pro Des* Mike Moon *Pro* Donna Castricone

Cartoon Network / Warner Bros
73 mins. US 2002. Rel: 18 October 2002. Cert. U.

Puckoon ★★★

Writer/director Terence Ryan is not a name to conjure with (more one to forget after *The Brylcreem Boys*), but he makes a reasonable fist of adapting Spike Milligan's Irish phantasmagoria, published as a novel in 1963. As a satirical take on military tactics, border divisions and the like this piece remains topical, but more bite and less crudity would be welcome. It's only fair to say that I venerate *The Goon Show* without being a fan of Milligan's books, and those who relish them may enjoy this more than I did. Sean Hughes is joined by Elliott Gould, who probably regrets it. However, there are reliable contributions from Nickolas Grace and David Kelly, plus a cameo from Richard Attenborough as the supposed writer/director arguing with his characters. MS

• *Dan Madigan* Sean Hughes *Dr Goldstein* Elliott Gould *Father Rudden* Daragh O'Malley *O'Brien* John Lynch *Col Stokes* Griff Rhys Jones *Foggerty* Nickolas Grace *Rafferty* B J Hogg *O'Toole* David Kelly *Sgt McGillikuddie* Milo O'Shea *Sir John Meredith* Freddie Jones *Alex Walker* Richard Rickings *writer-director* Richard Attenborough *Surveyor White* Marc Sinden *Lenny* Frankie McCafferty *Shamus* Conor Mullen
• *Dir* Terence Ryan *Scr* Ryan, based on the novel by Spike Milligan *Pro* Ken Tuohy, Ryan Ex *Pro* Jamie Brown, Stephen Margolis, Kevin Menton, Rainer Mockert, Brooks Riley *Co Pro* David McLoughlin *M* Pol Brennan, Richard Hartley *Ph* Peter Hannan *Ed* Dermot Diskin *Pro Des* John Bunker *Costumes* Hazel Webb-Crozier

Bórd Scannán na hÉireann / Distinguished Features / Insight Ventures Limited / MBP (Germany) / NatWest Ventures / National Lottery / Northern Ireland Film Commission / VCL Communications GmbH / Y2K Productions / Guerrilla
83 mins. UK/Ireland/Germany 2003. Rel: 4 April 2003.

Punch-Drunk Love ★★★

It's not easy to bring off a blend of black comedy, unease and violence, but Martin Scorsese did it brilliantly in 1985 with *After Hours.* Paul Thomas Anderson is one of America's most interesting younger talents but here fails to make comparable elements cohere. The story of a lonely oddball (Adam Sandler) finding the girl of his dreams (Emily Watson), but being menaced by a man running a sex line, combines off-beat humour with suggestions of loneliness and something approaching psychosis. It's a bizarre mix, although that very fact could give the film cult status. Technically it's first-class in every way (photography, editing, music, use of sound) and Watson is enchanting. But because the overall impression is of a film that has been misconceived, the good things about it cannot overcome a strong feeling of disappointment. MS

• *Barry Egan* Adam Sandler *Lena Leonard* Emily Watson *Dean Trumbell* Philip Seymour Hoffman *Lance* Luis Guzmán *Elizabeth* Mary Lynn Rajskub *Latisha* Ashley Clark *Kathleen* Julie Hermelin
• *Dir / Scr* Paul Thomas Anderson *Pro* Joanne Sellar, Daniel Lupi and Anderson *Ph* Robert Elswit *Ed* Leslie Jones *M* John Brion *Pro Des* William Arnold

Ghoulardi Film Company / New Line Cinema / Revolution Studios / Columbia Tristar
95 mins. US 2002. Rel: 7 February 2003. Cert 15.

Below: Molly Parker in Gillies MacKinnon's *Pure* (from Artificial Eye)

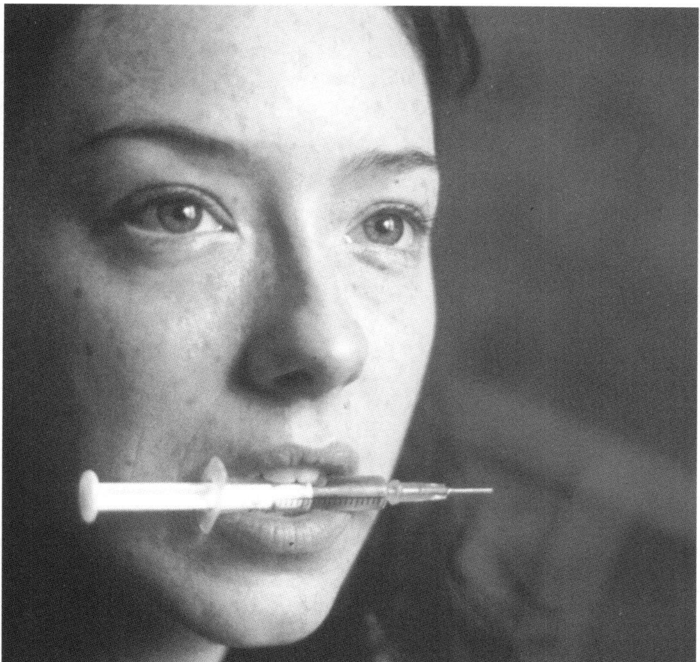

Pure ★★★

Any film centred on the wretched life of an East End boy (Harry Eden) coping as best he can with the drug addiction of his mother (Molly Parker) smacks of material that impresses audiences on TV but can't persuade the same people to part with money at the cinema. For the first half of *Pure* one regrets that fact because it's so well acted, with John de Borman's widescreen colour photography making the most of the locations. Unfortunately, though, the second half of Gillies MacKinnon's film suffers from weaknesses in Alison Hume's screenplay. Two characters are drawn without any subtlety, several plot developments lack conviction and the climax, backed by a dreadful music score, is appallingly manipulative. But the disappointments cannot destroy the film's good features, most especially the performances of Molly Parker and young Harry Eden. MS

• *Mel* Molly Parker *Lenny* David Wenham *Det Inspector French* Gary Lewis *Louise* Keira Knightley *Nanna* Geraldine McEwan *Paul* Harry Eden *Helen* Kate Ashfield *Grandad* Karl Johnson *Vicki* Marsha Thomason *Lee* Vinnie Hunter *Abu* Nitin Chandra Ganatra
• *Dir* Gillies MacKinnon *Scr* Alison Hume *Pro* Howard Burch *Ex Pro* Amit Barooah, Robert Bevan, Amanda Coombes, Jane Featherstone, Stephen Garrett, Keith Hayley, Charlie Savill *M* Nitin Sawhney *Ph* John de Borman *Ed* Pia di Ciaula *Pro Des* John Henson

A Bad Way / Kudos Productions / Little Wing Films / Artificial Eye
96 mins. UK 2002. Rel: 2 May 2003. Cert 15.

R

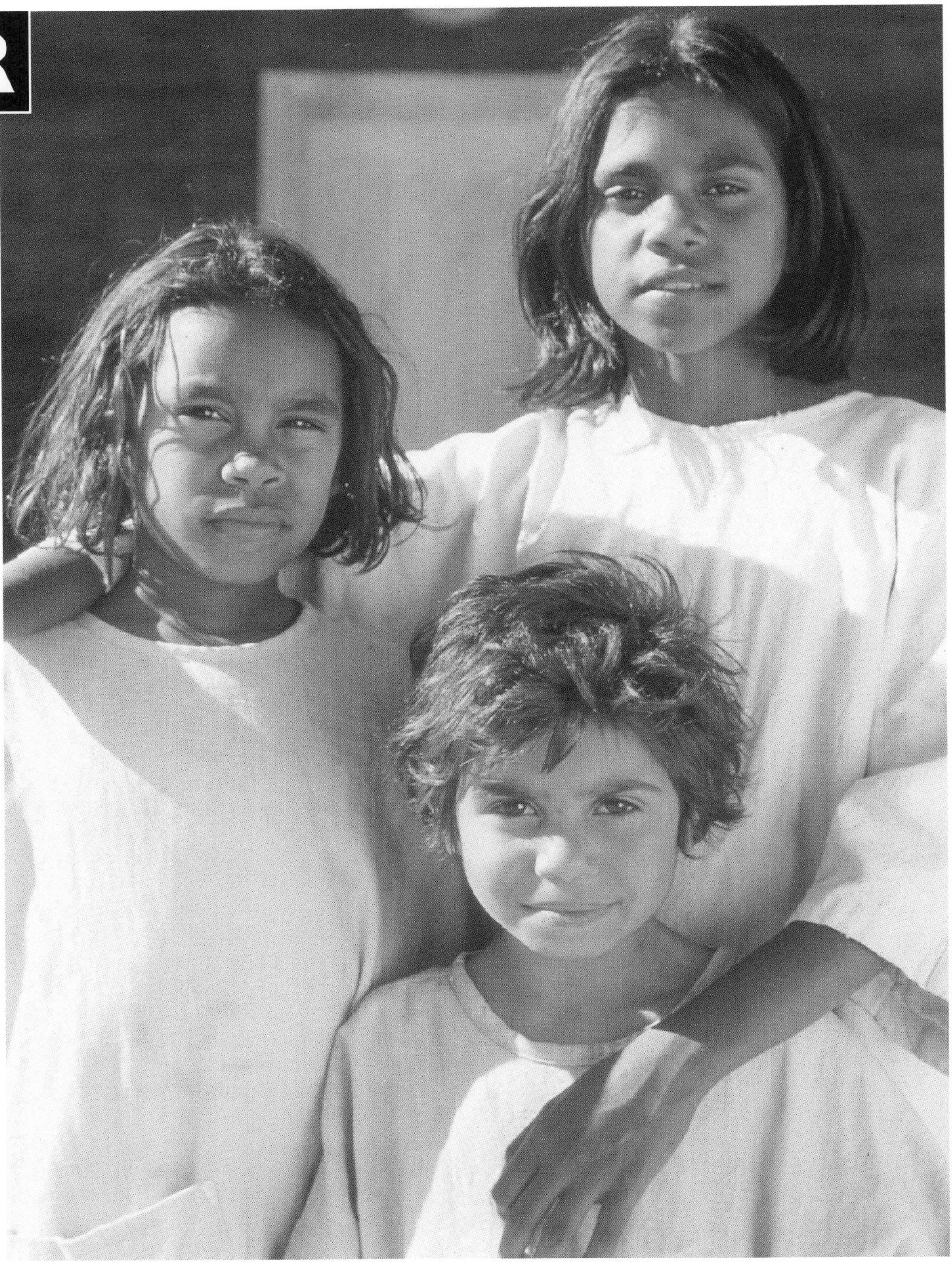

Left: Laura Monaghan, Tianna Sansbury and Everlyn Sampi in the controversial *Rabbit-Proof Fence* (from Buena Vista)

Rabbit-Proof Fence ★★★½

In easily the year's most controversial Australian film, Phillip Noyce returns to his homeland to tell the almost unbelievable story of how, up to the 1970s, Aboriginal children were being kidnapped from their families by government decree to have the 'black' bred out of them. Based on a true story of three very young girls who escaped the camps they were taken to and then survived a 1500-mile walk to their homes, what the film lacks in dramatic focus it makes up for in scale. Some have criticised Noyce for not making a more politically loaded film (he allows Kenneth Branagh to play the architect of the breeding policies, A O Neville, as a technocrat misguidedly serving his office), but that doesn't give credit to the sense of tragedy he has managed to create. The capture of the children inspired such profound grief among the Aboriginal members of Noyce's crew that some had to be physically restrained from intervening mid-take. How the

Australian Prime Minister, John Howard, can still refuse an apology to the Aboriginal communities for the 'Stolen Generations' is completely baffling. AK

• *Molly Craig* Everlyn Sampi *Daisy Craig* Tianna Sansbury *Gracie Fields* Laura Monaghan *Moodoo* David Gulpilil *Molly's mother* Ningali Lawford *Molly's grandmother* Myarn Lawford *Mavis* Deborah Mailman *Constable Riggs* Jason Clarke and *Mr A O Neville* Kenneth Branagh
• *Dir* Phillip Noyce *Scr* Christine Olsen, based on the book by Doris Pilkington Garimara *Ph* Christopher Doyle *Ed* John Scott, Veronika Jenet *M* Peter Gabriel *Pro Des* Roger Ford *Pro* Noyce, Olsen, John Winter.

Australian Film Commission / Australian Film Finance Corporation / Hanway / Lotteries Commission of Western Australia / Olsen Levy / Rumbalara / ScreenWest / Showtime Australia / South Australian Film Corporation / Buena Vista
93 mins. Australia 2002.
Rel: 8 November 2002. Cert PG.

Rain ★★★★½

This brilliant film poem from New Zealand gives notice of a potential major talent in writer/director Christine Jeffs. Her subject, taken from a novel by Kirsty Gunn, is the onset of sexual awareness in a 13-year-old girl, superbly played by Alicia Fulford-Wierzbicki. The approach is to eschew standard dramatics thereby avoiding melodrama, even though the girl's unfocused feelings are linked to her realisation that her hard-drinking mother is cheating on her father. The everyday is here heightened by an artist's eye and ear: John Toon's remarkably tactile photography plays a vital role and certain scenes are designed for musical accompaniment rather than dialogue. The words are occasionally inaudible, but the one really serious failing is a dramatic climax that is far too oblique in its connection with the central theme. Not quite a masterpiece then, but exceptional. MS

Below: Colin Farrell and Al Pacino lock horns in the entertaining *The Recruit* (from Buena Vista)

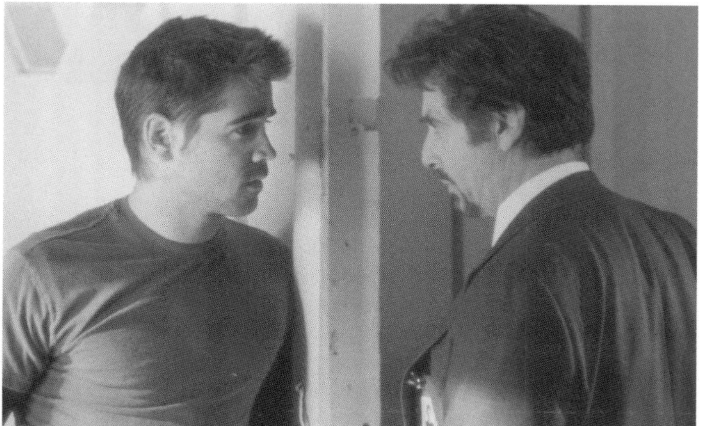

• *Janey* Alicia Fulford-Wierzbicki *Kate* Sarah Peirse *Cady* Marton Csokas *Ed* Alistair Browning *Jim* Aaron Murphy
• *Dir / Scr* Christine Jeffs, based on the novel by Kirsty Gunn *Ph* John Toon *Ed* Paul Maxwell *M* Neil Finn, Edmund McWilliams *Pro* Philippa Campbell *Pro Des* Kirsty Clayton

Communicado Productions / New Zealand Film Commission / Rain Film Productions / Rose Road / Circuit Films
91 mins. NZ 2002. Rel: 27 June 2003. Cert 15.

Raye Makhfi

See *Secret Ballot*

Real Women Have Curves ★★

Ana wants to be more than a seamstress in her mother, Carmen's, sweatshop. When she gets accepted for Columbia University, the conflicting aspirations collide. Although praised for its earthy simplicity and for tackling an ugly, limiting aspect of Latino culture, *Real Women Have Curves* simply never rises beyond its cable-movie format. Surly performances and flatly predictable jokes choke in mediocrity what could have been a rich and empowering family drama. AK

• *Ana* America Ferrera *Carmen* Lupe Ontiveros *Estela* Ingrid Oliu *Mr Guzman* George Lopez *Jimmy* Brian Sites *Pancha* Soledad St Hilaire *Rosali* Lourdes Perez *Raul* Jorge Cervera Jr *Grandfather* Filipe De Alba *Juan José* José Gerardo Zamora Jr *Juan Martin* Edgar Lujan *Norma* Lina Acosta
• *Dir* Patricia Cardoso *Scr* Josefina Lopez, George LaVoo *Ph* Jim Denault *Ed* Sloane Klevin *M* Margaret Guerra Rogers *Pro Des* Brigitte Broch *Pro* George LaVoo, Effie T Brown

HBO Independent Productions / LaVoo Productions / Optimum Releasing
86 mins. US 2002. Rel: 31 January 2002. Cert 12A.

The Recruit ★★★½

For much of its length, this thriller is fine for an evening out. It purports to tell a story based on the methods used by the CIA to recruit and train potential agents.Nevertheless, we take it all with a pinch of salt as we sit back to see how new recruit James Clayton (Colin Farrell) reacts when taken up in this way by a leading selector and trainer (Al Pacino). Pacino effortlessly dominates the screen once again, and Roger Donaldson knows how to direct this kind of caper. The misfortune is that, in keeping with today's tendency to push thrillers over the top, the last quarter of an hour becomes so preposterous that we can no longer suspend disbelief. However, by then we've had a fair measure of entertainment. MS

• *Walter Burke* Al Pacino *James Clayton* Colin Farrell *Layla Moore* Bridget Moynahan *Zack* Gabriel Macht *Ronnie Gibson* Mike Realba *instructor # 1* Dom Fiore *Alan* Ken Mitchell *Dennis Slayne* Karl Pruner
• *Dir* Roger Donaldson *Pro* Jeff Apple, Gary Barber, Roger Birnbaum *Scr* Roger Towne, Kurt Wimmer, Mitch Glazer *Ph* Stuart Dryburgh *Ed* David Rosenbloom *Pro Des* Andrew McAlpine *M* Klaus Badelt

Birnbaum-Barber / EIEIO Productions Inc / Spyglass Entertainment / Touchstone Pictures / Buena Vista
115 mins. US 2002. Rel: 21 March 2003. Cert 12A.

Red Dragon ★★½

Lacking any subtlety, this remake of Michael Mann's vastly superior *Manhunter* is a hollow, slavish paean to the worldwide popularity of Hannibal Lecter, the über-urbane gourmet-psychopath. Edward Norton plays FBI agent Will Graham, who is sent to entice Anthony Hopkins' Lecter into helping hunt down the deviously deranged serial killer known as the 'Tooth Fairy'. Wildly overblown melodramatics (and a soundtrack wielded like a cudgel) ensue as various people die in increasingly fantastic set-pieces. It's sad to see a quality cast betrayed by the purely commercial imperative of this Hollywood massacre. Only Emily Watson and Phillip Seymour Hoffman escape with their dignity. AK

• *Hannibal Lecter* Anthony Hopkins *Will Graham* Edward Norton *Francis 'Dee' Dolarhyde* Ralph Fiennes *Jack Crawford* Harvey Keitel *Reba McClane* Emily Watson *Molly Graham* Mary-Louise Parker *Freddy Lounds* Philip Seymour Hoffman *Dr Chilton* Anthony Heald *Barney* Frankie Faison
• *Dir* Brett Ratner *Scr* Ted Tally, based on the book by Thomas Harris *Ph* Dante Spinotti *Ed* Mark Helfrich *M* Danny Elfman *Pro Des* Kristi Zea *Pro* Dino De Laurentiis, Martha De Laurentiis

Dino De Laurentiis Company / MGM / Mikona Productions / Scott Free Productions / Universal Pictures / UIP
124 mins. US/UK/Germany 2002.
Rel: 11 October 2002. Cert 15.

Reign of Fire ★★★

Dungeons & Dragons meets *Apocalypse Now* in this thrilling beast of an actioner. Matthew McConaughey and Christian Bale grunt, growl and bark their way through a patchily organised script, with Izabella Scorupco doing duty as the tough-but-feeling eye candy. The premise: the remnants of humanity occupy a scorched Earth, hiding from flying, fire-breathing Godzillas until a group of crusading Yank dragon-slayers arrive with helicopters, machine guns and John Rambo's left-over exploding crossbolts. You want to believe it could happen, and you're mostly allowed to. If only the cast didn't all look like caricature 'action hero' steroid junkies. AK

• *Denton Van Zan* Matthew McConaughey *Quinn Albercrombie* Christian Bale *Alex* Izabella Scorupco *Creedy* Gerard Butler *Jared Wilde* Scott James Moutter
• *Dir* Rob Bowman *Scr* Gregg Chabot, Kevin Paterka, Matt Greenberg *Ph* Adrian Biddle *Ed* Thom Noble *Pro Des* Wolf Kroeger *M* Edward Shearmur *Ex Pro* Jonathon Glickman *Pro* Richard D Zanuck, Lili Fini Zanuck, Gary Barber, Roger Birnbaum

Barber / Birnbaum / The Zanuck Company / Tripod Entertainment / Touchstone Pictures / Spyglass Entertainment / Buena Vista
102 mins. US/Ireland 2002.
Rel: 23 August 2002. Cert 12A.

Above: Ralph Fiennes in the overblown *Red Dragon* (from UIP)

Resident Evil ★★★

In another step on the road to multimedia convergence, the 'hi-tech zombies versus military specialists' premise that has spawned a gigantic video games empire makes the transition to the big screen in Paul Anderson's elaborately faithful sci-fi horror thriller. (Anderson took over the reins after George A Romero, no less, left the project.) It opens in an underground laboratory called the Hive, controlled by an AI computer called The Red Queen, where scientists are doing illegal viral research. An act of sabotage unleashes one of their deadly viral pets and The Red Queen proceeds to kill off the entire complex. But being a zombie movie, chances are they won't stay dead. Layered with references to the (already quite movie-like) games, the film builds a relentless sense of dread and boasts furious action sequences and suitably horrific make-up. Jovovich makes a beautiful heroine and puts in a physical performance that compensates for her non-existent dialogue. Fans of the game might prefer a harder, gorier look, but they couldn't ask for a slicker one. FYI: The film was originally titled *Resident Evil: Ground Zero* but renamed after the 11 September bombing. AK

• *Alice* Milla Jovovich *Rain Ocampo* Michelle Rodriguez *Matt* Eric Mabius *Spence* James Purefoy *Kaplan* Martin Crewes *Number One* Colin Salmon *narrator/scientist* Jason Isaacs (uncredited)
• *Dir / Scr* Paul W S Anderson, from a story by Alan McElroy and Anderson, based on the Capcom computer game series *Ph* David Johnson *Ed* Alexander Berner *M* Marco Beltrami, Marilyn Manson *Pro Des* Richard Bridgland *Pro* Bernd Eichinger, Samuel Hadida, Jeremy Bolt, Anderson

Constantin Film-Produktion / Davis-Films / Impact Pictures / New Legacy / Pathé 100 mins. UK/US/Germany 2002. Rel: 12 July 2002. Cert 15.

Right: Milla Jovovich is sexy enough to wake the dead in *Resident Evil* (from Pathé)

Revengers Tragedy ★★★½

Alex Cox uses a modern setting for this adaptation of the classic Jacobean play thought to be by Thomas Middleton. Cox and writer Frank Cottrell Boyce have taken a hint from the way the original gives stylised names to such characters as Ambitioso and Supervacuo. What they serve up is the original plot in a Liverpool location, with male sibling rivalry at its heart against a context of plotting and general foul play. However, its Grand Guignol trappings (almost all of the characters end up dead) blend with elements of black comedy to provide a diverting entertainment not to be taken too seriously. Derek Jarman could well be the inspiration for this approach, where period text fuses with expletives and post-punk adornments. It's hardly memorable and sometimes pretentious, but by no means unenjoyable. MS

• *Vindici* Christopher Eccleston *Lussurioso* Eddie Izzard *The Duke* Derek Jacobi *The Duchess* Diana Quick *Carlo* Andrew Schofield *Lord Antonio* Anthony Booth
• *Dir* Alex Cox *Scr* Frank Cottrell Boyce, based on the play by Thomas Middleton *Pro* Tod Davies, Margaret Matheson *Ph* Len Gowing *Ed* Ray Fowlis *Pro Des* Cecilia Montiel *Costumes* Monica Aslanian

Bard Entertainments / Exterminating Angel Production / Northcroft Films / Metro Tartan 109 mins. UK 2002. Rel: 14 February 2003. Cert 15.

The Ring ★★★

On the evidence of *Nightwatch* you would think the received wisdom – that all American adaptations of foreign horror films are rubbish – was correct. But now we have *Ring*, or rather *The Ring*, which has acquired the definite article mid-Pacific as if to prove that it is... well, the definite article. The story, of a cursed videotape investigated by reporter Rachel Keller, follows a similar route to the Japanese original, but the sci-fi trappings are played down. Here, the telepathic child at the bottom of it all is called Sumara rather than Sadako and her powers remain unspecified, though she retains Sadako's curtain of long black hair. Unfortunately, we see rather too much of her as a 'normal' child peering out from under her fringe; all we saw of Sadako was one baleful eye. But the discovery of Sumara's lonely eyrie, a child's bedroom perched impossibly high in the eaves of a vast stable, is one of the most powerful new punches in Verbinski's film. Without the mythic references to water-creatures that permeated the original, this film can't be as frightening, but it is an intelligent interpretation of the material, with a few neat touches of its own. DM

• *Rachel Keller* Naomi Watts *Noah Clay* Martin Henderson *Richard Morgan* Brian Cox *Aidan Keller* David Dorfman *Samara Morgan* Daveigh Chase *Ruth Embry* Lindsay Frost *Katie Embry* Amber Tamblyn
• *Dir* Gore Verbinski *Scr* Ehren Kruger *Ex Pro* Mike Macari, Roy Lee, Michele Weisler, Neal Edelstein, J C Spink *Pro* Laurie MacDonald *Pho* Bojan Bazelli *Ed* Craig Wood

Asmik-Ace / Bender-Spink / Kuzui / MacDonald-Parkes / DreamWorks SKG 115 mins. Japan/US 2002. Rel: 21 February 2003. Cert: 15

Ripley's Game ★★★½

An adaptation of the Patricia Highsmith novel previously filmed by Wim Wenders in 1978 as *The American Friend*, this story about Tom Ripley presents him as an older character than the one seen in *The Talented Mr Ripley*. As amoral as ever, he's now rich and married and living in Italy with his criminal days behind him. Nevertheless, resentment at being criticised for his artistic taste leads him to play a game with the man who insulted him. He puts forward this respectable Englishman as a potential assassin for hire, this being done as a test since Ripley knows that the man is dying of leukaemia, and it is his belief that anyone so placed, and with a wife and child to support, can be bought. Unfortunately, the story becomes increasingly improbable and changes of heart by two characters are inadequately investigated. But director Liliana Cavani is on fine form, the film looks great and John Malkovich's Ripley is, without doubt, a collector's item. MS

• *Tom Ripley* John Malkovich *Jonathan Trevanny* Dougray Scott *Reeves* Ray Winstone *Sarah Trevanny* Lena Headey *Luisa Ripley* Chiara Caselli
• *Dir* Liliana Cavani *Scr* Cavani, Charles McKeown, based on the novel by Patricia Highsmith *Pro* Riccardo Tozzi, Simon Bosanquet, Ileen Maisel *Ex Pro* Marco Chimenz, Cam Galano, Rolf Mittweg, Mark Ordesky, Russell Smith *M* Ennio Morricone *Ph* Alfio Contini *Ed* Job Harris *Pro Des* Francesco Frigeri

Baby Films / Cattleya / Dogstar Films / Fine Line Features / Mr. Mudd / Entertainment
110 mins. USA/UK/Italy 2002. Rel: 30 May 2003. Cert 15.

Road to Perdition ★★★★

1931, Depression-era America, somewhere in the Midwest. Michael Sullivan's 12-year-old son discovers that his father is a hitman for the Irish mob. This leads eventually to the murder of his mother and brother, and puts father and son on the run from a shutterbug hitman… Sam Mendes' follow-up to *American Beauty* boasts exceedingly heavyweight casting. Beneath the holographic camerawork and the visceral, fast-cutting imagery is a core theme of fathers and sons. Paul Newman, as John Rooney, may rule the town 'like God rules the Earth' but he is also a father figure torn between a genuine love for his adopted son, Michael, and the ties that bind him to his blood heir, Connor.

Left: John Malkovich takes on the mantle of Patricia Highsmith's amoral protagonist in *Ripley's Game* (from Entertainment)

Strangely, the highly polished aesthetic actually diminishes the emotional impact the film could have had. Jude Law's ratty hitman, Maguire, is a glaring example of caricature instead of character, and Tyler Hoechlin as Michael Jr just fails to make the narration coalesce. But these faults are glaring only because the rest of the film is so beautifully executed. AK

• *Michael Sullivan* Tom Hanks *John Rooney* Paul Newman *Maguire* Jude Law *Annie Sullivan* Jennifer Jason Leigh *Frank Nitti* Stanley Tucci *Connor Rooney* Daniel Craig *Michael Sullivan Jr* Tyler Hoechlin *Finn McGovern* Ciarán Hinds *Alexander Rance* Dylan Baker *Peter Sullivan* Liam Aiken
• *Dir* Sam Mendes *Scr* David Self, based on the graphic novel by Max Allan Collins and Richard Piers Rayner *Pro* Richard D Zanuck, Dean Zanuck, Mendes *Ph* Conrad L Hall *Ed* Jill Bilcock *M* Thomas Newman *Pro Des* Dennis Gassner

20th Century Fox / DreamWorks SKG / The Zanuck Company / Fox
117 mins. US 2002. Rel: 27 September 2002. Cert 15.

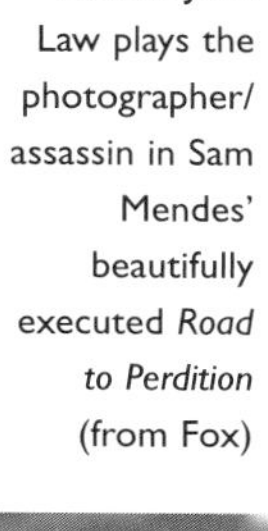

Below: Jude Law plays the photographer/ assassin in Sam Mendes' beautifully executed *Road to Perdition* (from Fox)

Le Roi danse

See *The King is Dancing*

Rokugatsu No Hebi

See *A Snake of June*

The Rookie ★★★★

Based on the true story of big league pitcher Jimmy Morris, this is two distinct, inspirational shorts combined in one film. After a shoulder injury sidelines Morris early in his career, he chooses to coach high-school ball in West Texas. The perennial losers strike a deal with their coach. If they can manage to become district champs, he will go back and try out for the big leagues. With grim determination and mutual support, they do just that. When Jimmy goes back to pitching, we get our second tale of comeback success. The baseball theme is almost peripheral to the heart-warming joy of *The Rookie*. It is, instead, a story of love, support and second chances proving that it's never really too late to make your dreams come true. The same should be said for actor Dennis

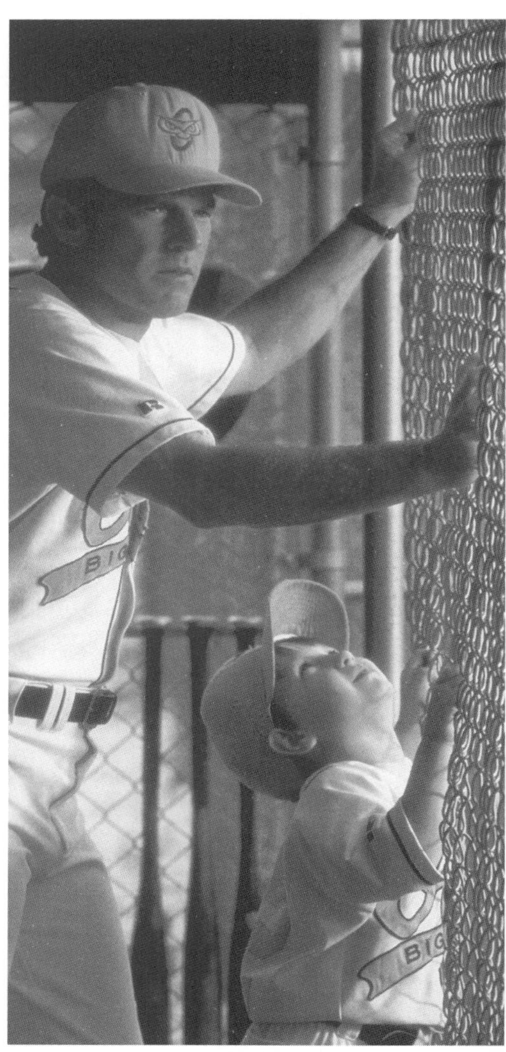

Quaid. This is his finest work to date. SWM

• *Jimmy Morris* Dennis Quaid *Lorri Morris* Rachel Griffiths *Joaquin Campos* Jay Hernandez *Jimmy's mother* Beth Grant *Hunter* Angus T. Jones *Jim Sr* Brian Cox *Rudy Bonilla* Rick Gonzalez *Joe David West* Chad Lindberg
• *Dir* John Lee Hancock *Scr* Mike Rich *Ph* John Schwartzman *Ed* Eric L Beason *M* Carter Burwell *Pro Des* Barry Robison *Pro* Gordon Gray, Mark Ciardi, Mark Johnson

**98 MPH Productions / Gran Via / Walt Disney Pictures / Buena Vista
127 mins. US 2002.
Rel: 11 October 2002. Cert U.**

Russian Ark ★★★

(*Russkij kovcheg*)

It's a feat to carry off successfully a film consisting of a single tracking shot. However, an audience drawn to a movie pondering Russian history as it takes the spectator through the rooms of the Hermitage may well be expecting something more meaningful and less avant-garde than this. The historical element boils down to little more than recognising representations of historic figures and the dialogue, largely between the unseen director and a foreign visitor whom the camera follows (Sergey Dreiden), is less interesting than one would hope. In contrast, the later scenes, using this setting to evoke the last balls before the Revolution, find the filmmaker providing a spectacle touched by sadness which is capable of comparison with Visconti. Director Sokurov's admirers will be fascinated, but less specialist audiences need to be warned about the nature of this film. MS

• *The Marquis* Sergey Dreiden *Catherine the Great* Maria Kuznetsova *The Spy* Leonid Mozgovoy *himself* Mikhail Piotrovsky *Orbeli* David Giorgobiani
• *Dir* Alexander Sokurov *Scr* Anatoly Nikiforov, Alexander Sokurov *Ph* Tilman Büttner *M* Sergey Yevtuschenko *Pro Des* Yelena Zhukova, Natalia Kochergina *Pro* Andrey Deryabin, Jens Meurer, Karsten Stöter

**Egoli Tossell Film AG / Fora Film / The Hermitage Bridge Studio / Artificial Eye
99 mins. Russia/Germany/Japan 2002.
Rel: 4 April 2003. Cert U.**

Left: Dennis Quaid in the elegiac *The Rookie* (from Buena Vista)

Below: Nicholas I (Yuli Zhurin) in *Russian Ark* (from Artificial Eye)

S

Safe Conduct ★★★½

(*Laissez-passer*)

Made with love and passion, this is Bertrand Tavernier's balanced take on the French film industry during the Occupation. His central figures are the director Jean Devaivre (Jacques Gamblin) and the writer Jean Aurenche (Denis Podalydès). Tavernier examines in detail the conflicting attitudes of those who refused to work for studios controlled by the Germans and those who accepted the situation for the sake of preserving the industry and sometimes to smuggle through films with coded messages hostile to the aggressors. It's a fine period piece and well acted, but its length (170 minutes) seems self-indulgent and Tavernier is so keen to comment fairly that he stuffs the film with references to cinema personages of the forties that will mystify all but the most knowledgable of film buffs. The misjudgments weaken the film, but it is unquestionably a work to respect. MS

• *Jean Devaivre* Jacques Gamblin *Jean Aurenche* Denis Podalydès *Olga* Marie Gillain *Suzanne Raymond* Charlotte Kady *Simone Devaivre* Marie Desgranges *Reine Sorignal* Maria Pitarresi *Jean-Paul Le Chanois* Ged Marlon *Maurice Tourneur* Philippe Morier-Genoud *Dr Grebe* Christian Berkel *Roger Richebé* Olivier Gourmet
• *Dir* Bertrand Tavernier *Scr* Jean Cosmos, Tavernier *Ph* Alain Choquart *Ed* Sophie Brunet *M* Antoine Duhamel *Pro Des* Émile Ghigo *Pro* Alain Sarde, Frédéric Bourboulon

France 2 Cinéma / France 3 Cinéma / KC Medien AG / Les Films Alain Sarde / Little Bear / Studio Canal/ Vertigo / Artificial Eye 170 mins. France 2002. Rel: 8 November 2002. Cert 12A.

Right: Tim Allen packs on the pounds in Michael Lembeck's light-hearted *The Santa Clause 2* (from Buena Vista)

The Santa Clause 2 ★★★

Scott Calvin (Tim Allen) has been the newest Santa Claus for the past eight years and, while the elves love him, it's taking its toll on his son Charlie. In order to help his son as well as seek out a new wife, Scott leaves the North Pole after the elves create a toy Santa to fill in for him. Toy Santa is a stickler for the rules, however... Tim Allen manages to muster a bit more Christmas magic in this light-hearted holiday product-placement vehicle. The tedious bits are more than offset by the charm of the story. The subtext of the need for a humanistic approach to the law is refreshing and genuine. SWM

• *Scott Calvin/Santa/Toy Santa* Tim Allen *Carol* Elizabeth Mitchell *Bernard* David Krumholtz *Charlie Calvin* Eric Lloyd *Neil Miller* Judge Reinhold *Laura Miller* Wendy Crewson *Curtis* Spencer Breslin
• *Dir* Michael Lembeck *Scr* Don Rhymer, Cinco Paul, Ken Daurio, Ed Decter, John J Strauss, from a story by Leo Benvenuti, Steve Rudnick *Ph* Adam Greenberg *Ed* David Finfer *M* George S Clinton *Pro Des* Tony Burrough *Pro* Brian Reilly, Bobby Newmyer, Jeffrey Silver

Boxing Cat Films / Outlaw Productions / Walt Disney Pictures / Buena Vista 105 mins. US 2002. Rel: 29 November 2002

S Club – Seeing Double ★★

Victor is an evil man but, being willing to settle for less than world domination, he sets out instead to clone S Club (all six of them) and an array of other pop singers so that they will be his creatures... Given such an inane plot-line, it's absurd that the second half of this feature film, built around S Club, should emphasise the story at the expense of the music. Even if the tale had merit it would have been an unwise decision, since there's little evidence that any members of the group can act. The first half is at least lively, with far more music, sharp editing and potted tours of the two main locations, Barcelona and LA, as S Club set out to uncover what is going on and to put an end to Victor's cloning. Director Nigel Dick is at least realistic: at the outset he told S Club: "This film isn't about making the critics happy, and I can tell you now what the reviews will be like." MS

• *Hannah* Hannah Spearritt *Jo* Jo O'Meara *Rachel* Rachel Stevens *Jon* Jon Lee *Bradley* Bradley Mcintosh *Tina* Tina Barrett *Gareth Gates clone* Gareth Gates *Victor* David Gant *Alistair* Joseph Adams *Scalper* Alec Von Bargen
• *Dir* Nigel Dick *Scr* Paul Alexander, Kim Fuller *Pro* John Steven Agoglia, Alan Barnette, Simon Fuller, Aaron Sandler *Ex Pro* Gayla Aspinall *Ph* Juan Benet (as Joan Benet) *Ed* Mark Henson *Pro Des* Laia Colet

Columbia Tristar 91 mins. UK 2003. Rel: 11 April 2003. Cert PG.

Scooby Doo ★★★

The world's favourite dog finally gets the Jessica Rabbit treatment in this live-action-plus-CGI summer pleaser. Touching on all the fan favourite references ("I would-a gotten away with it, too, if it wasn't for you pesky kids and that durned dog!"), the movie does take a chance by breaking up the Scooby gang when Fred, Velma and Daphne disagree over who gets the credit for their famous paranormal detections. When they are individually invited to solve the mysterious brainwashing of Spooky Island's guests by its owner, the reclusive Emile Mondavarious, they realise that only by working together (sigh) will they overcome the wonderfully chosen villain behind the mystery. Undeniably enjoyable, given a certain age or childhood fandom, the movie tries to balance the free-spirited nature of the original cartoon with a knowing irony that works best when Sarah Michelle Gellar is on screen. And the CGI Scooby is nigh on perfect. AK

• *Fred Jones* Freddie Prinze Jr *Daphne Blake* Sarah Michelle Gellar *Norville 'Shaggy' Rogers* Matthew Lillard *Velma Dinkley* Linda Cardellini *Emile Mondavarious* Rowan Atkinson *Scooby Doo's voice* Neil Fanning *Mary Jane* Isla Fisher *Scrappy Doo's voice* Scott Innes
• *Dir* Raja Gosnell *Scr* James Gunn, based on characters created by Hanna-Barbera Productions *Ph* David Eggby *Ed* Kent Beyda *M* David Newman *Pro Des* Bill Boes *Visual FX* Peter Crosman *Pro* Charles Roven, Richard Suckle

Atlas Entertainment / Hanna-Barbera Productions / Mosaic Media Group / Village Roadshow Productions
87 mins. US/Australia 2002. Rel: 12 July 2002. Cert PG.

Scratch ★★★

Welcome to the history of the hip-hop DJ in 91 minutes. *Scratch* takes its name from the basic move in 'turntablism' that involves moving the vinyl back and forth on the needle while juggling with the fader to create... well, to hear The Invisibl Skratch Pklz explain it, "music like they would listen to in outer space." Everybody is here. Grand Wizard Theodore, who claims to have invented it in mid-conversation with his Mum; Afrika Bambaataa, who took it to the streets in the name of urban transformation; DJ Shadow, whose star turn is an anorak's confession in a basement stuffed with half-a-million dusty records. A short segment also showcases the DJ stars of tomorrow, who look like 12-year-old Nintendo junkies... which they probably are. For all the fervid interest the filmmakers clearly have in their subject, the narrow focus eventually becomes a little too intense, and the talking heads sound less like musical heroes than obsessive-compulsives who have spent far too much time indoors. AK

• *themselves* Afrika Bambaataa, Grand Mixer DXT, Yoga Frog, DJ Krush, Lucas MacFadden (as Cut Chemist), Mix Master Mike, DJ Q-Bert, DJ Shadow, DJ Swamp, Grand Wizard Theodore, DJ Z-Trip (uncredited)
• *Dir* Doug Pray *Pr* Brad Blondheim, Ernest Meza *Ex Pro* Allen Hughes, Albert Hughes *Co Pro* Heidi Rataj Addison *Ass Pro* John Carluccio *Ph* Robert Bennett *Ed* Doug Pray *M* Carol Sue Baker, Jonathan Hafter, Herbie Hancock, DJ Shadow (uncredited)

Firewalks Film / Magic Lamp / Ridgeway Entertainment / Momentum
91 mins. US 2001. Rel: 30 August 2002. Cert 15.

Secret Ballot ★★★

(*Raye Makhfi*)

This clever, down-tempo political satire starts with a ballot box falling from the sky onto an Iranian island. A soldier is ordered to guard an election agent who will be collecting ballots on voting day. The punchline is that the agent is a woman, which is mystifying enough for the misogynist soldier, but her problems are amplified when she attempts to convince the island's other residents that voting in a new democracy will benefit their lives... Babak Payami's film is beautiful to look at and strides through its scenic disjointedness with unusual confidence. Something of a docu-fiction, the film engineers various encounters between half-baked political ideals and the brute fact of communities unprepared for the promised modernism and democracy. However, in spite of some genuinely hilarious moments arising out of the agent's idealism clashing with the stolid pragmatics of her bodyguard soldier, it is not quite an entertainment. MS

• *Girl* Nassim Abdi *Soldier* Cyrus Abidi
• *Dir* Babak Payami *Scr* Payami, based on an idea by Moshen Makhmalbaf *Ph* Farzad Jodat *Ed* Babak Karimi *M* Michael Galasso *Pro* Marco Müller and Payami

Fabrica / Payam / Rai Cinemafiction / Sharmshir / Televisione Svizzera Italiana / Artificial Eye
105 mins. Iran/Canada/Switzerland/Italy.
Rel: 13 September 2002. Cert U.

Secretary ★★★★

A girl is released from psychiatric therapy and finds her first job in the office of a highly eccentric lawyer. As his secretary, however, her job appears to require more than a measure of light bondage and sexy mind games... The arrestingly original opening scene sets the pace for this breathtakingly confident study of a very different kind of love. James Spader and Maggie Gyllenhaal completely occupy their claustrophobic private world with standout performances (in Gyllenhaal's case, a potentially career-making one).

Above: No laughing matter – Grégoire Colin and Roxanne Mesquida in *Sex is Comedy* (from Artificial Eye)

Their openness goes a long way to justifying scenes with, on the surface at least, are as politically correct as kicking nice old grannies. But get beyond the taboos and *Secretary* becomes a sweet confection about two misfits who find their soulmate against all the odds – in other words, *Amélie* in an S & M wonderland. AK

• *Mr Grey* James Spader *Lee Holloway* Maggie Gyllenhaal *Peter* Jeremy Davies *Joan Holloway* Lesley Ann Warren *Burt Holloway* Stephen McHattie *Dr Twardon* Patrick Bauchau
• *Dir* Steven Shainberg *Scr* Erin Cressida Wilson, based on the story by Mary Gaitskill *Ph* Steven Fierberg *Ed* Pam Wise *M* Angelo Badalamenti *Pro Des* Amy Danger *Pro* Shainberg, Andrew Fierberg and Amy Hobby.

Double A Films / Slough Pond / TwoPoundBag Productions / Metro Tartan
111 mins. US 2002. Rel: 16 May 2003. Cert 18.

Sex is Comedy ★★★★

Although this is less intense than most films by France's Catherine Breillat, the title should not be taken as indicating that you will find big laughs here. What you do get is a kind of self-portrait, as a woman filmmaker (Anne Parillaud) deals with the problems of shooting a film akin to Breillat's own *A ma soeur!*. It covers not only the temperament displayed by the actors, but the difficulties of handling sex scenes due to be played out between performers who dislike each other. Things are further complicated by the responses of the male lead, simultaneously nervous of the shoot but excited by it. Grégoire Colin's performance plays up to this unflattering portrait admirably, but the film's main interest is for anyone fascinated by Breillat's work. Those who see her dramas as criticising male dominance in sexual relationships will be intrigued to find that here her alter-ego seems to gain vicarious sexual stimulation through the power she exercises as a filmmaker. MS

• *Jeanne* Anne Parillaud *the actor* Grégoire Colin *the actress* Roxane Mesquida *Leo, the first assistant* Ashley Wanninger *Willy* Dominique Colladant *Ph* Bart Binnema *sound engineer* Yves Osmu *continuity girl* Elisabete Piecho
• *Dir / Scr* Catherine Breillat *Pro* Jean-François Lepetit, António da Cunha Telles *Ph* Laurent Machuel Film *Ed* Pascale Chavance *Pro Des* Frédérique Belvaux

CB Films / Canal+ / Centre National de la Cinématographie / Flach Film / France Télévision Images 2 / Le Studio Canal+ / Studio Images 2 / Arte France Cinéma / Artificial Eye
94 mins. France 2002. Rel: 25 July 2003. Cert 18.

Shanghai Knights ★★★★

Jackie Chan revisits the fertile ground broken by his partnership with Owen Wilson in *Shanghai Noon*. This time, ex-Imperial Guard Chon Wang and the bulletless gunfighter Roy O'Bannon find themselves in London searching for Chon Wang's sister. There is a sneering English baddie and a backflip every other scene, so all is well with the franchise. The breeziness

Left: Owen Wilson and Jackie Chan take their London sightseeing to extremes in *Shanghai Knights* (from Buena Vista)

that runs through the fight choreography, and Owen Wilson's anachronistic commentary, is a captivating mixture that is a delight all the way. And as Jackie gets older, one can but wonder how many more of these he has left in him before he makes the inevitably fatal error of 'going serious'. AK

• *Chon Wang* Jackie Chan *Roy O'Bannon* Owen Wilson *Charlie* Aaron Johnson *Artie Doyle* Thomas Fisher *Artie Gillen* Aidan Gillen *Chon Lin* Fann Wong *Wu Chan* Donnie Yen *Jack the Ripper* Oliver Cotton
• *Dir* David Dobkin *Scr* Alfred Gough, Miles Millar *Ph* Adrian Biddle *Ed* Malcolm Campbell *M* Randy Edelman *Pro Des* Allan Cameron *Action choreography* Jackie Chan *Pro* Roger Birnbaum, Gary Barber, Jonathan Glickman

All Knight Productions / Birnbaum/Barber / Jackie Chan Films Limited / Roger Birnbaum Productions / Spyglass Entertainment / Stillking / Touchstone Pictures / Buena Vista
114 mins. US/UK 2003. Rel: 4 April 2003. Cert 12A.

Shiri ★★★½

Kang Je-gyu may not be a name in Britain, but this prize-winning movie made by him in 1999 put Korean cinema on the map in both Hong Kong and Japan. Although there are echoes of *The Maltese Falcon* and *Black Sunday*, this is essentially a modern-style thriller in which violent action exists for its own sake. The hero is an agent working for intelligence in South Korea, and both he and a close colleague are in awe of the woman assassin who leads a terrorist group from North Korea. They have to trace her to save the world from a newly developed bomb described as the most dangerous in existence. Although over-long, the film is adroitly handled and the lead actress Kim Yoon-Jin impresses. It can be recommended to fans of the genre, even if it's bad timing to offer killing for entertainment in the year of the Iraq war. It's also where you have to go to hear 'Guys and Dolls' performed in Korean. MS

• *Ryu* Han Suk-Gyu *Lee* Song Kang-Ho *Hyun* Kim Yun-Jin *Park* Choi Min-Sik
• *Dir Scr* Kang Je-Gyu *Ph* Kim Seong-Bok *Ed* Park Gok-Ji *M* Lee Dong-Jun *Pro Des* Oh Sang-Man *Pro* Lee Kwan-Hak, Byun Moo-Rim

Kang Je-Kyu Film Co Ltd / Samsung Entertainment / Metro Tartan
125 mins. South Korea/HK 1999. Rel: 2 May 2003. Cert 18.

Signs ★★★½

Signs continues M Night Shyamalan's fascination with ordinary people experiencing close encounters with the extraordinary. Mel Gibson plays Graham Hess, a pastor who has lost faith in God since the death of his wife and is now raising two young children with the help of his younger brother Merrill in rural Bucks County, 45 miles outside Philadelphia. When crop circles appear in his fields, Graham struggles to hang on to a sense of normality while the world around him becomes hysterical with ET fever. Buoyed by a classic soundtrack that recalls the slow burn of a Hitchcock thriller, Shyamalan revels in a story he clearly loves. The tricks he uses are simple, almost archaic manoeuvres, like the sudden silence of crickets and the off-screen strangulation of a barking dog. However, compared to *The Sixth Sense* and *Unbreakable*, *Signs* is the Shyamalan film most vulnerable to the charge of over-indulgence. Shyamalan loads the early part of the film with heavy drama, stifling the excitement we should feel about the aliens-invading-the-earth story arc. Then, a rubbish alien and a clunky series of flashbacks mangle the finale, leaving *Signs* feeling much too... well, ordinary. AK

• *Graham Hess* Mel Gibson *Merrill Hess* Joaquin Phoenix *Morgan Hess* Rory Culkin *Bo Hess* Abigail Breslin *Officer Paski* Cherry Jones *Ray Reddy* M Night Shyamalan *Colleen Hess* Patricia Kalember
• *Dir / Scr* M Night Shyamalan *Pro* Shyamalan, Frank Marshall, Sam Mercer *Ph* Tak Fujimoto *Ed* Barbara Tulliver *M* James Newton Howard *Pro Des* Larry Fulton

Blinding Edge Pictures / The Kennedy/Marshall Company / Touchstone Pictures / Buena Vista
106 mins. USA 2002. Rel: 13 September 2002. Cert 12A.

S1m0ne ★★½

Plagued by the prima donna antics of his own star, has-been director Viktor Taranksy adopts a mad scientist's imaging technology to produce the world's first virtual superstar. As he assiduously keeps her non-humanity a secret, the distinction between the creator and the created begins to blur, especially when Taransky starts to sacrifice his personal life for that of his ethereal star... Pacino mugs all over this fanciful romantic farce, almost on autopilot. The dubious merits of the Hollywood star system get a gentle prodding, accompanied by some light riffs about pretentious autuerism and the prospect of videogame 'synthespians'. The film never quite rises to the occasion and is finally corrupted by the graceless manoeuvres it makes to secure a happy ending, more or less putting into practice everything it tried to satirise in theory. AK

• *Viktor Taransky* Al Pacino *Elaine Christian* Catherine Keener *Nicola Anders* Winona Ryder *Hank Aleno* Elias Koteas *Max Sayer* Pruitt Taylor Vince *Hal Sinclair* Jay Mohr *Milton* Jason Schwartzman *Frank Brand* Stanley Anderson *Lainey Christian* Evan Rachel Wood *Chief Detective* Daniel von Bargen *Simulation One / Simone* Rachel Roberts
• *Dir / Scr / Pro* Andrew Niccol *Ph* Edward Lachman, Derek Grover *Ed* Paul Rubell *M* Carter Burwell *Pro Des* Jan Roelfs *Costumes* Elisabetta Beraldo

New Line Cinema / Niccol Films / Entertainment
117 mins. US 2002. Rel: 25 October 2002. Cert PG.

Slap Her, She's French ★★★

Splendona, Texas; the present. Serial succeeder Starla Grady wins the local beauty pageant with a promise to play host to this year's French exchange student. When Genevieve Le Flouf arrives, a mousy mass of clichés, Starla takes her under her wing, introducing her to the notoriously tough society of the average middle-American high school. But Genevieve is not what she appears and soon usurps Starla's position at the top of the social ladder, stealing her boyfriend and robbing her cheerleading captaincy. Her vindictiveness even puts Starla in prison on the night she is meant to appear on television to win a journalism scholarship. But with the help of her precocious little brother Randolph, Starla makes her comeback... Wildly uneven but relentlessly enthusiastic, this is a teen movie that ironically denies itself a teen audience by being a little too smart. Sarcastic gags about the parochial stink of the Texan community provide the bassline beat for hard stabs at various aspects of American culture that are both satisfying and funny. AK

• *Genevieve Le Flouf / Clarissa Vog* Piper Perabo *Starla Grady* Jane McGregor *Edwin Mitchell* Trent Ford *Bootsie Grady* Julie White *Arnie Grady* Brandon Smith *Randolph Scot Grady* Jesse James *Tanner Jennings* Nicki Aycox *Ashley Lopez y Lopez* Alexandra Adi *Kyle Fuller* Matt Czuchry
• *Dir* Melanie Mayron *Scr* Lamar Damon, Robert Lee King *Pro* Beau Flynn, Jonathon King, Matthias Emcke *Ph* Charles Minsky *Ed* Marshall Harvey *Ex Pro* Matthias Deyle, Volker Shauz, Thomas Augsberger, Stefan Simchowitzh, Bernd Eichinger *Pro Des* Anne Stuhler, Roswell Hamrick *M* David Michael Frank

Bandeira Entertainment / Constantin Film Produktion GmbH / IMF Internationale Medien und Film GmbH & Co 2. Produktions KG / InterMedia Film Equities Ltd / Key Entertainment / Winchester Films
92 mins. Germany/UK/US 2002.
Rel: 18 October 2002. Cert 12A.

Små ulykker

See *Minor Mishaps*

A Snake of June ★★★½

(*Rokugatsu No Hebi*)
Tsukamoto, famous for the futuristic horror of the *Tetsuo* movies, here provides weirdness of a different kind. This is a contemporary Japanese take on sexual themes, telling the story of a wife who finds herself the target of a blackmailer. Possessing explicit photographs of her masturbating, he demands not cash but the carrying out of actions (wearing provocative clothing, buying a sex aid) which express her repressed sexual desires. The blackmailer's enjoyment of domination extends to subjecting the

husband to violence more suggestive of assault than sado-masochism. To its disadvantage the film is at times obscure and pretentious, even if the unexpectedly happy ending clearly suggests the positive side of overcoming sexual inhibitions. However, this is a film with real edge, thanks to fine performances and to quality filmmaking. The latter is evidenced by a highly atmospheric soundtrack and by very effective blue-toned monochrome photography. MS

• *Rinko Tatsumi* Asuka Kurosawa *Shigehiko* Yuji Kohtari *Iguchi* Shinya Tsukamoto *with* Mansaku Fuwa, Tomorowo Taguchi, Susumu Terajima
• *Dir / Scr / Pro / Ed / Ph / Pro Des* Shinya Tsukamoto *Ass Pro* Shin-Ichi Kawahara *M* Chu Ishikawa

Kaijyu Theater / Metro Tartan
77 mins. Japan 2002. Rel: 13 June 2003. Cert 18.

Sobibor: 14 October 1943, 16.00

★★★★★

A pendant to Claude Lanzmann's mammoth masterpiece about the Holocaust, *Shoah* of 1985, this standard-length feature documentary deals with a single incident identified as regards time and place by the film's title. This event was the only uprising against their Nazi persecutors by Jewish prisoners in a concentration camp. It is told through an interview given to Lanzmann in 1979 by one of the participants, Yehuda Lerner. Veracity is vital, so Lerner's words – he spoke in Polish – are often heard prior to subtitled translation. The pause in taking in the words allows us to contemplate the man, while footage of Sobibor itself adds to the impact. Reserved yet powerful, the film uses detail to make us experience intimately what Lerner lived through. Art at its most discreet plays a vital role in Lanzmann's splendidly realised historical document. MS

• *Dir / Scr* Claude Lanzmann *Ph* Caroline Champetier, Dominique Chapuis *Ed* Chantal Hymans, Sabine Marnou *interviewee* Yehuda Lerner

France 2 Cinéma / Les Films Aleph / Why Not Productions / ICA
95 mins. France 2001. Rel: 3 January 2003. Cert n/a

Solaris ★★★½

Steven Soderbergh, both writer and director here, regards this as a fresh take on Stanislaw Lem's science fiction novel – in other words less a remake of Tarkovsky's classic Russian film of 1971 than a variation, and a shorter one too (no excessive length here). George Clooney, on good form, plays a psychologist sent to investigate strange happenings on the planet Solaris. But this is no conventional action film. Demanding and sometimes obscure, it faces the hero with the figure of his dead wife (Natascha McElhone) and finally emerges as a tale about salvation through faith. It's interesting, but not coherent enough to satisfy fully. However, Soderbergh does have a triumph here. Under the name Peter Andrews he is responsible for some of the best and most atmospheric widescreen photography of recent years. MS

• *Chris Kelvin* George Clooney *Rheya* Natascha McElhone *Gordon* Viola Davis *Snow* Jeremy Davies *Gibarian* Ulrich Tukur *Gibarian's son* Shane Skelton

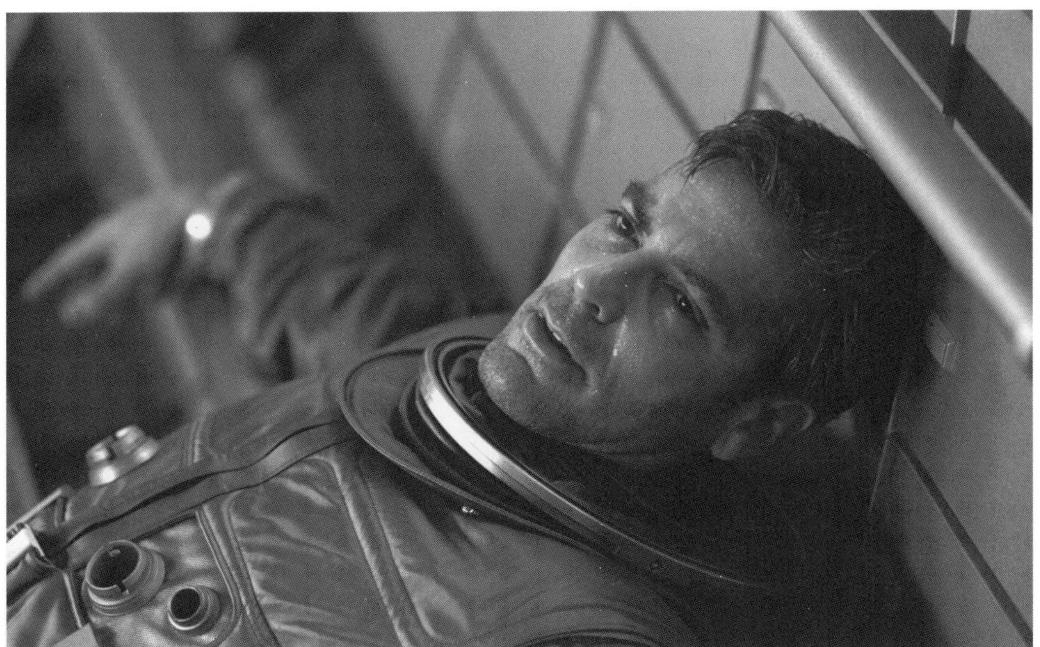

Left: George Clooney faces some psychological truths in Steven Soderbergh's triumphant *Solaris* (from Fox)

• *Dir / Scr* Steven Soderbergh, based on the book by Stanislaw Lem *Ph* Peter Andrews *Ed* Mary Ann Bernard *M* Cliff Martinez *Pro Des* Philip Messina *Pro* James Cameron, Rae Sanchini, Jon Landau *Costumes* Milena Canonero

Lightstorm Entertainment / Section Eight Ltd / USA Films / Twentieth Century Fox
98 mins. US 2002. Rel: 28 February 2003. Cert 12A.

Son of the Bride ★★½

(*El hijo de la novia*)
Absurdly over-extended at two hours, this tale of life in Buenos Aires is a comedy about a restaurant owner experiencing a mid-life crisis, while other characters are aware of guilt and failure in their lives. In other words, it should be real enough to be the kind of tragi-comedy that moves us. Instead, it's superficial and exaggerated, with a second half veering between broad and ridiculous comedy on the one hand and gross sentimentality on the other. The climax illustrates this when it shows the hero's father going through a religious marriage ceremony with the wife to whom he had previously denied this, despite the fact that she is now suffering from Alzheimer's. Add a smooth-it-over happy ending, and you can see why even a talented cast (especially Héctor Alterio and Norma Aleandro as the old couple) can't save it. MS

• *Rafael Belvedere* Ricardo Darín *Nino Belvedere* Héctor Alterio *Norma Belvedere* Norma Aleandro *Juan Carlos* Eduardo Blanco *Naty* Natalia Verbeke *Vicky* Gimena Nobile *Sandra* Claudia Fontan *Nacho* David Masajnik *Francesco* Atilio Pozzobon
• *Dir* Juan José Campanella *Scr* Campanella, Fernando Castets *Ph* Daniel Shulman *Pro* Fernando Blanco, Adrian Suar, Pablo Bossi, Jorge Estrada Mora, Gerardo Herrero, Mariela Besuievsky *Ed* Camilio Antolini *Pro Des* Mercedes Alfonsin *Costumes* Cecilia Monti *M* Ángel Illarramendi, Iván Wyszogrod

JEMPSA / Patagonik Film Group / Pol-Ka Producciones / Tornasol Films SA / Pathé
125 mins. Argentina/Spain 2001.
Rel: 23 May 2003. Cert 12A.

Le Souffle

See *Deep Breath*

Spider ★★★★

Although the initial build-up is slow, this intriguingly atmospheric drama becomes a compelling work hinging on the concept of the unreliable narrator. Here it's Dennis, known as Spider (Ralph Fiennes), through whose memories, presented in flashback, we learn of an unhappy childhood and a mother betrayed by an unfaithful husband (Gabriel Byrne). With Miranda Richardson appearing as both mother and mistress, the viewer comes to realise that we are being shown the schizoid fantasies of somebody who has never come to terms with sex. Bradley Hall justly shares star billing as the young Spider and David Cronenberg tames his excesses to direct with real sensitivity. A few scenes misfire prior to the degree of fantasy involved becoming manifest, but this is an effective and original work extremely well acted by all. MS

• *Dennis Cleg* Ralph Fiennes *Mrs Cleg* Miranda Richardson *Bill Cleg* Gabriel Byrne *Mrs Wilkinson* Lynn Redgrave *Terrence* John Neville *Freddy* Gary Reineke *Dennis as a boy* Bradley Hall
• *Dir* David Cronenberg *Scr* Patrick McGrath, based on his novel *Ph* Peter Suschitzky *Ed* Ronald Sanders *M* Howard Shore *Pro Des* Andrew Sanders *Pro* Cronenberg, Samuel Hadida and Catherine Bailey

Artists Independent Network / CBL / Capitol Films / Catherine Bailey Ltd / Davis-Films / Grosvenor Park Productions [uk] / Metropolitan Films / Helkon SK
98 mins. France/Canada/UK 2002. Rel: 3 January 2003. Cert 15.

Spirit: Stallion of the Cimarron ★★½

Spirit is the alpha mustang in a herd that lives an idyllic life on the green Cimarron plains. But when he is captured by the army, his life takes a rough turn into the world of men, where his only friend is the Red Indian boy Little Creek. Untameable, he escapes the army and nearly settles down with Rain, Little Creek's faithful mare. He decides to find his way home, however, but is again recaptured and this time put to work building a railway that would bring men into the heart of his family's untouched pastures... "The story of the Wild West told from the heart of a horse" sounds like a desperately silly idea, even for an animated feature, but at times it looks as if *Spirit: Stallion of the Cimarron* might work. But the curiously spiritless narration and the deeply banal soft-rock soundtrack (care of MOR king Bryan Adams) lock the film into two dimensions, both visually and emotionally. AK

• voices: *Spirit/narrator* Matt Damon *the Colonel* James Cromwell *Little Creek* Daniel Studi *Sergeant Adams* Chopper Bernet *Murphy* Jeff LeBeau *soldier* John Rubano
• *Dir* Kelly Asbury and Lorna Cook *Scr* John Fusco *Animation Supervisor* Kristof Serrand *Ed* Nick Fletcher *M* Hans Zimmer, with songs by Bryan Adams *Pro Des* Kathy Altieri *Pro* Mireille Soria and Jeffrey Katzenberg

DreamWorks SKG / UIP
83 mins. US 2002. Rel: 5 July 2002.
Cert U.

Springtime in a Small Town ★★★

(*Xiao cheng zhi chun*)

This is a remake of a belatedly acclaimed Chinese movie of 1948. The story it tells is one of the hoary chestnuts of melodrama: a husband in an ailing, childless arranged marriage welcomes an old friend into his house unaware that the visitor had been in love with his wife in years gone by. The slow pace means that the audience is half an hour ahead of the film in anticipating plot developments, and the director's misjudgment is confirmed by his statement that "We felt that a present-day audience would need more distance from the characters and the story." On the contrary, what is needed is a depth of characterisation to make us respond to the emotional core of the tale, however familiar. The cast is able and the film is visually stunning, but if you don't care about the characters you are left with a beautiful, empty shell. MS

• *Yuwen* Jingfan Hu *Dai Liyan* Jun Wu *Zhang Zhichen* Bai Qing Xin *Lao Huang* Xiao Keng Ye *Dai Xiu* Si Si Lu
• *Dir* Tian Zhuangzhuang *Pro* Li Xiaowan, Bill Kong, Ting Yatming *Scr* Ah Cheng, based on the story by Li Tianji and on the 1948 screenplay by Fei Mu *Ph* Mark Lee Pingbin *Ed* Xu Jianping

Beijing Film Studio / Beijing Rosart Film / China Film Group Corporation / Fortissimo Film Sales / Fortissimo Film / Orly Films / Paradis Films / Artificial Eye
116 mins. China/Hong Kong/France 2002. Rel: 13 June 2003. Cert PG.

Spy Kids 2: The Island of Lost Dreams ★★

The merchandising empire masquerading as a film series returns with barely enough time for the cast to finish promoting Robert Rodriguez's last attack of juvenilia. Juni and Carmen Cortez are this time sent to a mysterious island to recover a McGuffin of immense destructive power stolen from the President, a tragedy which the head of the OSS blames on them. So, to redeem themselves, they have to match wits with fellow OSS agents, the very blonde Gary and Gerti Giggles. There is no doubt the Spy Kids films have a box-office-busting audience. This kind of untrammelled crash-bang-wallop that portrays kids as heroes in a world of clueless adults has exactly the same compulsive appeal to under-12s as nutritionless candy. But I'll play the Grinch on this one, and wish it would all just go away. AK

• *Gregorio Cortez* Antonio Banderas *Ingrid Cortez* Carla Gugino *Carmen Cortez* Alexa Vega *Juni Cortez* Daryl Sabara *Romero* Steve Buscemi *Donnagon* Mike Judge *Machete* Danny Trejo *Felix Gumm* Cheech Marin *Gary Giggles* Matthew O'Leary *Gerti Giggles* Emily Osment *Grandfather* Ricardo Montalban *Grandmother* Holland Taylor *Fegan Floop* Alan Cumming *Alexandra* Taylor Momsen *President of the USA* Christopher McDonald
• *Dir / Scr / Ed / Ph / Pro Des* Robert Rodriguez *M* Rodriguez, John Debney *Pro* Elizabeth Avellan, Rodriguez

Dimension Films / Troublemaker Studios / Buena Vista
99 mins. US 2002. Rel: 16 August 2002. Cert U.

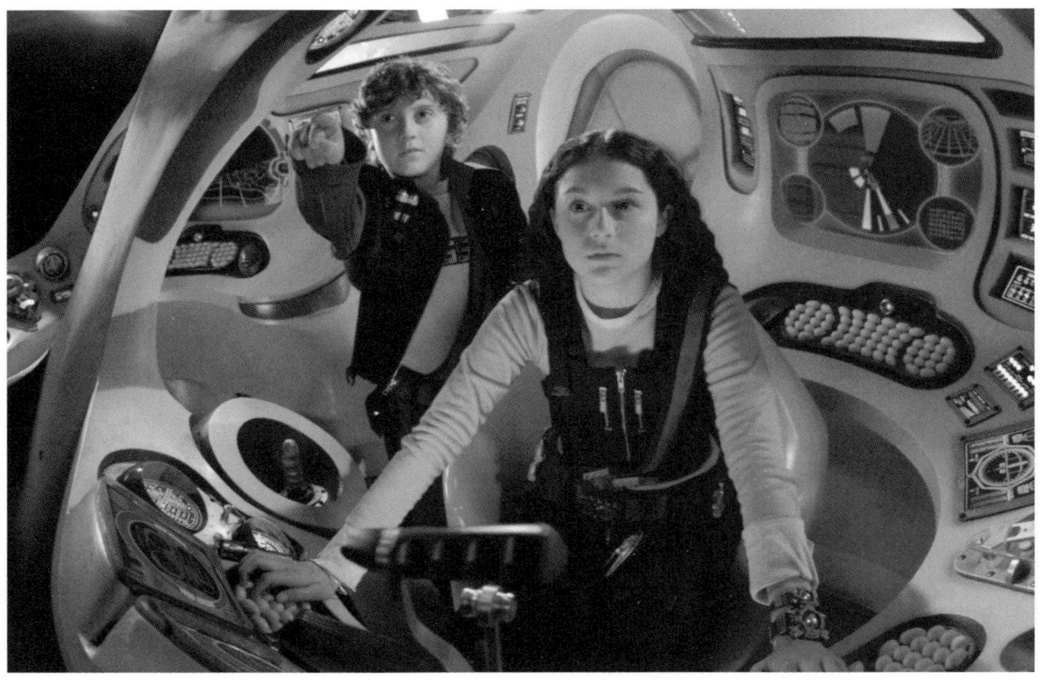

Left: Daryl Sabara and Alexa Vega in Robert Rodriguez' lacklustre *Spy Kids: The Island of Lost Dreams* (from Buena Vista)

Above: Michael Dorn, Brent Spiner, Jonathan Frakes, LeVar Burton (seated) and Patrick Stewart are still trekkin' in the disappointing *Star Trek: Nemesis* (from UIP)

Star Trek: Nemesis ★½

The tenth Trek film sees the Enterprise caught up again in a bid to save the Federation from an insidious plan to destroy it. This time, the crew members are lured into a Romulan plot by a clone of Captain Jean-Luc Picard, the bitter and charismatic Shinzon. While Picard and the crew are dealing with the revelation that Picard has been doubled, Commander Data comes to grips (literally) with a prototype of himself that was salvaged from space. By a long and bumpy warp, we arrive at a cataclysmic finale that feels like an extended traffic safety video for Federation starships. The film pays homage to the first TV series, which consistently had James T Kirk wrestling with some aspect of his own psyche. Appropriately, Picard's verbal fencing with Shinzon is pseudo-psychology at its worst, and the Data-meets-Beta side-plot is a thin parallel. Despite the circumstances, Patrick Stewart has no excuse for turning in such a flabby and disappointing performance. AK

• *Captain Jean-Luc Picard* Patrick Stewart *Data / Beta-4* Brent Spiner *Geordi La Forge* LeVar Burton *William Riker* Jonathan Frakes *Commander Suran* Jude Ciccolella *Senator Tal'aura* Shannon Cochran *Preator Hiran* Alan Dale *Reman officer* Robertson Dean *Worf* Michael Dorn *Shinzon* Tom Hardy *Beverly Crusher* Gates McFadden *Commander Donatra* Dina Meyer *Kathryn Janeway* Kate Mulgrew *Deanna Troi* Marina Sirtis *Guinan* Whoopi Goldberg *computer* Majel Barrett
• *Dir* Stuart Baird *Scr* John Logan, Brent Spiner, Rick Berman *Pro* Rick Berman *Co Pro* Peter Lauritson *Ed* Dallas Puett *Ph* Jeffrey Kimball *Ex Pro* Marty Hornstein *M* Jerry Goldsmith

Paramount Pictures / UIP
116 mins. US 2002. Rel: 3 January 2003. Cert 12A.

Stark Raving Mad ★★

There's obviously an audience for this sort of film, but it's not going to give Guy Ritchie any sleepless nights. Set in a rave club in the heart of Chinatown, the movie stars Seann William Scott as a hustler indebted to a ruthless mobster (Lou Diamond Phillips with spectacles and peroxide hair-do). The idea is that Scott will use the club as a cover for his break into the bank next door, the pounding music disabling the vault's sonic detector alarm system. However, there are a few personal, sexual, criminal and drug-related complications… Although directed with some style and energy, the film's real saving grace is Scott (last seen in *Evolution* and *American Pie 2*), who makes a tough, sexy leading man, not unlike a young Patrick Swayze with edge. JC-W

• *Ben McGewen* Seann William Scott *Jeffrey Jay* Patrick Breen *Jin Sun* Terry Chen *Jake Nealson* John Crye *Roy* Dave Foley *Scott* Paul Hungerford *Vanessa* Monet Mazur *Mr Gregory* Lou Diamond Phillips *Don Partridge* Adam Arkin *with* Suzi Nakamura, Reagan Dale Neis, Timm Sharpe, Kavan Smith, Jody Racicot, Ty Olsson
• *Dir / Scr* Drew Daywalt and David Schneider *Pro* John Baldecchi *Ex Pro* Christopher Ball, Lawrence Bender, Aaron Ryder and William Tyrer *Ass Pro* Nicole Pennington *Ph* Chuck Cohen *Pro Des* Keith Brian Burns *Ed* Hughes Winborne *M* John Digweed *Costumes* Alisa Krost

Newmarket / Summit Entertainment / Lawrence Bender Prods-Helkon SK
101 mins. USA 2002. Rel: 24 January 2003. Cert 15.

Stealing Harvard ★★½

Directed by *Kids in the Hall* alumnus Bruce McCulloch, *Stealing Harvard* is a hit and miss comedy about a man torn between two promises. Years ago, John Plummer promised his niece that he'd pay for her college education. Now she needs the $30,000 he's saved up with his fiancé to buy their first house just prior to their wedding. Under the dubious tutelage of best friend Walter 'Duff' Duffy (Tom Green), John and Duff decide to steal the money necessary for John to fulfil both his commitments. A series of comical misadventures ensues, most of it genuinely funny and showcasing the excellent comedic chemistry between Jason Lee and Tom Green. Moreover, the story never really goes exactly where you'd expect, which is a delight. SWM

• *Walter 'Duff' Duffy* Tom Green *John Plummer* Jason Lee *Elaine Warner* Leslie Mann *Patty Plummer* Megan Mullally *Mr Warner* Dennis Farina *Noreen Plummer* Tammy Blanchard *Honorable Emmet Cook* Richard Jenkins *David Loach* Chris Penn *Detective Charles* John C McGinley
• *Dir* Bruce McCulloch *Scr* Peter Tolan; story by Martin Hynes and Tolan *Ph* Ueli Steiger *Ed* Malcolm Campbell *M* Christophe Beck *Pro Des* Gregory Keen *Pro* Susan Cavan

Imagine Entertainment / Revolution Studios / Columbia TriStar
85 mins. US 2002. Rel: 14 March 2003. Cert 12A.

Stuart Little 2 ★★★

If the idea of two grown-ups adopting a mouse as a son wasn't weird enough, the rodent is now attending high school alongside a herd of non-judgmental homo-sapien kids. In this age of predetermined cynicism, one has to doff one's hat to the twee innocence of this franchise. Nevertheless, it is the sardonic wisecracks of the Littles' cat Snowbell (superbly timed by Nathan Lane) that win the biggest laughs. Having said that, scenarist Bruce Joel Rubin (who previously penned the nightmarish *Jacob's Ladder*) does come up with a decent story. Now that Mr and Mrs Little have a baby daughter and George Little has a new best friend, Stuart is feeling left out of the domestic fold. He then meets a bird with a wounded wing, invites her home and grows desperately fond of her. But the pretty little stranger has an ulterior motive... Cute. JC-W

• *Mrs Little* Geena Davis *Mr Little* Hugh Laurie *George Little* Jonathan Lipnicki *voice of Stuart Little* Michael J Fox *voice of Snowbell* Nathan Lane *voice of Margalo* Melanie Griffith *voice of Monty* Steve Zahn *voice of Falcon* James Woods
• *Dir* Rob Minkoff *Pro* Douglas Wick and Lucy Fisher *Ex Pro* Minkoff, Jason Clark, Jeff Franklin and Steve Waterman *Scr* Bruce Joel Rubin, from a story by Rubin and Wick *Ph* Steven B Poster *Pro Des* Bill Brzeski *Ed* Priscilla Nedd-Friendly *M* Alan Silvestri *Costumes* Mona May

Global Entertainment Prods/Columbia Pictures-Columbia TriStar.
77 mins. USA 2002. Rel: 19 July 2002. Cert U.

Above: French connection – Jacques Dutronc and Charlotte Rampling prepare for *les vacances* in *Summer Things* (from UGC)

Summer Things ★★★★

(*Embrassez qui vous voudrez*)

This stylish French farce from an unlikely source (it's based on a British novel) breaks the rules of the genre to good effect. Set principally in the holiday resort of Le Touquet, it plays around with a large cast of characters (friends, business associates, teenagers, couples) and entertains us with unexpected new permutations and other surprises. What is truly startling, however, is that instead of being puppets the characters grow in emotional credibility until, albeit with a light touch, the film becomes a comment on the absurdity of human behaviour. Director Michel Blanc draws the short straw as a jealous husband, but there are fine contributions from those in better roles, including Carole Bouquet and, best of all, Charlotte Rampling. The latter's sense of style is more than a surface matter, bringing together elegance and emotion and giving meaning to both. MS

• *Elizabeth Lannier* Charlotte Rampling *Bertrand Lannier* Jacques Dutronc *Lulu* Carole Bouquet *Jean Pierre* Michel Blanc *Véronique* Karin Viard *Jérôme* Denis Podalydès *Julie* Clotilde Courau *Maxime* Vincent Elbaz *Emilie* Lou Doillon *Kevin* Sami Bouajila *Loïc* Gaspard Ulliel *Carole* Mélanie Laurent *Romain* Mathieu Boujenah *Rena/Nanou* Mickaël Dolmen *Pauline* Barbara Kelsch *Dr Davy* Nicolas Briançon *Mme Davy* Jade Phan-Gia *Samuel* Serge Brincat *Clotilde* Hélène Pecqueur
• *Dir / Scr* Michel Blanc, based on *Summer Things* by Joseph Connolly *Pro* Julie Baines, Enzo Porcelli (as Franco Vincenzo Porcelli) *M* Mark Russell *Ph* Sean Bobbitt *Ed* Maryline Monthieux *Pro Des* Benoît Barouh

Alia Film / Canal+ / Dan Films / France 2 Cinéma / La Sofica Sofinergie 5 / Le Studio Canal+ / Mercury Film Productions / UGC Images / UGC YM / UGC Films UK
103 mins. France/UK 2003. Rel: 20 June 2003. Cert 15.

Sunshine State ★★½

John Sayles' curiously nostalgic ensemble drama (about a sleepy Florida island community kicked awake by a big developer's plans to buy it out) has going for it a cast that acts its collective socks off. Sitting on the other end of the see-saw is an irony far too subtle to justify its extended running time, forcing an audience to look far too closely at the subverted stereotypes that usually make up the 'small community vs big developer' genre. Sayles abides by some conventions: the developers are uncaring and the small-towners are substantial, idiosyncratic and charming. But the social ideals that are supposed to stand against capitalism are not so clear. The most prominent character, motel manager Marly Temple, actually welcomes the thought of selling up. In fact, without the subtext, this is simply a decent, low-budget social drama looking for a shorter edit. AK

• *Marly Temple* Edie Falco *Delia Temple* Jane Alexander *Furman Temple* Ralph Waite *Desiree Perry* Angela Bassett *Reggie Perry* James McDaniel *Eunice Stokes* Mary Alice *Dr Lloyd* Bill Cobbs *Earl Pickney* Gordon Clapp *Francine Pickney* Mary Steenburgen *Jack Meadows* Timothy Hutton *Flash Phillips* Tom Wright *Scotty Duval* Marc Blucas *Lester* Miguel Ferrer *Loretta* Charlayne Woodard *Murray Silver* Alan King *Steve Tregaskis* Richard Edson *Terrell Bernard* Alexander Lewis
• *Dir / Scr / Ed* John Sayles *Ph* Patrick Cady *M* Mason Daring *Pro Des* Mark Ricker *Pro* Maggie Renzi

Anarchist's Convention Films / Green/Renzi / Columbia TriStar
140 mins. US 2002. Rel: 26 July 2002. Cert 15.

Super Troopers ★★★★

The State Troopers patrolling the highways outside Spurbury fight a running feud with the local police force, led by Chief Grady. When budget cuts threaten to close down the State Troopers, its fun-lovin', pot-smokin', tail-chasin' officers realise they have to impress the Governor if they are to survive. When huge shipments of marijuana start appearing under the brand of an Afghanistani cartoon monkey (prompting the lame but tenaciously memorable line "Afghanimation! It's great!"), they get their chance, though only if Chief Grady doesn't beat them to it… If *Monthy Python's Flying Circus* mated *Smokey & The Bandit* with *Police Academy*, and dosed the results with a dash of *South Park*'s anti-Canadianism (for that inbred Vermont flavour), *Super Troopers* would be the idiot savant love-child of that union. The members of Broken Lizard, the comedy group who created and star in the film, deliver the most infectious piss-take comedy to come out of America since *Best in Show*. AK

• *Thorny* Jay Chandrasekhar *Farva* Kevin Heffernan *Mac* Steve Lemme *Foster* Paul Soter *Rabbit* Erik Stolhanske *Capt John O' Hagan* Brian Cox *Chief Grady* Daniel Von Bargen *Ursula* Marisa Coughlan *Governor Jessman* Lynda Carter *Mayor Timber* John Bedford Lloyd *Larry Johnson* Jim Gaffigan
• *Dir* Jay Chandrasekhar *Scr* Broken Lizard *Ed* Jumbulingam Chandrasekhar, Kevin Heffernan *Ph* Joaquin Baca-Asay *M* 38 Special *Pro* Richard Perello

Broken Lizard Productions / Cataland Films / Fox Searchlight Pictures / Jersey Shore / Twentieth Century Fox
100 mins. US 2002. Rel: 15 November 2002. Cert 15.

Sweet Home Alabama ★★★

When the New York mayor's son proposes to Melanie Carmichael, the ingenue fashionista and Alabama refugee is forced to return to her hometown to secure her divorce from Jake Perry, her childhood sweetheart, whom she left at the altar many moons ago. But she finds that Jake is not so eager to sign on the dotted line. Things are complicated further when the suspicious mayor investigates her past, because Melanie's folks aren't quite the gentrified bluebloods she made them out to be… A by-the-numbers romcom that lifts itself above the usual level via Reese Witherspoon's smile alone, *Sweet Home Alabama* coasts through the clichéd otherness of a South that annually re-enacts the Civil War and is stubbornly proud of its apparent backwardness. But there's enough charm here to overcome the gooey sweetness of an improbably painless ending. AK

Left: Reese Witherspoon lands on the wrong side of the law in *Sweet Home Alabama* (from Buena Vista)

• *Melanie Carmichael/Smooter* Reese Witherspoon *Jake Perry* Josh Lucas *Andrew Hennings* Patrick Dempsey *Kate Hennings* Candice Bergen *Pearl Smooter* Mary Kay Place *Earl Smooter* Fred Ward *Stella Kay* Jean Smart *Bobby Ray* Ethan Embry *Lurlynn* Melanie Lynskey
• *Dir* Andy Tennant *Scr* C Jay Cox, based on a story by Douglas J Eboch *Ph* Andrew Dunn *Ed* Troy Takaki, Tracey Wadmore-Smith *M* George Fenton *Pro Des* Clay A Griffith *Pro* Neal H Moritz, Stokely Chaffin

**D&D Films / Original Film / Pigeon Creek Films / Touchstone Pictures / Buena Vista
108 mins. US 2002. Rel: 20 December 2002.
Cert 12A.**

Sweet Sixteen ★★★½

Anybody who's seen a film by Ken Loach will know not to expect a slick, feel-good comedy. And in the tradition of *Ladybird Ladybird*, *My Name is Joe* and *Bread and Roses*, Loach again focuses on disorientated, under-privileged, salt-of-the-earth people. *Sweet Sixteen*, filmed in and around the former shipbuilding town of Greenock, outside Glasgow, is, if anything, one of his least compromising works to date. To make his point, Loach steers clear of any shadow of Hollywood artifice, not only hiring unknowns but also non-professionals. His ace card is that he can connect with these people and draw extraordinary performances out of them. *Sweet Sixteen* is the story of a 15-year-old lad, Liam, who routinely flouts the law but has found a centre of decency in spite of his parents' criminal activities. With two months to go before his mother is released from prison, Liam decides to save up for a caravan, so that he and she can live away from the abuse of his father. Much of the film is unintelligible (it starts out with subtitles), but is redeemed by a rare spontaneity and human warmth and, above all, a remarkable central performance from Martin Compston, whose first acting stint this is. JC-W

• *Liam* Martin Compston *Pinball* William Ruane *Chantelle* Annmarie Fulton *Suzanne* Michelle Abercromby *Jean* Michelle Coulter *Stan* Gary McCormack *Rab* Tommy McKee *Calum* Calum McAlees *Scullion* Robert Rennie
• *Dir* Ken Loach *Pro* Rebecca O'Brien *Co Pro* Ulrich Felsberg and Gerardo Herrero *Line Pro* Peter Gallagher *Scr* Paul Laverty *Ph* Barry Ackroyd *Pro Des* Martin Johnson *Ed* Jonathan Morris *M* George Fenton *Costumes* Carole K Millar

**Sixteen Films / Road Movies / Tornasol / Alta Films / Scottish Screen / BBC Films-Icon
106 mins. UK/Germany/Spain 2002.
Rel: 4 October 2002.
Cert 18.**

Swimf@n ★★

Swimf@n aims to be a psychological thriller for teenysomethings, and succeeds well enough in terms of mood and casting. However, the lack of psychological depth plus plastic dialogue and confused editing hobbles its dynamics. So much rides on Erika Christensen as Madison, the femme fatale who stalks Ben, the school swimming stud, but her drugged-out slacker delivery melts the necessary menace into a puddle of soapy made-for-TV goop. And the final act is laughably rushed. AK

• *Ben* Jesse Bradford *Madison* Erika Christensen *Amy* Shiri Appleby *Carla* Kate Burton *Josh* Clayne Crawford *Randy* Jason Ritter *Rene* Kia Joy Goodwin *Coach Simkins* Dan Hedaya
• *Dir* John Polson *Scr* Charles Bohl and Phillip Schneider *Pro* John Penotti, Allison Lyon Segan and Joe Caracciolo Jr *Ph* Giles Nuttgens *Ed* Sarah Flack *M* Louis Febre, John Debney *Pro Des* Kalina Ivanov

Cobalt Media Group / Forrest Films / Further Films / GreeneStreet Films Inc / Icon 85 mins. US 2002. Rel: 20 September 2002. Cert 12A.

The Sum of All Fears ★★½

A wayward Israeli warhead is recovered by a European cartel that wants to start World War III. It falls to young CIA analyst Jack Ryan, the ubiquitous hero of the political thrillers based on Tom Clancy's novels, to unmask this Machiavellian plan and prevent the detonation of a nuclear bomb on US soil... Given the reality of terrorism in modern-day America, *The Sum of All Fears* falters on almost every front. Neither dark enough to be taken seriously, nor glossy enough to distance itself from recent history, it goes through the motions like a shadowboxing fighter, making the devastation in its third act feel oddly inconsequential. Good actors abound but aren't given enough to do. We should at least be grateful that the filmmakers kept gung-ho American patriotism at a palatable level. AK

• *Jack Ryan* Ben Affleck *William Cabot* Morgan Freeman *President Fowler* James Cromwell *Dressler* Alan Bates *Defense Secretary Becker* Philip Baker Hall *Secretary of State Owens* Ron Rifkin *Revell* Bruce McGill *President Nemerov* Ciaran Hinds *Cathy Muller* Bridget Moynahan
• *Dir* Phil Alden Robinson *Scr* Paul Attanasio and Daniel Pyne, based on the novel by Tom Clancy *Ph* John Lindley *Ed* Neil Travis *M* Jerry Goldsmith *Pro Des* Jeannine Oppewall *Pro* Mace Neufeld

MFP Munich Film Partners GmbH & Company I. Produktions KG / Mace Neufeld Productions / Paramount Pictures / UIP
123 mins. US/Germany 2002.
Rel: 16 August 2002.
Cert 12A.

The Sweetest Thing ★

Three hip singletons despair of ever meeting Mr Right and decide to beat the lads at their own game by being cruder, louder and more aggressive on a road trip into the suburbs, where they finally admit to themselves that what they really want is 'love'. That is the wafer-thin excuse for perhaps the worst movie ever to feature three such beautiful (and pretty talented) actresses. The grinding run of bewilderingly bad jokes includes a po-faced musical number titled 'The Penis Song', a fellatio accident (the old 'cock-piercing stuck on dental work' trick) and a group feel-up in the ladies' room to prove whose fake boobs are the most 'real'. Both cast and crew are sucked up in the implosion of bad taste and have no means of escape. AK

• *Christina* Cameron Diaz *Courtney* Christina Applegate *Peter* Thomas Jane *Jane* Selma Blair *Roger* Jason Bateman *Judy* Parker Posey
• *Dir* Roger Kumble *Scr* Nancy M Pimental *Ph* Anthony B Richmond *Ed* Wendy Greene Bricmont, David Rennie *M* Edward Shearmur *Pro Des* Jon Gary Steele *Pro* Cathy Konrad

Columbia Pictures Corporation / Konrad Pictures / Columbia TriStar
88 mins. US 2002. Rel: 30 August 2002.

Below: Morgan Freeman lends his usual gravitas to *The Sum of All Fears* (from UIP)

Tableau de famille / Le fate ignoranti

See *His Secret Life*

Tadpole ★★★

It seems to have been the year for upper-Manhattan sex comedies starring precocious Holden Caulfield clones. But alongside the very impressive *Igby Goes Down*, this digitally shot, low-budget black comedy looks very much like a poor relation. The tyro of the piece is Voltaire-quoting Oscar Grubman, who is set on losing his virginity to his ideal woman, his stepmother Eve. He is, ahem, waylaid by Eve's best friend Diane, who treats him like a 15-year-old sex toy, at one point recommending his services to her other friends. Meanwhile, Oscar is undergoing all kinds of sophisticated, angsty crises about 'betraying' his one true love. Beneath the urbane and pseudo-intellectual setting, this is really a French sex farce that owes more to the sensibilities of Woody Allen than it wants to admit. Amusing, fabulously cast and deliciously risqué, it still falls well short of the excellent film it could have become given more money and another polish on the script. AK

• *Oscar Grubman* Aaron Stanford *Eve Grubman* Sigourney Weaver *Stanley Grubman* John Ritter *Diane* Bebe Neuwirth
• *Dir* Gary Winick *Pro* Dolly Hall, Alex Alexanian, Winick *Ex Pro* Jonathan Sehring, Caroline Kaplan, John Sloss *Scr* Heather McGowan, Niels Mueller *Ph* Hubert Taczanowski *Ed* Susan Littenberg *M* Renaud Pion *Costumes* Suzanne Schwarzer *Pro Des* Anthony Gasparro *Art Director* Sara Parks

Dolly Hall Productions / IFC Productions / InDigEnt / Buena Vista
78 mins. US 2002. Rel: 20 June 2003. Cert 15.

Take Care of My Cat ★★★½

(*Goyangileul butaghae*)
To have a feature from Korea is something of a novelty in itself and Jeong Jae-eun's film is an agreeable piece, set in Seoul and Inchon, contrasting the fates of five girls, all in their twenties and from the same school. One is a career girl, another has her wings clipped by belonging to a family dominated by the father, the third is being brought up by poor grandparents and the other two are twins with a Chinese mother repudiated by their grandfather. A cat passes from hand to hand, further linking these friends as their individual tales develop. The acting is good and the film brings out the contrasting lifestyles, but ultimately it seems rather thin and overstretched at 112 minutes. That's why, pleasant though it is, it leaves one with a faint sense of disappointment. MS

• *Yoo Tae Hee* Bae Doo Na*Shin Hye Joo* Lee Yo WanSeo Ji young Ok Ji Young *Biryu* Lee Eun Shil *Onjo* Lee Eun Joo and *Uhm Chan Yong* Oh Tae Kyung.
• *Dir / Scr* Jeong Jae-eun *Ph* Choi Young Hwan *Ed* Lee Hyun Mee *M* M & F *Art Dir* Kim Jin Chul *Pro* Oh Gi Min

Masulpiri Films / Millennium Film Distribution
112 mins. South Korea 2001. Rel: 27 December 2002. Cert PG.

Above: Pedro Almodóvar directs a scene from his stylish, flamboyant *Talk to Her* (from Pathé)

Talk to Her ★★★★½

(*Hable con ella*)
At one time talented but overrated, Pedro Almodóvar has reached maturity as evidenced by *All About My Mother* and now confirmed by the stylish *Talk to Her*, a fine film brilliantly acted. Its tale of two women in a coma, one a bullfighter, and of the men who yearn for them (a journalist, a nurse and another bullfighter) features flamboyant, even controversial, elements. But the potential melodrama is played down, allowing us to sense a broad range of sympathy reminiscent of Renoir. Fans may pick out the surrealistic and erotic film within the film, but that's the bit which doesn't quite belong (it suggests the Woody Allen of *Everything You Wanted to Know About Sex But Were Afraid to Ask*). More importantly, though, this is at heart a film about loneliness, even more subtle and affecting than Mike Leigh's *All Or Nothing*. Not quite perfect, but very, very impressive. MS

• *Benigno* Javier Cámara *Marco* Darío Grandinetti *Alicia* Leonor Watling *Lydia* Rosario Flores *Katarina* Geraldine Chaplin *Rosa* Mariola Fuentes *Matilde* Lola Dueñas
• *Dir / Scr* Pedro Almodóvar *Ph* Javier Aguirresarobe *Ed* José Salcedo *M* Alberto Iglesias *Pro Des* Antxon Gómez *Pro* Agustín Almodóvar

El Deseo SA / Antena 3 Televisión / Good Machine / Vía Digital / Pathé
113 mins. Spain 2002. Rel: 23 August 2002. Cert 15.

Tape ★★½

Set entirely in a dark motel room in Lansing, Michigan, *Tape* explores the resentments built up over the years in two male friends, both of whom once loved the same woman. Claustrophobic, self-consciously theatrical and passionately determined, there is nevertheless the strong suspicion that Richard Linklater and his three actors should have put in a little more time honing their lo-fi exercise before unleashing it in so raw a state. It doesn't take long for Ethan Hawke's character to establish his pathetic and angry insecurity, but it is a theme replayed to the detriment of the ensemble, obscuring the subtler emotions. The heavy, relentless tone and lack of sympathetic focus in a piece this sustained is eventually too much for the otherwise committed performances to bear, making a short film feel grindingly long. AK

• *Vince* Ethan Hawke *Johnny* Robert Sean Leonard *Amy* Uma Thurman
• *Dir* Richard Linklater *Scr* Stephen Belber *Ph* Maryse Alberti *Ed* Sandra Adair *Pro Des* Stephen J Beatrice *Pro* Alex Alexanian, John Sloss, Anne Walker-McBay, Gary Winick

Detour Film Production / IFC Productions / InDigEnt / Tape Productions Inc / Metrodome
88 mins. US 2001. Rel: 12 July 2002. Cert 15.

Ted Bundy

See *Bundy*

Ten ★★★★½

The Circle is just one of several examples of recent Iranian cinema concentrating on the situation of women in that country. Consequently, Abbas Kiarostami's latest, in which a divorced woman taxi driver in Tehran is the central figure, is not in the vanguard. It's also the case that the decision to keep the largely static camera in the taxi throughout is a formal device that can seem wearing, even if it does represent the constraint in the lives of the female characters. But, in portraying ten journeys, the film becomes startlingly direct in advocating attitudes for women that break wholly with traditional Iranian ways. There's also a marvellously arresting scene between the mother and her critical young son. Regardless of minor criticisms, it's clearly a major work by one of the world's best directors, but with content even more important than style. MS

• *driver* Mania Akbari *Amin* Amin Maher *passengers* Roya Arabshahi, Katayoun Taleidzadeh, Mandana Sharbaf, Amene Moradi
• *Dir / Scr* Abbas Kiarostami *Ed* Abbas Kiarostami, Morteza Tabatabaii, Bahman Kiarostami, Mastaneh Mohajer, Mazdak Sepanlu, Reza Yadzdani, Vahid Ghazi Kamran Adl *M* Howard Blake *Pro* Marin Karmitz, Abbas Kiarostami

Abbas Kiarostami Productions / MK2 Productions / ICA
93 mins. France/Iran 2002. Rel: 27 September 2002. Cert 12A.

They ★★★

When Billy was six, he was afraid of the dark. Once his bedroom light was turned out, he'd imagine strange beings shifting in the shadows, waiting to pounce. Now that Billy is 25 he knows that his childhood impressions were not the stuff of an over-active imagination. Now 'They' have come to reclaim him. Or so he tells his childhood friend, Julia Lund. Julia was also haunted by 'night terrors' as a child but, now that she's a psychology student, she knows that these fears are merely paranoid delusions. Silly girl. 'They' have come to get her, too... There's the germ of a good idea here and Laura Regan is a photogenic guide to our worst fears (she was last terrorised in *My Little Eye*). The film is also competently directed, working on the assumption that what we don't see is scarier than what we do. The sound effects do a lot of the work and while the cumulative effect is unsettling, it's a shame that the plot is so underdeveloped. JC-W

• *Julia Lund* Laura Regan *Paul* Marc Blucas *Sam* Ethan Embry *Terry* Dagmara Dominczyk *Billy* Jon Abrahams *Mrs Levin* Wanda Cannon *Mary Parks* Desiree Zurowski *young Billy* Alexander Gould *little girl* Jessica Amlee
• *Dir* Robert Harmon *Pro* Tom Engelman and Scott Kroopf *Ex Pro* Ted Field and David Linde *Co Pro* Barbara Kelly and Tony Blain *Scr* Brendan William Hood *Ph* Rene Ohashi *Pro Des* Douglas Higgins *Ed* Chris Peppe *M* Elia Cmiral, *Costumes* Karen Matthews *Sound* Anne Bakker *Creature design* Patrick Tatopoulos *Visual effects* Kyle Menzies

Dimension Films / Focus Features / Wes Craven / Radar Pictures-Entertainment
89 mins. USA 2002. Rel: 1 November 2002. Cert 15.

Thorns ★★

(*Kaante*)

Notable for being the first contemporary Bollywood potboiler, but universally condemned for its lack of focus, there is nevertheless something deliciously charming about the idea of an all-singing, all-dancing Hindi rehash of *Reservoir Dogs*, *The Usual Suspects* and *Rififi*. The rather long and, yes, occasionally tedious film about six shady types who meet up in a jail cell and decide to rob the bank that holds the police payroll, only to be betrayed by one of their own, is a shameless crib from the Tarantino style-book. Were it not for director Sanjay Gupta's lack of discipline and imagination, it could have been a kitsch classic, boasting some fine performances. AK

• *Yashvardhan Rampal/Major* Amitabh Bachchan *Jay Rehan/Ajju* Sanjay Dutt *Marc Isaak/the bouncer* Sunil Shetty *Anand Mathur/Andy* Kumar Gaurav *Raj Yadav/Baali* Mahesh Manjrekar *Maqbool Haider/Mak* Lucky Ali
• *Dir* Sanjay Gupta *Scr* Gupta, Milap Zaveri, Anurag Kashyap *Ph* Kurt Brabbee *Ed* Bunty Nagi *M* Viju Sha, Lucky Ali, Anand Raj Anand, Gregor Narholz, Vishal-Shekhar *Pro* Gupta, Raju Sharad Patel *Pro Des* Peter Jamison, Linda Spheeris *Costumes* Akbar Gabbana, Jerry Ross *Choreography* Neisha Folkes-LeMelle

Pritesh Nandy Communications / Bollywood Pictures
151 mins. India 2002. Rel: 19 December 2002. Cert 15.

Time of Favour ★★★★

(*Hahesdar*)
Israel, the present. Menachem and Pini are best friends in a religious Torah academy run by the charismatic Rabbi Meltzer. The Rabbi looks to army officer Menachem to train a special army unit made up of recruits from his school, but favours the scholar Pini with his daughter Michal's hand in marriage. But Michal rejects Pini for Menachem, causing rifts in their friendship that lead to extreme consequences… Joseph Cedar's film shifts confidently from naturalism to soapy drama, the former being far more interesting, examining the tensions between the secular and religious in Israeli society. Essentially, though, the film is really about the fight to stay human in an atmosphere polluted by warring ideologies. Because of this emotional core, *Time of Favour* feels remarkably honest in spite of its rather plain 'psychological thriller' skin. MS

• *Menachem* Aki Avni Michal *Tinkerbell Pini* Edan Alterman *Rabbi Meltzer* Assi Dayan *Itamar* Micha Selektar *Mookie* Amnon Volf
• *Dir / Scr* Joseph Cedar *Pro* David Mandil, Eyal Shiray *Ph* Ofer Inov *Ed* Tova Asher *Costumes* Etiti Lugassi. *M* Yonatan Bar-Giora *Pro Des* Yair Greenberg, Ofer Rachanim

Cinema Factory Production Ltd / Israel Film Fund / Yes Productions / Blue Dolphin
102 mins. Israel 2000. Rel: 2 August 2002. Cert 12A.

To Kill a King ★★★

But for the determination of its star Dougray Scott, this romantic dramatisation of Oliver Cromwell's short-lived republic could have been subtitled *To Kill a Movie*. The demise of FilmFour reined in the film's already slim budget, and it was only through Scott's bloody-minded determination to see a decent script get made that a new financier was unearthed. And 'bloody' is a good word for it; the opening frame pans down from a decomposed corpse on a gibbet,

Below: Rupert Everett makes an unlikely Charles I in *To Kill a King* (Pathé)

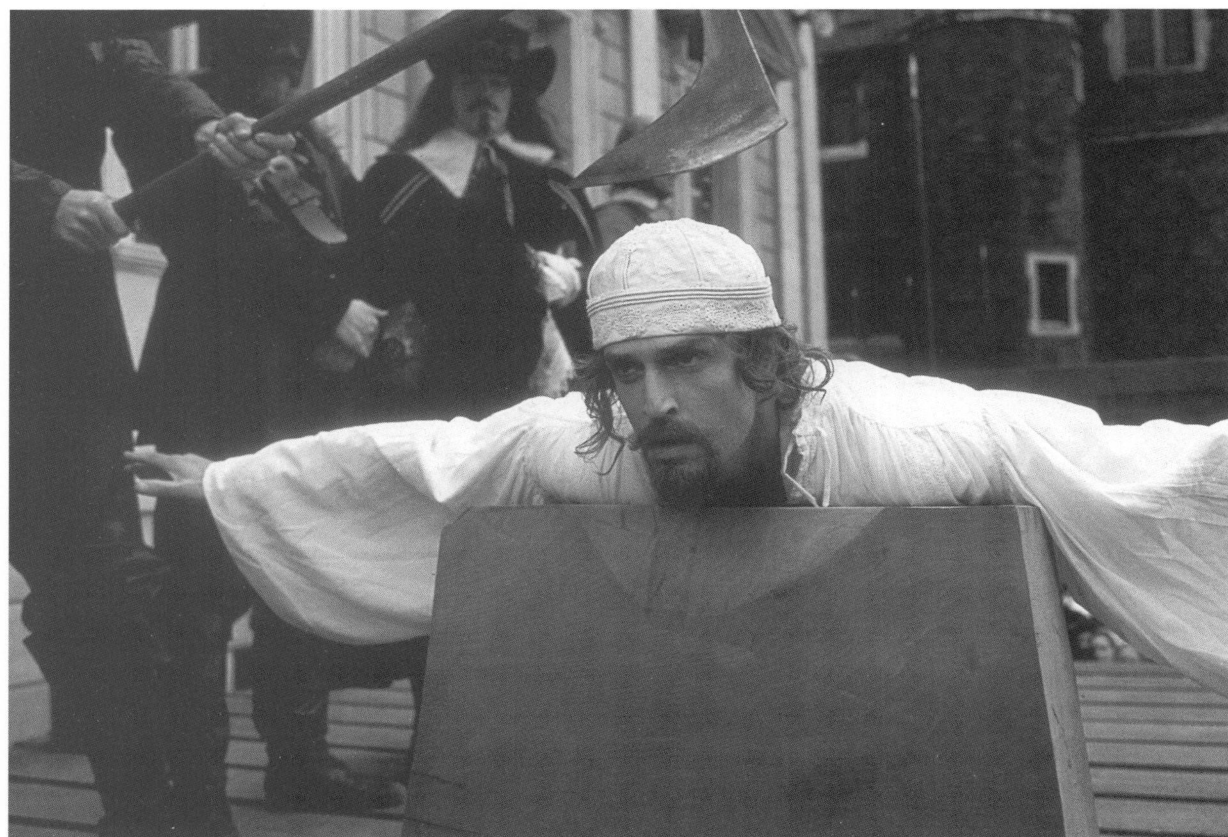

then downshifts the years to one of the final battles of 1645. Cue corpses piled high, field surgeons with sharp saws, loud screaming in Dolby Surround. First impressions aside, the film is not about pitched battles against the King's troops. Instead it blends political intrigue with a liberally dramatised 'buddy' interpretation of the relationship between Lord General Fairfax and Oliver Cromwell (played by Tim Roth with his usual rat-like intensity). The heavy brooding leans a bit too much towards melodrama, but the film does eventually find its centre in the tortured triangle of Oliver Cromwell, Lord Fairfax and Lady Anne Fairfax, delivering a historical pageant to match most of its ambitions. AK

• *General/Lord Protector Oliver Cromwell* Tim Roth *General Thomas Fairfax* Dougray Scott *King Charles I* Rupert Everett *Lady Anne Fairfax* Olivia Williams *Baron Denzil Holles* James Bolam *Lord de Vere* Corin Redgrave *Cousin Henry* Finbar Lynch *James* Julian Rhind-Tutt *Sergeant Joyce* Adrian Scarborough
• *Dir* Mike Barker *Scr* Jenny Mayhew *Ph* Eigil Bryld *Ed* Guy Bensley *Pro Des* Sophia Becher *Pro* Kevin Loader, Richard G Mitchell *M* Mitchell

FilmFour / Future Film Financing / HanWay Films / IAC Film / Natural Nylon / Entertainment / Rockwood Edge / Screenland Movieworld GmbH / Pathé
102 mins. UK/Germany. 2002. Rel: 16 May 2003. Cert 12A.

Tortilla Soup ★★★

Imagine Ang Lee's Oscar-winning family drama *Eat Drink Man Woman* set in a Hispanic LA neighbourhood. The homage is deliberate in *Tortilla Soup*, which builds on the basic themes of food and family fissures but with a change of cuisine. Lacking Lee's delicate touch, it is nevertheless a warm and earthy relationship-comedy about three sisters breaking for independence from a dominating dad. As with *Eat Drink Man Woman*, the real star turns are provided by the cooking, making the film torture to watch on an empty stomach. AK

• *Martin* Hector Elizondo *Carmen* Jacqueline Obradors *Maribel* Tamara Mello *Andy* Nikolai Kinski *Antonio Urgell* Joel Joan *Orlando* Paul Rodriguez *Letitia* Elizabeth Peña *Gomez* Julio Oscar Mechoso *Hortensia* Raquel Welch
• *Dir* María Ripoll *Scr* Tom Musca, Ramón Menéndez, Vera Blasi, based on the film *Eat Drink Man Woman* by Ang Lee *Ph* Xavier Perez Grobet *Ed* Andy Blumenthal *M* Bill Conti *Food consultants* Mary Sue Milliken, Susan Feniger *On-set chef* Monique King *Pro Des* Alicia Maccarone *Pro* John Bard Manulis

Samuel Goldwyn Films / Starz! Encore Entertainment / Optimum Releasing
103 mins. US 2001. Rel: 23 August 2002. Cert PG.

Trapped ★★½

A wealthy doctor's wife is held hostage and her asthmatic daughter is kidnapped by a mercilessly efficient gang led by the devilishly charismatic Joe Hickey. She needs to survive the next 24 hours trapped in her own home until the kidnappers get their money. But Karen Jennings is no ordinary trophy wife, and as the hours wind down she pits her cunning against her captors, knowing that one false move will mean her child's death... *Trapped*'s strong cast, tantalising premise and gripping pace promise a taut, stylish thriller until a complete failure of common sense results in a showdown ripped from a bad episode of *The A-Team*, involving a careless plot device, a highway pile-up and a stunningly banal final twist. AK

• *Karen Jennings* Charlize Theron *Cheryl Hickey* Courtney Love *Will Jennings* Stuart Townsend *Joe Hickey* Kevin Bacon *Marvin* Pruitt Taylor Vince *Abby Jennings* Dakota Fanning
• *Dir* Luis Mandoki *Scr* Greg Iles, based on his novel *24 Hours Ph* Frederick Elmes, Piotr Sobocinski *Ed* Jerry Greenberg *M* John Ottman *Pro Des* Richard Sylbert *Pro* Mimi Polk Gitlin, Mandoki

Mandolin Entertainment / Propaganda Films / Senator Film Produktion / The Canton Company / Columbia TriStar
105 mins. US/Germany 2002. Rel: 25 April 2003. Cert 15.

Treasure Planet ★★★★

Pirates and treasure hunting... in *space!* This beautifully animated update of Robert Louis Stevenson's classic does just about everything right. We are introduced to our hero with an X-sports inspired sequence showing James Pleiades Hawkins shooting through the clouds on a rocket-powered solar-skateboard-surfer thingee, establishing Skywalker-esque pilot skills. But he is busted by the robo-police and dragged home to his harried mother. Then the map to the legendary Treasure Planet lands on his doorstep, pirates burn down their home in search of it, a dotty professor funds an expedition and suddenly the galaxy is a holiday camp of quirky, chatty, alien characters. Everyone knows (or ought to know) how it all ends so the narrative line is not the attention-grabber here. Instead there are fabulous helpings of eye-candy, standard-issue hero-building, and just enough zing in the script to keep the grown-ups amused. AK

• *Voices: Jim Hawkins* Joseph Gordon-Levitt *John Silver* Brian Murray *Captain Amelia* Emma Thompson *Doctor Doppler* David Hyde Pierce *B. E. N.* Martin Short *Morph* Dane A Davis *Scroop* Michael Wincott *Sarah* Laurie Metcalf *Mr Arrow* Roscoe Lee Browne *Billy Bones* Patrick McGoohan
• *Dir* John Musker, Ron Clements *Scr* Clements,

Musker, Rob Edwards, based on the novel *Treasure Island* by Robert Louis Stevenson *Ed* Michael Kelly *M* James Newton Howard, with songs written and performed by John Rzeznik *Pro Des* Steven Olds, Frank Nissen *Pro* Roy Conli, Musker, Clements

Walt Disney Pictures / Buena Vista
95 mins. US 2002. Rel: 14 February 2003. Cert U.

Trembling Before G-d ★★★★

Judged simply as filmmaking this documentary is structurally weak, but its subject matter and its approach make it an important work. It was created by Orthodox and Hasidic Jews who believe that their homosexuality is wrongly condemned by those who interpret the Rabbinic teachings of the Torah and the Talmud as inviolable on a word-by-word basis. They suggest that Judaism should be treated as a form of belief legitimately able to adjust to human needs in the wake of understanding. What might have been didactic is instead a platform expressing a range of views to encourage debate. By showing the culture of these believers as central to their lives, it explains why gays and lesbians in this situation would not wish to turn to a different form of Judaism. Wishing to accept the validity of both their faith and their sexuality, they invite talk and discussion. MS

• *with* David, Michelle, Devorah, Mark, Israel,Malka, Leah, Rabbi Steven Greenberg, Shlomo Ashkinazy, Chaim, Ben Aaron, Sue, Tova and Shmuel *[some are pseudonyms]*
• *Dir* Sandi Simcha DuBowski *Ph* Donna Binder, Sandra Chandler, Mik Cribben, Jim Denault, Ken Druckerman, DuBowski, Kirsten Johnson, Kevin Keating, Karen Kramer, Jennifer Lane, David Leitner, Marie Pederson, Ben Speth, Fawn Yacker and Andrew Yarme, Noski DeVille, Nili Aslan, Issa Freij, Jackie Matithau, Yoram Milo, Yitzak Portal, Abigail Sperber *Ed* Susan Korda *M* John Zorn *Pro* DuBowski, Marc Smolowitz

Cinephil / Keshet Broadcasting / Pretty Pictures / Simcha Leib Productions / Turbulent Arts / Miracle Communications
84 mins. US/France/Israel 2001. Rel: 30 May 2003. Cert 15.

The Trespasser ★★★½

(*O invasor*)

Giba and Ivan are two engineers whose appetites have outstripped their ethics. They hire Anisio, a weasel of a hitman, to dispose of their partner, who is standing in the way of a lucrative scam. Anisio does the job but then decides to force his way into their upper middle-class milieu... The bleached atmosphere and thumping hip-hop soundtrack emphasise the spiritual wretchedness at the core of this story. Nobody with money comes off well, and the criminal underclasses are given sympathetic treatment as a gang of rogues who at least know how to have a good time and can be trusted in a tight spot. How clearly this subtext plays to a non-Brazilian audience testifies to the power behind the images and the excellent performances. AK

• *Ivan* Marco Ricca *Gilberto/Giba* Alexandre Borges *Anísio* Paulo Miklos *Marina* Mariana Ximenes *Claudia/Fernanda* Malu Mader *Cecília* Chris Couto *Estevao* George Freire *Dr Araujo* Tanah Correa *Norberto* Jayme del Cueto *Sabotage* Sabotage *Marina's friend* Marina Franco *Luisa* Daniela Tramujas *Giba's daughter* Thavyne Ferrari *Lucia* Priscila Luz *nightclub manager* Marcos Azevedo *Rangel* Silvio Luz *Alessandra* Amanda Santos *Silvana* Ida Sztamfater *Dr Luchesi* Tom Curti *Romao* Manoel Freitas *Leo* Joeli Pimentel *Debi* Audreia Regina *Jaime* Piero Sarjentelli *Ale* Arthur Marsan *clerk* Walmir Pinto *investigator* Mario Bortolotto *Claude's friend (voice)* Viétia Rocha *Rogerinho* Black Gero
• *Dir* Beto Brant *Scr* Marçal Aquino, Beto Brant, Renato Ciasca *Pro* Bianca Villar, Renato Ciasca *Ass Pro* Mariana Ximenes, Marco Ricca, Paulo Miklos, Malu Mader, Alexandre Borges *M* Paulo Miklos, Sabotage *Ph* Toca Seabra *Ed* Manga Campion

Drama Filmes / Gala Films
97 mins. Brazil 2002. Rel: 13 September 2002. Cert 18.

Trouble Every Day ★★★

Critics who overpraised Claire Denis for *Beau Travail* went to the other extreme here. Visually striking, *Trouble Every Day* is technically accomplished but its weakness lies in its failure to say anything. The material, something of a variant on both werewolf movies and Jekyll and Hyde, would need a different treatment to appeal to horror fans but fails also to build in other directions. Béatrice Dalle plays a wife who can't control her sexual and killing urges due to being a victim of misguided scientific experimentation to harness the human libido; Vincent Gallo is a honeymooner out to expose what has happened, but finding himself sharing the same uncontrollable urges. Despite echoes of *Psycho* and a touch of cannibalism, the film needs to play as a metaphor for human relationships and a lover's need to trust. But this is not developed sufficiently in what is, nevertheless, an interesting and distinctly sensual film. MS

• *Shane* Vincent Gallo *June* Tricia Vessey *Coré* Béatrice Dalle *Léo* Alex Descas
• *Dir* Claire Denis *Scr* Denis, Jean-Pol Fargeau *Ph* Agnes Godard *Ed* Nelly Quettier *Pro Des* Arnaud de Moléron *Pro* Georges Benayoun, Philippe Liégeois, Jean-Michael Rey
Centre National de la Cinématographie / Dacia Films /

Kinetique Inc / Le Studio Canal+ / Messaouda Films / Rézo Films / Rézo Productions / Zweites Deutsches Fernsehen / arte France Cinéma / arte / Metro Tartan 101 mins. France/Germany/Japan 2002. Rel: 27 December 2002. Cert 18.

The Truth About Charlie ★★★

The first half of Jonathan Demme's remake of Stanley Donen's Hitchcockian homage *Charade* is lightweight but diverting. The Paris setting, superbly photographed by Tak Fujimoto, has been retained, but now becomes the excuse for playful references to Nouvelle Vague cinema (brief appearances by Anna Karina and Agnès Varda, some Godardian camera movement, references to Truffaut). Despite some alterations, the original plot is largely followed: an innocent young widow is menaced by crooks trying to recover a fortune purloined and hidden by her dead husband. As the attractive stranger who offers help but may not be trustworthy, Mark Wahlberg is no Cary Grant (the age difference is one of the changes), but Thandie Newton does well by the Audrey Hepburn role. Sadly, though, the second half is over-extended and boring, and the story's final forseeable twist, which could have been altered to advantage, is still in place. MS

• *Joshua Peters* Mark Wahlberg *Regina Lambert* Thandie Newton *Mr Bartholomew* Tim Robbins *Il-Sang Lee* Joong-Hoon Park *Emil Zadapec* Ted Levine *Lola Jansco* Lisa Gay Hamilton *Commandant Dominique* Christine Boisson *Charlie* Stephen Dillane *Karina* Anna Karina *mysterious woman in black* Magali Noël *the Widow Hyppolite* Agnès Varda • *Dir* Jonathan Demme *Scr* Demme, Steve Schmidt, Peter Joshua and Jessica Bendinger, based on the motion picture screenplay *Charade* by Peter Stone *Ph* Tak Fujimoto *Ed* Carol Littleton *M* Rachel Portman *Pro Des* Hugo Luczyc-Wyhowski *Pro* Demme, Peter Saraf, Edward Saxon

Clinica Estetico / Mediastream Film / Universal Pictures / UIP
104 mins. US 2003. Rel: 16 May 2003. Cert 12A.

28 Days Later ★★★★

The world is becoming a scary place and Danny Boyle – director of *Shallow Grave*, *Trainspotting* and *The Beach* – wants to up the ante. Not content to explore the hazards of flat-sharing, heroin and tourism, the Manchester-born filmmaker now turns his attention to animal experimentation, viral plague, the end of the world as we know it and military ethics. All this and more jumps out of the screen in his latest, harrowing vision of Britain. It starts promisingly, then cruises along on routine suspense and ends on a note of knee-weakening violence. When Jim, a bicycle courier, wakes up in hospital after an accident, he finds the world a changed place. The streets of London are totally deserted, double-

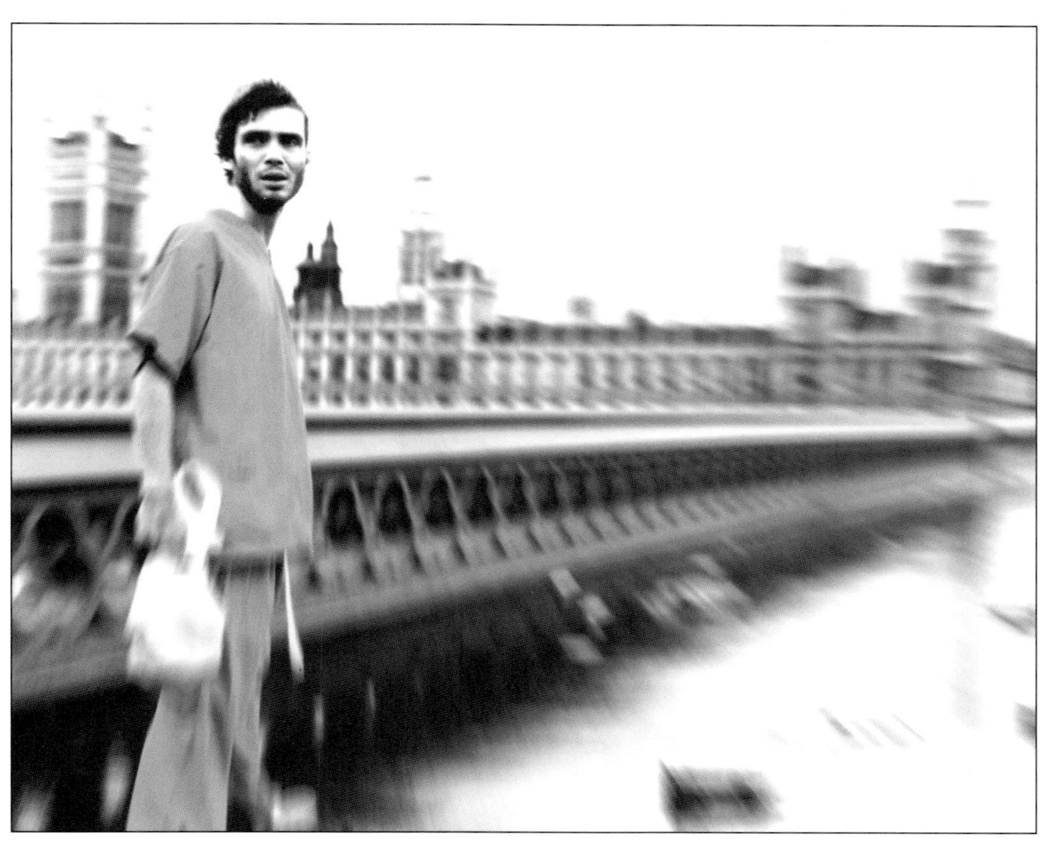

Right: Cillian Murphy in Danny Boyle's harrowing *28 Days Later* (from Fox)

decker buses lie on their sides and paper money is left blowing in the wind. Soon he realises that a horrible virus has wiped out the population, leaving only a few stragglers in a demonic state of rage. Eventually Jim hooks up with two other survivors and contemplates whether or not there is any reason to live. Shot on digital video, the film is actually an accomplished revision of George A Romero's *Night of the Living Dead* (via Richard Matheson's novel *I Am Legend*) and is every bit as unsettling. JC-W

• *Jim* Cillian Murphy *Selena* Naomie Harris *Hannah* Megan Burns *Frank* Brendan Gleeson *Major Henry West* Christopher Eccleston *Private Jones* Leo Bill *Private Mitchell* Ricci Harnett *with* Stuart McQuarrie, Noah Huntley, Jukka Hiltunen
• *Dir* Danny Boyle *Pro* Andrew Macdonald *Line Pro* Robert Howe *Scr* Alex Garland *Ph* Anthony Dod Mantle *Pro Des* Mark Tildesley *Ed* Chris Gill *M* John Murphy *Costumes* Rachael Fleming *Sound* Glenn Freemantle

Figment Films / DNA Films / Fox Searchlight / Film Council-Fox.
113 mins. UK/USA 2002. Rel: 1 November 2002. Cert 18.

Left: Barry Pepper and Philip Seymour Hoffman come to terms with the plight of Edward Norton in Spike Lee's *25th Hour* (from Buena Vista)

25th Hour ★★★

There's no reason why Spike Lee should not move away from racial themes but misguidedly he's chosen for this purpose David Benioff's adaptation of his own novel. A well-shot New York movie, its dialogue sounds more literary than real at times, but the central drawback is that a talented cast can only leave us wondering why we should care and what the point is. Edward Norton plays a man about to be imprisoned for drug-dealing and spending his last hours of freedom with his girl (Rosario Dawson) and his two best friends (Philip Seymour Hoffman and Barry Pepper), who have their own problems. There's also the question of who betrayed our anti-hero to the police. The film gets by thanks to the cast, although it seems disturbingly obsessed with gay rape and can hardly be said to hang together meaningfully. MS

• *Monty Brogan* Edward Norton *Jacob Elinsky* Philip Seymour Hoffman *Francis Xavier Slaughtery* Barry Pepper *Naturelle Riviera* Rosario Dawson *Mary D'Annunzio* Anna Paquin *James Brogan* Brian Cox *Kostya Kovotny* Tony Siragusa
• *Dir* Spike Lee *Scr* David Benioff, based on his novel *Ph* Rodrigo Prieto *Ed* Barry Alexander Brown *M* Terence Blanchard *Pro Des* James Chinlund *Pro* Lee, Jon Kilik, Tobey Maguire, Julia Chasman

40 Acres & a Mule Filmworks / Gamut Films / Industry Entertainment / Touchstone Pictures / Buena Vista
134 mins. US 2002. Rel: 25 April 2003.
Cert 15.

2 Fast 2 Furious ★★★

Ex-undercover cop Brian O'Connor is the only man fast enough to catch the ultra-smooth Miami mobster Carter Verone, so the authorities call the street racer back into the fold, offering to expunge his criminal record and that of his childhood buddy Roman Pearce. But even with the help of another sexy undercover agent, Monica Clemente, also in Verone's entourage, Brian may have bitten off more than he can chew... John Singleton takes a break from serious filmmaking to indulge in some serious fun in this all-adrenaline, nitro-charged road movie that is as much about the shiny, souped-up toys as it is the stunt-packed action sequences. A weirdly camp script suits the irony-free performances surprisingly well, not that any of the film's huge army of car-tuning fans will notice, given the sumptuous parade of eye-candy plastered all over the screen, both human and mechanical. AK

• *Brian O'Connor* Paul Walker *Roman Pearce* Tyrese Gibson *Monica Clemente* Eva Mendes *Carter Verone* Cole Hauser *Suki* Devon Aoki *Chris* Ludacris *Agent Markham* James Remar
• *Dir* John Singleton *Scr* Michael Brandt and Derek Haas, based on a story by Gary Scott Thompson *Ph* Matthew F Leonetti *Ed* Bruce Cannon and Dallas Puett *M* David Arnold *Pro Des* Keith Brian Burns *Pro* Neil H Moritz

Original Film / Neal H Moritz Productions / Universal Pictures / UIP
107 mins. USA 2002. Rel: 20 June 2003. Cert 12A.

Two Can Play That Game ★★

The beautiful, successful and somewhat vicious Shanté catches her man in a club with another woman, and decides to teach him a lesson or ten about love. A black romantic comedy in both senses, Mark Brown's essay on buppie love shimmers with middle-class African-Americans assailing the *When Harry Met Sally* genre with their own twist on the game. The cast look like models at a *Cosmo* fashion shoot, and the typically 'earthy' humour (penis and

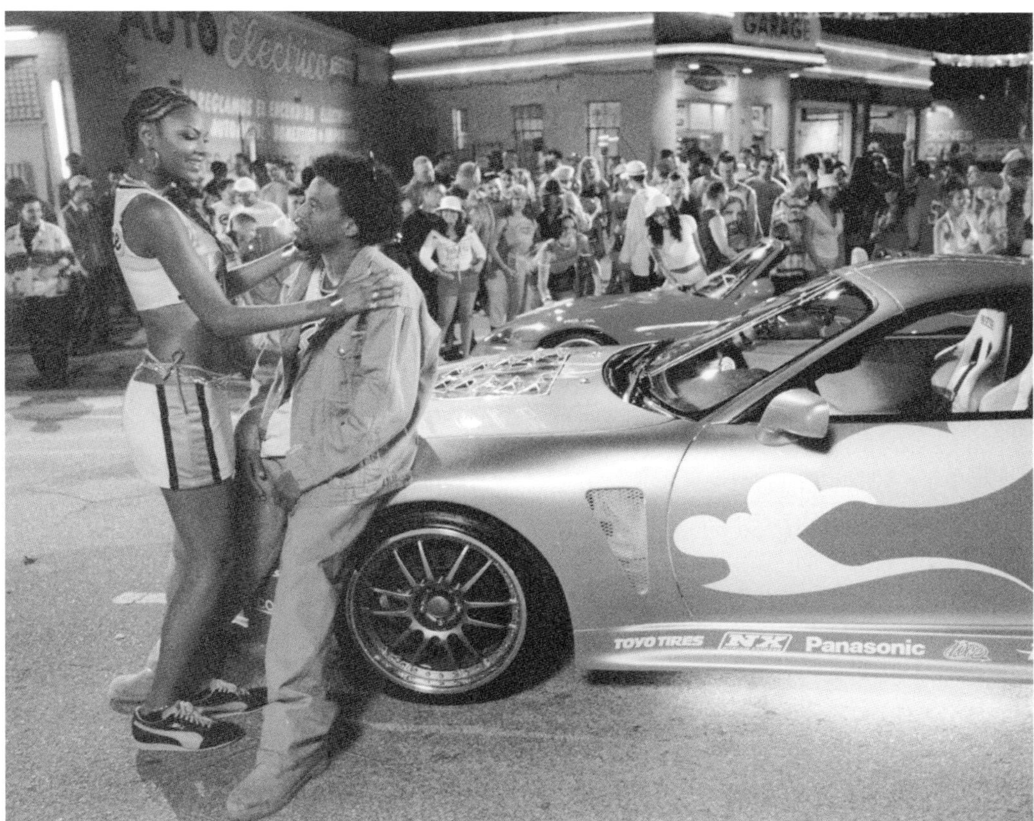

Right: The wheels steal every scene in 2 *Fast 2 Furious* while Michael Ealy is otherwise occupied (from UIP)

breast jokes) supply what I suppose is the Richard Pryor element. The combination, however, feels artificial. AK

• *Shanté Smith* Vivica A Fox *Keith Fenton* Morris Chestnut *Tony* Anthony Anderson *Karen* Wendy Raquel Robinson *Tracye Edwards* Tamala Jones *Diedre* Mo'Nique *Bill Parker* Ray Wise *Michael* Bobby Brown *Dwain* Dondré T Whitfield *Conny Spalding* Gabrielle Union
• *Dir / Scr* Mark Brown *Ph* Alexander Gruszynski *Ed* Earl Watson *M* Marcus Miller *Pro Des* Amy Ancona *Pro* Doug McHenry, Mark Brown, Paddy Cullen

Blue Train Productions / DreamWorks SKG / Parkes/MacDonald / Vanguard Films Production / UIP 98 mins. US 2002. Rel: 9 January 2003. Cert 12A.

Two Men Went to War ★★★

With the momentous, bloody battles of the Second World War so well documented by the cinema, it's refreshing to encounter a little-known episode of more intimate endeavour. Here, we have two conscripts of the Army Dental Corps at Aldershot, both of whom yearn to taste the adrenaline of combat. When Sergeant Peter King is passed over for being too old for active duty, he decides to commandeer trainee dental mechanic Leslie Cuthbertson for a private assault on occupied France. After a shaky start, *Two Men Go to War* settles into its stride and evolves into a funny and diverting tale that is all the more remarkable for being true. Newcomer Leo Bill overplays the gormless act (too often he recalls Private Pike from *Dad's Army*), but Kenneth Cranham is wonderful as the bitter veteran determined to do his bit for King and Country. True, the film drags at times, but its eccentric charm wins through, illuminating an extraordinary story that just had to be told. JC-W

• *Sgt Peter King* Kenneth Cranham *Private Leslie Cuthbertson* Leo Bill *Major Desmond Merton* Derek Jacobi *Faith* Phyllida Law *Major Bates* James Fleet *Colonel Hatchard* Julian Glover *Sgt Major Dudley* Anthony Valentine *Emma Fraser* Rosanna Lavelle *Winston Churchill* David Ryall *with* Richard Sutton, Anthony O'Donnell, Brian Bosley, Mossie Smith, Barbara Massey, Richard Everett, Christopher Villiers
• *Dir* John Henderson *Pro* Ira Trattner and Pat Harding *Ex Pro* Keith Hayley, Robert Bevan, Charlie Savill, Amanda Coombes and Amit Barooah *Co Pro* Sally French *Ass Pro / Scr* Christopher Villiers and Richard Everett *Ph* John Ignatius, *Pro Des* Steve Carter *Ed* David Yardley *M* Richard Harvey *Costumes* Jill Taylor

**Little Wing-Guerilla Films
109 mins. UK 2002. Rel: 1 November 2002. Cert PG.**

U

Above: Eddie Griffin busts some righteous moves as the *Undercover Brother* (from Universal)

Undercover Brother ★★½

Austin Powers meets James Brown in *Undercover Brother*, an afroed spy spoof that is a bit of a mixed bag. The Undercover Brother is a platform-wearing, Caddy-driving, pimped-out superhero for the black nation who is sartorially trapped in a 70s time-warp. His exploits bring him to the attention of the B.R.O.T.H.E.R.H.O.O.D., a secret organisation working out of a neighbourhood barbershop's cavernous basement. They recruit the Undercover Brother to bring down 'The Man', a segregationist, Blofeld-type villain who is distributing mind-control drugs through a fried chicken franchise as part of a plan to degrade black people. Ultra-broad humour and an inability to pass over any blaxploitation gag, no matter how weak, let down what is undoubtedly a winning idea. Racism is uncool, and Eddie Griffin's fluorescent-flared creation goes some way to prove it can be fought with the profound power of a funky disco beat and an enormous bling-bling medallion. Solid! AK

• *Undercover Brother* Eddie Griffin *Mr Feather* Chris Kattan *Penelope Snow / White She-Devil* Denise Richards *Conspiracy Brother* David Chappelle *Sistah Girl* Aunjanue Ellis *Lance* Neil Patrick Harris *the Chief* Chi McBride *Mr Elias* Jack Noseworthy *Smart Brother* Gary Anthony Williams *General Boutwell* Billy Dee Williams
• *Dir* Malcolm D Lee *Scr* John Ridley and Michael McCullers, based on Ridley's UrbanEntertainment.com website *Ph* Tom Priestley Jr *Ed* William Kerr *M* Stanley Clarke *Pro Des* William Elliott *Pro* Michael Jenkinson, Damon Lee

Imagine Entertainment / Universal Pictures / Urban Media / Winchester Films
86 mins. US 2002. Rel: 14 February 2003.
Cert 12A.

Van Wilder: Party Liaison ★★★½

It is spring semester in the seventh year of Van Wilder's college career. The undisputed king of the Coolidge campus, Wilder's 24/7 party lifestyle is jeopardised when his father cuts him off without tuition. Can his preternatural talent for fun save him from expulsion? And are massage oils and open flames a bad combination? A cross between *Ferris Beuller's Day Off* and *American Pie*, this was the first decent teen comedy of the year and wallows in its appetite for bad taste. The jokes are hilarious and profoundly juvenile, while Ryan Reynolds projects the cool aura of Wilder ("Like, the raddest dude in the history of the world, man!") with laid-back perfection, allowing us to stare adoringly at his magnificence without feeling too stupid. AK

• *Van Wilder* Ryan Reynolds *Gwen* Tara Reid *Taj* Kal Pen *Van Wilder Sr* Tim Matheson *Casey* Kim Smith

Right: Ryan Reynolds plans his next scheme in Walt Becker's *Van Wilder: Party Liaison* (from Momentum)

Richard Bragg Daniel Cosgrove *Elliot Grebb* Tom Everett Scott *Timmy the Jumper* Chris Owen • *Dir* Walt Becker *Pro* Robert L Levy, Peter J Abrams, Andrew Panay, Jonathon Komack-Martin *Scr* Brent Goldberg, David T Wagner *Ph* James Bagdonas *Ed* Dennis M Hill *Costumes* Alexis Scott *M* Christopher Violette *Pro Des* Rachel Kamerman

Artisan Entertainment / Myriad Pictures / In-Motion AG / WMF V / Tapestry Films / Momentum
92 mins. US 2002. Rel: 27 September 2002. Cert 12A.

Villa des Roses ★★★

In war-torn Paris, love blooms between an unsophisticated chambermaid and a raffish, opportunistic painter. But this is not a typical love story told in nostalgic tones. An adaptation of Willem Elsschot's 1913 Flemish classic, *Villa des Roses* surrounds the central romance with playfully eccentric detail, mostly about the dilapidated hotel where the lovebirds work and live, and their delightfully nutty neighbours. Lavishly designed and beautifully lensed, the biggest thrill is that Frank Van Passel and his cast successfully preserve the emotional honesty of the film while indulging in various fantastical motifs. AK

• *Louise Créteur* Julie Delpy *Richard Grünewald* Shaun Dingwall *Ella* Shirley Henderson *Olive* Harriet Walter *Hugh* Timothy West *Aasgaard* Frank Vercruyssen *Brizard* Jan Decleir *Craxi* Alfredo Pea *O'Connor* Gary Whelan *De Kerros* Stéphane Excoffier *Gendron* Dora van der Groen *Kuprinski* Maya van den Broecke *Natsje* Halina Reijn *Radsky* Rifka Lodeizen *Mrs Bunny Wimhurst* Toni Barry *Eustache Lejeune* John Dobrynine *Maurice* Albert Delpy *Lucien* Simon Chefnourry *Maurice* Jean Hayet *Bernard* Michel Franssen *bellboy* Michel Jurowicz • *Dir* Frank Van Passel *Scr* Van Passel, Christophe Dirickx, Willem Elsschot *Pro* Julie Baines, Jason Newmark, Jani Thiltges, Rudy Verzyck *Co Pro* Wilfried Depeweg, Dirk Impens, Els Vandevorst, Claude Waringo *M* Paul M van Brugge *Ph* Jan Vancaillie *Ed* Ludo Troch, Karin Vaerenberg *Pro Des* Willem Klewais

Favourite Films / Dan Films / Isabella Films / Samsa Film S.a.r.l. / Eurimages / Miracle Communications
119 mins. Belgium/Luxembourg/UK 2002.
Rel: 11 October 2002. Cert 12A.

Virgil Bliss ★★★

Ex-film critic and sound mixer Joe Maggio impresses with his debut feature film, a modern parable about a sensitive but evil-tempered ex-con, played well by Clint Jordan, who stubbornly hangs on to his naïveté despite a sleaze-ridden, drugged-up environment that wants to drag him back into itself. A low-budget, indie-noir look adds graphic weight to the tragedy of Virgil Bliss. However, shallow characterisations by the supporting cast don't quite match up to the fine atmosphere the film successfully projects elsewhere. AK

• *Virgil Bliss* Clint Jordan *Ruby* Kirsten Russell *Manny* Anthony Gorman *Devo* Marc Romeo *Gillette* Greg Amici
• *Dir / Scr* Joe Maggio *Ph* Harlan Bosmajian *M* Greta Gaines, Clint Jordan, Anthony Gorman *Pro* Maggio, John Maggio *Ex Pro* Thierry Cagianut, Matthew Myers *Ed* Elizabeth Downer

Concrete Films / P-Kino
93 mins. US 2002. Rel: 14 March 2003. Cert 15.

A Walk to Remember ★★

Beaufort, North Carolina; the present. Landon Carter has always enjoyed his role as the school rebel without a cause, and he doesn't care who knows it. However, his strutting attitude never impressed Jamie Sullivan, who, being the daughter of the town's Baptist minister, puts her faith first. Then, when Landon is forced to partake in his school's drama class, he finds himself sharing quality time with Jamie, which is just too uncool... As a love story aimed squarely at the demographic of young teenage girls, this is a handsome, well-acted slice of Mills & Boon. There are good performances from most concerned (although Daryl Hannah looks like a man in drag) and Mandy Moore, on the coat-tails of her bitchy Valley Girl in *The Princess Diaries*, shows she has some real range, even though she looks uncannily like Phoebe Cates. It's all terribly familiar stuff, and as predictable as hell, but its earnestness wins it serious Brownie points. JC-W

• *Landon Carter* Shane West *Jamie Sullivan* Mandy Moore *Rev Sullivan* Peter Coyote *Cynthia Carter* Daryl Hannah *Belinda* Lauren German *Dean* Clayne Crawford *Eric* Al Thompson *Tracie* Paz de la Huerta *with* Jonathan Parks Jordan, Matt Lutz, David Andrews, David Lee Smith, Paula Jones
• *Dir* Adam Shankman *Pro* Denise Di Novi and Hunt Lowry *Ex Pro* E.K. Gaylord II, Casey La Scala, Edward L McDonnell and Bill Johnson *Scr* Karen Janszen, based on the novel by Nicholas Sparks *Ph* Julio Macat *Pro Des* and *Costumes* Doug Hall *Ed* Emma E Hickox *M* Mervyn Warren; songs performed by The Breeders, Mandy Moore, Soul Hooligan, Extra Fancy, Cold, Jars of Clay, Switchfoot, Fuel, Noogie, Rachel Lampa, Matthew Hager, New Radicals, Missy 'Misdemeanor' Elliott, Toploader, 311, etc.

Pandora / Warner / Di Nova Pictures-Helkon SK 102 mins. USA 2002. Rel: 13 September 2002. Cert PG.

The War Bride ★★½

Set during the Second World War, this is the story of two friends who go to Canada as war brides and find life more difficult than they had anticipated. In particular, Lily has to put up with a hostile mother-in-law (Fricker) and a crippled sister-in-law (Parker). The actresses are as good as you would expect, but as Lily's errant husband, Aden Young is wholly inadequate, especially when he has to suggest a man traumatised by war experience (a crucial plot point). In any case, Angela Workman's script is superficial and many plot details fail to convince, including the Pollyanna-like manner in which Lily ultimately wins over the family. The film won two Canadian genie awards, but it's not easy to understand why. MS

• *Lily* Anna Friel *Betty* Brenda Fricker *Charlie* Aden Young *Sophie* Julie Cox *Joe* Loren Dean *Sylvia* Molly Parker *Peggy* Caroline Cave *Moira* Keeley Gainey
• *Dir* Lyndon Chubbock *Pro* Douglas Berquist *Scr* Angela Workman *Ph* Ron Orieux *Pro Des* Ken Rempel *M* John Sereda

DB Entertainment / Random Harvest Pictures / Vanguard Entertainment / Miracle Communications 107 mins. UK/Canada 2001. Rel: 29 November 2002. Cert PG.

Welcome to Collinwood ★★★

In the crummy 'burb of Collinwood, a gang of desperate lifelong losers team up to pull off a sure-fire score (a 'Bellini'). But the ineptitude they bring to the caper transforms it into a farcical nightmare of bad luck (a 'Mullinski'). *Welcome to Collinwood* is the exuberant, shiny, mugging cousin to Woody Allen's dry satire of the caper genre, *Small Time Crooks*, though it's based on another caper-disaster, *Big Deal on Madonna Street*. An excellent cast combine with a raucous script of wrong turns and idiot players to mostly hilarious effect. The lack of restraint, however, begins to tell after a while, particularly with the uneven romantic duel between Sam Rockwell and Jennifer Esposito's characters. The final notes (consisting of a long shot lining up the despondent faces of the would-be master criminals and then the derelict, vandalised 'Welcome' sign) are also played too heavily to serve the supposed irony of its title. AK

• *Riley* William H Macy *Leon* Isaiah Washington *Pero* Sam Rockwell *Toto* Michael Jeter *Cosimo* Luis Guzman *Rosalind* Patricia Clarkson *Basil* Andrew Davoli *Jerzy* George Clooney *Carmela* Jennifer Esposito *Michelle* Gabrielle Union

Below: George Clooney (in wheelchair), Sam Rockwell, the late Michael Jeter and William H Macy (with baby) in *Welcome to Collinwood* (from Helkon)

• *Dir / Scr* Anthony and Joe Russo, based on the film *Big Deal on Madonna Street* by Suso Cecchi d'Amico, Mario Monicelli, Agenore Incrocci and Furio Scarpelli *Ph* Lisa Rinzler, Charles Minsky *Ed* Amy Duddleston *M* Mark Mothersbaugh *Pro Des* Tom Meyer *Pro* George Clooney, Steven Soderbergh

Gaylord Pictures / HSBS Media / Pandora Cinema / Section Eight Ltd / Helkon SK
86 mins. US 2002. Rel: 25 April 2003. Cert 15.

Werckmeister Harmonies ★★★½

Here's a film to make us wonder afresh at the gradations that can be found in images photographed in black and white. This is a long work (145 minutes) made by a true artist, Hungary's Béla Tarr, who is not afraid to make immense demands of his audience (he has been compared with Tarkovsky). Avant-garde enthusiasts can safely be recommended to try this, a piece with symbolism reminiscent of Fellini and wondrous camera movement echoing Janscó. The setting is a provincial town on the Hungarian plains where a promised Prince fails to arrive, although a tent is set up in t he square containing the carcass of a whale. For whatever reason, a mass revolt follows, but the film's meaning remains obscure. Enigmatic, breathtaking, bleak, very hardgoing – all of these descriptions fit. MS

• *Janos Valushka* Lars Rudolf *Gyorgy Eszter* Peter Fitz *Tunde Eszter* Hanna Schygulla *man in broadcloth coat* Janos Derzi *man in western boots* Djoko Rossich
• *Dir* Béla Tarr *Scr* Tarr, Laszlo Krasznahorkai, based on the novel *The Melancholy of Resistance* by Krasznahorkai *Ph* Gabor Medvigy *Ed* Agnes Hranitzky *M* Mihaly Vig *Pro* Miklos Szita, Franz Goess

13 Productions / Fondazione Montecinemaverita / Goëss Film / Magyar Mozgókép Alapítvány / Magyar Televízió / Nemzeti Kultúrális Alapprogram / Országos Rádió és Televízió Testület / Radiotelevisione Italiana / Studio Babelsberg / Von Vietinghoff Filmproduktion GmbH / Zweites Deutsches Fernsehen / arte / Artificial Eye
145 mins. Hungary/Italy/Germany/France 2000.
Rel: 18 April 2003.
Cert 12A.

Windtalkers ★★½

A scarred and cynical marine is chosen to guard a Navajo Indian 'Windtalker', so called for the radio code based on their language which the Japanese cannot yet break. His secret primary objective is to protect the code, even at the expense of his charge's life. But come the moment of truth, will he stay true to his orders or to the friendship that has grown up between them? Based on the real Windtalkers, whose codes were never broken and were thus crucial to the Allied victories in the Pacific, the film feels less like a proper war movie than a cartoon conception of a war movie, stuffed with melodrama and overcooked atmosphere. Elaborately staged on a panoramic scale, John Woo volleys the story off the screen with the subtlety of a charging tank division. Nicholas Cage's performance survives the bombsite setting and allows the film to limp off into the sunset with some dignity – and a severe case of tinnitis. AK

• *Joe Enders* Nicolas Cage *Ben Yahzee* Adam Beach *Hjelmstad* Peter Stormare *Chick* Noah Emmerich *Pappas* Mark Ruffalo *Harrigan* Brian Van Holt *Nellie* Martin Henderson *Charlie Whitehorse* Roger Willie *Rita* Frances O'Connor *Ox Henderson* Christian Slater *Major Mellitz* Jason Isaacs
• *Dir* John Woo *Scr* John Rice and Joe Batteer *Ph* Jeffrey Kimball *Ed* Steven Kemper, Jeff Gullo and Tom Rolf *M* James Horner *Pro Des* Holger Gross *Pro* Woo, Terence Chang, Tracie Graham, Alison Rosenzweig
Lion Rock / Metro-Goldwyn-Mayer / Twentieth Century Fox
134 mins. US 2002. Rel: 30 August 2002. Cert 15.

Wrong Turn ★★½

On his way to a job interview, Chris Finn (Desmond Harrington) is driving through the mountains of West Virginia. Diverting to avoid a chemical spill, he turns down a side road and runs in to (literally) a group of hikers whose own car has broken down. Looking for help, they come across a lone cabin in the Appalachian woods inhabited by three in-bred, cannibalistic horrors. The race is on to see who can make it out of the woods alive... Eliza Dushku is the new 'It' girl and dominates *Wrong Turn* as surely as every other movie she's done of late. She alone makes watching it worthwhile. Throw in three *Deliverance*-style mutants named Three Finger, Saw-Tooth and One-Eye and you get a modern-day *The Hills Have Eyes*. Anyone who's driven in the West Virginia wilderness can all too easily relate to the premise here. It's every driver's nightmare come to life. SWM

• *Chris Finn* Desmond Harrington *Jessie Burlingame* Eliza Dushku *Carly* Emmanuelle Chriqui *Scotr* Jeremy Sisto *Evan* Kevin Zegers *Francine* Lindy Booth *Three Finger* Julian Richings *Saw-Tooth* Garry Robbins *One-Eye* Ted Clark
• *Dir* Rob Schmidt *Scr* Alan McElroy *Ph* John S Bartley *Ed* Michael Ross *M* Elia Cmiral *Pro Des* Alicia Keywan *Effects and make-up* Stan Winston Studio *Pro* Erik Feig, Robert Kulzer, Winston, Brian Gilbert

DCP Wrong Turn Productions / Summit Entertainment / Constantin Film Produktion / Stan Winston Studio / Media Cooperation One / Newmarket Capital Group / Regency Enterprises / Pathé
84 mins. US/Germany 2002. Rel: 27 June 2003. Cert 18.

X

Left: Wheels of misfortune – Patrick Stewart loses his mind in Bryan Singer's *X2* (from Fox)

Y

X2 ★★★★½

(aka *X-Men 2*, *X²*, *X-2*)

An attempt on the American president's life sparks off a war against mutants led by government scientist William Stryker. Troops break into Charles Xavier's school for 'gifted youngsters' (read: 'mutants') to corral the secret base of the X-Men. But Stryker has an agenda, and it will be up to the X-Men allied with Magneto to prevent him from killing every mutant on the planet... From the first thrilling punch thrown by the teleporting Nightcrawler in the stunning pre-credits action sequence, to the final hint as to where the next movie will take us, Bryan Singer's second film about the world's coolest superheroes is a breathless, leather-clad triumph. Singer focuses on delivering action adventure in its purest form. Every battle is a spectacle and the characters are swiftly and surely defined, and importantly come across as three-dimensional rather than comic caricatures; this is not an action flick that downgrades the subtlety of the performances to make way for the explosions. Not that the movie really aims for emotional naturalism; this is escapist entertainment of the highest order invoking the fevered adolescent dreams and comic book 'Ker-Pows' of youth. AK

• *Prof Charles Xavier* Patrick Stewart *Logan/Wolverine* Hugh Jackman *Eric Lensherr/Magneto* Ian McKellen *Storm* Halle Berry *Jean Grey* Famke Janssen *Scott Summers/Cyclops* James Marsden *Mystique* Rebecca Romijn-Stamos *William Stryker* Brian Cox *Kurt Wagner/Nightcrawler* Alan Cumming *Senator Kelly* Bruce Davison *Rogue* Anna Paquin *Yuriko Oyama* Kelly Hu *John Allerdyce/Pyro* Aaron Stanford *Bobby Drake/Iceman* Shawn Ashmore
• *Dir* Bryan Singer *Scr* Michael Dougherty, Dan Harris, from a story by Singer, David Hayter and Zak Penn based on the Marvel Comics' characters *Ph* Newton Thomas Sigel *Ed/M* John Ottman *Pro Des* Guy Hendrix Dyas *Pro* Lauren Shuler Donner, Ralph Winter *Ex Pro* Avi Arad, Stan Lee, Tom De Santo, Singer *Co Pro* Ross Fanger, Kevin Feige *Ass Pro* David Gorder *Visual Effects Supervisor* Michael Fink *Visual Effects Producer* Joyce Cox *Art Director* Helen Jarvis *Set Design* Lawrence Hubbs *Costumes* Louise Mingenbach *Make-up* Norma Hill-Patton, Gordon Smith

Ames Entertainment / XM2 Productions / 20th Century Fox / Bad Hat Harry Productions / Frantic Films / Marvel Entertainment / The Donners' Company / Fox
133 mins. US 2003. Rel: 2 May 2003.
Cert 12A.

Xiao cheng zhi chun

See *Springtime in a Small Town*

xXx ★★★½

A new millennium calls for a new kind of super-spy, and Xander Cage is just the ultra-cool extreme athlete for the job. The pre-credits teaser shows the CIA's top Bond lookalike eliminated by the Anarchy 99 syndicate in Prague. A tough, ex-Russian paramilitary group apparently dressed by Galliano in retro-survivalist chic, they are developing a plan to reduce the world to chaos, and after a Darwinian selection program the CIA picks Xander Cage as the only man capable of infiltrating them. Working on the basis that you cannot have an explosion too big, or a situation that cannot be defused by the riskiest solution available, *xXx* feeds the espionage genre into the MTV/freesports grinder to produce a smooth yet meaty action flick that works better than it should, thanks mostly to its rumblingly cool star. AK

• *Xander Cage* Vin Diesel *Agent Augustus Gibbons* Samuel L Jackson *Yelena* Asia Argento *Yorgi* Marton Csokas *El Jefe* Danny Trejo *Toby Lee Shavers* Michael Roof *Senator Dick Hotchkiss* Tom Everett
• *Dir* Rob Cohen *Scr* Rich Wilkes *Ph* Dean Semler *Ed* Chris Lebenzon, Paul Rubell and Joel Negron *M* Randy Edelman *Pro Des* Gavin Bocquet *Pro* Neal H Moritz

Original Film / Revolution Studios / Columbia Tristar
124 mins. US 2002. Rel: 18 October 2002.
Cert 12A.

Right: Asia Argento and Vin Diesel in *xXx* (from Columbia Tristar)

Xingfu Shiguang

See *Happy Times*

Yadon Ilaheyya

See *Divine Intervention*

Video Releases

A selection of films released direct to video/DVD in the UK between July 2002 and June 2003.

by Danny Graydon

After the Storm
Based on a story by Ernest Hemingway, this passable melodrama involves a luxury yacht, a violent storm and two sets of salvage hunters. Dwelling on the theme of romantic betrayal, director Guy Ferland gets things off to a slow start, building up the tension and dramatic force in the last half hour. There's a case for arguing that Hemingway's work doesn't really lend itself to cinematic treatment. For all its merits, *After the Storm* won't silence the doubters. Leading man Benjamin Bratt, best known as Julia Roberts' ex-boyfriend, is a solid actor but lacks star power. The Belize locations are easy on the eye, though.
• Also starring Armand Assante, Stephen Lang, Jennifer Beals, Mili Avital.
High Fliers, November 2001. Cert 15.

The Anarchist's Cookbook
An admirably ambitious social drama by debut feature director Jordan Susman, this film centres on a self-proclaimed anarchist and his like-minded friends. Susman attempts to mix drama and comedy, but unfortunately with little of the assurance or bite of something like *Trainspotting*. It's somewhat contrived and one-dimensional in places, but there are flashes of real innovation, and like *Traffic*, you get all sides of the story and get to judge for yourself.
• *Director: Jordan Susman*
Mosaic, June 2003

The Angel Doll
A nostalgic drama in the *Stand By Me* mould, this story of two childhood friends, Jerry and Whitey, who search for an angel doll to give to Whitey's terminally ill sister, may soak up every opportunity for outright sentiment, but it does provide a charmingly honest view of 1950s American home life. Only a mixed view on prejudice leads to a few bumps in the story.
• *Director: Alexander Johnston*
Odyssey, September 2002

Bangkok Haunted
This Thai film puts together three unrelated ghost stories, but people expecting the same shocks as the more widely known Japanese horror, *Ring*, will be disappointed. Neither as gore-intensive as *The Evil Dead* nor possessing the brooding chills of *The Sixth Sense*, the three tales nonetheless maintain a spooky atmosphere – but they're never overly frightening.
• *Directors: Oxide Pang Chun, Pisut Praesangeam*
Tartan, March 2003

Black Cadillac
Essentially trading on the modest success of John Dahl's *Duel* update *Joyride* (or *Roadkill* as it was known in the UK), this traverses much the same territory, with a group of teens being terrorised by a mysterious, unrelenting Cadillac. Randy Quaid is effective as a cop and, despite a profusion of plot holes and the occasional failure to maintain suspense, it does what it says on the tin.
• *Director: John Murlowski*
Mosaic, June 2003

City of Lost Souls
An example of what happens to directors when they become cult items and the hype overtakes them. This typically violent Takashi Miike mis-step sees Japanese-Brazilian Mario and Chinese hairdresser Kei about to be deported. His plan is to stow away on a ship and to steal money from the Mafia. Kei is captured by Yakuza and he must save her. Randomly violent and with poor CGI, it's hard to get into.
• *Director: Takashi Miike*
Tartan, November 2002

Clay Pigeons
In this grisly noir, Joaquin Phoenix is the small-minded hick who inadvertently befriends serial killer Vince Vaughn, who is being pursued by diligent FBI agent Janeane Garofalo. Well-crafted by Ridley Scott protégé David Dobkin, the suspense levels are kept high and the film is infused with a wealth of warped humour and excellent performances – particularly from Vaughn.
• *Director: David Dobkin*
Momentum, April 2003

Country Bears
Based on a Disneyland fairground attraction, this live-action affair revolves around the idea that humans and talking bears co-exist in harmony. A young bear comes across a legendary band and helps them reunite for one final concert. Basically a parody of endlessly reuniting bands like The Eagles, what it lacks in wit it makes up for in typical Disney sugar.
• *Director: Peter Hastings*
Buena Vista, July 2003

Cube 2
The original *Cube* was a particularly innovative and clever mix of SF and horror, in which a group of strangers find themselves trapped in a giant block of interlocked booby-trapped cubes – with only one escape route. The sequel loses the more overt gore factor, instead favouring a state of bewilderment – for the audience as well as the characters! Even so, the scrappy charm is intact, if not the cunning.
• *Director: Andrzej Sekula*
Mosaic, April 2003

Dagon
(aka *H P Lovecraft's Dagon*)
From Brian Yuzna's so-called 'Fantastic Factory' in Barcelona comes this extremely gory H P Lovecraft adaptation, telling the story of Paul Marsh, a young man who discovers that the truth will not set him free; instead, it condemns him to a waking nightmare of unrelenting horror. Occasionally lacking in plot, it

Dagon (from Metrodome)

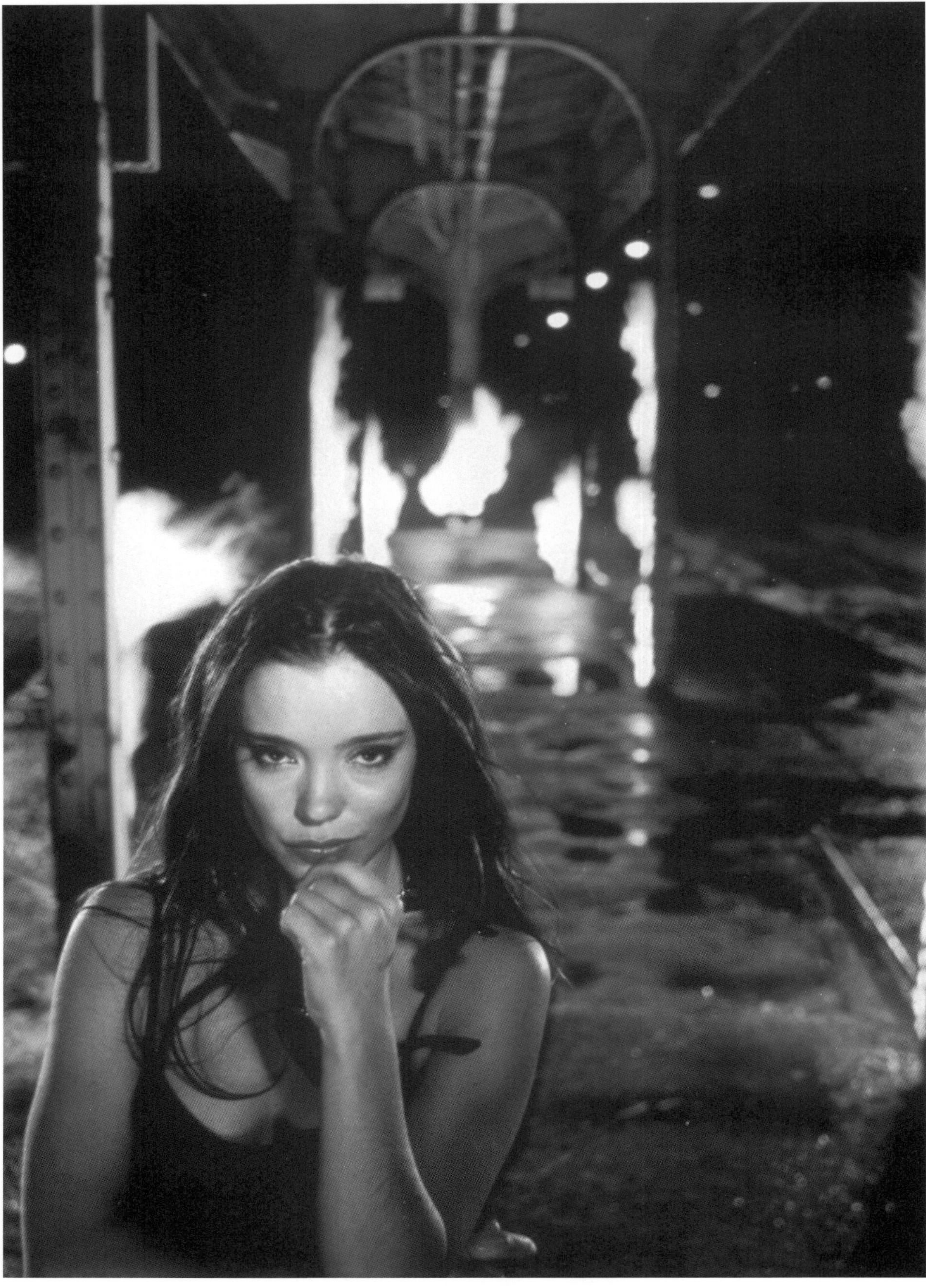

Left: *Firestarter Rekindled* (from Universal)

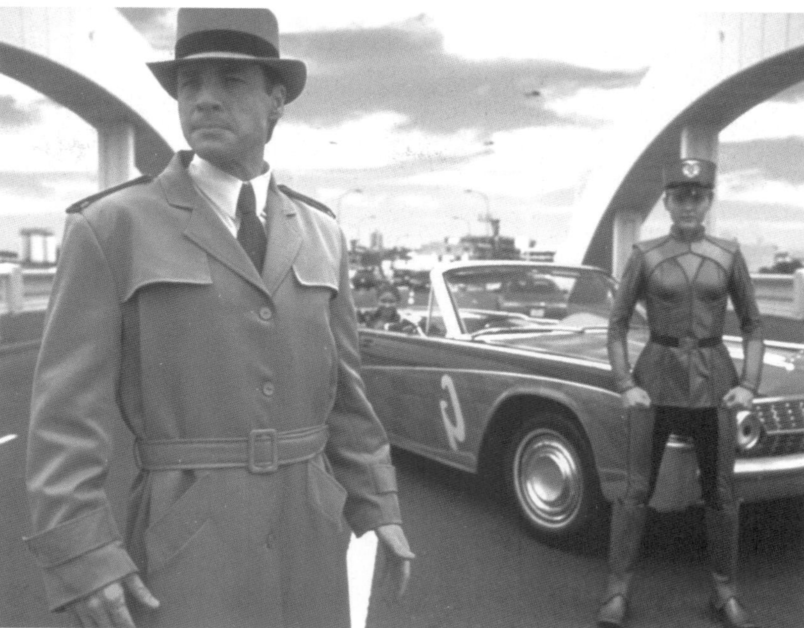

Above: *Inspector Gadget 2* (from Buena Vista)

nevertheless delivers the goods where shocks are concerned. Not bad for what is essentially B-movie material.
• *Director: Stuart Gordon*
Metrodome, May 2003

Dawg

As you'd expect from something proclaiming 'Starring Liz Hurley', *Dawg* has very little to recommend it. To inherit a million dollars, egotistical Denis Leary (one reason to watch at least) must find the women he's betrayed and convince them to forgive him. Culminating in a welter ofquite unbelievably achieved changes of character, it drowns in its own lack of humour.
• *Director: Victoria Hochberg*
Metrodome, April 2003

Deadly Engagement

A by-the-numbers action adventure of the kind that fills every video shop's bottom shelf. The fact that it contains a Balkan warlord character who inexplicably sports an Irish accent should indicate the quality of what's on offer here. Deplorable on every level.
• *Director: Lloyd A Simandl*
Third Millennium, January 2003

Firestarter Rekindled

The original *Firestarter* is widely considered one of the worst adaptations of a Stephen King novel – which is saying something – and is a good indication of what you can expect from this tepid sequel. A three-hour TV miniseries featuring Malcolm McDowell and Dennis Hopper, it's clueless in virtually every respect and the special effects are depressingly cheap.
• *Director: Robert Iscove*
Universal, Feb 2003

The Forsaken

This lame-brained horror flick (usefully subtitled *Desert Vampires* on the cover) never approaches the class of its obvious models, *Near Dark* and *From Dusk Till Dawn*. There are plenty of teen TV stars – Brendan Fehr from *Roswell*, Kerr Smith from *Dawson's Creek*, Phina Oruche from *Buffy the Vampire Slayer* – together with lots of cheesy gore and nudity. Surprisingly, this gained a US theatrical release back in April 2001.
• *Director: J S Cardone*
Columbia TriStar, July 2002

Guilt By Association

In this TV movie made for US cable channel Court TV, Mercedes Ruehl shines as Susan Walker, a single mother who is sentenced to 20 years in federal prison simply because her live-in boyfriend and his cronies were trafficking marijuana. For such a small-scale production, this is a commendable study of the various injustices inflicted by America's mandatory minimum sentencing laws – all framed by Ruehl's excellent performance.
Director: Graham Campbell
Odyssey, October 2002

The Guilty

Bill Pullman offers another of his characteristically measured performances in this enjoyable legal thriller. Pullman plays a corrupt lawyer who is blackmailed by his assistant, and in response convinces his estranged ex-con son to murder her. With a suitable array of twists and turns as opposed to blunt violence, it's a well-constructed story. Superbly supported by Joanne Whalley, Gabrielle Anwar and Devon Sawa, this is another small-screen triumph for Pullman.
• *Director: Anthony Waller*
Mosaic, Feb 2003

Harvard Man

James Toback's semi-autobiographical tale of heinous hedonism, in which a young graduate tries to raise money for his parents illegally in between bouts of LSD abuse, unfortunately fails to spark like you hope it will. Instead, it careers wildly through its 100 minutes, ending up as a decidedly awkward trip. Sarah Michelle Gellar shows none of the depth she tapped into in *Cruel Intentions*, while Joey Lauren Adams is somewhat miscast as a Harvard professor.
• *Director: James Toback*
Mosaic, Jan 2003

Inspector Gadget 2

Free of original stars Matthew Broderick and Rupert Everett, the gadget-enhanced police inspector once again takes on his arch-nemesis Claw. French Stewart is an excellent replacement for Broderick and the effects are still impressive. Ultimately, it's no better or worse than its predecessor, and will only really satisfy undemanding kids. Neither is as good as the cartoon series.
• *Director: Alex Zamm*
Buena Vista, May 2003

K9 PI

James Belushi's career has been dogged by bad choices, and this needless second retread of a modest hit from 1988 provides him with another one – a shame, as Belushi is hardly a talent-free performer. As it is, this sees him give another personable performance as nearly-retired maverick cop Dooley, who, with canine partner Jerry Lee in tow, takes on a gang of techno-thieves. Belushi puts in the effort, but he's completely undermined by gross-out material.

• *Director: Richard J Lewis*
Universal, March 2003

The Land Before Time 8

Clearly, they're trying to make this franchise last as long as the prehistoric period it covers. The 1988 original was a feel-good hit, but what we have here is a mediocre tale suffused with the kind of undiluted sentimentality only the most sensitive kids will endure. The plot – such as it is – sees young Dino 'Spike' and friends trying to combat a natural disaster – but in a terribly jaunty way. The worst entry, hands down.

• *Director: Charles Grosvenor*
Universal, September 2002

Protection

Despite a hoary old premise – a mobster moves to a new town as a protected witness and tries to start over, only to find he can't escape his old ways – this thriller is elevated by a strong central performance by Stephen Baldwin as Sal Veronica. All the clichés are present and correct: shoot-outs, betrayals, death threats etc, but are offset by notable support from Peter Gallagher as Sal's new business partner.

• *Director: John Flynn*
Momentum, Dec 2002

The Santa Clause Bros

This made-for-TV animated feature sees Santa Clause approaching retirement. He sends his three sons in search of the true meaning of Christmas, in the hope that the quest will divulge his rightful successor. However, a mischievous elf, Snorkel, has plans to take over himself. The film's main selling point is its outstanding animation, combined with CGI to create a richly detailed 3-D production.

• *Director: Mike Fallows*
Momentum, December 2002

Say Nothing

After having a brief affair with Natassja Kinski, wealthy and mentally unstable William Baldwin begins to stalk her, systematically unravelling her life. Despite a wealth of implausibility, this psychodrama is at least buoyed up by decent acting from the leads – although Hart Bochner doesn't make the most engrossing hero. This is all-too-familiar fare, but by no means a complete waste of time.

• *Director: Allan Moyle*
Odyssey, June 2002

Sharing a Secret

A purposely heart-tugging TV movie, this is a sensitive and effective exploration of the effects of bulimia. The mother-daughter dynamic between Mare Winningham and Alison Loihman is particularly effective, with able support from Tim Matheson. Only the ending takes an unfortunate turn into familiar sugar-coated territory.

• *Director: Katt Shea*
Odyssey, February 2003

Silent Justice

This passable rip-off of *The Star Chamber* sees a conspiracy between rogue cop Richard Tyson, state judge Robert Vaughn and several businessmen resulting in vigilante action against criminals. In order to cover their actions, the conspirators have also offed many innocent victims, including the family of a former DA. The latter, joined by an inquisitive female attorney, unravels the conspiracy only for the pair to become a target themselves.

• *Director: James Dalthorp*
Odyssey, August 2002

The Skulls 2

A pedestrian retread of the 2000 Josh Jackson-starring tale of Ivy League intrigue, which was only mildly diverting anyway. This time (again) a band of Young, Pretty, Rich, White Males get caught up in the dubious dealings of a campus secret society, only this time with even less suspense and excitement than the original – hi and relying on gratuitous nudity to spice things up.

• *Director: Joe Chapelle*
Universal, August 2002

Slapshot 2

This inexplicable sequel to a little-seen 1977 Paul Newman vehicle about ice hockey sees Stephen Baldwin as the team coach who faces off against rival team bad guy Gary Busey, simultaneously dealing with the new female manager, Jessica Steen. Frankly, they all look utterly bewildered. Ice hockey fans will probably derive an added 'Ooooh!' factor from the 'Spot The Real Life Players' game – but only if they want to waste their time watching it.

• *Director: Steve Boyum*
Universal, October 2002

Snow Job

Released as *Sheer Bliss* in the States, this is an above-average teen flick in which four 'dudes' (*American Pie*'s Eddie Kaye Thomas the most recognisable) spend their gap year in ski resort Aspen doing the usual: partying, hi-jinks, chasing chicks, etc etc. Typical stuff, but it manages to strike a good balance. Watch out for an appearance by one-time 007 George Lazenby.

Right: *The Skulls 2* (from Universal)

Above: Tarzan and Jane (from Buena Vista)

• *Director: Marni Banack*
Mosaic, June 2003

Tarzan and Jane

Though it doesn't come close to hitting the tree-swinging heights of the Oscar-winning 1999 original, this sequel is an adequate second helping of jungle action. In actuality it's three combined episodes of the Tarzan cartoon series, which take place around the duo's first year of marriage. It manages to look slick, despite the inevitable budgetary restriction to 2-D animation, and is blessed with a decent voice cast.
• *Directors: Victor Cook, Steve Loter*
Buena Vista, July 2002

Tremors 3

The original became a cult favourite, spawning an enjoyable sequel, but with this third entry the once enticing B-movie pastiche has become somewhat tired. Michael Gross' engaging gun-nut Bert Gummer is the sole remaining character from the first film, leading the resistance against another wave of attacking 'Graboids' and their mutant offsring 'The Shriekers'. Only dedicated fans need apply.
• *Director: Brent Maddock*
Universal, October 2002

Vampires: Los muertos

Unnecessary follow-up to John Carpenter's interesting but generally unloved *Vampires*, with Jon Bon Jovi a poor substitute for James Woods. More a watered-down remake, if truth were told, garnished with a few directorial flourishes from Tommy Lee Wallace, who 20 years ago concocted a much more intriguing Carpenter sequel, *Halloween III: Season of the Witch*.
• *Director: Tommy Lee Wallace*
Columbia TriStar, November 2002

Versus

This is undiluted Fanboy Heaven: a frenzied, super-stylised, hyper-kinetic mix of *The Evil Dead*, *Highlander* and *The Matrix* – with added zombies. Two escaped convicts rendezvous with a carload of super-cool Yakuza and their female captive in the woods. But, when the Yakuza heavies refuse to free her, prisoner KSC2-303 guns down one of the gangsters, only to discover that in The Forest Of Resurrection, the dead don't always stay dead. Enormous fun – in an utterly gratuitous way.
• *Director: Ryuhei Kitamura*
Tartan, June 2003

The Weight of Water

With a decent cast (Sean Penn, Catherine McCormack and, ahem, Liz Hurley) and an intriguing if unoriginal plot – a newspaper photographer, Jean, researches the lurid and sensational axe murder of two women in 1873 as an editorial tie-in with a brutal modern double-murder – this is a competent thriller tailor-made for easy consumption.
• *Director: Kathryn Bigelow*
Momentum, December 2002

Faces of the Year

ORLANDO BLOOM

Born: 13 January 1977, Canterbury, Kent.
Big screen: *Wilde* (1997), *The Lord of the Rings: The Fellowship of the Ring* (2001), *Black Hawk Down* (2001), *The Lord of the Rings: The Two Towers* (2002), *Pirates of the Caribbean* (2003) *Ned Kelly* (2003).
Next up: *The Lord of the Rings: The Return of the King* (2003), *Troy* (2003).
Small screen: *Midsomer Murders* (1997), *Smack the Pony* (1999), *Denim Invasion* (2002: Gap clothing ads with Kate Beckinsale, directed by Cameron Crowe).
Quick study: 'Orli' Bloom rocketed to stardom almost as soon as he left drama school, when he began work on Peter Jackson's epic *Lord of the Rings* trilogy. 18 months in New Zealand wearing pointy elf ears and a blonde barnet was part adventure camp, part stellar career launchpad. When the first *LOTR* film was released, Bloom was an instant sensation, idolised by (mostly female) fans worldwide for his smooth blend of action hero and fantasy dreamboat. Having, in his time, broken his back, ribs, nose, both legs, arm, wrist, a finger and a toe (not to mention cracking his skull three times), he was the ideal choice to play the first casualty in *Black Hawk Down*, while his teen idol status made him a natural for Disney's old-fashioned pirate flick *Pirates of the Caribbean.*
Furthermore: He originally auditioned for the role of Faramir in the *Lord of the Rings* trilogy, but lost out to Viggo Mortensen. His 'almost A-list' status was confirmed by Academy Award organisers, who refused him a ticket for the 2002 Oscars because the stadium was full.
He said it: On his part in *Black Hawk Down* – "My character breaks his back, and I had mentioned I had done that when I was up for the part. Who knows why one actor gets a job and another doesn't? I think it was just good timing that I happened to be there and I had had the experience – I mean, I was lucky."

ADRIEN BRODY

Born: 14 April 1973, New York.
Previous occupation: As a child, performed magic shows at children's birthdays as 'The Amazing Adrien', later attending New York's prestigious

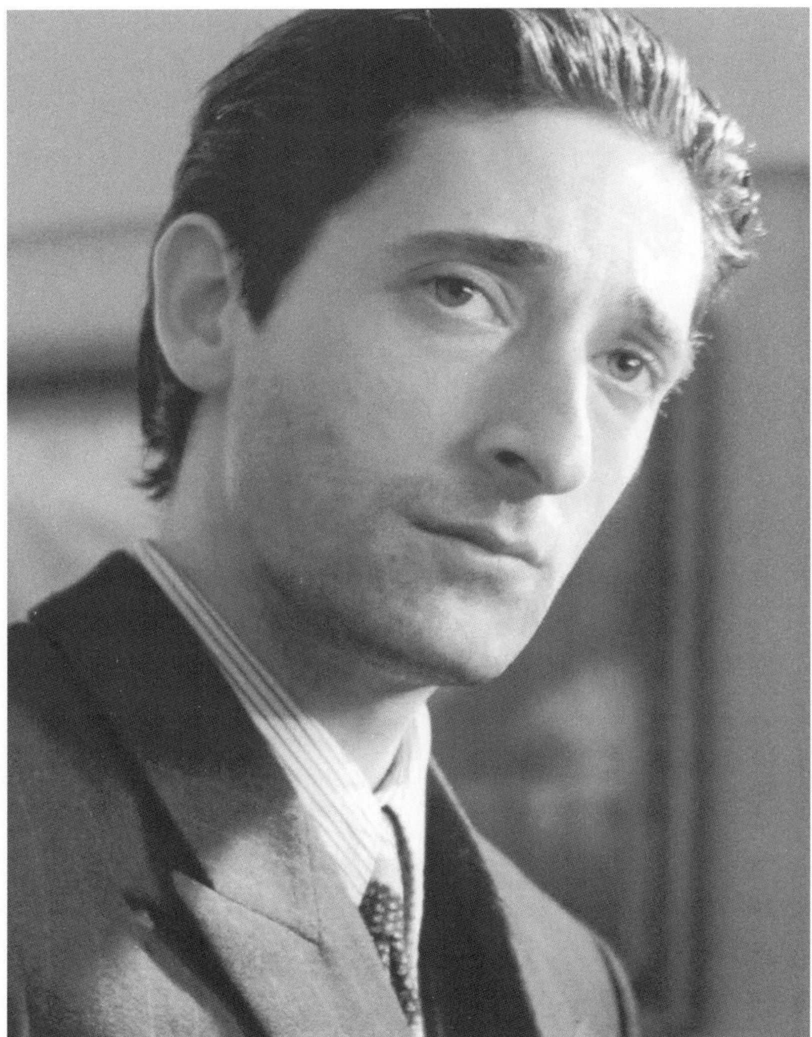

High School of Performing Arts aka 'The *Fame* School'.
Big screen: *Liberty Heights* (1999), *Harrison's Flowers* (2000), *The Affair of the Necklace* (2001), *The Pianist* (2002).
Next up: *The Singing Detective*, where his character exists only in Robert Downey Jr's head. "I basically sing and dance and beat the shit out of Robert over the course of the movie!"
Off screen: After picking up his Oscar, the sharply dressed actor was chosen for an ad campaign by Peter Lindbergh for designer Ermenegildo Zegna.
Quick study: Tall, dark and sharply handsome, Brody's mother is the Hungarian-born photojournalist Sylvia Plachy, longtime staff snapper for *The Village Voice*. He credits her with making him feel comfortable in front of the camera. His character was shaved into insignificance in the final cut of Terence Malick's war epic *The Thin Red Line*, and while he remained an underground favourite for his magnetic performances in Spike Lee's *Summer of Sam* and Ken Loach's socalist drama *Bread and Roses*, it looked like his bid for young stardom had passed. Until, that is, Roman Polanski cast him in the title role of *The Pianist*, where Brody drew on the Eastern European heritage (and rare dialect) of his Polish grandmother, losing nearly 20lbs from his already lean frame for the role. "I've been offered roles in big movies," he says. "And I've been offered a lot of money, which I haven't taken – not yet, anyway. I'm not saying that doing a big picture is something I disrespect. But I've been fortunate enough to stick to what's important to me. I like projects that have a certain degree of social relevance – whether it's a point of view I agree with or not."
Furthermore: Brody is the only actor to win a Best Actor Oscar when nominated alongside four previous Oscar winners, and, at the age of 29, replaces Richard Dreyfuss as the youngest actor ever to win.
He said it: After a lengthy kiss with presenter Halle Berry, he started his acceptance speech by admitting his sadness at accepting an award at "such a strange time," referring to the American war on Iraq. "My experiences of making this film made me very aware of the sadness and the dehumanisation of people at times of war and the repercussions of war. Whoever you believe in, whether it's Allah or God, may he watch over you and let's pray for a peaceful and swift resolution. I have a friend from Queens who is a soldier in Kuwait and I hope you and your boys make it back real soon. I love you."

GERARD BUTLER

Born: 13 November 1969, Glasgow.
Previous occupation: Reluctant, high-powered solicitor.
Big screen: *Timeline* (2003), *Lara Croft Tomb Raider: The Cradle of Life* (2003), *Reign of Fire* (2002), *Dracula 2000*

(2000), *Harrison's Flowers* (2000), *One More Kiss* (1999), *Tomorrow Never Dies* (1997), *Mrs Brown* (1997).
Next up: Playing the title role in the film adaptation of hit musical *The Phantom of the Opera*, and starring in *The Game of Their Lives* (2003). Favourite to be the next James Bond.
Small screen: *The Jury* (2002), *Attila* (2001).
Quick study: The ex-law society president of Glasgow University began his acting career when he was approached in a London coffee shop by Steven Berkoff and offered a role in *Coriolanus*. Bitten by the bug, he went on to play Renton in the stage adaptation of *Trainspotting*, and made his film debut as Billy Connolly's younger brother in *Mrs Brown* (1997). Butler's career took off in two breakthrough roles, both capitalising on his dark, strong features: as 'Attila the Hun' in the USA then as Wes Craven's alpha-bloodsucker in *Dracula 2000*. At 6' 2", with a thick Scots brogue and a lawyer's affinity for a good suit, Butler's name moved to the top of the list as a potential James Bond. In the meanwhile, he is building his action hero credentials in the second *Tomb Raider* movie and in the swords-and-science thriller based on Michael Crichton's novel, *Timeline*.
Furthermore: Honoured by the Royal Humane Society for saving a drowning swimmer from the River Tay, possibly while getting into training for Her Majesty's Secret Service.
He said it: "I wouldn't be an actor now if I hadn't been such an awful lawyer then."

ZOOEY DESCHANEL

Born: 17 January 1980, Los Angeles.
Previous occupation: Graduated from Crossroads School for Arts and Sciences in Santa Monica.
Big screen: *Eulogy* (2003), *Elf* (2003), *House Hunting* (2003), *It's Better to be Wanted for Murder Than Not to Be Wanted at All* (2003), *Whatever We Do* (2003), *All the Real Girls* (2003), *Abandon* (2002), *Sweet Friggin' Daisies* (2002), *The New Guy* (2002), *Big Trouble* (2002), *The Good Girl* (2002), *Manic* (2001), *Almost Famous* (2000), *Mumford* (1999).
Quick study: Named after the male character in J D Salinger's *Franny and Zooey*, Zooey Claire Deschanel is well-pedigreed for Hollywood, as daughter of cinematographer Caleb Deschanel and *Twin Peaks* actress Mary Jo Deschanel. She attended the elite Northwestern University for a year, studying theatre and leaving when her complex performance in Lawrence Kasdan's *Mumford* landed her a role in Cameron Crowe's *Almost Famous* (supporting her old high-school classmate, Kate Hudson). Her insouciant, pouting slacker in *The Good Girl* established her scene-stealing credentials, and announced her as the perfect mix of indie-cred and popular accessibility.
Furthermore: She was featured in the video of *She's Got Issues* by rock band The Offspring and plays ukulele for the band If All the Stars Were Pretty Babies.
She said it: "Part of being an actor is having no fear, or at least having a lot of courage. My only fear is playing the same part, over and over again."

ROMOLA GARAI

Born: 1 July 1982, Hong Kong.
Previous occupation: She abandoned her BA in English Literature at Queen Mary's College after a year to take the

lead role in *I Capture the Castle.*
Big screen: *Nicholas Nickleby* (2002), *I Capture the Castle* (2003).
Next up: *Vanity Fair* (2004), *Dirty Dancing II: Havana Nights* (2004) and *Dance With the Devil*, an adaptation of Raymond Radiguet's *The Devil in the Flesh*, in development by Ecosse.
Small screen: *Daniel Deronda* (2002), *Perfect* (2001), *Attachments* (2000) and *The Last of the Blonde Bombshells* (2000).
Quick study: Young, posh and slightly exotic beauty Romola Garai was spotted in a school play and invited to act as the younger version of Judi Dench's character in *The Last of the Blonde Bombshells* (2000). Her big break came with the part of the not-quite-naïve Zoe in the BBC internet office drama *Attachments* (2000). Her ability to be girlish yet sexy, and sophisticated yet endearing, have won her choice parts in some remarkably substantial films, when you consider that Garai has had no real formal training as an actor.
Furthermore: She was born and raised in Hong Kong and Singapore until she was eight, before moving back to Wiltshire. She plays the violin, and loves her horses.
She said it: "My family is mad. I think everybody's family is eccentric, in different ways. Families by their very nature are dysfunctional."

MAGGIE GYLLENHAAL

Born: 16 November 1977, Los Angeles.
Previous occupation: Waitressing, where her affair with the chef gave her some useful insights into the naughtiness she practised in *The Secretary.* "He would call me in from working on the restaurant floor and give me spoonfuls of whatever he was making."
Big screen: *Riding in Cars with Boys, Adaptation, 40 Days and 40 Nights, Donnie Darko* and *Secretary.* Dates required for all these.
Quick study: After years of being frustrated at playing second fiddle to her younger brother, Jake Gyllenhaal, in a series of slight appearances (albeit in good movies), the daughter of screenwriter Naomi Foner and director Stephen Gyllenhaal rocketed to stardom with a stunningly bold lead performance in the S&M romance, *The Secretary*: layered, sensitive and seductively subtle, effortlessly ranging from girlish innocence to feline sexuality. A degree from Columbia University, and a stint with the Royal Academy of Dramatic Art in London, suggest a serious intellect and her acting proves it. With a National Board of Review Award, an Independent Spirit Award and a Golden Globe nomination under her garter belt, this one should run and run.
Furthermore: Maggie once tried to 'kill' her brother Jake for refusing to sing along to a Cyndi Lauper song.
She said it: "My first bad review almost destroyed me. I wept and wept, and when I realised I had to go do the play that night and for several more weeks, I wept some more. I almost quit acting but realised all I could do was focus, get better and stop reading reviews."

ALISON LOHMAN

Born: 18 September 1979, Palm Springs, California.
Big screen: *Matchstick Men* (2003), *White Oleander* (2002), *White Boy* (2002), *Menace* (2002), *Alex in Wonder* (2001), *Delivering Milo* (2000), *The Million Dollar Kid* (1999), *Planet Patrol* (1999), *The Auteur Theory* (1999), *The Thirteenth Floor* (1999), ... *Kraa! The Sea Monster* (1998).
Next up: *Big Fish* (2003).
Small screen: *Tucker* (2000), *Sharing the Secret* (2000), *Pasadena* (2001).
Quick study: Alison Marion Lohman was a veteran of 12 different stage and musical productions by the time she turned 17. Awarded a scholarship by the National Foundation for the Advancement of the Arts to NYU's Tisch School, Lohman decided to skip directly to Los Angeles to pursue a Hollywood career. She cracked the big time playing Michelle Pfeiffer's troubled daughter in *White Oleander*, and bagged another showcase role as a nubile grifter in *The Matchstick Men* opposite Nicholas Cage and Sam Rockwell. "I don't know why these directors trust me with these intense, wonderful parts," she remarks. "I don't even think I'm that good."
Furthermore: While still in high school, Lohman also enjoyed a career as a solo vocalist, appearing with such heavy-hitters as Frank Sinatra and Bob Hope. She did a stint at RADA and starred in Kenneth Lonergan's play *This Is Our Youth* in London's West End in 2002.
She said it: "Acting always seemed like an odd choice for someone as shy as I am. I don't really start conversations with strangers. I am a big homebody. But I get so excited about bringing a character to life and imagining what their world is like that I forget to be nervous. I guess I hide behind a role."

DEREK LUKE

Born: 24 April 1974, Jersey City, New Jersey.
Previous occupation: Waiting tables and working at the Sony Pictures LA gift shop, selling candy for five years.
Big screen: *Biker Boyz* (2003), *Pieces of April* (2003), *Antwone Fisher* (2002).
Next up: *Pieces of April* (2003), *Spartan* (2004).
Small screen: *The Kind of Queens* (1998), *Moesha* (1996).
Quick study: An unstoppable determination, more than his magnetic good looks or rough-edged screen presence, is the secret to Derek Luke's success. He barged his way into a screen test when he found out that Denzel Washington was casting his directorial debut, and bombed so badly he broke down in front of Christian Kaplan, Fox's casting director. Lucky thing, because raw emotion was what Denzel was looking to bring to his hard-luck biopic of *Antwone Fisher*. Luke auditioned for the title role five times over a four-year period before he finally won his big break into feature films. His guileless and unvarnished performance won universal acclaim, and Luke won another lead opposite Lawrence Fishburne in *Biker Boyz* (2003), which didn't set the box-office alight but did his reputation no harm.
Furthermore: When he won his Independent Spirit Award for *Antwone Fisher* he brought his wife Sophia on stage and gave it to her. He then revealed that, four years ago, he was waiting tables at the 1999 Spirit Awards.
He said it: "I come from a place where people died young and dreams went unfulfilled. I've had to accomplish everything on faith."

QUEEN LATIFAH

Born: 18 March 1970, Newark, New Jersey.
Previous occupation: Burger King chef, management company CEO, recording star, daytime TV host.
Big screen: *Bringing Down the House* (2003), *Chicago* (2002), *Pinocchio* (2002), *Brown Sugar* (2002), *Seven Days* (2002), *The Country Bears* (2002), *Bringing Out the Dead* (1999), *The Bone Collector* (1999), *Living Out Loud* (1998), *Sphere* (1998), *Hoodlum* (1997), *Set It Off* (1996), *My Life* (1993), *Juice*

(1992), *Angel Town 2* (1992), *House Party 2* (1991), *Jungle Fever* (1991).
Next up: *Taxi* (2004), *Barbershop 2* (2004), *Scary Movie 3* (2003).

Small screen: *Living Single* (1993), *My Girls* (1993), *Mama Flora's Family* (1998), *Living with the Dead* (2002), *The O.Z.* (2002), *Talking to Heaven* (2002), *Queen Latifah Show* (1999).
Quick study: Born Dana Owens, she renamed herself Queen Latifah at eight years of age, liking its meaning in Arabic: 'delicate and sensitive'. She was anything but delicate as a rap star, winning a Grammy on the way to becoming one of the genre's most influential female artistes, crowned the 'First Lady of Rap'. HRH exercised her entrepreneurial talents and started a successful talent management company called Flavor Unit Entertainment, and made several bids to front her own TV show with only middling success. Her film roles were usually in small supporting parts; sometimes only her rich voice made the final cut, as in Scorsese's *Bring Out The Dead.* Then came an Oscar nomination for supporting in *Chicago* and a starring role in *Bringing Down the House* (which she also produced) – and these were the first two films of 2003 to pass the $100m mark. Her larger-than-life personality just about fits the big screen (her breast reduction from an E to a DD cup may have helped her along), and she still carries with her the drive, discipline and energy that has got her this far.
Furthermore: Coming from a family of police officers has influenced Queen Latifah's personal philosophy on many levels. Her older brother, Lance Owens, died in an accident on the motorcycle Latifah bought for him as a present. She still wears the motorcycle key around her neck in his memory.
She said it: "Freedom is not free. You have to speak up on what's important to you. We're all Americans and we're still affected by what happens in this country. I'm the daughter of a Vietnam veteran, so I've lived with the effects of what happens to a person who goes to war."

SAM ROCKWELL

Born: 5 November 1968, Daly City, California.
Previous occupation: Busboy, waiter, burrito delivery guy, trendy restaurant delivery guy, soap opera extra.
Big screen: *Last Exit to Brooklyn* (1989), *Basquiat* (1996), *The Search for One-eye Jimmy* (1996), *Glory Daze* (1996), *Mercy* (1996), *Box of Moon Light* (1996), *Lawn Dogs* (1997), *Safe Men* (1998), *Jerry and Tom* (1998), *Celebrity* (1998), *A Midsummer Night's Dream* (1999), *Heist* (2001), *Confessions of a Dangerous Mind* (2002), *Welcome to Collinwood* (2002), *Matchstick Men* (2003).
Next up: *Piccadilly Jim* (2004).
Small screen: *Clownhouse* (1988), *Over the Limit* (1990), *Law & Order* (1990) *Subway Stories: Tales from the Underground* (1997).
Quick study: A chameleon-like ability to inhabit almost any character he comes across has, after ten years in the bit-part/guest-role wilderness, finally given Sam Rockwell the recognition he deserves. Sam debuted early, while still a teen, in Francis Ford Coppola's TV movie *Clownhouse* (1988). He was picked up for the NBC TV series *Dream Street* in 1989 but was fired, which meant paying his dues in a string of meantime jobs, taking whatever roles he could pick up (he was 'Head Thug' in *Teenage Mutant Ninja Turtles*, for instance). In 1994, a Miller Ice beer commercial enabled him to concentrate on his acting career, and in 1996 he had five movies to his name. *Lawn Dogs* (1997) won him Best Actor gongs at the Montreal and Barcelona film fests, lending substance to the rumour that Rockwell was a whiz with offbeat, marginal characters like drunks, savants, and social outcasts. The crime-comedies *Safe Men* (1998) and *Jerry and Tom* (1998) proved him a good man with a punchline. *The Green Mile* (1999) and *Galaxy Quest* (1999) moved him up further and he landed the part of the chief baddie in *Charlie's Angels* (2000), which turned on his ability to shift characters in the blink of an eye. However, it took the support of George Clooney and Steven Soderbergh to really make him a heavyweight contender, starring him in two difficult movies which they released almost simultaneously: *Confessions of a Dangerous Mind* and *Welcome to Collinwood* (both 2002). Suddenly, Rockwell is the new Sean Penn, without the temper.
Furthermore: Rockwell won a Silver Berlin Bear for his performance in *Confessions of a Dangerous Mind.*
He said it: "I'd like to be an action hero, but I don't think they'd ever make me that type of leading man. I'm too quirky. If they put me in *Speed 3*, two days later they'd go, 'Yep, we're gonna have to fire him now. Can we get someone more mainstream?' … [But if he were really given the lead in *Speed 3*?] … I'd take it. But I'd play it like Hamlet."

Film World Diary

July 2002 – June 2003

JULY 2002

Julia Roberts marries movie cameraman **Daniel Moder** in a star-studded midnight ceremony at her ranch in New Mexico. Moder left his wife of five years – make-up artist **Vera Steinberg** – to marry 34-year-old Ms Roberts. • Animal rights protesters in Sicily hiss and jeer as **Pedro Almodóvar** collects a special *European Nastro d'Argent* prize at Italy's oldest film awards for his film *Talk To Her*. • **Angelina Jolie** and **Billy Bob Thornton** file for divorce after two years of marriage, citing irreconcilable differences, just months after adopting a 20-month-old Cambodian refugee they named Maddox. "I'm angry. I'm sad. It's a very difficult and sad time," she said. "It was a real deep connection, a deep marriage." • **Jennifer 'J-Lo' Lopez** files for divorce from dancer **Chris Judd** just ten months after marrying him – and just one night after her 32nd birthday bash in New York where she hooked up with **Ben Affleck**. • The Blockbuster video rental chain boycotts Warner Bros films because of a price hike in rental DVDs. • *Austin Powers* star **Mike Myers** gets his star on the Hollywood Walk of Fame. The location is neatly located in front of the International Love Boutique. • Survivors of the Russian K-19 submarine accuse director **Kathryn Bigelow** of stabbing them in the back. "She promised us we'd be portrayed as heroes, but we're shown as a bunch of alcoholics and illiterates," says Yury Mukhin, 71, a former lieutenant-commander. • China's best-known actress, **Gong Li**, is picked to head the Venice Film Festival jury. • **Steven Spielberg** discloses that his friend and *Star Wars* creator **George Lucas** will not allow him to make a *Star Wars* film. "I wanted to do one 15 years ago and he didn't want me to do it. I understand why – *Star Wars* is George's baby." • **Sam Peckinpah**'s banned film *Straw Dogs*, notorious for a harrowing double-rape scene, has been passed uncut by censors for video release. The BBFC decide to allow the 1971 film a certificate only after advice from clinical psychologists that it will not be harmful to viewers. • India's film censors have decided to screen pornographic films in dedicated cinemas to try to control the huge popularity of adult films in the country. "Since we are unable to control it, we might as well try to regulate it." • **Charlton Heston** reveals that he "has symptoms similar to Alzheimer's disease".

AUGUST 2002

Right: Lisa Marie Presley and Nicolas Cage at the Los Angeles premiere of *Windtalkers* (Rex Features)

Disney's income slides a further seven per cent in the third quarter of what is shaping up as a disastrous year. Total revenue fell by three per cent and the firm's share price has tumbled 21per cent in the last 12 months. The losses are being blamed on a theme park slump in the wake of September the 11th. A Bombay court restrains the media from publicising a taped conversation alleged to be between major Bollywood star **Sanjay Dutt** and **Chota Shakeel**, a leading member of an organised crime syndicate. The recording was submitted as evidence in the ongoing trial of one of Bollywood's biggest film financiers, **Bharat Shah**. • **Priscilla Presley** unveils plans to turn her romance with **Elvis Presley** into a musical, to coincide with the upcoming 25th anniversary of Presley's death. Meanwhile, **Lisa Marie Presley** and **Nicolas Cage** tie the knot in a very private ceremony in Hawaii just a week before the same anniversary. • **Sir Quentin Thomas** – who played a key part in securing peace in Northern Ireland – is named the new president of the British Board of Film Classification. He replaces **Andreas Whittam Smith**, who left to take up a post at the Church of England. • **Leonardo DiCaprio** urges US president George W Bush to attend the Earth Summit in South Africa at a rally organised by Global Green USA, an affiliate of Green Cross International. "Mr Bush, we're asking for your support, to be the president that looks towards the future." • **Jason Priestley** is involved in a crash during a race at the Kentucky Speedway – he suffers a spinal fracture, a head injury, broken bones in both his feet and amnesia. "We have no indication from any of the scans that he's had that he has any further damage to his head," doctors say. "He has his eyes open, he looks around and will follow commands." They later announce that Priestley should make a full recovery. • **Virgin Records** apparently renege on a promise to cover the costs of preparing and shipping the bodies of singer-actress **Aaliyah** and eight others back to the United States. Lawsuits, many lawsuits, are in progress.

SEPTEMBER 2001

Over 5000 people apply to play extras in **Mel Gibson's** new film about Christ, *The Passion*, at an open casting call in the Italian town of Matera. • **Laurence Fishburne** and **Gina Torres** marry after seven years as a couple. • **John Travolta** and **Olivia Newton-John** thrill guests at a Hollywood party by reliving scenes from *Grease* to celebrate the film's DVD release. It is later reported they are to star in a sequel that will feature the children of the original characters, set in the 1970s disco era and imaginatively titled *Grease 3*. • **Paul Newman** returns to Broadway after 40 years off stage to appear in a revival of Thornton Wilder's classic play, *Our Town*. • **Steven Soderbergh**, **Robert Altman**, **Martin Scorsese** and **Steven Spielberg** launch a lawsuit against CleanFlicks, an American company that releases expurgated versions of well-known films on video, taking out sex, violence and swearing. They are among the plaintiffs in a class action filed by the Directors Guild of America. "It is unconscionable, and unethical, to take someone else's hard work, alter it and profit from it," Soderbergh said. • **Tom Hanks** announces he is giving up directing films, saying he would rather leave the job to **Steven Spielberg** after several (quite good) directorial efforts. "You're always thinking about what you've got to do. As soon as you say you're gonna direct a motion picture, the risks just keep piling up. It just goes on, and on, and on, and never lets up until the movie comes out. The stuff of your worst nightmares, you know." • **Nick Nolte** is arrested for driving under the influence • **Sarah Jessica Parker** and **Matthew Broderick** are the proud parents of a baby son, David. • **Matt Damon** criticises the rating given to his movie *The Bourne Identity*. Damon thinks the film is unsuitable for youngsters due to its violent content, and pushed for a '15' classification. "I would urge parents to be very mindful, and maybe go see the movie first before they let a 12-year-old see it." • Bollywood star **Salman Khan** is charged with rash and negligent driving after his car jumps onto a pavement, killing one person and injuring three others who were sleeping there.

OCTOBER 2001

Jackie Chan unveils his star on the Hollywood Walk of Fame, but also admits that he is tired of being the world's greatest action star and wants to be, sigh, a "real actor". • Because of serial sniper killings in Maryland, 20th Century Fox shelve the US release of the similarly themed *Phone Booth* indefinitely. • **Jude Law** and **Sadie Frost** suffer a serious scare when their two-year-old toddler **Iris Law** accidentally swallows Ecstasy at a children's party at an exclusive West End club.

NOVEMBER 2001

Spider-Man creator **Stan Lee** sues comic book publishers Marvel Entertainment for £6.5 million, claiming they cheated him out of "jackpot" film profits. The 80-year-old cartoonist wants ten per cent of all takings from movies about his characters, which also include the Incredible Hulk, the X-men and Daredevil. • **Ben Affleck** and **Jennifer Lopez** are set to marry. J-Lo's pre-nuptial agreement includes "sex at least four times a week; a £3 million fine should Affleck have an affair; as many children as J-Lo wants; access to his film set when Affleck is filming a love scene; a £600,000 fine every time he is caught lying; and to be surprised with gifts on a regular basis." • **Nicolas Cage** files for divorce from **Lisa Marie Presley** after only three months of marriage, citing 'irreconcilable differences'.

Right: Jennifer Lopez and Ben Affleck at the New York premiere of *Maid in Manhattan* (Rex Features)

DECEMBER 2001

Kathleen Turner enters rehab. • **Michael J Fox** gets his Hollywood star. • **Mel Gibson** gets $25 million to return to the *Mad Max* franchise, to be directed by its original director **George Miller**. • **Steven Spielberg** announces that Indiana Jones IV *is* going ahead with **Harrison Ford** and **Sean Connery** on board. • **Dobby**, **Gollum** and **Yoda** become the first computer-generated characters up for an industry award. The US Broadcast Film Critics Association institute a Best Digital Acting Performance category to recognise the advent of the 'synthespian'. The winner is … Gollum, unnaturally. • **Winona Ryder** is sentenced to 480 hours' community service, three years' probation and a fine of $10,000. She is then offered a modelling contract by Mark Jacobs, the company whose clothes Ms Ryder stole from Saks Fifth Avenue in Beverly Hills. • **Brian Cox** reveals that he nearly turned down a CBE because he disagreed with the British honours system. • **Jean-Paul Belmondo**, 69, marries a former dancer in Paris. • **Rosie O'Donnell** marries her girlfriend Kellie Carpenter in a private ceremony over Christmas.

JANUARY 2002

Alan Bates and **Ridley Scott** are knighted in the New Year's Honours, while **Edward Fox** is awarded an OBE. • **Julianne Moore** announces her engagement to longtime boyfriend, film director **Bart Freundlich**. • **Paul Bettany** and **Jennifer Connelly** tie the knot in a quiet ceremy in Scotland. • **Steven Spielberg** gets his star on the Hollywood Walk of Fame. • **Jude Law** and **Sadie Frost** withdraw from the production company Natural Nylon because they're "too busy." Co-founder Ewan McGregor pulled out last year. • Maori tribes demand that **Tom Cruise** pay a tribute to their sacred Mount Taranaki, which is to be transformed into Japan's Mount Fuji for his new film *The Last Samurai*. • **Danny Boyle** reveals that *Porno*, the sequel to *Trainspotting*, could face problems because the cast look too healthy to play the burnt-out heroin addicts ten years on from the first film. "They look as if they've been using face cream. They all look great." • *Gremlins* star **Zach Galligan** is arrested for allegedly stealing a CD by Deep Purple from a Tower Records store in Los Angeles. • **Britney Spears** and **Colin Farrell** are caught by cameras in a very public smooch. • **Dennis Quaid**, 48, announces his engagement to former sales rep Anna Poche, who is 28 years his junior.

FEBRUARY 2002

Courtney Love is detained at Heathrow airport for 11 hours, arrested on charges of "verbal abuse". • The 2001 British census reveals that 390,000 people in the UK gave their religion as *Jedi*, equivalent to 0.7 per cent of the population. • **John Cleese** is awarded £13,500 in damages and a full apology from the *Evening Standard* after the newspaper claimed he was no longer funny. • **Helena Bonham Carter** reveals that she is expecting her first child, courtesy of **Tim Burton** (who made a monkey out of her in *Planet of the Apes*). • **Nicole Kidman** reveals that she is phobic about acting: "I've tried to pull out of almost every one I've done because of sheer terror. I can always come up with a list of actresses who would be better, and try to convince the director to cast someone else by showing the list." • **Angelina Jolie** reveals the removal of her 'Billy Bob' tattoo at the Orange British Academy Film Awards.

MARCH 2002

Anthony Hopkins marries the antiques dealer **Stella Arroyave**, 46, in a St David's Day wedding at his cliff-top mansion in Malibu, California. • "Dear Catherine/Mom, we know how hard you worked and we know what a joy it turned out to be. We love you, Michael and Dylan." This is the text of a £12,000 ad that **Michael Douglas** took out in *Variety* to praise his wife for her work in *Chicago*. • **Samantha Morton** reveals she once turned down a $1 million film deal because she was asked to wear a skirt. "There was an instruction to my manager to wear a skirt. I just said 'Fuck off.' I didn't say no, I said fuck off. I was like, 'How dare you say that?' – I probably would have worn a skirt that night but, because I was told to,
I was like 'Go f*** yourself.'" • **Brett Ratner**, who took over the project from *Charlie's Angels* director **McG**, quits the new *Superman* project, frustrated at his failure to find a leading man. **Josh Hartnett**, **Brendan Fraser**, **Paul Walker** and **Matthew Bomer** were all candidates for the role, but could not commit to the trilogy of films written by **J J Abrams**. • **Will Smith** boycotts the Oscars to protest against the war in Iraq. • *The Oscars* (which cancelled its red carpet parade because of the ongoing war in Iraq) receives its lowest TV viewing figures since the 1950s. With just 33.1 million viewers it's the lowest on record since Nielsen Media Research started monitoring the event in 1974. Viewers were apparently more interested in the 24-hour news coverage of *Gulf War: Part II*.*
• **Kirk Douglas** reveals an attempted suicide attempt following his recent stroke. He admits he put the gun he used in the movie *Gunfight at the OK Corral* in his mouth but it hit a bad tooth – which made him forget suicide. The 86-year-old actor says suicidal impulses are natural after suffering a debilitating stroke.*

APRIL 2002

In a Caribbean ceremony, **Liv Tyler** marries **Royston Langdon**, the lead singer of the band Spacehog. • **Russell Crowe** marries the British-born **Danielle Spencer** at a chapel built for the occasion on his ranch in New South Wales, Australia, on his birthday. • **Jude Law** and **Sadie Frost** split up amid rumours that **Nicole Kidman** might have had an affair with Jude. Kidman is not amused and extracts apologies from British papers which accused her of being a home-wrecker by threatening them with lawsuits.
• **Bob Hope** is named 'Hollywood Citizen of the Century' but is too frail to attend the unveiling of his new, improved star on the Walk of Fame. • New York lawyer **Marie Flaherty**, who claims she had the original idea for **Steve Martin's** latest movie *Bringing Down The House*, files a £9.6 million lawsuit against the film's producers, including **Queen Latifah**.*
• **Jim Carrey's** ex-wife insists that $6000 a month is not enough to give their 15-year-old daughter Jane the same luxuries as her dad. **Melissa Womer** wants **Jane Carrey** to have a personal trainer, her own Pilates studio, a car and ski-ing trips to prepare her for a life in showbiz.* • *The Pianist* grosses $100m worldwide, and star **Adrien Brody** lands himself a modelling contract with Ermenegildo Zegna, who provided the suits he wore to collect his best actor Oscar for the film.* • *Anger Management* grosses $100m and also scores the highest debut of the year so far, spanking *Daredevil's* new record for an April opening.
• **Michael Douglas** and **Catherine Zeta-Jones** obtain a partial victory in their £3

million High Court action over unauthorised photographs of their November 2000 wedding being published in *Hello!* magazine. Mr Justice Lindsay ruled *Hello!* breached the couple's rights of confidence but they had no legal claim on an invasion of privacy. During the trial **Zeta-Jones** testified that the couple felt like hunted animals and that the photos taken by the magazine were "sleazy and unflattering" and made her look unnaturally "large".

MAY 2002

Catherine Zeta-Jones and **Michael Douglas** threaten Clear Channel Worldwide with legal action over topless pictures of the heavily pregnant star which have appeared on over 1200 US websites – showing her smoking while carrying their daughter Carys. • *Johnny English* grosses $100 million worldwide – prior to its opening in the US. • **Brooke Shields** gives birth to her first child, a baby girl, at the age of 37. • **Roger Moore** is admitted to hospital after reportedly fainting from exhaustion and dehydration during a Broadway performance of a song and dance number in the comedy *The Play What I Wrote*, but emerges weeks later with a new pacemaker for his heart.* • **Demi Moore**'s ex-ranch manager claims she tried to seduce him and then sacked him when he turned her down, and has sued for £120,000 as damages for sexual harrassment and discrimination. Is this life imitating *Disclosure*, or was Lawrence Bass just dreaming?* • London university lecturer **Sue Clayton** reveals the blueprint for a perfect blockbusting feature: action 30 per cent, comedy 17 per cent, good v evil 13 per cent, love/sex/romance 12 per cent, special effects 10 per cent, plot 10 per cent and music 8 per cent. In a study commissioned by Diet Coke to help it decide on what films to sponsor, *Toy Story* is named the closest to perfection according to the formula, with *Shakespeare in Love* coming a close second, only losing out because of a lack of special effects. • **Sandra Bullock** wins a restraining order against a mentally ill man she claims stalked her in three states across America. • **Jennifer Garner** files for divorce from actor **Scott Foley** after three years of marriage. • **Tobey Maguire** reveals how a back injury led producers of the *Spider-Man* sequel to replace him with **Jake Gyllenhaal**. **Ron Meyer**, the head of Universal and father of Maguire's girlfriend **Jennifer Meyer**, convinced the actor to fight for his role, and lobbied to have him reinstated. Maguire had to undergo a physical examination that included swinging from a harness before he was allowed to resume the role. • **Jennifer Lopez** is sued for £3 million by **Adam Shankman**, her director in *The Wedding Planner*, who claims she stole his idea for a film based on the opera *Carmen*. • **Halle Berry** breaks her ulna during a stunt in the supernatural thriller *Gothika*, forcing her off set for several weeks. This girl is unlucky; she was also wounded by a grenade while filming *Die Another Day*. • The premiere of *Matrix Reloaded* becomes the most expensive event in the history of Cannes. An estimated £2 million was spent on the prestigious party, including more than £600,000 on private jets and hotel rooms for the film's stars, £900,000 on computer equipment to recreate the film's special effects, and £250,000 for the F & B. • Filming of **Baz Luhrmann**'s *Alexander the Great* in Morocco has been suspended after a car bomb killed 41 in Casablanca. The Macedonian epic – starring **Leonardo DiCaprio** and **Nicole Kidman** – will resume shooting once new locations have been set up. • **Kenneth Branagh** marries art director **Lindsay Brunnock** in a small and secret ceremony. • *Matrix Reloaded* breaks box-office records around the world, taking more than £68 million in its second week of release in 62 countries outside the US. It is the first time the US$100m mark has been broken in a film's second week. But the film lost pole position at the US box-office to **Jim Carrey's** divine comedy *Bruce Almighty*.* • **Keanu Reeves** plans to donate £50 million in profits from the two Matrix sequels to effects and costume designers who worked on the movies. Based on his contract giving him 15 per cent of the box-office takings, expected to pull in about £450 million worldwide, Reeves can expect a payout of nearly £70 million. "Money is the last thing I think about. I could live on what I've already made for the next few centuries." While filming the sequels in Australia, he surprised 12 stuntmen by giving them Harley-Davidson motorbikes. • **Sean Connery** takes charge of the big-budget blockbuster film *The League Of Extraordinary Gentlemen*. He has been overseeing the editing process of the film from bases in the Bahamas, New York and Los Angeles. Filming of the movie, which ended earlier this year, was dogged by a series of arguments between the actor and director **Stephen Norrington**. It was also disrupted when flooding on location in Prague damaged sets worth £7 million. • **Renée Zellweger** signs up to star in *Bridget Jones 2* in a deal reported to be worth £15 million.

JUNE 2002

Mancunian **Andy Green** is being plagued by calls asking for God because his phone number is the same as that of the fictional God in **Jim Carrey**'s *Bruce Almighty*. "At weekends I'm getting up to 70 calls a day. Most people ring off when they hear my voice. They don't expect God to have a Manchester accent." He added: "The problem is I'm starting to believe I'm God. I might have to go into therapy." • **Kevin Costner** reveals he is to marry his long-term girlfriend **Christine Baumgartner.** • Sussex-based writer **Alan Davidson** sues Steven Spielberg's DreamWorks studio and animators **Peter Lord** and **Nick Park**, claiming *Chicken Run* was based on his 1995 novel *Escape From Cold Ditch*.

• **Adam Sandler** marries his model girlfriend **Jackie Titone** in a star-studded Malibu ceremony. Sandler goes to great lengths to keep the ceremony private, using giant balloons to keep helicopters at a distance. Sandler's pet bulldog attends the ceremony dressed in a dinner jacket. Sandler met Jackie in 1999 on the set of his film *Big Daddy*. • *Hulk* sets a June opening record of $62.6 million, surpassing the previous record ($54.9 million) for *Austin Powers: The Spy Who Shagged Me*, although the latter actually sold more tickets.

• *The Exorcist* author **William Peter Blatty** and director **William Friedkin** file a lawsuit against Warner Bros, alleging the studio didn't do enough to make them money. They claim Warner Bros breached its fiduciary duty by self-dealing the rights for a newer version of the film and sold the rights to its sister cable networks, TNT and TBS, for little to no profit. Fiduciary? • A month after opening his easyCinema in Milton Keynes (offering no-frills cinema seats for as little as 20 pence), **Stelios Haji-Ioannou**, founder of the Easy Group of companies, complains that the six large companies which control 90 per cent of film distribution have refused to sell 'first run' rights to him. The tycoon says he did not have evidence of a cartel but felt there was "tacit collusion" in the industry against easyCinema and the idea of price competition.

• **Sharon Stone** says suffering a brain haemorrhage has had one advantage – curbing her temper.

• **Arnold Schwarzenegger** confirms that he is considering running for the governorship of the state of California, but would decide only after the 2 July opening of *Terminator 3: Rise of the Machines*, perhaps to make sure that his fans are still out there. • **Harrison Ford** is lost for words as he receives a star on the Hollywood Walk of Fame. When asked to make a speech outside the Kodak Theatre in Los Angeles, he stammers and finally says, "I'm grateful for this treasure here in front of the Kodak Theatre, grateful for the attention and the kind words and this honour."

Left: The next Governor of California at the Los Angeles premiere of *Terminator 3: Rise of the Machines* (Rex Features)

Movie Quotations of the Year

QUOTES ON SCREEN

'It is an historical fact, sharing has never been humanity's defining attribute.'
Professor Xavier, *X-Men 2*

Michal: 'Idealists do not suffer.'
Menachem: 'But around any idealist there are people who suffer much.'
From *Time of Favor*

'Natural law. Sons are put on this earth to trouble their fathers.'
John Rooney, *Road to Perdition*

'A man can lose his soul. He can lose his life. But the worst thing he can lose is his teeth.'
Frank Sanger, *Novocaine*

Roxie Hart: 'God that''s beautiful!'
Billy Flynn: 'Cut out God. Stay where you're better acquainted.'
From *Chicago*

Roxie Hart: 'It''ll never work ... I HATE YOU!'
Velma Kelly: 'There's only one business where that's no problem at all.'
From *Chicago*

Frida Kahlo: 'What do you think matters most for a good marriage?'
Guillermo Kahlo: 'A short memory.'
Frida Kahlo: 'Why did you get married?'
Guillermo Kahlo: 'I can't remember.'
From *Frida*

Paul Denton: 'Do you have any E?'
Harry: 'That shit makes your spinal fluid run backwards.'
From *Rules of Attraction*

Lara: 'It's amazing how much weight you lose when you go off The Pill.'
Lauren: 'Which is nothing compared to the 50 pounds you gain when you get knocked up.'
From *Rules of Attraction*

Hannibal Lecter: 'You're a remarkable boy. You're so courageous. I think I'll eat your heart. '
From *Red Dragon*

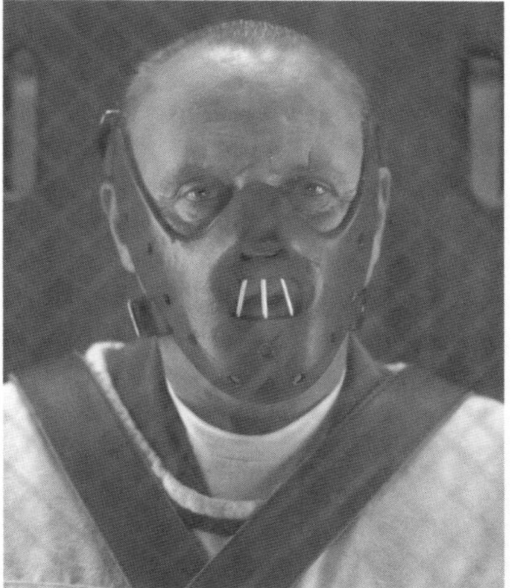

Above: Nicole Kidman arrives at the premiere of *The Others* at the end of October

Frank Abagnale Jr: 'I don't want to lie to you anymore, all right. I'm not a doctor. I never went to medical school. I'm not a lawyer, or a Harvard Graduate, or a Lutheran. I ran away from home a year and a half ago when I was 15.'
Brenda Strong: 'Frank? You're not a Lutheran?'
From *Catch Me If You Can*

Helen: 'What does your therapist say about all of this?'
Jessica: 'Oh, I could never tell my therapist.'
Helen: 'Why not?'
Jessica: 'Because it's private.'
From *Kissing Jessica Stein*

Johnny English: 'The only thing that France is adept at hosting is an invasion.'
From *Johnny English*

Ginny: 'Read the brochure in there ... it's all around us. 100 years ago the government moved these Indians here. They all died because there was no water.'
Rhodes: 'Well, now they're coming back to life! Like sea monkeys, huh?'
From *Identity*

Thomas Ripley: 'You know the most interesting thing about doing something terrible? That after a few days, you can't even remember it.'
From *Ripley's Game*

Daphne: 'Those creatures are taking over the world? That's *so* mean!'
From *Scooby-Doo*

QUOTES OFF-SCREEN

'My husband asked,'Are you going to wear pointy ears?' I said,'Yes.' He said,'Do it!''
Cate Blanchett on playing an elf in the *The Lord of the Rings: The Two Towers*

'My training has been total: I've done everything except rodeos and porn.'
Bea Arthur, 82

'It just makes you feel permanently like a girl walking past construction workers.'
Brad Pitt on female adulation

'I don't want to be emotionally provoked all the time. If I had to do an intense black comedy every day, I would kill myself, my friends would abandon me, and no one would want to be near me.'
Rachel Weisz

Soundtracks

by James Cameron-Wilson

What was the best soundtrack of the 2002/2003 period? **John Williams**' *Catch Me if You Can*, for which he was bestowed with his 42nd Academy Award nomination? No. **Thomas Newman**'s Oscar-nominated *Road to Perdition*? No way. Well, how about **Elliot Goldenthal**'s inspirational, Oscar-winning score for *Frida*? Very close, but no Havana. In my humble opinion the most effortlessly enjoyable soundtrack was a jazzy recreation of a 27-year-old work: *Chicago*. One of the year's most unexpected successes (at the time of writing it has grossed over $300 million worldwide), the film dumbfounded its detractors and waltzed off with a staggering 13 Oscar nominations, winning a total of six, including the gong for Best Picture. Following in the star-spangled wake of *Moulin Rouge!*, this spelled a healthy resurgence for the musical.

While the genre has been a money-spinning staple of the New York and London stage, film versions have proved to be notoriously difficult to pull off. Since the exceptional popularity of *Grease* 25 years ago, such celluloid musicals as *A Chorus Line*, *Hair*, *Popeye*, *The Wiz* and *Xanadu* all perished at the box-office. But with a brand-new audience reared on MTV and with such crossover stars as Madonna and Jennifer Lopez ripe for the picking, the musical is primed for a renaissance. In addition, new technology has brought down the costs of producing what was previously a prohibitively expensive art form, while ancillary benefits range from FM-friendly air play, music videos and, of course, the movie soundtrack.

Musicals also invite repeat viewings, which is more than can be said for story-driven films like *Identity* and *The Recruit*. With such major works as *The Phantom of the Opera*, *Guys and Dolls*, *Rent* and *Urinetown* already in pre-production, the future of the musical soundtrack seems in good hands. Of course, *Chicago* was blessed with an exceptional array of good tunes, including a new one written especially for the film ('I Move On'). However, with savvy musicianship and state-of-the-art production values, the show tune could once again become a regular chart-topper.

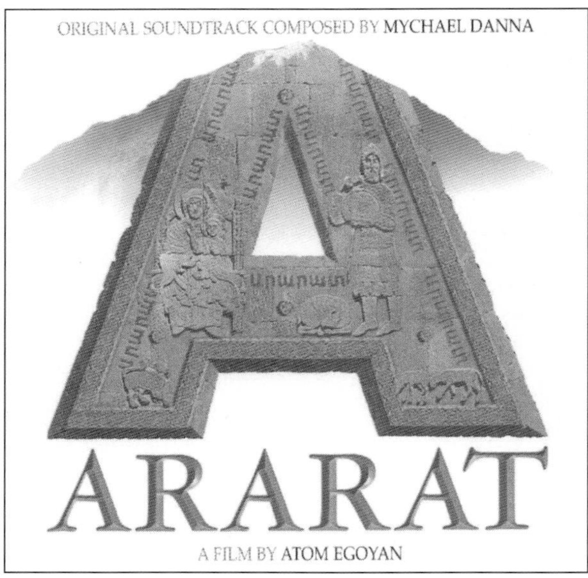

ORIGINAL SOUNDTRACK COMPOSED BY MYCHAEL DANNA
ARARAT
A FILM BY ATOM EGOYAN

Ararat

Mystical, mournful and haunting soundtrack from the endlessly inventive **Mychael Danna**, who collaborates with director Atom Egoyan for the ninth time. Blending the exotic sounds of Armenia with a Western flavour where appropriate, Danna recorded much of the music in a sixth century Armenian church. Standouts include the ethereal voice of the Canadian-Armenian soprano Isabel Bayrakdarian and the simple, penetrating lament of a solitary duduk (a traditional Armenian wind instrument). Profound.

Catch Me If You Can

John Williams' score is a polished, enjoyable evocation of the progressive jazz of the 1960s but it hardly merits an Oscar nomination. Like so many Williams compositions, it draws on some of the composer's old tricks, most notably snatches of

the jollier parts of *Jaws* and *ET*, but merely receives the Academy's approval out of habit.

Chicago

Fabulous, razzle-dazzling, dark-edged, witty and dynamic companion to the Oscar-winning film, one of the best musical soundtracks in aeons. There's even a new song specially penned by the legendary **Fred Ebb** and **John Kander** – the swinging, exuberant (and Oscar-nominated) 'I Move On', delivered with pizzazz by Catherine Zeta-Jones and Renée Zellweger. Seventy minutes of pure, gilt-edged Broadway.

Die Another Day

A highly energised composition from **David Arnold**, initially drawing heavily on variations of Monty Norman's legendary theme (essential), but then introducing some fine new sounds, including the spirited 'Welcome to Cuba', the musing, seductive 'Jinx Jordan' and the downright epic 'Icarus'. Oh, and Madonna's title song rocks.

Far from Heaven

With his effective recreation of the swooping, agitated phrasing of Bernard Herrmann, **Elmer Bernstein** was a shoo-in for an Oscar nomination this year. He's also 83 years old, which gives the old boy a sentimental edge. However, besides the soundtrack's spot-on evocation of rising melodrama, it does get a tad tedious after repeated listenings.

Frida

'Evocative' is an adjective much abused to describe film soundtracks, but in the case of **Elliot Goldenthal**'s Oscar-winning score it is genuinely applicable. Packed with colourful, passionate songs and bridged by Goldenthal's richly nuanced, guitar-led music, this is Mexican Heaven on a plate. Salma Hayek herself sings on 'La Bruja', while Frida Kahlo's former lover – the 83-year-old Chavela Vargas – provides a blood-chilling rendition of 'Paloma Negra.' A very special album, indeed.

Gangs of New York

A microcosm of the entire musical history of the United States, this extraordinary CD showcases 18 of the 86 pieces of music used in the film. Combining archive recordings from the private collections of Martin Scorsese and Robbie Robertson with new works from U2, Peter Gabriel and snippets of **Howard Shore**'s moody score, this is a soundtrack that towers over most others.

Good Bye Lenin!

On the heels of *Amélie*, Yann Tiersen provides another exquisite soundtrack, leading with some simple melodies on piano (played by himself) and backed up by frenzied work from the string section. At times recalling the rich sound of **Michael Nyman**, this is terrific music, both deeply affecting and spiritually rousing. With luck, we'll be hearing a lot more from M Tiersen.

Harry Potter and the Chamber of Secrets

There is an enormous professionalism to **John Williams**' music that makes it so easy to listen to. *The Chamber of Secrets* is another solid work from the 71-year-old composer who, it would seem, can whip up a score in his sleep. In fact, this composition works much better on CD, as it tended to swamp the film it was written for.

Heartlands

This parcel of aural honey is more than this dismal film deserves. With the clear, lyrical voice of rising folk star Kate Rusby (on nine soul-stirring numbers) and the affecting melodies of composer **John McCusker** (etched out on piano, fiddle and accordion), the soundtrack is really quite disarming.

The Hours

This is music of a different kind, a rolling wall of melody that infiltrates every pore. Apparently, the music of **Philip Glass** actually influenced much of the emotional texture of Michael Cunningham's original novel, so it really does serve as one of the cornerstones of this brilliant movie. While some found the score a little intrusive, its fundamental connection to the images painted by Stephen Daldry merely serve to heighten the colour – and pleasure – of this exceptional soundtrack.

The Life of David Gale

Novelty value aside, this is an accomplished score by any standards. Having written temporary tracks for their father's films in the past, musical siblings **Jake** and **Alex Parker** have been given carte blanche with this underrated drama. With Jake's grounding in classical composition and Alex's work as an audio engineer, the brothers complement each other perfectly, providing a rounded, resonant and dramatic score. Alan Parker should be proud.

The Lord of the Rings: The Two Towers

There are a lot of unusual musical instruments on this soundtrack (including the Norwegian fiddle and the rhaita, a North African oboe), the London Philharmonic, hordes of ominous voices and the odd angelic choir. Of course, all this is prize company for a truly unique vision, but you really have to be in the mood to appreciate it. Nevertheless, fans of the Tolkien phenomenon will no doubt relish **Howard Shore**'s surging dark mood swings.

The Matrix Reloaded

If you have to bang your head open, you might as well do it to the year's coolest hard rock compilation. In keeping with everything about the Wachowskis' head-tripping movie, this ensemble boasts some major acts of shrapnel: Linkin Park, Marilyn Manson, POD, Oakenfold and, appropriately, Rage Against the Machine.

My Big Fat Greek Wedding

As sweet as a baklava and thoroughly uplifting, this is a fine match for one of the year's great cinematic joys. A breezy melange of traditional and exotic melodies, the soundtrack – co-produced by Tom Hanks – is further enhanced by an exquisite score from **Alexander Janko** and **Chris Wilson**, played out on piano, guitar, flute and string section.

The Pianist

Considering that the 'pianist' himself, Wladislaw Szpilman, specialised in the compositions of fellow Pole Chopin, it seems apt that this soundtrack is virtually all Chopin. And that is a good thing. Janusz Olejniczak (who doubled for Adrien Brody in the film) dominates the proceedings, in particular bringing a clear poetry to Chopin's ethereal 'Nocturne in C-sharp Minor'. Szpilman himself is represented on the final track, 'Mazurka in A Minor, Op 17, No 4', while **Wojciech Kilar**'s incidental score is reduced to one minute and 52 seconds. So, Chopin rules.

Rabbit-Proof Fence

Moody, dark and undeniably strange, this really does fit **Peter Gabriel**'s pioneering ethnic template. Drawing on the haunting vocals of Pakistan's redoubtable Nusrat Fateh Ali Khan, the percussion of the Adzido Pan African Dance Ensemble and the 'wails' of one Sherry Carter, this is something else, being an evocative, dream-like hymn to the otherworldly universe of the Australian Outback. Unsettling and intense.

Road to Perdition

While much of this lengthy soundtrack is padded out with repetition and functional cues, there is much to commend **Thomas Newman**'s evocative, elegiac score. Baring its Irish soul from the outset, the album draws on the considerable range of the violin, while harnessing the emotional fabric of the film with some excellent pieces on piano. There's even a hesitant, moving duet on the old joanna supplied by none other than Tom Hanks and Paul Newman.

The Wild Thornberrys Movie

In a year of unimpressive song soundtracks, it took the offshoot of a TV cartoon to make an impact. Indeed, this is better than most, being a joyous combination of Western and African sounds, with top acts including Hugh Masekela, Youssou N'Dour, Hijas del Sol, Dave Matthews, Peter Gabriel, Sting and, of course, Paul Simon with his Oscar-nominated 'Father and Daughter'.

Awards and Festivals

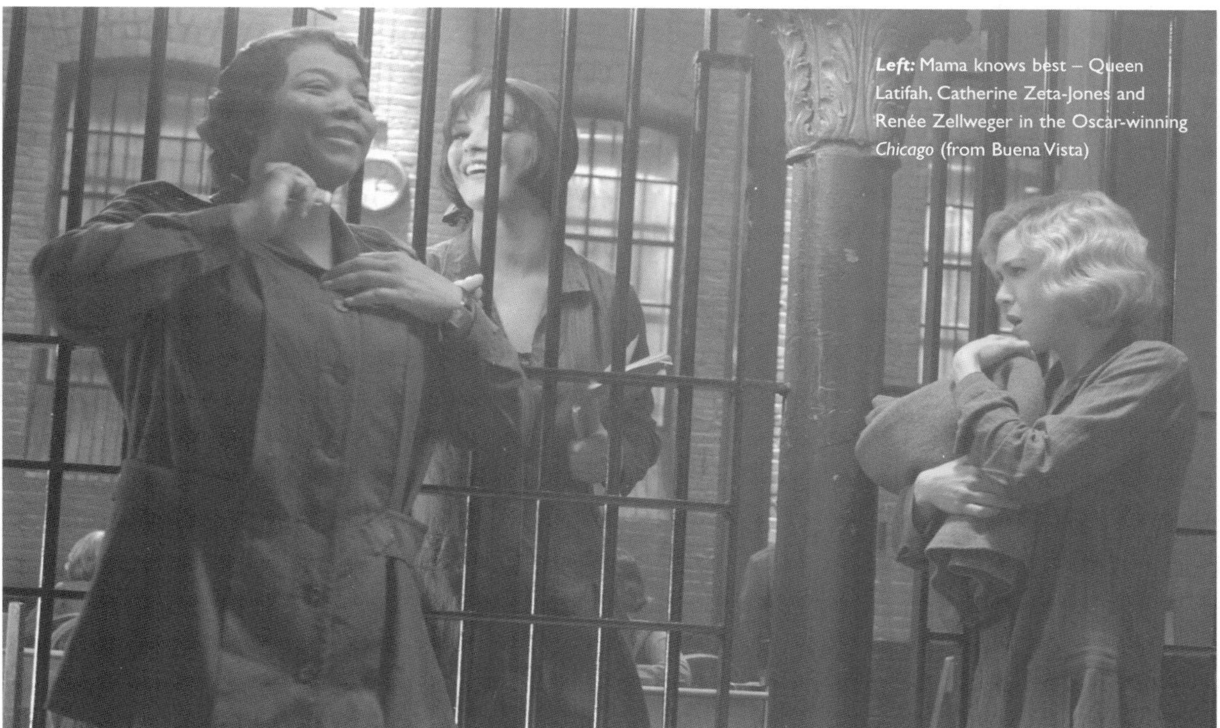

Left: Mama knows best – Queen Latifah, Catherine Zeta-Jones and Renée Zellweger in the Oscar-winning *Chicago* (from Buena Vista)

The 75th American Academy of Motion Picture Arts and Sciences Awards ('The Oscars') and nominations for 2002, Los Angeles, 23 March 2003.

• **Best Motion Picture:** *Chicago.*
Nominations: *Gangs of New York*; *The Hours*; *The Lord of the Rings: The Two Towers*; *The Pianist.*
• **Best Director:**
Roman Polanski, for *The Pianist.*
Nominations: Pedro Almodóvar, for *Talk to Her*; Stephen Daldry, for *The Hours*; Rob Marshall, for *Chicago*; Martin Scorsese, for *Gangs Of New York.*
• **Best Actor:**
Adrien Brody, for *The Pianist.*
Nominations: Nicolas Cage, for *Adaptation*; Michael Caine, for *The Quiet American*; Daniel Day-Lewis, for *Gangs of New York*; Jack Nicholson, for *About Schmidt.*
• **Best Actress:**
Nicole Kidman, for *The Hours.*
Nominations: Salma Hayek, for *Frida*; Diane Lane, for *Unfaithful*; Julianne Moore, for *Far from Heaven*; Renée Zellweger, for *Chicago.*
• **Best Supporting Actor:**
Chris Cooper, for *Adaptation.*
Nominations: Ed Harris, for *The Hours*; Paul Newman, for *Road to Perdition*; John C Reilly, for *Chicago*; Christopher Walken, for *Catch Me If You Can.*
• **Best Supporting Actress:**
Catherine Zeta-Jones, for *Chicago.*
Nominations: Kathy Bates, for *About Schmidt*; Julianne Moore, for *The Hours*; Queen Latifah, for *Chicago*; Meryl Streep, for *Adaptation.*
• **Best Original Screenplay:**
Pedro Almodóvar, for *Talk to Her.*
Nominations: Todd Haynes, for *Far from Heaven*; Jay Cocks, Steven Zaillian and Kenneth Lonergan, for *Gangs of New York*; Nia Vardalos, for *My Big Fat Greek Wedding*; Carlos Cuarón and Alfonso Cuarón, for *Y tu Mamá también.*
• **Best Screenplay Adaptation:**
Ronald Harwood, for *The Pianist.*
Nominations: Peter Hedges, Chris Weitz and Paul Weitz for *About a Boy*; Charlie Kaufman and Donald Kaufman for *Adaptation*; Bill Condon, for *Chicago*; David Hare, for *The Hours.*
• **Best Cinematography:**
Conrad L Hall, for *Road to Perdition.*
Nominations: Dion Beebe, for *Chicago*; Edward Lachman, for *Far from Heaven*; Michael Ballhaus, for *Gangs of New York*; Pawel Edelman, for *The Pianist.*
• **Best Editing:**
Martin Walsh, for *Chicago.*
Nominations: Thelma Schoonmaker, for *Gangs of New York*; Peter Boyle, for *The Hours*; Michael Horton, for *The Lord of the Rings: The Two Towers*; Hervé de Luze, for *The Pianist.*
• **Best Original Score:**
Elliot Goldenthal, for *Frida.*
Nominations: John Williams, for *Catch Me If You Can*; Elmer Berstein, for *Far from Heaven*; Philip Glass, for *The Hours*; Thomas Newman, for *Road To Perdition.*
• **Best Original Song:**
'Lose Yourself' by Eminem, Jeff Bass and Luis Resto, lyrics by Eminem, from *8 Mile.*

Left: Orlando Bloom in Best Visual Effects winner *The Lord of the Rings: The Two Towers* (from Entertainment)

Right Meryl Streep in Silver Bear winner *Adaptation* (from Columbia Tristar)

Nominations: 'Burn It Blue' by Elliot Goldenthal, lyrics by Julie Taymor, from *Frida*; 'Father and Daughter' by Paul Simon, from *The Wild Thornberrys Movie*; 'The Hands That Built America' by Bono, The Edge, Adam Clayton and Larry Mullen, from *Gangs of New York*; 'I Move On' by John Kander, lyrics by Fred Ebb, from *Chicago*.

• **Best Art Direction:** John Myhre (art direction) and Gord Sim (set decoration), for *Chicago*. Nominations: Felipe Fernandez del Paso (art direction) and Hannia Robledo (set decoration) for *Frida*; Dante Ferretti (art direction) and Francesca Lo Schiavo (set decoration), for *Gangs of New York*; Grant Major (art direction) and Dan Hennah and Alan Lee (set decoration), for *The Lord of the Rings: The Two Towers*; Dennis Gassner (art direction) and Nancy Haigh (set decoration) for *Road to Perdition*.

• **Best Costume Design:** Colleen Atwood, for *Chicago*. Nominations: Julie Weiss, for *Frida*; Sandy Powell, for *Gangs of New York*; Ann Roth, for *The Hours*; Anna Sheppard, for *The Pianist*.

• **Best Sound:** Michael Minkler, Dominick Tavella and David Lee, for *Chicago*. Nominations: Tom Fleischman, Eugene Gearty and Ivan Sharrock, for *Gangs of New York*; Christopher Boyes, Michael Semanick, Michael Hedges and Hammond Peek, for *The Lord of the Rings: The Two Towers*; Scott Millan, Bob Beemer and John Patrick Pritchett, for *Road to Perdition*; Kevin O'Connell, Greg P Russell and Ed Novick, for *Spider-Man*.

• **Best Sound Editing:** Ethan Van der Ryn and Michael Hopkins, for *The Lord of the Rings: The Two Towers*. Nominations: Richard Hymns and Gary Rydstrom, for *Minority Report*; Scott A Hecker, for *Road to Perdition*.

• **Best Visual Effects:** Jim Rygiel, Joe Letteri, Randall William Cook and Alex Funke, for *The Lord of the Rings: The Two Towers*. Nominations: John Dykstra, Scott Stokdyk, Anthony LaMolinara and John Frazier, for *Spider-Man*; Rob Coleman, Pablo Helman, John Knoll and Ben Snow, for *Star Wars: Episode II - Attack Of The Clones*.

• **Best Documentary Feature:** *Bowling for Columbine* by Michael Moore and Michael Donovan. Nominations: *Daughter from Danang*, by Gail Dolgin and Vincente Franco; *Prisoner of Paradise*, by Malcolm Clarke and Stuart Sender; *Spellbound*, by Jeffrey Blitz and Sean Welch; *Winged Migration*, by Jacques Perrin.

• **Best Documentary Short:** *Twin Towers*, by Bill Guttentag and Robert David Port. Nominations: *The Collector of Bedford Street*, by Alice Elliott; *Mighty Times: The Legacy of Rosa Parks*, by Robert Hudson and Bobby Houston; *Why Can't We Be a Family Again?*, by Roger Weisberg and Murray Nossel.

• **Best Foreign Language Film:** *Nowhere in Africa* (Germany). Nominations: *The Crime of Father Amaro* (Mexico); *Hero* (China); *The Man Without a Past* (Finland); *Zus & Zo* (The Netherlands).

• **Best Makeup:** John Jackson and Beatrice De Alba, for *Frida*. Nominations: John M Elliott, Jr and Barbara Lorenz, for *The Time Machine*.

• **Best Animated Film:** *Spirited Away*, directed by Hayao Miyazaki. Nominations: *Ice Age*, directed by Chris Wedge; *Lilo & Stitch*, directed by Chris Sanders; *Spirit: Stallion of the Cimarron*, directed by Jeffrey Katzenberg; *Treasure Planet*, directed by Ron Clements.

• **Best Animated Short:** *The Chubbchubbs!*, by Eric Armstrong. Nominations: *The Cathedral*, by Tomek Baginski; *Das Rad*, by Chris Stenner and Heidi Wittlinger; *Mike's New Car*, by Pete Docter and Roger Gould; *Mt Head*, by Koji Yamamura.

• **Best Live Action Short Film:** *This Charming Man (Der Er En Yndig Mand)*, by Martin Strange-Hansen and Mie Andreasen. Nominations: *Fait d'Hiver*, by Dirk Beliën and Anja Daelemans, *I'll Wait for the Next One... (J'attendrai le suivant...)*, by Philippe Orreindy and Thomas Gaudin, *Inja (Dog)*, by Steven Pasvolsky and Joe Weatherstone, *Johnny Flynton*, by Lexi Alexander and Alexander Buono.

• **Honorary Award:** Peter O'Toole, actor.

44th Australian Film Institute Awards, 7 December 2002.

• **Best Film:**
Rabbit-Proof Fence
• **Best Actor:**
David Gulpilil, for *The Tracker*
• **Best Actress:**
Maria Theodorakis, for *Walking on Water*
• **Best Supporting Actor:**
Nathaniel Dean, *Walking on Water*
• **Best Supporting Actress:**
Judi Farr, for *Walking on Water*
• **Best Director:**
Ivan Sen, for *Beneath Clouds*
• **Best Original Screenplay:**
Roger Monk, for *Walking on Water*
• **Best Screenplay Adaptation:**
Phillip Gwynne and Paul Goldman, for *Australian Rules*
• **Best Cinematography:**
Allan Collins, for *Beneath Clouds*
• **Best Editing:**
Reva Childs, for *Walking on Water*
• **Best Foreign Film:**
The Lord of the Rings: The Fellowship of the Ring (USA)
• **Best Music:**
Peter Gabriel, for *Rabbit-Proof Fence*
• **Best Documentary:**
A Wedding in Ramallah
• **Young Actors Award:** Emily Browning, for *Halifax f.p (Playing God)*
• **Global Achievement Award:**
Mel Gibson

The 53rd Berlin International Film Festival, 16 February 2003

• **Jury President:** Atom Egoyan
• **The Golden Bear for Best Film:**
In This World (UK)
• **Silver Bear for Jury Grand Prize:**
Adaptation (USA)
• **Silver Bear for Best Actor:**
Sam Rockwell, for *Confessions of a Dangerous Mind*
• **Silver Bear for Best Actress:**
Meryl Streep, Nicole Kidman, and Julianne Moore, for *The Hours*
• **Silver Bear for Best Director:**
Patrice Chéreau, for *Son frère*
• **Golden Bear for Best Short Film:**
Best Short Film *(A)Torzija* (Slovenia)
• **Silver Bear for Best Short Film:**
En ausencia (Argentina);
Ischov tramwai N°9 (Ukraine)
• **Blue Angel Prize:**
Wolfgang Becker, for *Goodbye, Lenin!*
• **Silver Bear for Outstanding Artistic Achievement:** Screenwriter and Director Yang Li, for *Mang jing*
• **Ecumenical Jury Prize:**
Best Film: *In This World* (UK)
New Cinema Forum: *Edi* (Poland)
Panorama: *Knafayim Shvurot* (Israel)

• **FIPRESCI Prizes (International Film Critics' Association):**
• Best Film: *Lichter*
• **New Cinema Forum:** *Edi* (Poland)
• **Panorama:** *Wolfsburg* (Germany)
• **Wolfgang Staudte Prize:**
Rengeteg (Hungary)
• **CICAE Award (international confederation of art cinemas):**
New Cinema Forum: *Amarelo Manga* (Brazil)
• **Panorama:** *Knafayim Shvurot* (Israel)
German Art House Cinemas Guild:
My Life Without Me (Spain/Canada)
• **Gay Teddy Bear Award, Best Feature:**
Mil nubes de paz cercan el cielo, amor, jamás acabarás de ser amor (Mexico)
• **Peace Film Prize:** *In This World* (UK)
• **Panorama Audience Award:**
Knafayim Shvurot (Israel)

• **Honorary Golden Berlin Bear:**
Anouk Aimée

The 23rd Canadian Film Awards ('Genies'), Toronto, Ontario, 13 February 2002.

• **Best Film:**
Ararat
• **Best Director:**
David Cronenberg, for *Spider*
• **Best Actor:**
Luc Picard, for *Savage Messiah*
• **Best Actress:**
Arsinée Khanjian, for *Ararat*
• **Best Supporting Actor:**
Elias Koteas, for *Ararat*
• **Best Supporting Actress:** Pascale Montpetit, for *Savage Messiah*
• **Best Screenplay:**
Deepa Metha, for *Bollywood/Hollywood*
• **Best Screenplay Adaptation:**
Sharon Riis, for *Savage Messiah*
• **Best Art Direction/Production Design:**
François Seguin, for *Almost America*
• **Best Cinematography:**
Paul Sarossy, for *Perfect Pie*
• **Best Costume Design:**
Beth Pasternak, for *Ararat*
• **Best Editing:**
Lara Mazur, for *Suddenly Naked*
• **Best Original Score:**
Mychael Danna, for *Ararat*
• **Best Original Song:**
'Com Estas Asas' by Carlos Lopes, for *Saint Monica*
• **Best Sound:**
Tom Hidderley, Todd Beckett, Keith Elliott, Mark Zsifkovitz, for *Between Strangers*
• **Best Sound Editing:**
Fred Brennan, Roderick Deogrades, Barry Gilmore, Andy Malcolm, David McCallum, Jane Tattersall, for *Max*

• **Best Feature-Length Documentary:**
Gambling, Gods and LSD, by Ingrid Veninger and Peter Mettler
• **Best Animated Short:**
The Hungry Squid, by Marcy Page and John Weldon
• **Best Live-Action Short Drama:**
I Shout Love, by Meredith Caplan, Sarah Polley, and Jennifer Weiss

2002 Golden Reel Award for Box-Office Performance: *Les Boys III*, which grossed $5.3 million at the Canadian box-office between 21 October 2001 and 20 October 2002

• **Special Awards:**
Robert Daudelin, Sheila Copps

The 56th Cannes Film Festival Awards: 14-24 May 2003.

• **Jury:** Patrice Chéreau (president); Aishwarya Rai, Meg Ryan, Karin Viard , Erri De Luca, Jean Rochefort, Steven Soderbergh, Danis Tanovic, Wen Jiang.
• **Palme d'Or for best Film:**
Elephant (USA), by Gus Van Sant
• **Grand Prix du Jury:**
Uzak (Turkey), by Nuri Bilge Ceylan
• **Best Actor:**
Nuri Bilge Ceylan, for *Uzak*
• **Best Actress:**
Marie-Josée Croze, for *Les Invasions barbares – le déclin continue*
• **Best Director:**
Gus Van Sant, for *Elephant* (USA)
• **Best Screenplay:**
Denys Arcand, for *Les Invasions barbares – le déclin continue*
• **Palme d'Or for Best Short Film:**
Cracker Bag (Australia), by Glendyn Ivin
• **Prix du Jury for Best Film:**
Panj é asr (Iran/France), by Samira Makhmalbaf
• **Prix du Jury for Best Short Film:**
L'Homme sans tête (France), by Juan Diego Solanas
• **Cinefondation Award:**
First Prize: *Bezi zeko bezi* (Yugoslavia), by Pavle Vuckovic
• **Second Prize:**
Historia del desierto (UK), by Celia Galan Julve
• **Third Prize (tied):** *Rebeca a esas alturas* (Mexico), by Luciana Jauffred Gorostiza; *TV City* (Germany), by Alberto Couceiro, Alejandra Tomei
• **Camera d'Or (for First Feature):**
Reconstruction (Denmark), by Christoffer Boe

FIPRESCI Prizes (International Film Critics' Association):
• **Director's Fortnight:**
Las horas del día (Spain), by Jaime Rosales
Competition: *Otets i syn* (Russia), by Aleksandr Sokurov
• **Un Certain Regard:**
American Splendor (USA), by Shari Springer Berman and Robert Pulcini
• **Ecumenical Prizes:**
Panj é asr (Iran/France), by Samira Makhmalbaf
• **Critics' Week Awards Grand Prize:**
Depuis qu'Otar est parti (France/Belgium), by Julie Bertucelli
• **Honorary Golden Palm:** Jeanne Moreau

15th Annual European Film Awards ('The Felixes'), Teatro dell'Opera, Rome, 7 December 2002.

• **Best European Film 2002:**
Hable con ella (Talk to Her) (Spain), by Pedro Almodóvar
• **Best European Director:**
Pedro Almodóvar, for *Hable con ella (Talk to Her)*
• **Best European Actor:**
Sergio Castellitto, for *Bella Martha (Mostly Martha)* and *L'ora di religione (My Mother's Smile)*

• **Best European Actress(es):** the ensemble cast of *8 Femmes*: Catherine Deneuve, Isabelle Huppert, Emmanuelle Béart, Fanny Ardant, Virginie Ledoyen, Danielle Darrieux, Ludivine Sagnier, Firmine Richard
• **Best Screenwriter:**

Below: Adrien Brody in *The Pianist* (from Universal). Both were Cesar winners

Pedro Almodóvar, for *Hable con ella (Talk to Her)*
• **Best Cinematographer:**
Pawel Edelman, for *The Pianist*
• **Achievement in World Cinema:**
Victoria Abril
• **Discovery of the Year (the Fassbinder Award):** Director György Palfi, for *Hukkle*
• **Best Documentary (Prix Arte):**
Etre et avoir (To Be and To Have) (France), by Nicolas Philibert
• **Best Short Film:**
10 Minuta (10 Minutes) (Bosnia and Herzegovina), by Ahmed Imamovic
• **Best non-European Film:**
Divine Intervention (Palestine), by Elia Suleiman
• **Lifetime Achievement Award:**
Tonino Guerra

• **People's Awards:**
• **Best Director:**
Pedro Almodóvar, for *Hable con ella (Talk to Her)*
• **Best Actor:**
Javier Cámara, for *Hable con ella (Talk to Her)*
• **Best Actress:**
Kate Winslet, for *Iris*

28th French Academy ('Cesar') Awards, Champs Elysées Theatre, Paris, 22 February 2003.

• **Best Film:**
The Pianist
• **Best Actor:**
Adrien Brody, for *The Pianist*
• **Best Actress:**
Isabelle Carre, for *Se souvenir des belles choses*
• **Best Supporting Actor:**
Bernard Le Coq, for *Se souvenir des belles choses*
• **Best Supporting Actress:**
Karin Viard, for *Embrassez qui vous voudrez*
• **Best Director:**
Roman Polanski, for *The Pianist*
• **Best Foreign Film:**
Bowling for Columbine (USA), directed by Michael Moore
• **Best European Union Film:**
Talk to Her
• **Best Art Direction:**
Allan Starski, for *The Pianist*
• **Best Costume:**
Philippe Guillotel, Tanino Liberatore, and Florence Sadaune, for *Astérix et Obélix: Mission Cléopâtre*
• **Best Sound:**
Jean-Marie Blondel, Gerard Hardy, and Dean Humphreys, for *The Pianist*
• **Best First Feature Film:**
Se souvenir des belles choses, by Zabou Breitman
• **Best Short Film:**
Peau de vache, by Gerald Hustache-Mathieu

• **Best Screenplay:**
Costa-Gavras and Jean-Claude Grumberg, for *Amen*
• **Best Cinematography:**
Pawel Edelman, for *The Pianist*
• **Best Editing:**
Nicolas Philibert, for *Etre et avoir*
• **Best Music:**
Wojciech Kilar, for *The Pianist*
• **Best Newcomer, Actor:**
Jean-Paul Rouve, for *Monsieur Batignole*
• **Best Newcomer, Actress:**
Cecile de France, for *L'Auberge Espagnole*
• **Honorary Cesars:**
Bernadette Laffont, Spike Lee, Meryl Streep

23rd Annual Golden Raspberry (RAZZIE) Award 'Winners'

• **Worst Film:**
Swept Away
• **Worst Actor:**
Roberto Benigni (dubbed by Breckin Meyer), for *Pinocchio*
• **Worst Actress (shared):**
Madonna, for *Swept Away* and Britney Spears, for *Crossroads*
• **Worst Supporting Actor:**
Hayden Christensen, for *Star Wars: Episode II – Attack of the Clones*

• **Worst Supporting Actress:**
Madonna, for *Die Another Day*
• **Most Flatulent Teen-Targeted Movie (New Category):** *Jackass: The Movie*
• **Worst Screen Couple:**
Adriano Giannini and Madonna, for *Swept Away*
• **Worst Director:**
Guy Ritchie, for *Swept Away*
• **Worst Remake or Sequel:**
Swept Away
• **Worst Screenplay:**
George Lucas and Jonathan Hales, for *Star Wars: Episode II – Attack of the Clones*

60th Hollywood Foreign Press Association ('Golden Globes') Awards, 19 January 2003

• **Best Motion Picture – Drama:**
The Hours
• **Best Motion Picture – Musical/Comedy:**
Chicago
• **Best Actor – Drama:**
Jack Nicholson, for *About Schmidt*
• **Best Actress – Drama:**
Nicole Kidman, for *The Hours*
• **Best Actor – Comedy/Musical:**
Richard Gere, for *Chicago*
• **Best Actress – Comedy/Musical:**
Renée Zellweger, for *Chicago*
• **Best Supporting Actor:**
Chris Cooper, for *Adaptation*
• **Best Supporting Actress:**
Meryl Streep, for *Adaptation*
• **Best Director – Motion Picture:**
Martin Scorsese, for *Gangs of New York*
• **Best Screenplay – Motion Picture:**
Alexander Payne and Jim Taylor, for *About Schmidt*
• **Best Foreign Language Film:**
Talk to Her
• **Best Original Score:**
Elliot Goldenthal, for *Frida*
• **Best Original Song:**
'The Hands That Built America' from *Gangs of New York*, music and lyrics by U2
• **Cecil B DeMille Award:**
Gene Hackman

23rd Annual London Film Critics Circle Awards. (The 'Alfs') 2002, The Dorchester Hotel, 12 February 2003

• **Best British Film:**
All or Nothing
• **Best Film:**
About Schmidt
• **Best British Actor:**
Hugh Grant, for *About A Boy*
• **Best Actor:**
Michael Caine, for *The Quiet American*
• **Best British Actress:**
Lesley Manville, for *All or Nothing*
• **Best Actress:**
Stockard Channing, for *The Business of Strangers*
• **Best British Supporting Actor:**
Kenneth Branagh, for *Harry Potter and the Chamber of Secrets*
• **Best British Supporting Actress:**
Emily Watson, for *Red Dragon*
• **Best British Director:**
Christopher Nolan, for *Insomnia*
• **Best Director:**
Phillip Noyce, for *The Quiet American*
• **Best British Screenwriter:**
Steven Knight, for *Dirty Pretty Things*
• **Best Screenwriter:**
Andrew Bovell, for *Lantana*
• **Best Foreign Language Film:**
Y tu Mamá también (Mexico)
• **Best British Newcomer:** Martin Compson, for *Sweet Sixteen* and Keira Knightley, for *Bend It Like Beckham.*

The 28th Los Angeles Film Critics Association Awards: 15 December 2002.

• **Best Picture:**
About Schmidt
• **Best Actor (shared):**
Daniel Day-Lewis, for *Gangs of New York* and Jack Nicholson, for *About Schmidt*
• **Best Actress:**
Julianne Moore, for *Far from Heaven* and *The Hours*
• **Best Supporting Actor:**
Chris Cooper, for *Adaptation*
• **Best Supporting Actress:**
Edie Falco, for *Sunshine State*
• **Best Director:**
Pedro Almodóvar, for *Talk to Her*
• **Best Screenplay:**
Alexander Payne and Jim Taylor, for *About Schmidt*
• **Best Foreign-Language Film:**

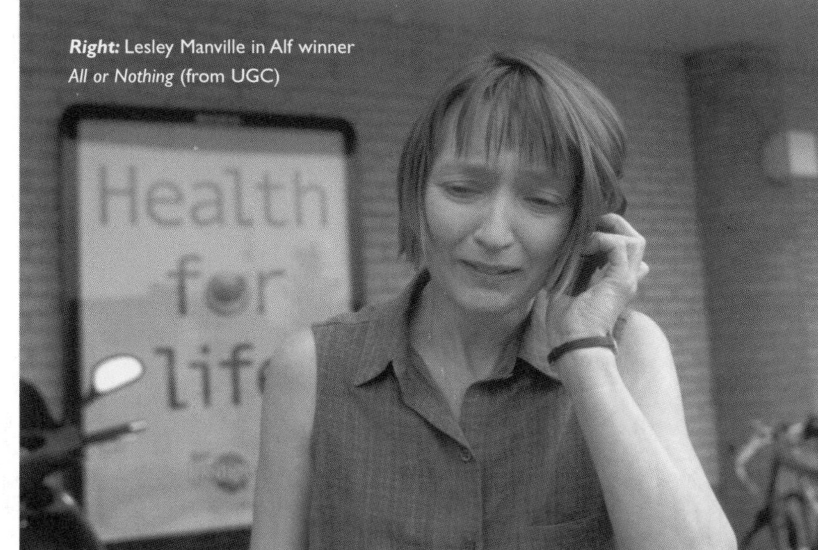

Right: Lesley Manville in Alf winner *All or Nothing* (from UGC)

Y tu Mamá también (Mexico)
• **Best Documentary:**
The Cockettes, by Bill Weber
and David Weissman
• **Best Cinematography:**
Edward Lachman, for *Far from Heaven*
• **Best Production Design:**
Dante Ferretti, for *Gangs of New York*
• **Best Music:**
Elmer Bernstein, for *Far from Heaven*
• **Best Animation Feature:**
Spirited Away, by Hayao Miyazaki
• **Special Citation:**
Lilo & Stitch, by Chris Sanders
and Dean DeBlois
• **New Generation Award:**
Lynne Ramsey, for *Morvern Callar*

The 94th National Board Of Review Awards: 4 December 2002

• **Best Film:**
The Hours
• **Best Director:**
Phillip Noyce, for *The Quiet American* and *Rabbit-Proof Fence*
• **Best Actor:**
Campbell Scott, for *Roger Dodger*
• **Best Actress:**
Julianne Moore, for *Far from Heaven*
• **Best Supporting Actor:**
Chris Cooper, for *Adaptation*
• **Best Supporting Actress:**
Kathy Bates, for *About Schmidt*
• **Best Foreign Film:**
Talk to Her (Spain)
• **Best Documentary:**
Bowling for Columbine, by Michael Moore
• **Best Animated Feature:**
Spirited Away, by Hayao Miyazaki
• **Best Screenwriter:**
Charlie Kaufman, for *Confessions of a Dangerous Mind, Adaptation* and *Human Nature.*
• **Special Achievement Award in Filmmaking:**
George Clooney as director, producer, and star, for *Confessions of a Dangerous Mind*
• **Best Ensemble Performance:**
the cast of *Nicholas Nickleby*
• **Breakthrough Performance:**
Derek Luke, for *Antwone Fisher*
and Maggie Gyllenhaal, for *Secretary*
• **Best Directorial Debut:**
Rob Marshall, for *Chicago*
• **Special Award for Visionary Cinematic Achievement:**
George Lucas
• **William K Everson Award for Film History:**
Annette Insdorf, for her book *Indelible Shadows: Films and the Holocaust*
• **Career Achievement Award:** Christopher Plummer
• **Career Achievement:**
Elmer Bernstein,
for excellence in film music scoring
• **Career Achievement in Cinematography:**
Conrad L Hall
• **Humanitarian Award:**
Sheila Nevins

The 37th National Society of Film Critics' Awards: 4 January 2003.

• **Best Film:**
The Pianist
• **Best Actor:**
Adrien Brody, for *The Pianist*
• **Best Actress:**
Diane Lane, for *Unfaithful*
• **Best Supporting Actor:** Christopher Walken,
for *Catch Me If You Can*
• **Best Supporting Actress:**
Patricia Clarkson,
for *Far from Heaven*
• **Best Director:**
Roman Polanski, for *The Pianist*
• **Best Screenplay:**
Ronald Harwood, for *The Pianist*
• **Best Foreign Film:**
Y tu Mamá también (Mexico),
by Alfonso Cuarón
• **Best Non-Fiction Film:**
Standing in the Shadows of Motown
• **Best Cinematography:**
Edward Lachman, for *Far from Heaven*

• **Special Citation:**
UCLA's film and television archives, "for long-lived and heroic work in film preservation, restoration
and resurrection"
• **Film Heritage Award:**
Kino International, "for releasing restored versions of *Metropolis* and box sets of D W Griffith
silent films"

68th Annual New York Film Critics' Circle Awards: 16 December 2002.

• **Best Picture:**
Far from Heaven
• **Best Actor:**
Daniel Day-Lewis,
for *Gangs of New York*
• **Best Actress:**
Diane Lane, for *Unfaithful*
• **Best Supporting Actor:**
Dennis Quaid, for *Far from Heaven*
• **Best Supporting Actress:**
Patricia Clarkson,
for *Far from Heaven*
• **Best Director:**
Todd Haynes, for *Far from Heaven*
• **Best Screenplay:**
Charlie (and Donald) Kaufman,
for *Adaptation*
• **Best Foreign Film:**
Y tu Mamá también,
directed by Alfonso Cuarón
• **Best Cinematography:**
Edward Lachman,
for *Far from Heaven*
• **Best First Narrative Feature Film:** *Roger Dodger,*
directed by Dylan Kidd
• **Best Non-Fiction Film:**
Standing in the Shadows of Motown
• **Best Animated Film:**
Spirited Away,
directed by Hayao Miyazaki

• **Special Award:**
Kino International, for the restoration of Fritz Lang's *Metropolis*

2003 British Academy Film and Television Arts Awards ('BAFTAs'): Odeon Leicester Square, London, 23 February 2003.

• **Outstanding Film of the Year:** *The Pianist*
• **Alexander Korda Award for Outstanding British Film of the Year:** *The Warrior*
• **Best Actor:**
Daniel Day-Lewis, for *Gangs of New York*
• **Best Actress:** Nicole Kidman, for *The Hours*
• **Best Supporting Actor:** Christopher Walken, for *Catch Me If You Can*
• **Best Supporting Actress:** Catherine Zeta-Jones, for *Chicago*
• **David Lean Award for Achievement in Direction:**
Roman Polanski, for *The Pianist*
• **Best Original Screenplay:**
Pedro Almodóvar, for *Talk to Her*
• **Best Screenplay Adaptation:** Charlie Kaufman (and Donald Kaufman), for *Adaptation*
• **Best Foreign Language Film:**
Talk to Her
• **Best Cinematography:**
Conrad L Hall, for *Road to Perdition*
• **Best Costume Design:**
Ngila Dickson and Richard Taylor, for *The Lord of the Rings: The Two Towers*
• **Best Editing:**
Daniel Rezende, for *City of God*
• **Best Make-Up/Hair:**
Judy Chin and Beatrice D'Alba, for *Frida*
• **Anthony Asquith Award for Achievement in Film Music:**
Philip Glass, for *The Hours*
• **Best Production Design:**
Dennis Gassner, for *Road to Perdition*
• **Best Sound:**
Michael Minkler, Dominick Tavella, David Lee, Maurice Schell, for *Chicago*
• **Best Special Visual Effects:**
Jim Rygiel, Joe Letteri, Randall William Cook, Alex Funke, for *The Lord of the Rings: The Two Towers*
• **Best Short Film:** *My Wrongs 8245-8249 and 117*, by Mark Herbert, Chris Morris
• **Best Short Animation:**
Fish Never Sleep, by Gaelle Denis
• **Carl Foreman Award for Special Achievement by a Director, Screenwriter or Producer in their First Feature Film:**
Asif Kapadia, director and co-writer, for *The Warrior*
• **Orange Audience Award:** *The Lord of the Rings: The Two Towers*
• **BAFTA Fellowships:**
David Jason, David Tomblin, Michael Stevenson, Saul Zaentz

The 24th Sundance Film Festival: Park City, Utah, 25 January 2003.

• **Jury:** dramatic – Steve Buscemi; Emanuel Levy; David O Russell; Tilda Swinton; Forest Whitaker; documentary – Nanette Burstein; Susan Frömke; Avon Kirkland; Lesli Klainberg; Doug Pray

• **Dramatic Grand Jury Prize:** *American Splendor*, directed by Shari Springer Berman and Robert Pulcini, produced by Ted Hope
• **Documentary Grand Jury Prize:**
Capturing the Friedmans, directed by Andrew Jarecki, produced by Andrew Jarecki and Marc Smerling
• **Audience Award for Documentary:** *My Flesh and Blood*, directed by Jonathan Karsh, produced by Jennifer Chaiken
• **Audience Award for Dramatic Feature:** *The Station Agent*, directed by Tom McCarthy, produced by Mary Jane Skalski, Robert May, and Kathryn Tucker
• **Audience Award for World Cinema:** *Whale Rider* (New Zealand) directed by Niki Caro, produced by Tim Sanders, John Barrett, and Frank Hubner
• **Documentary Directing Award:** Jonathan Karsh, for *My Flesh and Blood*
• **Dramatic Directing Award:** Catherine Hardwicke, for *Thirteen*
• **Best Cinematography Award (Documentary):** Dana Kupper, Gordon Quinn, and Peter Gilbert, for *Stevie*
• **Excellence in Cinematography Award (Dramatic):** Derek Cianfrance, for *Quattro Noza*
• **Freedom of Expression Award:** *What I Want My Words To Do To You*, directed by Judith Katz, Madeleine Gavin, and Gary Sunshine, produced by Judith Katz
• **Waldo Salt Screenwriting Award:** Tom McCarthy, *The Station Agent*
• **Alfred P Sloane Feature Film Award (scientific subjects):**
Mark Decena, for *Dopamine*
• **Special Jury Prize for Documentary (shared):** *The Murder of Emmett Till*, directed by Stanley Nelson, produced by Mark Samels; and *A Certain Kind of Death*, directed and produced by Blue Hadaegh and Grover Babcock
• **Special Jury Prize for Outstanding Dramatic Performance (shared):**
Patricia Clarkson, for *The Station Agent*, *Pieces of April* and *All The Real Girls*; and Charles Busch, for *Die Mommie Die*
• **Special Jury Prize for Emotional Truth (Dramatic):** *All The Real Girls* and *What Alice Found*
• **Jury Prize in Short Filmmaking:**
Terminal Bar, directed by Stefan Nadelman
• **Sundance Online Film Festival Viewers Awards:** *Broken Saints*, by Brooke Burgess (Animation)

and *One*, by Stewart Hendler (Short Subject)
• **Sundance/NHK International Filmmakers Award:** Michael Kang, for *The Motel* (USA); Juan Pablo Rebella and Pablo Stoll, for *Whisky* (Latin America); Mai Tominaga, for *100% Pure Wool* (Japan); Yesim Ustaoglu, for *Waiting for the Clouds* (Europe)
• **Tribute to Independent Vision Award:** Holly Hunter

The 59th Venice International Film Festival Awards: 28 August-7 September 2002.

• **Jury:** Li Gong (China) [head of jury]; Jacques Audiard (France); Yevgeni Yevtushenko (Russia); Ulrich Felsberg (Germany); László Kovács (Hungary); Francesca Neri (Italy); Yesim Ustaoglu (Turkey)

• **Golden Lion for Best Film:** *The Magdalene Sisters*, directed by Peter Mullan
• **Grand Special Jury Prize:** *Dom durakov*, by Andrei Konchalovsky
• **Silver Lion Best Short Film:** *Clown*, by Irina Efteeva
• **Volpi Cup for Best Actor:** Stefano Accorsi, for *Un viaggio chiamato amore*
• **Volpi Cup for Best Actress:** Julianne Moore, for *Far from Heaven*
• **Outstanding Individual Contribution:** Edward Lachman, for cinematography on *Far from Heaven*
• **Marcello Mastroianni Award for Emerging Actor or Actress:** So-ri Moon, for *Oasis*
• **Luigi De Laurentiis Award for Best First Feature:** *Due amici*, by Spiro Scimone (director) and Francesco Sframeli (director); and *Roger Dodger*, by Dylan Kidd (director/producer).
• **Career Golden Lion:** Dino Risi
• **Audience Award for Best Film:** *L'Homme du train.*
• **Audience Award for Best Actor:** Jean Rochefort, for *L'Homme du train*
• **Audience Award for Best Actress:** Julianne Moore, for *Far from Heaven*
• **UIP Venice Award for Best European Short Film:** *Kalózok szeretöje*, by Zsofia Péterffy

Controcorrente (Upstream) Awards for International Film

• **Jury:** Ghassan Abdul Khalek (President), Catherine Breillat, Peggy Chiao, Klaus Eder and Enrico Ghezzi
• **San Marco Award:** *Xiao Cheng Zhi Chun (Springtime in a Small Town)*, by Tian Zhuangzhuang
• **Jury's Special Award:** *Rokugatsu No Hebi (A Snake of June)*, by Shinya Tsukamoto.
• **Special Mentions:** *La virgen de la lujuria,* by Arturo Ripstein and *Renmin Gongche (Public Toilet)*, by Fruit Chan

FIPRESCI International Critics' Awards

David Stratton (Australia) [head of jury]; Luciano Monteagudo (Argentina); Milan Vlajcic (Yugoslavia); Meenakshi Shedde (India); Eva af Geijerstam (Sweden); Evgenija Tirdatova (Russia); Rolf Rüdiger Hamacher (Germany); Noel Tinazzi (France); Marco Lombardi (Italy)

• **Best Film:** *Oasis*, by Chang-dong Lee (for the audacity and courage of its imaginative exploration of the difficulties of communication, and for its remarkable actors)
• **Best Short Film:** Ken Loach's segment of *11'09"01 – September 11* (for the clarity and passion with which challenging ideas are presented)
• **Parallel Section:** *Roger Dodger*, by Dylan Kidd (for the wit and precision of its depiction of the education of a jaded roué by a young ingenue)
• **UNESCO Award:** *11'09"01 – September 11*, by Youssef Chahine; Amos Gitai; Alejandro González Iñárritu; Shohei Imamura; Claude Lelouch; Ken Loach; Samira Makhmalbaf; Mira Nair; Idrissa Ouedraogo; Sean Penn; Danis Tanovic
• **Future Film Festival Digital Award:** *Blood Work*, by Clint Eastwood
• **Future Film Festival Digital Award – Special Mention:** *My Name is Tanino*, by Paolo Virzì
• **Special Director's Award:** *Oasis*, by Lee Chang-dong

In Memoriam

by James Cameron-Wilson, Adam Keen, Daniel O'Brien and Jonathan Rigby

AALIYAH

Born: 16 January 1979 in Brooklyn, New York.
Died: 25 August 2001, in a private plane as it crashed on take-off from the Bahamas.
Full name: Aaliyah Haughton.
• R&B singer Aaliyah co-starred in two mediocre films, the gangland romance *Romeo Must Die* (2000) and the horror movie *Queen of the Damned* (2002), in which she played a vampire.

JOHN AGAR

Born: 31 January 1921, in Chicago, Illinois.
Died: 7 April 2002 in Burbank, California, from emphysema.
• Best known for his marriage to Shirley Temple, actor John Agar never looked cut out for movie stardom. With no training or experience, he appeared opposite John Wayne and former child star Temple in John Ford's *Fort Apache* (1948). Agar also stood tall with Wayne in Ford's *She Wore a Yellow Ribbon* (1949) and *The Sands of Iwo Jima* (1949). Agar's divorce from Shirley Temple marked a sharp decline in his film career. Universal-International offered him leading roles in shockers like *Revenge of the Creature* (1955) and *Tarantula* (1955), followed by further parts in science fiction schlock.

SAMUEL Z ARKOFF

Born: 12 June 1918 in Fort Dodge, Iowa.
Died: 16 September 2001 in Burbank, California, of natural causes.
• Samuel Z Arkoff was the co-founder of American International Pictures, specialists in cheaply made exploitation aimed at the lucrative teenage market Alongside business partner James H Nicholson (1916-1972), Arkoff financed and distributed such luridly titled movies as *Reform School Girl* (1957), *Terror from the Year 5000* (1958) and *I Was a Teenage Werewolf* (1957). AIP moved upmarket with the hit Gothic thriller *House of Usher* (1960), which revived Vincent Price's career and established director Roger Corman as a significant talent. The ensuing Edgar Allan Poe series included *The Masque of the Red Death* and *The Tomb of Ligeia* (both 1964), now regarded as classics of the genre. AIP also flogged beach party movies, Hell's Angels fodder, rural gangster films and blaxploitation.

GEORGE AXELROD

Born: 9 June 1922 in New York City.
Died: 21 June 2003 in Los Angeles, California, of heart failure.
• Oscar-nominated screenwriter of *Bus Stop*, *Breakfast at Tiffany's* (1961) and *The Manchurian Candidate* (1962). The son of silent film actress Betty Carpenter, Axelrod made his name on Broadway with the plays *The Seven Year Itch* (1953) and *Will Success Spoil Rock Hunter?* (1957), both subsequently filmed.

CARMELO BENE

Born: 1 September 1937 in Campi Salentina, Italy.
Died: 16 March 2002 in Rome, from cancer.
• Actor-writer-director-producer-composer-costume designer Carmelo Bene devoted most of his career to the stage, where he earned a reputation as a bold iconoclast. An admirer of Buster Keaton and Sergei Eisenstein, Bene made five feature films between 1968 and 1973, supervising every aspect of their production. The first, *Nostra signora dei turchi/Our Lady of the Turks* (1968), was based on his novel and play. Set in 15th Century Otranto, during the Turkish invasion, the film was praised for its avant-garde style.

BERRY BERENSON

Born: 14 April 1948 in New York City.
Died: 11 September 2001, when her American Airlines plane from Boston to Los Angeles was hijacked by terrorists and crashed into the World Trade Centre, New York.
Real name: Berinthia Berenson.
• A professional fashion photographer and occasional actress, Berry Berenson's best-known connection to the film world was through her long marriage to actor Anthony Perkins. Berenson acted in three movies, two of them opposite Perkins: *Remember My Name* (1978), a psychological thriller, and *Winter Kills* (1979), a satirical black comedy. The other was Paul Schrader's torrid revamp of *Cat People* (1982).

MILTON BERLE

Born: 12 July 1908 in the Bronx, New York City.
Died: 27 March 2002 in Los Angeles, California, of colon cancer.
Real name: Mendel Berlinger.
• Having dominated the fledgling field of US TV in the 1950s, comedian Milton Berle made cameo appearances in films as diverse as *Let's Make Love* (1960), *The Muppet Movie* (1980) and *Broadway Danny Rose* (1984). His best movie role was as one of the many crazed loot hunters in *It's a Mad Mad Mad Mad World* (1963), in which he shared several delightful confrontations with Britain's own Terry-Thomas.

MONTY M BERMAN

Born: 16 February 1912 in London.
Died: 15 July 2002 in Monte Carlo, Monaco, 'after a short illness'.
• Often confused with Monty Berman the cinematographer and producer, Monty M Berman was the costumier for innumerable films, notably *30 is a Dangerous Age, Cynthia* (1968), *The Guns of Navarone* (1961), *Around the World in 80 Days* (1956) and *While the Sun Shines* (1947).

JULIE BISHOP

Born: 30 August 1914 in Denver, Colorado.
Died: 30 August 2001 (on her 87th birthday) of natural causes in Mendocino, California.
Real name: Jacqueline Brown.
• A former child actress, Julie Bishop never made it as an adult star. Her best film (billed as Jacqueline Wells) is Edgar G Ulmer's cult horror movie *The Black Cat* (1934), in which she shared the screen with king ghouls Boris Karloff and Bela Lugosi. She also appeared opposite Laurel and Hardy (*The Bohemian Girl* 1936) and, having changed her name to Julie Bishop, John Wayne (*Sands of Iwo Jima* 1949, *The High and the Mighty* 1954), before retiring from the screen in 1957.

SERGEI BODROV JR

Born: 27 December 1971 in Moscow, USSR (now Russia).
Died: 20 September 2002 in Karmadon Canyon in the Caucasus Mountains, Russia – in an avalanche while working on his last film, *The Messenger.*
• The son of producer and director Sergei Bodrov, Bodrov Jr debuted in his father's *Kavkazskij Plennik (Prisoner of the Mountains)* (1996), for which he won a Nika. In 1997 he played a lead role in Alexei Balabanov's *Brat* (1997), which made him a star in Russia as a gangster heart-throb, a role he reprised in *Brat 2* (2000). He made his directorial debut with *Syostry* (2001), acclaimed for its naturalistic and unsparing vision of modern Russia.

BUDD BOETTICHER

Born: 19 July 1916 in Chicago, Illinois.
Died: 29 November 2001 in Ramona, California, of multiple organ failure.
Real name: Oscar Boetticher Jr.
• Director Budd Boetticher is best known for a series of modestly budgeted Westerns, made for Columbia Pictures in association with producer Harry Joe Brown, writer Burt Kennedy and star Randolph Scott. Films such as *The Tall T* (1957), *Ride Lonesome* (1959) and *Comanche Station* (1960) have a taut pace, strong linear narrative and keen visual sense. Boetticher quit Hollywood for Mexico in 1960, to make a documentary about Carlos Arruza, a champion matador and personal friend. Seven years in production, *Arruza* (1971) proved a disappointment. Boetticher's feature film career never recovered.

MARGARET BOOTH

Born: 14 January 1898 in Los Angeles, California.
Died: 28 October 2002 in Los Angeles, of complications from a stroke.
• Margaret Booth received an Honorary Oscar for her 30 years at MGM as the studio's supervising editor. She took sole charge of the editing on some of MGM's finest films of the 30s, including *Susan Lenox: Her Fall and Rise* (1931), *Strange Interlude* (1932), *Bombshell, Dancing Lady* (both 1933), *The Barretts of Wimpole Street* (1934), *Reckless, Mutiny on the Bounty* (both 1935), George Cukor's *Romeo and Juliet* (1936) and his version of *Camille* (1937). As supervising editor, she worked (sometimes uncredited) on such films as *A Yank at Oxford* (1938) and *The Wizard of Oz* (1939). Latterday credits include *The Owl and the Pussycat* (1970), *Fat City* (1972), *The Way We Were* (1973), *The Black Bird* (1975), *Funny Lady* (1975) and John Huston's *Annie* (1982).

ROY BOULTING

Born: 21 November 1913 in Bray, Buckinghamshire.
Died: 5 November 2001 in Eynsham, Oxfordshire, of cancer.
• Along with his twin brother John (1913-1985), writer-producer-director Roy Boulting worked hard to raise the profile of British movies. The Boultings came to prominence with the bold anti-fascist dramas *Pastor Hall* (1939) and *Thunder Rock* (1942), both directed by Roy. However, the box-office failure of *Fame is the Spur* (1947), an ambitious political fable, prompted him to concentrate on commercially safe projects. During the 1950s, the Boultings made a series of enjoyable satirical comedies, notably *Private's Progress* (1955), *Lucky Jim* (1957) and *I'm All Right Jack* (1959). The Boultings' joint career declined in the 1960s.

EDDIE BRACKEN

Born: 7 February 1915 in Astoria, New York City.
Died: 14 November 2002 in Montclair, New Jersey, of complications from surgery.

• After a childhood spent in vaudeville and silent shorts, and an adolescence on Broadway, Bracken found his niche as a nervous but lovable comic Everyman in films like *Brother Rat* (1938, his film debut), *Too Many Girls* (1940), *Life with Henry*, *Caught in the Draft* (both 1941), *The Fleet's In*, *Sweater Girl* and *Star Spangled Rhythm* (all 1942). Preston Sturges cast him as Norval Jones in *The Miracle of Morgan's Creek* (1942) and together they refined the character in *Hail the Conquering Hero* (1944). Many years later, Bracken made good again in the family films *Home Alone 2: Lost in New York* (1992), *Rookie of the Year* (1993) and *Baby's Day Out* (1994).

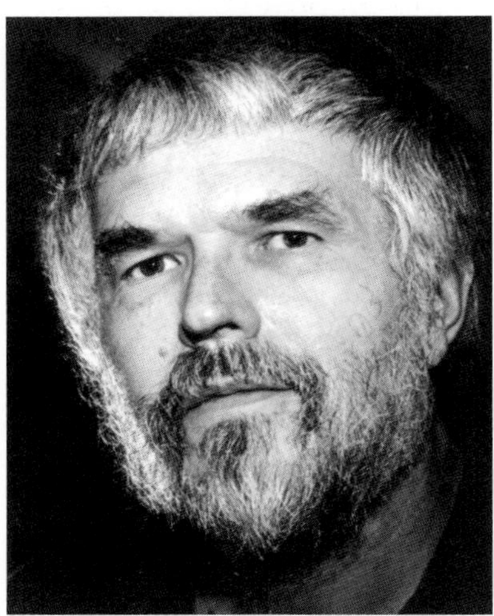

STAN BRAKHAGE

Born: 14 January 1933 in Kansas City, Missouri.
Died: 9 March 2003 in Victoria, British Columbia, from cancer.
Real name: Robert Sanders.
• This American auteur made the astounding avant-garde cycle of short films, *Dog Star Man* (1961-4), as well as some 380 other films ranging in length from a matter of seconds to several hours. A Film Studies professor at the University of Colorado, he was and remains a totemic figure to indie filmmakers. Quote: "The capacity to be intrinsic and vulgar is American."

VLASTIMIL BRODSKY

Born: 15 December 1920 in Hrusovany, now part of the Czech Republic.
Died: 20 April 2002 in Prague, a suicide.
• A star of the short-lived 1960s Czech New Wave, Vlastimil Brodsky excelled in tragi-comic characters. For director Jiri Menzel, he appeared in a series of political satires, playing a conceited Nazi official in the Academy Award-winning *Closely Observed Trains* (1966). Brodsky and Menzel continued their successful association with *Capricious Summer* (1968) and *Larks on a String* (1969), the latter rapidly banned by the Communist authorities. Brodsky's performance in the title role of *Jacob the Liar* (1975), an East German production, earned him the Best Actor Award at the Berlin Film Festival.

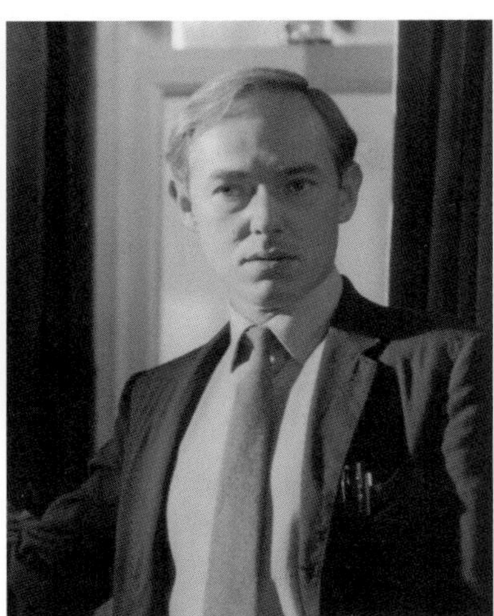

MICHAEL BRYANT

Born: 5 April 1928 in London.
Died: 25 April 2002 in Richmond, London.
• One of Britain's most accomplished stage actors, Michael Bryant contributed sterling performances to a number of films. He was cast as one of the Titanic's ill-fated crew in *A Night to Remember* (1958) and later had his head eaten by a demonic cat in *Torture Garden* (1967). In *Nicholas and Alexandra* (1971) he played an icy Lenin, coolly threatening Brian Cox's dissident Trotsky. Bryant's strangest film is the black comedy *Mumsy, Nanny, Sonny and Girly* (1969), where his character is imprisoned by an insane family.

HORST BUCHHOLZ

Born: 4 December 1933 in Berlin.
Died: 3 March 2003 in Berlin, of pneumonia.
• Horst Werner Buchholz was once labelled the 'James Dean of German cinema' for his early roles as an angry young teen, a character he reprised brilliantly as Chico, the wannabe gunslinger, in *The Magnificent Seven* (1960). A journeyman career followed in romantic leads on both sides of the Atlantic, but never quite realised the promise that won him an award at the Cannes Film Festival for his performance in only his second film, *Himmel ohne Sterne/Sky Without Stars* (1955).
Other notable credits: *The Great Waltz* (1972) and *La vita è bella/Life is Beautiful* (1997).

JULES BUCK

Born: 30 July 1917 in St Louis, Missouri.
Died: 19 July 2001 in Paris, from complications with Alzheimer's Disease.
• Producer Jules Buck worked with actor Peter O'Toole for nearly two decades. Based in London from 1957 onwards, Buck founded Keep Films with O'Toole and they scored a hit with *Becket* (1964), followed by *Lord Jim* (1964), *What's New Pussycat?* (1965), *Great Catherine* (1968) and *The Ruling Class* (1972). Producer and star went their separate ways after *Man Friday* (1975), an ill-conceived reworking of *Robinson Crusoe*.

PHYLLIS CALVERT

Born: 18 February 1915 in London.
Died: 8 October 2002 in London, of natural causes.
• Born Phyllis Hannah Bickle, Calvert started in quota quickies and got her first break in *Kipps* (1941). She was the nice girl in *The Man in Grey* (1943) and quickly became one of Britain's most popular actresses, playing genteel (but often sardonic) characters in Gainsborough melodramas like *Fanny by Gaslight*, *Madonna of the Seven Moons* (both 1944) and *They Were Sisters* (1945). An unsatisfactory spell in Hollywood (including Robert Siodmak's *Time Out of Mind*, 1947) was followed by a BAFTA nomination for her performance in Alexander Mackendrick's *Mandy* (1952). She later acted mainly in the theatre and on television, playing the title role in Yorkshire TV's early 1970s drama, *Kate*.

KATRIN CARTLIDGE

Born: 15 May 1961 in London.
Died: 7 September 2002 in London, of complications from pneumonia and septicaemia.
• A bright, bold and independent actress who graduated from TV's *Brookside* to a notable film career. A Mike Leigh favourite, her films include *Eat the Rich* (1987), *Breaking the Waves* (1996), *Career Girls* (1997), *Claire Dolan* (1998), *Topsy-Turvy* (1999) *The Weight of Water* (2000), *From Hell* and *No Man's Land* (both 2001). She died suddenly, a week prior to shooting *Helen of Peckham* and being cast in Alejandro Gonzalez Inarritu's *21 Grams*.

ANTHONY CARUSO

Born: 7 April 1916 in Frankfort, Indiana.
Died: 4 April 2003 in Brentwood, California.
• Dark features and a craggy demeanour made Caruso a natural 'heavy' character actor, whether as a city mobster, a safari hunter or American Indian chiefs. His resumé of menaces included roles in hundreds of films and TV shows, notably *Johnny Apollo* (1940), *Tarzan and the Leopard Woman* (1946), *The Asphalt Jungle* (1950), *A Cry in the Night* (1956, where he played a cop for a change), *Baby Face Nelson* (1957), *The Badlanders* (1958) and *Mean Johnny Barrows* (1976).

TONINO CERVI

Born: 14 June 1929 in Milan.
Died: 31 March 2002 in Siena, from a heart attack.
Full name: Antonio Cervi.
• Producer Tonino Cervi worked with such noted Italian filmmakers as Pier Paolo Pasolini, Michelangelo Antonioni and Federico Fellini. He gave budding director Bernardo Bertolucci his big break with *The Grim Reaper* (1962), based on a story by Pasolini. Antonioni's *Red Desert* (1964), an expensive commercial failure, nearly bankrupted Cervi, who then switched to low-budget programmers. Cervi produced, co-scripted and directed the intriguing spaghetti western *Today It's Me... Tomorrow It's You* (1968), partly inspired by his love of Japanese samurai films.

JOHN CHAMBERS

Born: 12 September 1922 in Chicago.
Died: 25 August 2001 in a retirement home in Woodland Hills, California, from complications with diabetes.
• A pioneering make-up artist, John Chambers secured a place in cinema history with his groundbreaking work for *Planet of the Apes* (1968). Chambers' humanoid-ape designs are still impressive today, despite over 30 years of progress in the field of special make-up. Chambers also worked on the western *A Man Called Horse* (1970), building the fake chest worn by Richard Harris when his character undergoes the excruciating Sundance ritual.

CHANG CHEH

Born: 1923 in China.
Died: 22 June 2002 in Hong Kong, of pulmonary disease.
• Chang Cheh directed a series of stylish, if bloody, swordplay films for Hong Kong's Shaw Brothers studio during the 1960s and 1970s. His best known titles include *One Armed Swordsman* (1967), *Golden Swallow* (1968), *New One Armed Swordsman* (1970), *Blood Brothers* (1973) and *Five Deadly Venoms* (1978).

HELEN CHERRY

Born: 24 November 1915 in Manchester.
Died: 27 September 2001 in London.
• Long married to Trevor Howard, stage actress Helen Cherry turned up in films as diverse as *Morning Departure* (1950), *The Naked Edge* (1961) and *Flipper's New Adventure* (1964). She also acted alongside Howard in a few movies, notably Tony Richardson's satirical *The Charge of the Light Brigade* (1968) and the courtroom drama *Conduct Unbecoming* (1975).

LESLIE CHEUNG

Born: 12 September 1956 in Hong Kong.
Died: 1 April 2003, committing suicide by jumping from the 24th floor of Hong Kong's Mandarin Oriental Hotel.
• A flamboyant Asian film and pop-music star who masked his homosexuality via a career in romantic lead roles, Cheung dominated the 1980s and 90s Hong Kong film scene. He worked with the likes of Chen Kaige, Wong Kar-wai, Tsui Hark and John Woo in every genre, from popular kung-fu flicks like *The Bride with White Hair* (1993) to actioners like *A Better Tomorrow*. There were also dozens of romantic comedies and epic historical dramas like *Farewell, My Concubine* (1993), which made him an international star. A graduate of Leeds University, his last words were reportedly "I'll be right down."

ROSEMARY CLOONEY

Born: 23 May 1928 in Maysville, Kentucky.
Died: 29 June 2002 in Beverly Hills, of complications from lung cancer.
• Cabaret singer Rosemary Clooney starred in a handful of films during the 1950s, including the sentimental favourite *White Christmas* (1954). Then, following a breakdown in 1968, she was nominated for an Emmy for playing a

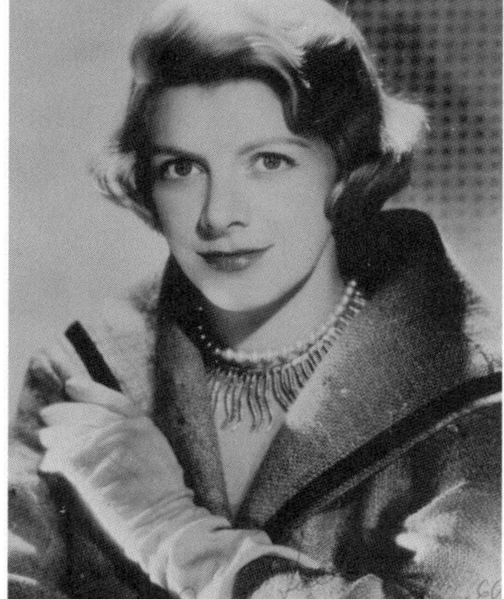

patient with Alzheimer's (who could only communicate through song) on the TV series *ER*, starring her nephew George Clooney.

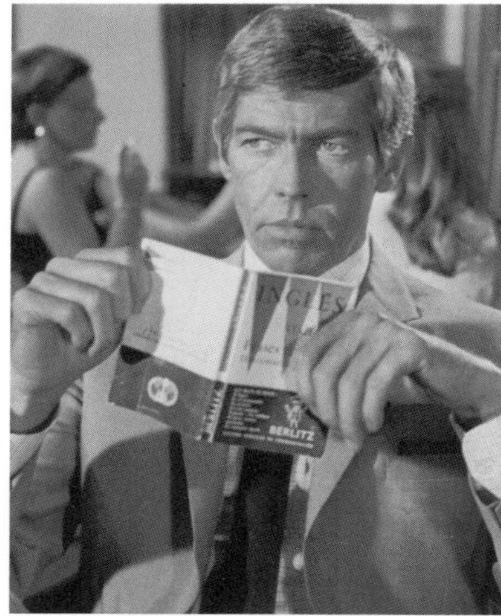

JAMES COBURN

Born: 31 August 1928 in Laurel, Nebraska.
Died: 18 November 2002 in Beverly Hills, of a heart attack.
• Coburn's star-making performance in *The Magnificent Seven* (1960) marked him out as a lean and dangerous lead. He later gained cult status in the James Bond spoofs *Our Man Flint* (1966) and *In Like Flint* (1967), and starred in several Peckinpah films, including *Pat Garrett and Billy the Kid* (1973) and *Cross of Iron* (1977), as well as being his 2nd unit director on *Convoy* (1978). Hampered in later years by rheumatoid arthritis, he nevertheless scored a 1990s renaissance in films like *Young Guns II* (1990), *Deadfall* (1993), *Maverick* (1994), *Eraser* (1996) and *Payback* (1999). He also picked up a Best Supporting Actor Oscar for *Affliction* (1999).

HERMAN COHEN

Born: 27 August 1928 in Detroit, Michigan.
Died: 2 June 2002 in Los Angeles, California, of throat cancer.
• A specialist in low-budget schlock horror – and sometime associate of Sam Arkoff [qv] – producer Herman Cohen enjoyed early success with the drive-in classics *I Was a Teenage Werewolf* (1957) and *I Was a Teenage Frankenstein* (1957). He subsequently relocated to England, where his output included the fascinating, if frequently terrible, *Horrors of the Black Museum* (1959) and the colourful Sherlock Holmes v Jack the Ripper shocker, *A Study in Terror* (1965). He retired from filmmaking after the early 1970s.

CHARLOTTE COLEMAN

Born: 3 April 1968 in London.
Died: 14 November 2001 in London, of an asthma attack.
• A professional actress since childhood, Charlotte Coleman achieved major recognition as an adult for her outstanding performance in the BBC television drama *Oranges Are Not the Only Fruit* (1990). The actress' best-known film role arrived with *Four Weddings and a Funeral* (1993), in which she played Scarlett, Hugh Grant's wacky, punkish flatmate. The performance

earned Coleman a BAFTA nomination. She later had strong roles in *The Young Poisoner's Handbook* (1994) and *Beautiful People* (1999).

PAT COOMBS

Born: 27 August 1926 in Camberwell, south London.
Died: 25 May 2002 in west London, of emphysema.
Full name: Pat Doreen Coombs.
• A graduate of LAMDA, where she also taught, actress Pat Coombs specialised in nervy comic roles. Her films include *Follow a Star* (1959), *Carry On Doctor* (1968) and *Adolf Hitler: My Part in His Downfall* (1972).

JEFF COREY

Born: 10 August 1914 in Brooklyn, New York.
Died: 16 August 2002 in Santa Monica, California, of complications from a fall.
• After a promising start in a wide range of character roles in the 1940s, Corey became an acting teacher after being blacklisted in the 1950s. His students included Jack Nicholson, Sally Kellerman, Barbra Streisand, Anthony Perkins, Rita Moreno, Richard Chamberlain and Robin Williams. He returned to acting with memorable supporting roles in films like *The Cincinnati Kid* (1965), *In Cold Blood* (1967), *Butch Cassidy and the Sundance Kid* (1969), *True Grit* (1969), *They Call Me MISTER Tibbs!* (1970), *Little Big Man* (1970), *Conan the Destroyer* (1984), *Bird on a Wire* (1990) and *Color of Night* (1994).

RICHARD CRENNA

Born: 30 November 1926 in Los Angeles, California.
Died: 17 January 2003 in Los Angeles, from pancreatic cancer.
• Famous for playing Col Samuel Trautman in the *Rambo* films, Crenna was a network radio star from the age of 10 and graduated to playing 'heavies' in films like *Wait Until Dark* (1967). He gained a Golden Globe nomination for his sleazy card sharp in *The Flamingo Kid* (1984) and satirised his *Rambo* character in *Hot Shots! Part Deux* (1993). Other notable films include *The Sand Pebbles* (1966), *Star!* (1968), *Midas Run*, *Marooned* (both 1969) and *Body Heat* (1981).

HUME CRONYN

Born: 18 July 1911 in London, Ontario.
Died: 15 June 2003 in Fairfield, Connecticut, of prostate cancer.
• Hume Cronyn co-wrote screenplays for Hitchcock's *Rope* (1948) and *Under Capricorn* (1949) while giving masterly supporting performances in roles that capitalised on his very ordinary features (a legacy of an early career in Canadian boxing). He won an Oscar nomination for the death-camp escapee drama *The Seventh Cross* (1944) and played in quality films like *The Postman Always Rings Twice* (1946) and *Brute Force* (1947). He left Hollywood for Broadway during the 1950s, often playing alongside his wife Jessica Tandy, later returning to the big screen with the hit *Cocoon* (1985) and its 1988 sequel.

ANDRÉ DELVAUX

Born: 21 March 1926 in Heverlee, Brabant, Belgium.
Died: 4 October 2002 in Valencia, Spain, of a heart attack.
• After studying German philology, law, piano and composition, Delvaux proceeded to carve out an arthouse film career. He gained worldwide attention when his first film, *The Man Who Had His Hair Cut Short* (????), scooped a BAFTA. The international acclaim for his trademark 'magic realism' launched a new era in Belgian cinema. His other films include: *One Night ... a Train* (1968), *Rendez-vous à Bray* (1971), *To Woody Allen, From Europe With Love* (1980), and *L'Oeuvre au noir / The Abyss* (1988).

TED DEMME

Born: 26 October 1964 in New York.
Died: 14 January 2002 from a heart attack while playing basketball at a school in Santa Monica, California. Later, traces of cocaine were found in his system.
• Director Ted Demme was a filmmaker of promise, if limited achievement. The nephew of Jonathan Demme, he attracted attention with *The Ref* (1994),

a dark yuppie satire starring Denis Leary, Kevin Spacey and Judy Davis. Demme's last and probably best film was the controversial drama *Blow* (2001), starring Johnny Depp as a cocaine smuggler. The sad irony of Demme's own drug-related death is all too obvious.

MAURICE DENHAM

Born: 23 December 1909 in Beckenham, Kent.
Died: 24 July 2002 in Northwood, London.

• Star of some of Britain's most popular 1940s radio programmes, Denham later became a prolific TV and film character actor. He provided all the voices in the animated *Animal Farm* (1954) and appeared in over 100 films, including *The Blue Lagoon* (1949), *Night of the Demon* (1957), *Our Man in Havana* (1959), *Sink the Bismarck!* (1960), *Those Magnificent Men in Their Flying Machines* (1965), *Sunday Bloody Sunday* (1971), *Day of the Jackal* (1973) and *84 Charing Cross Road* (1987).

AMANDO DE OSSORIO

Born: 1918 in A Coruña, Spain.
Died: 13 January 2001 in Madrid.

• In the midst of the otherwise largely derivative Spanish horror boom of 1968 to 1975, writer/director Amando de Ossorio created a uniquely Spanish set of monsters – namely, the zombie Knights Templar, riding down their hapless victims in slow motion, their fine-tuned hearing acting as a substitute for their long-since-removed eyes. Their adventures began in the genuinely startling *La noche del terror ciego* (aka *Tombs of the Blind Dead*, 1971) and extended to three sequels. De Ossorio's other horrors included *Malenka* (1968, starring Anita Ekberg) and *Las garras de Lorelei* (1973), in which he turned his attention to German, rather than Hispanic, legendry.

ANDRÉ DE TOTH

Born: 15 May 1912 in Mako, Austria-Hungary.
Died: 27 October 2002 in Burbank, California, from an aneurysm.
Real name: Sasvrai Farkasfalvi Tothfalusi Toth Endre Anral Mihaly.

• De Toth fled a promising film career in Hungary when World War II broke out, first to England and then to America, where his penchant for depicting violence in as realistic a manner as possible earned him a 'controversial director' tag. Though he was predominantly a man for Westerns and actioners, he also made the 3-D Vincent Price hit *House of Wax* (1953), unhampered by having only one eye. He also shared an Oscar nomination for writing *The Gunfighter* (1950).

BRAD DEXTER

Born: 9 April 1917 in Goldfield, Nevada.
Died: 12 December 2002 in Rancho Mirage, California, of emphysema.
Real name: Boris Milanovich.

• A tough guy specialist of Serbian descent, Dexter debuted in *Winged Victory* under the stage name 'Barry Mitchell'. John Huston cast him as a bad hat in *The Asphalt Jungle* (1950), where he re-launched himself as Brad Dexter. His most famous role was Harry Luck in *The Magnificent Seven* (1960). He continued acting into the 1970s before becoming a producer.

JESÚS DÍAZ

Born: October 1941 in Havana, Cuba.
Died: 2 May 2002 in Madrid, Spain.

• A novelist, teacher, political activist and documentarist, Jesús Díaz made two feature films. *Polvo rojo/Red Dust* (1981) deals with the 1959 Cuban revolution, while *Lejania/Distance* (1985) focuses on Cuban exiles in the United States.

TROY DONAHUE

Born: 27 January 1936 in New York.
Died: 2 September 2001 in Santa Monica, California, from a massive heart attack.
Real name: Merle Joseph Johnson Jr.

• Blond-haired and blue-eyed, Troy Donahue was one of Hollywood's last studio-groomed hunks. However, leading roles in the Warner productions *Parrish* (1961) and *A Distant Trumpet* (1964) revealed his limitations as a screen performer. Without major studio support, his career drifted after the mid-1960s.

DANILO DONATI

Born: 1926 in Suzzara, Italy.
Died: 2 December 2001 in Rome, of heart failure.
Costume and set designer Danilo Donati worked with many of Italy's biggest film directors: Pier Paolo Pasolini (*The Gospel According to St Matthew* 1964, *The Canterbury Tales* 1972, *Salò* 1975), Franco Zeffirelli (*The Taming of the Shrew* 1967, *Romeo and Juliet* 1968), Federico Fellini (*Satyricon* 1969, *Roma* 1972, *Casanova* 1976) and Roberto Benigni (*Life is Beautiful* 1997). He won Academy Awards for *Romeo and Juliet* and *Casanova.*

MARY ELLIS

Born: 15 June 1897 in New York City.
Died: 30 January 2003 in London.
• The originator of the female leads in Ivor Novello's operettas, Mary Ellis was a member of the New York Metropolitan Opera at age 18. Also a Broadway star, she later moved to England and starred in films like *All the King's Horses* (1934), *Bella Donna* (1934), *Paris in Spring* (1935), *Fatal Lady* (1936) and *Glamorous Night* (1937), many scored by Novello. She was still acting in the 1990s.

MICHAEL ELPHICK

Born: 19 September 1946 in Chichester, Sussex.
Died: 7 September 2002 in Willesden, London, of a heart attack.
• Michael Elphick was a popular TV actor best remembered for playing the title character in *Boon.* His film career was not so prominent, but he lent his impressive barrel-chested presence to films like *Cry of the Banshee* (1969), *Quadrophenia* (1979), *The Elephant Man* (1980 – memorable as the nasty hospital porter who exploits the title character), *Privates on Parade* (1982), *Curse of the Pink Panther* (1983) and *Withnail and I* (1987).

JEAN-YVES ESCOFFIER

Born: 12 July 1950 in Lyon, France.
Died: 1 April 2003 in Los Angeles, California, from heart failure.
• A master behind the lens, cinematographer Escoffier cut his teeth on Coline Serreau's *3 Hommes et un couffin* (1985) (remade as *Three Men and a Baby*) and went on to make three striking films with Leo Carax, *Les Amants du Pont-Neuf* (1991), *Mauvais sang* (1995) and *Boy Meets Girl* (1997). His subsequent US films include: *Gummo* (1997), *Good Will Hunting* (1997), *Rounders* (1998), *Cradle Will Rock* (1999), *Nurse Betty* (2000) and *Possession* (2002). His last completed work was on Robert Benton's adaptation of the Philip Roth novel *The Human Stain,* and at the time of his death he was set to start shooting Wong Kar-Wai's *2054.*

ADAM FAITH

Born: 23 June 1940 in Acton, London.
Died: 8 March 2003 in Stoke-on-Trent, from a heart attack.
Real name: Terence Nelhams.
• A teen pop star of the 1960s who collaborated closely with John Barry, Faith transformed his career several times over, as, variously, music magnate,

financial expert and, in particular, actor. From 1959 to 1962, he appeared in disposable fodder like *Beat Girl, Never Let Go, What A Whopper!* and *Mix Me A Person.* He then starred in the cult TV series *Budgie* and made a serious impact playing the hardnosed rock manager in *Stardust* (1974). Other films included *McVicar* (1980).

MARÍA FÉLIX

Born: 8 April 1914 in Alamos, Mexico.
Died: 8 April 2002 in Mexico City, from congestive heart failure.
Full name: María de Los Angeles Félix Guerena.
• One of the Mexican cinema's biggest stars, actress María Félix came to prominence during its 'Golden Age' in the 1940s. Specialising in impassioned melodramas, Félix found her career-defining role in *Dona Barbara* (1943), cast as a ruthless female rancher with a tragic past. The comedy *Enamorada* (1947), co-starring Pedro Armendariz, reworked Shakespeare's *The Taming of the Shrew* against a backdrop of the Mexican Revolution. Active in Mexican films until 1970, Félix also made a few movies in Europe, notably Jean Renoir's *French Cancan* (1954).

JAMES FERMAN

Born: 11 April 1930 in New York City.
Died: 24 December 2002 in Hampstead, London, from acute pneumonia.

• James Alan Ferman headed the British Board of Film Classification for 23 years and came under frequent fire for his liberal leanings towards controversial films such as *Crash*, *Lolita* and *The Last Temptation of Christ*. He argued that explicit pornography should be legally sold through licensed outlets in order to stifle the black market. He was also responsible, however, for the decades-long suppression of mainstream titles like *The Exorcist*.

BARRY FOSTER

Born: 21 August 1931 in Beeston, Nottinghamshire.
Died: 11 February 2002 in Guildford, Surrey, of a heart attack.

• Actor Barry Foster achieved television stardom with *Van der Valk* (1972-73, 1977, 1991), cast as a Dutch police detective. On the big screen, he played an IRA man in *Ryan's Daughter* (1970), David Lean's epic Irish saga of adultery and gun-running. However, Foster's biggest film role came in Alfred Hitchcock's *Frenzy* (1972). Cast as Bob Rusk, the necktie strangler, Foster memorably conveyed the character's outward charm and psychopathic rage.

IVAN FOXWELL

Born: 22 February 1914 in London.
Died: 16 January 2002 in London.

• A screenwriter and producer of intelligence and taste, Ivan Foxwell made a solid contribution to British cinema. His films include *No Room at the Inn* (1948), a wartime melodrama involving evacuee abuse and prostitution, and *The Colditz Story* (1955), a fiercely patriotic POW tale.

JOHN FRANKENHEIMER

Born: 19 February 1930 in New York City.
Died: 6 July 2002 at Cedars-Sinai Medical Center, Los Angeles, California, after suffering a massive stroke due to complications following spinal surgery.

• An extensive career in TV preceded Frankenheimer's explosive entry into films with *The Manchurian Candidate* and *Birdman of Alcatraz* (both 1962). More quality pictures followed, notably *Seven Days in May* and *The Train* (both 1964). The 1968 assassination of close friend Robert F Kennedy drove Frankenheimer to the bottle, however, resulting in a string of disappointing projects broken only by titles like *The Horsemen* (1971) and *The French Connection II* (1974). He recovered his form in the 1990s, though mainly on Emmy-winning TV movies for HBO. Only the post-Cold War spy drama *Ronin* (1998) was reminiscent of his cinematic powers at their peak.

KATHLEEN FREEMAN

Born: 17 February 1919 in Chicago.
Died: 23 August 2001 in New York City, of lung cancer.

• Character actress Kathleen Freeman appeared in nearly 100 movies. Making her screen debut in *The Naked City* (1947), she was memorable as voice coach Phoebe Dinsmore in *Singin' in the Rain* (1952). Freeman acted in ten films with top comedy star Jerry Lewis, including *The Ladies' Man* (1961), *The Nutty Professor* (1963), *The Disorderly Orderly* (1965) and *Three on a Couch* (1966). She later added a touch of comedy expertise to the overblown chase movie *The Blues Brothers* (1980), cast as a fierce Mother Superior nicknamed 'The Penguin'.

BERNARD FRESSON

Born: 27 May 1931 in Reims, Marne, France.
Died: 20 October 2002 in Paris, France.

• Self-effacing French actor, best known internationally for his roles in *Hiroshima mon amour* (1959), *The French Connection II* (1974) and *Brotherhood of the Wolf* (2001). Physically imposing, Fresson won praise for his performances under demanding directors like Roman Polanski (*Le Locataire*, 1976), Costa-Gavras (*Z*, 1969) and Samuel Fuller (*Street Of No Return*, 1989). He spent a while in TV before returning with a powerful, Cesar-winning performance in *Place Vendôme* (1997) opposite Catherine Deneuve.

KINJI FUKASAKU

Born: 3 July 1930 in Mito, Japan.
Died: 12 January 2003 in Tokyo, of prostate cancer.
• A pillar of the Japanese film industry with over 60 films to his name, Kinji Fukasaku was launched to international fame by *Tora! Tora! Tora!* (1970), a brutal and passionate account of Japan's attack on Pearl Harbor. His last films included the two hit *Battle Royale* movies (2000 and 2003), crafted by Fukasaku as ironic comments on the breakdown of respect in Japanese society. Chairman of the Directors Guild of Japan since 1996, he continued work on the second *Battle Royale* film until his hospitalisation in December 2002. Other notable films include *War Without a Code* (1953) and *The Fall Guy* (1982).

MASSIMO GIROTTI

Born: 18 May 1918 in Mogliano (Macerata), Marche, Italy.
Died: 5 January 2003 in Rome, Italy, from a heart attack.
• A paragon of athletic Italian masculinity, Massimo Girotti bookended a series of so-so matinée action films and swashbucklers with early leads in Roberto Rossellini's *Desiderio*, Luchino Visconti's *Ossessione* (both 1943), Vittorio De Sica's *The Gate of Heaven* (1946) and Visconti's *Senso* (1954), followed at the other end of his career by films like *Teorema* (1968), *Last Tango in Paris* (1972), *L'innocente* (1976) and Roberto Benigni's *The Monster* (1996).

RON GOODWIN

Born: 17 February 1925 in Plymouth, Devon.
Died: 8 January 2003 in Brimpton Common, Reading, of complications from a longstanding asthma condition.
• Goodwin composed the music for films like *Village of the Damned* (1960) and the popular 'Miss Marple' series before his rousing score for *633 Squadron* (1964) brought him international acclaim. Other notable scores: *Of Human Bondage* (1964), *Those Magnificent Men in Their Flying Machines* (1965), *Operation Crossbow* (1965), *The Trap* (1966), *Where Eagles Dare* (1968), *Monte Carlo or Bust* (1969), *Battle of Britain* (1969, replacing a commissioned score from Sir William Walton), *Frenzy* (1972, this time supplanting Henry Mancini) and *Force 10 from Navarone* (1978).

CLIFF GORMAN

Born: 13 October 1936 in Queens, New York City.
Died: 5 September 2002 in New York City, from leukaemia.
• A consummately skilled actor who won a Tony Award for his dazzling stage portrayal of Lenny Bruce but was passed over in favour of Dustin Hoffman in Bob Fosse's film adaptation of the Bruce story. However, he enjoyed showy supporting roles in films like *The Boys in the Band* (1970), *Cops and Robbers* (1973), *Hoffa* (1992), *Ghost Dog: The Way of the Samurai* (1999) and *King Of The Jungle* (2001).

DOLORES GRAY

Born: 7 June 1924 in Chicago, Illinois.
Died: 26 June 2002 in Manhattan, of a heart attack.
Singer-actress Dolores Gray appeared in four films for M-G-M, including *It's Always Fair Weather* (1955), opposite Gene Kelly, and *Designing Woman* (1957), with Gregory Peck and Lauren Bacall.

DAVID GREENE

Born: 22 February 1921 in Manchester.
Died: 7 April 2003 in Ojai, California, of pancreatic cancer.
Real name: David Brian Lederman.
• Starting as an actor, David Greene crossed the Atlantic to carve out a remarkable directorial career in US and Canadian television, finally venturing into cinema with a stylish British shocker called *The Shuttered Room* (1966). The momentum gathered by subsequent films like *Sebastian* (1967), *I Start Counting* (1969) and *Godspell* (1973) petered out fairly rapidly, however, and, after the submarine melodrama *Gray Lady Down* (1976), Greene returned almost exclusively to making TV movies.

JANE GREER

Born: 9 September 1924 in Washington DC.
Died: 24 August 2001 in Los Angeles, of complications from cancer.
Real name: Bettejane Greer.
• Jane Greer was one of Hollywood's most beguiling leading ladies during the late 1940s. Her best film is undoubtedly Jacques Tourneur's *Out of the Past* (1947), a superior RKO film noir co-starring Robert Mitchum and Kirk Douglas. Greer plays Mitchum's duplicitous, coolly amoral ex-lover, who won't let him forget his criminal past. The actress made one of her last screen appearances in *Against All Odds* (1984), an inferior remake of *Out of the Past*, in which she played her original character's mother.

JAMES GREGORY

Born: 23 December 1911 in The Bronx, New York.

Died: 16 September 2002 in Sedona, Arizona, from natural causes.
• James Gregory gave up Wall Street for Broadway but kept in touch with his past by playing loud, brash businessmen and tough cops. He is best known for playing the Chief in the Matt Helm spoofs starring Dean Martin. His films include *The Manchurian Candidate* (1962), *Murderers' Row* (1966), *The Silencers* (1966) and *The Ambushers* (1967).

RACHEL GURNEY

Born: 5 March 1920 in Eton, Berkshire.
Died: 24 November 2001 in Holt, Norfolk, from natural causes.
Full name: Rachel Gurney Lubbock.
• Actress Rachel Gurney was best known for playing Lady Marjorie in the hit television series *Upstairs, Downstairs* (1971-73). She also appeared in a few British films, notably *Tom Brown's Schooldays* (1951), *A Touch of Larceny* (1959) and *Funeral in Berlin* (1966).

BUDDY HACKETT

Born: 31 August 1924 in Brooklyn, New York.
Died: 30 June 2003 in Los Angeles, California, from natural causes.
Real name: Lenny Hacker.
• Pudding-faced Buddy Hackett was a popular stand-up comic who cultivated a family-friendly persona in films like *It's A Mad, Mad, Mad, Mad World* (1963), *The Love Bug* (1968) and as the whiny voice of Scuttle the Seagull in Disney's *The Little Mermaid* (1989). But his live Las Vegas acts were the kind screened well past the watershed, showcased in the 1983 TV special *Buddy Hackett: Live And Uncensored*. In addition, his critically acclaimed Broadway career proved him a talented actor capable of much more than his film roles ever demanded.

CONRAD HALL

Born: 21 June 1926 in Papeete, Tahiti, French Polynesia.
Died: 4 January 2003 in Santa Monica, California, of complications from bladder cancer.
• Renowned for his rich and complex visual sensibility, Conrad Hall won an Academy Award for lensing *Butch Cassidy and the Sundance Kid* (1969). He later won two more, for *American Beauty* (1999) and *Road to Perdition* (2002). One of only five cinematographers to have a star on Hollywood Boulevard's Walk of Fame, his other films include *Saboteur: Code Name Morituri* (1965), *The Professionals* (1966) and *In Cold Blood* (1967), for all of which he received Oscar nominations, plus *Fat City* (1972), *The Day of the Locust* (1975, another Oscar nomination), *Marathon Man* (1976), *Black Widow* (1987), *Class Action* (1991), *Tequila Sunrise* (1988: yet another nomination), *Searching for Bobby Fischer* (1993: and another) and *Love Affair* (1994).

JONATHAN HARRIS

Born: 6 November 1914 in The Bronx, New York.
Died: 3 November 2002 in Encino, California, from a blood clot in the heart.
Real name: Jonathan Charasuchin.
• After over 100 appearances on Broadway, Harris made his film debut opposite Alan Ladd and James Mason in *Botany Bay* (1953). He was, however, irreversibly typecast as a posh villain after his cult TV portrayal of Dr Zachary Smith in *Lost in Space* (1965).

RICHARD HARRIS

Born: 1 October 1930 in Limerick, Ireland.
Died: 25 October 2002 in London, from Hodgkin's Disease.
• Born Richard St John Harris, this incorrigibly ornery Irishman offered support in *The Guns of Navarone* (1961) and *Mutiny on the Bounty* (1962) before earning his star with an electrifying performance in *This Sporting Life* (1963). But his run of good films quickly dried up, leaving his career in neutral until *A Man Called Horse* (1970) offered a (somewhat gory) return to the A-list. His wild habits worked to the detriment of his career and the next 20 years were marked by disappointingly pedestrian films, until his Oscar-nominated performance in *The Field* (1990) marked a latterday rebirth. Strong supporting roles followed in *Patriot Games* (1992), *Unforgiven* (1992) and *Wrestling Ernest Hemingway* (1993) before he took the

role which made him more famous than he had ever been, playing the wizard Albus Dumbledor in the Harry Potter films. Quote: "I don't care what I'm remembered for. I don't care if I'm remembered. I don't care if I'm not remembered. I don't care why I'm remembered. I genuinely don't care."

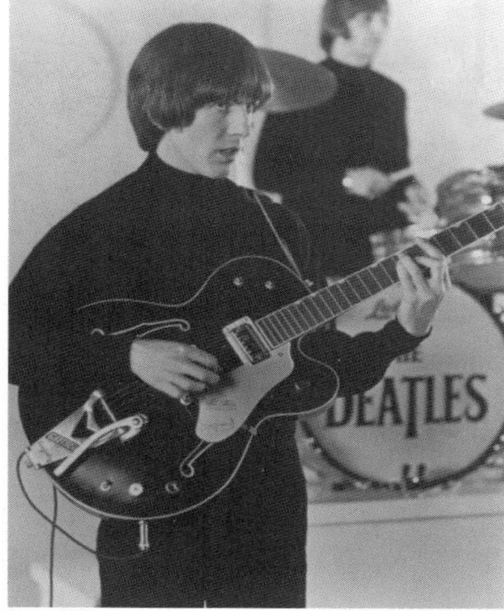

GEORGE HARRISON

Born: 25 February 1943 in Wavertree, Liverpool.
Died: 30 November 2001 in Los Angeles, from cancer.
• A film producer almost by chance, ex-Beatle George Harrison was always more comfortable as a singer, composer and guitarist. As one of the Fab Four, he appeared in *A Hard Day's Night* (1964) and *Help!* (1965). Fifteen years later, Harrison rescued *Monty Python's Life of Brian* (1979) after EMI dropped the project, setting up his own film company, HandMade. HandMade subsequently produced Terry Gilliam's Pythonesque fantasy *Time Bandits* (1981), Neil Jordan's *Mona Lisa* (1986) and Bruce Robinson's cult success *Withnail and I* (1987).

SIGNE HASSO

Born: 15 August 1910 in Stockholm, Sweden.
Died: 8 June 2002 in Los Angeles, California, from pneumonia brought on by lung cancer.
Maiden name: Signe Larsson.
• Signe Hasso spent much of the 1940s in Hollywood, touted as a new Garbo and lending her talents to Ernst Lubitsch's *Heaven Can Wait* (1943), Fred Zinnemann's *The Seventh Cross* (1944) and George Cukor's *A Double Life* (1948). She enjoyed a rare villainous role as a Nazi agent in Henry Hathaway's *The House on 92nd Street* (1945), later moving into Broadway roles, translating Swedish folk songs and setting up a Swedish national repertory.

ANTHONY HAVELOCK-ALLAN

Born: 28 February 1904 in Darlington.
Died: 11 January 2003 in London, from heart failure.
• Oscar-nominated writer/producer who in the 1930s took advantage of the government's quota system to push 23 films through at Paramount in only two years. First-rank actors like Vivien Leigh, Rex Harrison, Wendy Hiller, Alastair Sim, Margaret Rutherford and George Sanders all made their debuts in his films. He worked closely on many David Lean productions, including *In Which We Serve* (1942), *This Happy Breed* (1944), *Brief Encounter* (1945), *Great Expectations* (1946) and *Ryan's Daughter* (1970), which was his last film. He also produced Franco Zeffirelli's 1968 adaptation of *Romeo and Juliet.*

NIGEL HAWTHORNE

Born: 5 April 1929 in Coventry, West Midlands.
Died: 26 December 2001 of a heart attack at his 15th century manor house in Hertfordshire.
• An actor of skill and sensitivity, Nigel Hawthorne didn't become established in

films until the early 1990s. His few Hollywood credits range from the atrocious *Firefox* (1982) to the enjoyable *Demolition Man* (1993). Hawthorne's best film role, however, was as King George III in *The Madness of King George* (1994). He was also well loved on television as the scheming Sir Humphrey Appleby in the BBC's *Yes, Minister* and its sequel *Yes, Prime Minister.*

JAMES HAZELDINE

Born: 4 April 1947 in Salford, Lancashire.
Died: 17 December 2002 in London.
• Best known to British audiences for playing firefighter Mike 'Bayleaf' Wilson in the hit drama *London's Burning* (1988-95), stage actor Hazeldine had a sporadic film career, punctuated by occasional highlights like an appearance in the cult Pink Floyd film, *The Wall* (1982).

EILEEN HECKART

Born: 29 March 1919 in Columbus, Ohio.
Died: 31 December 2001 at her home in Norwalk, Connecticut, of cancer.
Real name: Anna Eckart Herbert.
• Stage actress Eileen Heckart made only a handful of films, including *The Bad Seed* (1956), *Bus Stop* (1956) and

Somebody Up There Likes Me (1957), and won an Oscar for Best Supporting Actress in *Butterflies are Free* (1972), reprising the role she'd played in the original 1969 Broadway production.

KATHARINE HEPBURN

Born: 12 May 1907 in Hartford, Connecticut.
Died: 29 June 2003 at her home in Old Saybrook, Connecticut, after a long illness.

• A spunky, classy, red-headed, trouser-clad, independent-minded role model and all-round Hollywood icon, Katharine Hepburn excelled at playing dominant women in pointed dramas, screwball comedies and historical melodramas. Married briefly to the well-heeled Ludlow Ogden Smith, 'Kate' was romantically linked with Spencer Tracy for 25 years, with whom she made eight films. She also goes down in the history books for winning an unprecedented four Oscars, for *Morning Glory* (1933), *Guess Who's Coming To Dinner?* (1967), *The Lion in Winter* (1968) and *On Golden Pond* (1981). Her last film appearance was in a supporting role, but a key one, as Warren Beatty's spirited aunt in *Love Affair* (1994), in which she used the f-word for the first time. Other triumphs include *Little Women* (1933), *Alice Adams* (1935), *Stage Door* (1937), *Bringing Up Baby* and *Holiday* (both 1938), *The Philadelphia Story* (1940), *Woman of the Year* (1942), *Adam's Rib* (1949), *The African Queen* (1951), *Pat and Mike* (1952), *Summertime* (1955), *The Rainmaker* (1956), *Suddenly Last Summer* (1959) and *Long Day's Journey Into Night* (1962). In her honour, Broadway dimmed its lights two days after her death.

GEORGE ROY HILL

Born: 20 December 1921 in Minneapolis, Minnesota.
Died: 27 December 2002 in New York, of complications from Parkinson's Disease.

• Having served as a pilot in both World War II and the Korean War, Hill arrived in Hollywood as a grown man of 40. His first film was the Tennessee Williams adaptation *Period of Adjustment* (1962), which he followed by directing Dean Martin in *Toys in the Attic* (1963) and Peter Sellers in *The World of Henry Orient* (1964). These were followed in turn by his knowingly ironic take on the outlaw Western in *Butch Cassidy and The Sundance Kid* (1969). His first Oscars came with *The Sting* (1973), for both Best Director and Best Film, but his whimsical fantasies *Slaughterhouse-Five* (1972) and *The World According to Garp* (1982) met with only muted box-office. His other films were: *Hawaii* (1966), *Thoroughly Modern Millie* (1967), *The Great Waldo Pepper* (1975), *Slap Shot* (1977), *A Little Romance* (1979), *The Little Drummer Girl* (1984) and *Funny Farm* (1989).

WENDY HILLER

Born: 15 August 1912 in Bramhall, Cheshire.
Died: 14 May 2003 in Beaconsfield, Buckinghamshire.

• Primarily a stage star, Dame Wendy Hiller's relatively sporadic film performances are remarkable for a high ratio of Oscar-worthy performances. Her first nod was for playing Eliza Doolittle in *Pygmalion* (1938), later winning a Best Supporting Actress award for *Separate Tables* (1958) and being nominated again for *A Man for All Seasons* (1966). Other notable films include *Major Barbara* (1941), *I Know Where I'm Going* (1945), *Sons And Lovers* (1960) and *Murder on the Orient Express* (1974).

THORA HIRD

Born: 8 May 1911 in Morecambe, Lancashire.
Died: 15 March 2003 in Twickenham, Middlesex, following a stroke.

• Undaunted by the fact that her break into films, aged 28, was thanks to George Formby calling his agent to recommend her for the role of his mother, the much-loved Dame Thora Hird carved out a rich career playing roles which simultaneously romanticised and precisely documented the nuances of working-class life in northern England. She was a favourite of playwrights John Osborne, cast at his request in *The Entertainer* (1960), and Alan Bennett, for whom she gave several memorable TV performances.

PETER HUNT

Born: 11 March 1925 in London.
Died: 14 August 2002 in Santa Monica, California, from heart failure.
• Film editor-turned-director Peter Hunt cut the first five James Bond films, developing a much-copied style he called 'crash cutting' for the first, *Dr. No* (1962), and directing the now much-admired sixth entry, *On Her Majesty's Secret Service* (1969). He also edited *The Ipcress File* (1965) and was associate producer on *Chitty Chitty Bang Bang* (1968). On the Bond films, which he likened to paperback novels: "My feeling was always that one should make the films seriously, but never *take* them seriously."

KIM HUNTER

Born: 12 November 1922 in Detroit, Michigan.
Died: 11 September 2002 in New York City, of a heart attack.
Real name: Janet Cole.
• Though immediately recognisable as Stella in Elia Kazan's adaptation of Tennessee Williams' *A Streetcar Named Desire* (1951), for which she won an Oscar, Kim Hunter remained masked in her most popular role, as the sympathetic lady-ape Dr Zira in *Planet of the Apes* (1968) and its first two sequels. She made an elegant screen debut in Val Lewton's 1943 horror film *The Seventh Victim.* Her other notable films include *A Matter of Life and Death* (1945), *The Young Stranger* (1957), *Lilith* (1964), *The Swimmer* (1968), *Midnight in The Garden of Good and Evil* (1997), *A Price Above Rubies* (1998) and *Here's to Life!* (2000), which won her a Genie award nomination for best actress. Her 60-year career included long periods of enforced inactivity because of her association with blackballed film directors during the McCarthyite era.

MICHAEL JETER

Born: 26 August 1952 in Lawrenceburg, Tennessee.
Died: 30 March 2003 in Los Angeles, California, of complications from HIV.
• A character actor who specialised in playing life's bullied losers, Jeter is most famous for his Emmy-winning role in Burt Reynolds' TV sitcom, *Evening Shade.* His first film appearance was a bit part in Milos Forman's *Hair* (1979), his last a starring role in George Clooney's heist comedy *Welcome to Collinwood* (2002). At the time of his death, Jeter was filming *Polar Express* with Tom Hanks. Quote: "I'm not dying of AIDS, I'm living with it."

JAROMIL JIRES

Born: 10 December 1935 in Bratislava, Czechoslovakia.
Died: 24 October 2001 in Prague, from head injuries sustained in a car crash two years earlier.
• A director of the Czech New Wave, Jires was best known for the Gothic, visually spectacular fantasy *Valerie and Her Week of Wonders* (1970).

DAVID JOHN

Born: 15 March 1945 in London. Bedford according to imdb
Died: 25 June 2002 in London, from cancer.
One of the best sound mixers in the business, David John worked on *The Long Good Friday* (1980), *Mona Lisa* (1986), *The Princess Bride* (1987) and *GoldenEye* (1995), among many others.

STRATFORD JOHNS

Born: 22 February 1925 in Pietermaritzburg, South Africa.
Died: 29 January 2002 in Heveningham, Suffolk, of a heart condition.
• A burly character actor specialising in gruff authority figures, Johns starred in the BBC police dramas *Z Cars* (1962-65) and *Softly Softly* (1966-72). His film credits include *The Ladykillers* (1955), *Cromwell* (1970), *The Lair of the White Worm* (1988) and *Splitting Heirs* (1993).

CHUCK JONES

Born: 21 September 1912 in Spokane, Washington.
Died: 22 February 2002 in Corona Del Mar, California, of congestive heart failure.
Full name: Charles Martin Jones.
• Chuck Jones was one of the best-known animation directors of Hollywood's golden era. Based at Warner Bros for most of his career, Jones developed the characters of Bugs Bunny, Daffy Duck, Porky Pig and Elmer Fudd

into their definitive versions. His original creations included Roadrunner and the long-suffering Wile E Coyote. Jones won Academy Awards for *For Scentimental Reasons* (1949) and *The Dot and the Line* (1965). His best work includes the brilliant musical parodies *Rabbit of Seville* (1950) and *What's Opera Doc?* (1957), both starring Bugs Bunny and Elmer Fudd.

KATY JURADO

Born: 16 January 1924 in Guadalajara, Jalisco, Mexico.
Died: 5 July 2002 in Cuernavaca, Morelos, Mexico, of a heart attack.
• Born María Cristina Jurado Garcia, Katy Jurado was an actress of arresting beauty and fiery temperament. Until Salma Hayek in *Frida* (2002), she was the only Mexican actress ever to be nominated for an Academy Award (for *Broken Lance*, 1954). She also won a Golden Globe for *High Noon* (1952) and three Ariels (Mexico's Oscars), including one for her role in Luis Buñuel's *El bruto* (1952). She learnt her dialogue phonetically for her first American films, but mastered English during her life in California as Mrs Ernest Borgnine from 1959 to 1964. Her American pictures include her debut in *Bullfighter and the Lady* (1951), *One-Eyed Jacks* (1961), *Stay Away, Joe* (1968), *Pat Garrett and Billy the Kid* (1973), *Under the Volcano* (1984) and *The Hi-Lo Country* (1998).

JOHN JUSTIN

Born: 24 November 1917 in London.
Died: 29 November 2002 in London.
• War experience as the real thing helped John Justin capture the role of test pilot Philip Peel in David Lean's *The Sound Barrier* (1952). His first film, however, was in the role of Prince Ahmad opposite Conrad Veidt and June Duprez in Alexander Korda's *The Thief of Bagdad* (1939). He had a long career on stage and screen, including appearances in three Ken Russell extravaganzas (*Savage Messiah* 1972, *Lisztomania* 1975, *Valentino* 1977) and as a very frightening zombie aristocrat in the BBC's *Schalcken the Painter* (1979).

PAULINE KAEL

Born: 19 June 1919 in Petaluma, Sonoma County, California.
Died: 3 September 2001 in Great Barrington, Massachusetts, after a prolonged battle with Parkinson's Disease.
Probably America's best-known and most influential film critic, Pauline Kael served as the *New Yorker*'s regular movie reviewer from 1968 to 1991. She used this position to promote the more radical and challenging style of film that arose – briefly – from the ashes of the studio system. Kael hailed the early work of Robert Altman, Francis Coppola, Martin Scorsese, Paul Schrader, Robert Towne, Steven Spielberg and Brian De Palma, though most subsequently fell from her favour.

RACHEL KEMPSON

Born: 28 May 1910 in Dartmouth.
Died: 24 May 2003 in Millbrook, New York City, from natural causes.
• The matriarch of the Redgrave clan, the widow of Sir Michael and mother of Vanessa, Lynn and Corin carved out a respectable career of her own on stage and screen, her film credits including *The Captive Heart* (1946), *Tom Jones* (1963), *Georgy Girl* (1966), *The Charge of the Light Brigade*, *The Virgin Soldiers* (both 1969) and *Out of Africa* (1985). Her grandchildren – Natasha Richardson, Joely Richardson and Jemma Redgrave – continue the family's illustrious thespian tradition.

DAVE KING

Born: 23 June 1929 in Twickenham.
Died: 15 April 2002.
• A comedian and singer once tipped for international stardom, Dave King turned to acting with limited success. He was given lead roles in the feeble swashbuckler *Pirates of Tortuga* (1961) and the flat comedy *Go to Blazes* (1962), both of which flopped. Briefly seen in *Up the Chastity Belt* (1971), a vehicle for Frankie Howerd, King played small parts in *The Ritz* (1976), *The Long Good Friday* (1980) and Warren Beatty's epic *Reds* (1981).

SYDNEY LASSICK

Born: 23 July 1922, Chicago, Illinois.
Died: 12 April 2003, Los Angeles,

California, of complications from diabetes.
• A cherubic character actor, Lassick is best known for his performance as Cheswick in *One Flew Over the Cuckoo's Nest* (1975) and for memorable roles in *Carrie* (1976) and *Deep Cover* (1992).

JACK LEE

Born: 27 January 1913 in Stroud, Gloucestershire.
Died: 15 October 2002, Sydney, Australia.
• Born Wilfrid John Raymond Lee, Lee's skills as a director crossed genre boundaries with ease, though his best works probably remain his war films *The Wooden Horse* (1950), *Circle of Deception* (1960) and the gritty classic *A Town Like Alice* (1956). Upon emigrating to Australia, he turned away from directing, concentrating instead on running his own production company.

BUDDY LESTER

Born: 6 January 1917 in Chicago, Illinois.
Died: 4 October 2002 in Los Angeles, California, from cancer.
• Deadpan stand-up comedian and character actor who worked with Frank Sinatra in Rat Pack films such as *Ocean's Eleven* (1960) and *Sergeants Three* (1962). He also appeared with Jerry Lewis in *The Nutty Professor* (1963), *The Patsy* (1964), *Three on a Couch* (1966) and *The Big Mouth* (1967).

LEO McKERN

Born: 16 March 1920 in Sydney, New South Wales, Australia.
Died: 23 July 2002 in Bath, after a long illness.
• McKern will always be remembered as TV's bulbously proportioned English barrister in *Rumpole of the Bailey.* Films include *Murder in the Cathedral* (1952), *A Tale of Two Cities* (1958), *The Mouse That Roared* (1959), *Scent of Mystery* (1960), *The Day the Earth Caught Fire* (1962), *The Horse Without a Head* (1963), *Help!* (1965), *A Man for All Seasons* (1966), *Ryan's Daughter* (1970), *The Adventure of Sherlock Holmes' Smarter Brother* (1975), *The Omen* (1976), *Candleshoe* (1977), *The Blue Lagoon* (1980), *The French Lieutenant's Woman* (1981), *Ladyhawke* (1985) and *Monsignor Quixote* (1989).

PEGGY MORAN

Born: 3 October 1918 in Clinton, Iowa.
Died: 24 October 2002 in Camarillo, California, of complications from injuries suffered in a car accident.
• Born Mary Jeanette Moran, Peggy Moran's career as a B-movie siren reached a peak with Universal potboilers *The Mummy's Hand* (1940) and *Horror Island* (1941), the films so establishing her cult status that she was still attending fan conventions all over the USA nearly 60 years after her retirement. After making *King of the Cowboys* in 1943 opposite Roy Rogers, she forsook films for marriage to director Henry Koster.

BRUCE PALTROW

Born: 26 November 1943 in Brooklyn, New York City.
Died: 2 October 2002 in Rome, Italy, while on holiday in Tuscany with his daughter to celebrate her 30th birthday, from a recurrence of throat cancer and pneumonia.
• An accomplished producer, director and writer of multi-Emmy-winning TV series *The White Shadow* and *St. Elsewhere*, Bruce Paltrow's stature was eventually overshadowed by the enormous popularity of his daughter Gwyneth. His last film, *Duets* (2000), actually suffered from unhelpful press arising from the disparity.

SUZY PARKER

Born: 28 October 1932 in Long Island, New York.
Died: 3 May 2003 in Montecito, California.
Real name: Cecilia Ann Renée Parker.
• A forerunner of today's supermodels, copper-haired Suzy Parker was one of the quintessential faces of the 1950s. Inevitably picked up by Hollywood, she featured in the 'Think Pink' number of Stanley Donen's *Funny Face* (1957), appeared opposite Cary Grant in *Kiss Them for Me* (1957, also for Donen) and Gary Cooper in *Ten North Frederick* (1958), and met her husband, Bradford Dillman, while working on the British film *A Circle of Deception* (1961). She also starred in such TV shows as *Burke's Law, The Twilight Zone, Dr Kildare* and *Night Gallery*; her last theatrically released film, *Chamber of Horrors* (1966), itself began life as a TV movie.

GREGORY PECK

Born: 5 April 1916 in La Jolla, California.
Died: 12 June 2003 at his home in Los Angeles, from natural causes.
Full name: Eldred Gregory Peck.
• An extraordinarily handsome and sincere leading man, Gregory Peck became a star in his very first film, *Days of Glory* (1943). His second picture, *The Keys of the Kingdom* (1944), netted him the first of five Academy Award nominations, a path that led to his

Oscar-winning performance as the immaculate lawyer, Atticus Finch, in *To Kill a Mockingbird* (1962). Such was Peck's clean-cut image of unimpeachable decency that he astounded cinemagoers worldwide when he played the Nazi surgeon, Josef Mengele, in *The Boys from Brazil* (1978). Other notable films: *Spellbound* (1945), *Duel in the Sun* (1946), *The Yearling* (1946, Oscar nomination), *Gentleman's Agreement* (1947, Oscar nomination), *Twelve O'Clock High* (1949, Oscar nomination), *The Gunfighter* (1950), *Captain Horatio Hornblower R.N.* (1951), *Roman Holiday* (1953), *Moby Dick* (1956), *The Big Country* (1958), *On the Beach* (1959), *The Guns of Navarone* (1961), *Cape Fear* (1962), *Arabesque* (1966), *MacKenna's Gold* (1969), *The Omen* (1976), *MacArthur* (1977), *The Sea Wolves* (1980), *Old Gringo* (1989) and *Other People's Money* (1991). Always active in liberal and charitable causes, he received the Academy's Jean Hersholt Humanitarian Award in 1967.

MAURICE PIALAT

Born: 31 August 1925 in Cunlhat, Puy de Dome, Auvergne, France.
Died: 11 January 2003 in Paris, France, of kidney failure.
• Painter-turned-actor-turned-award-winning-*enfant-terrible* auteurist whose exacting artistic instincts translated beautifully onto the big screen. He won the Cannes Golden Palm for *Sous le soleil de Satan / Under Satan's Sun* (1987). Gerard Depardieu became a company player in films that were almost always difficult or controversial but still meaningfully incisive. Pialat's other internationally important films include *Nous ne vieillirons pas ensemble (We Will Not Grow Old Together* aka *The Break-up)* (1972 debut), *Loulou* (1980), *À nos amours/To Our Loves* (1983), *Police* (1985) and *Van Gogh* (1991).

SIDNEY PINK

Born: 16 March 1916 in Pittsburgh, Pennsylvania.
Died: 12 October 2002 in Pompano Beach, Florida, after a long illness.
• Pink produced one of the first 3-D feature films, *Bwana Devil*, producing 50 other pictures over his continent-hopping career and discovering Dustin Hoffman when he hired him to star in *Madigan's Million.*

VERA RALSTON

Born: 12 June 1919 (or 1921) in Prague, Czechoslovakia (now Czech Republic)
Died: 9 February 2003 in Santa Barbara, California, from cancer.
• Sometimes billed as: Vera Hruba Ralston.
Born Vera Helena Hruba, this former skating champion became the butt of a hundred 'bad actress' jokes. Her accent and stiff mannerisms clashed with her physical grace, as showcased in *Ice Capades* (1941), *Ice Capades Revue* (1942), and *Lake Placid Serenade* (1944). Her marriage to Republic Studios boss Herbert J Yates accounts for a Hollywood career that also included *The Lady and the Monster* (1943), opposite Erich von Stroheim, plus *Dakota* (1945) and *The Fighting Kentuckian* (1949), in both of which she starred with John Wayne, who reportedly threatened to leave the studio if forced to work with her again.

KAREL REISZ

Born: 21 July 1926 in Ostrava, Czechoslovakia.
Died: 25 November 2002 in London, after suffering a blood disorder.
• A Czech Jew schooled in England, Karel Reisz was a war refugee at 12, orphaned when his parents were killed at Auschwitz. Author of a seminal text on aesthetics, *The Technique of Film*

Editing, Reisz was, along with fellow theorists Lindsay Anderson and Tony Richardson, a prime proponent of British Free Cinema. His impressive debut feature *Saturday Night and Sunday Morning* (1960) was a landmark of British social-realist filmmaking. Reisz's output was sporadic but included the remake of *Night Must Fall* (1964), the cult favorite *Morgan! A Suitable Case for Treatment* (1966), and the biographical drama *Isadora* (1968). His American films were similarly varied: *The Gambler* (1974), *Who'll Stop the Rain* aka *Dog Soldiers* (1978), *The French Lieutenant's Woman* (1981), *Sweet Dreams* (1985) and *Everybody Wins* (1990).

KENNETH RIVE

Born: 26 July 1918 in London.
Died: 30 December 2002 in Radlett, Hertfordshire, from natural causes.
• Rive was a child actor in German and British silent pictures but his true legacy was the foundation of Gala Film Distributors in 1952. The biggest British distributor of foreign films, Gala introduced British audiences to Bergman's *Cries and Whispers* and most of Truffaut's work.

MARTHA SCOTT

Born: 22 September 1912 in Jamesport, Missouri.
Died: 28 May 2003 in Van Nuys, California, from natural causes.
• Martha Scott's debut role in *Our Town* (1940) won her an Oscar nomination, launching her as a character actress of uncommon quality. Her natural warmth in *Cheers for Miss Bishop* and *One Foot in Heaven* (both 1941) contrasted well with the glamour-girl artificiality deemed de rigueur in the 1940s. Other notable films include *In Old Oklahoma* (1943), *So Well Remembered* (1947), *Strange Bargain* (1949), *When I Grow Up* (1951), *The Desperate Hours* (1955), *The Ten Commandments* (1956), *Sayonara* (1957) *Ben-Hur* (1959), *The Turning Point* (1977) and *Doin' Time on Planet Earth* (1988).

FRANCIS SEARLE

Born: 14 March 1909 in Putney, London.
Died: 31 July 2002 in Wimbledon, London.
• Director/producer Francis Searle will be remembered for his work with Hammer Film Productions in the late 1940s and as an indefatigable purveyor of second features over the next two decades. He directed his first feature film (and only 'A' picture) in 1946 – *A Girl in a Million*, starring Hugh Williams and Joan Greenwood – and later directed *Cloudburst* (1951), the first film ever made at Hammer's Bray Studios. He subsequently gave early breaks to Tommy Steele (*Kill Me Tomorrow*, 1957) and Jackie Collins (*Undercover Girl*, also 1957).

ALBERTO SORDI

Born: 5 June 1920 in Rome.
Died: 25 February 2003 in Rome, of a heart attack.
• One of Italy's best-loved comic stars, Sordi turned Italian life, especially the foibles of his fellow Romans, into hilarious, often bittersweet vignettes. Holder of Italy's highest film award, the David of Donatello, as well as a Golden Lion for Lifetime Achievement presented at the Venice Film Festival in 1995, he was made honorary mayor of Rome for a day in 1999. Films include *Il Conte Max* (1957), Mario Monicelli's *The Great War* (1959), Luigi Comencin's classic *Tutti a casa/Everybody Goes Home* (1960) and Dino Risi's *Una via difficile/A Hard Life* (1963). Less than a week after his death, one of Rome's main streets was renamed after him.

ROBERT STACK

Born: 13 January 1919 in Los Angeles, California.
Died: 14 May 2003 in Beverly Hills, California, from a heart attack.
• Tall, athletic and dashing, Robert Stack debuted in *First Love* (1939), in which he gave maturing child star Deanna Durbin her first 'adult' screen kiss, simultaneously launching himself as an overnight matinée idol. He made movie history starring in the 3-D pioneer *Bwana Devil* (1952), which broke box-office records, and won an Oscar nomination for *Written on the Wind* (1956). He remains most famous, however, for his clench-jawed Eliot

Ness in the long-running TV series *The Untouchables*. Quote: "It's not what you are in Hollywood – it's what people think you are."

ROD STEIGER

Born: 14 April 1925 in Westhampton, New York.
Died: 9 July 2002 in Los Angeles, California, from pneumonia and kidney failure.
• Best known for his Oscar-winning support turn as Sheriff Bill Gillespie in 1967's edgy racial crime-drama *In the Heat of the Night*, Rodney Stephen Steiger leaves behind an imposing range of meaty characters in films like *On the Waterfront* (1954), *Oklahoma!* (1955), *The Harder They Fall* (1956), *Al Capone* (1959), *The Longest Day* (1962), *Dr Zhivago* and *The Loved One* (both 1965). His tortured concentration camp survivor in Sidney Lumet's *The Pawnbroker* (1964) is considered one of his finest roles, winning him a Berlinale for best actor and another Oscar nomination, this time in the Best Actor category. Overweight and depressed in the 1980s, his career hit a slump, but the 1990s saw him busier than ever, taking on roles in dozens of TV movies and better-than-average films, including *Mars Attacks!* (1996), *Crazy in Alabama*, *The Hurricane*, *End of Days* (all 1999), *The Hollywood Sign* (2001) and *Poolhall Junkies* (2002), his last film.

PETER STONE

Born: 27 February 1930 in Los Angeles, California.
Died: 26 April 2003 in New York City, from pulmonary fibrosis.
• Stone became the first writer to win a Tony (holding a career total of three), an Oscar and an Emmy. A scathingly witty raconteur, he broke into films in 1963 with the script for Stanley Donen's *Charade*. The following year, he shared an Oscar for Best Original Screenplay for *Father Goose*. This was followed by another couple of flashy thrillers, *Mirage* (1965) and *Arabesque* (1966), both starring Gregory Peck. In 2002, he co-wrote *The Truth About Charlie*, Jonathan Demme's scattershot remake of *Charade*, under the pseudonym of Peter Joshua, which happened to be the name of Cary Grant's character in the original.

DANIEL TARADASH

Born: 29 January 1913 in Louisville, Kentucky.
Died: 22 February 2003 in Los Angeles, California, from pancreatic cancer.
• The widely respected and politically active Oscar-winning scriptwriter of *From Here to Eternity* (1952), Taradash directed one film, *Storm Center* (1956), starring Bette Davis as a librarian who refuses to remove a book about Communism from the shelves. A brave thing to deliver at the height of the Cold War. His other scripts included *Desirée* (1954), *Picnic* (1955), *Bell, Book and Candle* (1958), *Castle Keep* (1969), *Doctors' Wives* (1970) and *The Other Side of Midnight* (1977).

LYNNE THIGPEN

Born: 22 December 1948 in Joliet, Illinois.
Died: 12 March 2003 in Los Angeles, California, from a cerebral haemorrhage.
Real name: Lynne Richmond.
• A Tony and Obie award-winning stage actress with a stunning singing voice, Thigpen carved a niche for herself playing characterful black women in films such as *Anger Management* (2003), *Novocaine* (2001), *Shaft* (2000), *Bicentennial Man* (1999), *The Insider* (1999), *Random Hearts* (1999), *Blankman* (1994), *Just Cause* (1995), *Lean on Me* (1989), *Bob Roberts* (1992) and *Tootsie* (1982).

J LEE THOMPSON

Born: 1 August 1914 in Bristol.
Died: 30 August 2002 in Sooke, British Columbia, Canada, from congestive heart failure.
• A teenage prodigy who had two plays published and performed by the age of 20, Thompson was responsible as a film director for a series of edgy British neo-realist hits: *The Yellow Balloon* (1950), *The Weak and the Wicked* (1953), *Yield to the Night* (1956) and *Woman in a Dressing Gown* (1958), Thompson's career was apparently overwhelmed by the enormous success of *The Guns of Navarone* (1961), however, after which (except for *Cape Fear*, 1962) his

confident touch turned flabby with a slate of populist movies, including the Charles Bronson and Chuck Norris action flicks he pumped out in the 1970s and 80s.

RAF VALLONE

Born: 17 February 1916 in Tropea, Calabria, Italy.
Died: 31 October 2002 in Rome.
• A one-time journalist, Vallone stumbled into showbiz stardom at 31 with his electrifying stage performance as the hot-headed Italian-American, Eddie, in Arthur Miller's *A View from the Bridge*, reprised in Sidney Lumet's 1961 film. His Italian films include *Non c'è pace sotto gli ulivi (There's No Peace Under the Olive Trees)* (1950), *Cristo proibito (Forbidden Christ)* (1950), *Il cammino della speranza (The Road to Hope)* (1951), *Roma ore 11 (Rome 11 O'Clock)* (1952). Internationally, he had cameo roles in *Two Women* (1960), *El Cid* (1961), *The Cardinal* (1963), *Phaedra* (1962), *The Greek Tycoon* (1978) and *The Godfather Part III* (1990).

JEAN YANNE

Born: 18 July 1933 in Paris.
Died: 23 May 2003 in Morsains, Marne, France, from a heart attack.
Real name: Jean Gouyé.
• French songwriter, actor and director much-loved for his boorish style, made famous by Jean Luc Godard's *Weekend* (1967). His coarse persona struck a chord with audiences who embraced him as "a pathological cretin expressing leftwing ideas with rightwing vocabulary" (his own words). Claude Chabrol gave him two of his best roles, in *Le Boucher* and *This Man Must Die!/Que la bête meure!* (both 1969). Yanne's directorial debut, *Tout le monde il est beau, Tout le monde il est gentil/Everybody is Nice, Everybody is Beautiful* (1971), was a caustic satire on advertising and was a huge box-office hit in France. His films were usually scathing and parodic and include: *Moi y en a vouloir des sous (Me, I Want Money)* (1973), *The Chinese in Paris* (1974), *Je te tiens, tu me tiens par la barbichette (I Hold You and You Hold Me by the Small Goatee)* (1978), *Deux heures moins le quart avant Jésus-Christ (Quarter to Two Before Jesus Christ)* (1982) and *Liberté, Egalité, Choucroute* (1985).

Index

Names of films and videos appear in the index in *italics*. Page references for illustrations appear in **BOLD**.
The last separate word of an individual's name is used as the index entry. Thus Robert De Niro appears within 'N' as Niro, Robert De